Critical Essays on
Randall Jarrell

Critical Essays on Randall Jarrell

Suzanne Ferguson

G. K. Hall & Co. ● Boston, Massachusetts

Library of Congress Cataloging in Publication Data

Main entry under title.

Critical essays on Randall Jarrell.

  (Critical essays on American Literature)
  Includes bibliographical references and index.
  1. Jarrell, Randall, 1914–1965—Criticism and
interpretation—Addresses, essays, lectures. I. Ferguson,
Suzanne, 1939–   II. Series.
PS3519.A86Z62   1983   811'.52   82-12100
ISBN 0-8161-8486-0

CRITICAL ESSAYS ON AMERICAN LITERATURE

This series seeks to publish the most important reprinted criticism on writers and topics in American literature along with, in various volumes, original essays, interviews, bibliographies, letters, manuscript sections, and other materials brought to public attention for the first time. We are delighted to add to the series Suzanne Ferguson's volume on Randall Jarrell, a book that constitutes the most substantial collection of criticism ever published on this important American writer. The collection contains, along with reprinted essays and reviews by John Crowe Ransom, Karl Shapiro, Helen Vendler, John Berryman, John Updike, Michel Benamou, and others, five original essays by Helen Hagenbüchle, Keith Monroe, Suzanne Ferguson, Kathe Davis Finney, and Richard K. Cross. We are confident that this collection will make a permanent and significant contribution to American literary study.

JAMES NAGEL, GENERAL EDITOR

Northeastern University

CONTENTS

INTRODUCTION   1

REVIEWS

John Crowe Ransom, [From "Constellation of
    Five Young Poets"]   15

Ruth Lechlitner, "Music of Despair"   17

Delmore Schwartz, "The Dream from Which No
    One Wakes"   19

W. S. Graham and Hayden Carruth, "Jarrell's
    Losses: A Controversy"   21

Robert Lowell, "Randall Jarrell's Wild Dogmatism"   27

M. L. Rosenthal, "Of Pity and Innocence"   29

Karl Shapiro, "In the Forests of the Little People"   30

John Logan, "The Rilkean Sense"   32

Philip Booth, "The Poet Fulfills the Man"   33

William Meredith, "The Adventures of a Private
    Eye"   35

Helen Vendler, *"The Complete Poems"*   37

Delmore Schwartz, "Light on the Poet's
    Waste Land"   41

John Berryman, "Matter and Manner"   43

Helen Vendler, *"The Third Book of Criticism"*   45

John Lucas, "Arriving at Acceptance"   48

John Metcalf, [From "New Novels"]   54

P. L. Travers, "A Kind of Visitation"   55

John Updike, *"Fly by Night"*   57

ESSAYS

GENERAL ESSAYS

Sister M. Bernetta Quinn, [From "Randall Jarrell:
    His Metamorphoses"]   63

Jerome Mazzaro, "Between Two Worlds: The
Post-Modernism of Randall Jarrell"   82

Helen Hagenbüchle, "Blood for the Muse: A Study
of the Poetic Process in Randall Jarrell's
Poetry"   101

William H. Pritchard, "Randall Jarrell:
Poet-Critic"   120

THE POETRY

Parker Tyler, "The Dramatic Lyrism
of Randall Jarrell"   140

Richard Fein, "Randall Jarrell's World of War"   149

Frances C. Ferguson, "Randall Jarrell and
the Flotations of Voice"   163

Russell Fowler, "Randall Jarrell's 'Eland':
A Key to Motive and Technique in His Poetry"   176

Charlotte H. Beck, "Unicorn to Eland: The Rilkean
Spirit in the Poetry of Randall Jarrell"   191

Sister M. Bernetta Quinn, "Randall Jarrell:
Landscapes of Life and *Life*"   203

Mary Kinzie, [From "The Man Who Painted Bulls"]   228

Leven M. Dawson, "Jarrell's 'The Death of the Ball
Turret Gunner' "   238

David K. Cornelius, "Jarrell's 'The Death of the
Ball Turret Gunner' "   240

Michel Benamou, "The Woman at the Zoo's Fearful
Symmetry"   241

THE CRITICISM

Janet Sharistanian, "The Poet as Humanitarian:
Randall Jarrell's Literary Criticism as
Self-Revelation"   246

Keith Monroe, "Principle and Practice in the
Criticism of Randall Jarrell"   256

THE FICTION

Sylvia Angus, "Randall Jarrell, Novelist:
A Reconsideration"   266

Suzanne Ferguson, "To Benton, with Love and
Judgment: Jarrell's *Pictures from an Institution*"   272

Kathe Davis Finney, "The Poet, Truth, and
Other Fictions: Randall Jarrell as
Storyteller"   284

THE TRANSLATIONS

Ingo Seidler, [From "Jarrell and the Art
of Translation"]   298

Richard K. Cross, "Jarrell's Translations:
   The Poet as Elective Middle European"   310

INDEX   321

INTRODUCTION

To describe a "body" of criticism is to delineate a strange creature: a beast made by a committee that, like the camel, moves awkwardly but serviceably about its work in the world. The body of Jarrell criticism, moderate in size, lacking the dazzling virtuosity of style and range that characterized Jarrell's own body of criticism, nevertheless has a well-articulated skeleton and consistency among its parts. It can perform the useful task of guiding readers through the thickets and across the wider vistas of Jarrell's created world. In *Critical Essays on Randall Jarrell* I attempt to display the contours of this body, beginning with the reviews that constructed its skeleton and going on to essays—from the early 1950s to 1981—which give it substance, treating both general and particular aspects of Jarrell's work as poet, critic, writer of fiction, and translator. Although in *The Poetry of Randall Jarrell* (1971)[1] I studied Jarrell almost exclusively as a poet, it seems important to me now to attempt an assessment of the whole writer, to explore the various facets of his work and their interrelationship by juxtaposing selections from the best criticism available in an arrangement that shows both the range of Jarrell's achievement and its essential unity.

Despite the density of imagery in many of his earlier poems, Jarrell's most characteristic work does not lend itself to explication; his fundamental world view, shaped by Freud, Arnold, and Rilke, was perceived early on and has been increasingly well understood. The central figures and issues of his poetry—children and women; dreams and fairy tales; history and art; memory; and the experience and implications of modern warfare—have stimulated annotation, usually in the context of more general discussions of these themes, but little controversy about interpretation of passages or poems. Controversy has arisen, however, over something far more fundamental than the meaning of individual works: Jarrell's aesthetic, his basic approach to the writing of poetry or fiction, to transforming his vision of the world into poetic language or fictional form.

From the outset, Jarrell's poetic temperament was at odds with his environment. Deep as was his affection and respect for John Crowe Ransom, and much as he shared some of Ransom's theories of poetry, his mentor's style was as remote from Jarrell's as the "Blue Girls," "travelling the sward / Under the towers of [their] seminary" were from his "Girl in a Library." His attraction to the high modernist style as represented in Tate, to whom Blood for a Stranger² was dedicated, was mixed with repulsion (shown in his description of modernism prefixed to "The Rage for the Lost Penny").³ Though drawn to the ideas and the style of the early Auden, Jarrell had neither the inclination nor the gift to write in that idiom for long. The war confirmed his suspicion that existing styles were inadequate or inappropriate to express what he sensed *must* be communicated in poetry: the response of individuals to being caught up in a vast machine of destruction, a faceless Necessity that churned on while its expendable units—children, soldiers-like-children—were swept up, then disposed of: "When I died they washed me out of the turret with a hose." He sought a style plain but capable of accommodating figures of speech and occasional allusions; images of contemporary life and grandiose abstractions, sometimes used ironically; outrage and longing.

Whitman—the homely, not the oratorical Whitman—Frost, and to a lesser extent, Williams, were closer to what Jarrell wanted: a language that could expose the ordinary as something special, give a sense of mystery behind the mundane; but they, too, were so individual as to be impossible models. Corbière and, even more, Rilke suggested possibilities in the late forties, but it was not until the last years of his life that Jarrell arrived at the consistently perfect match of matter and manner in his autobiographical poems of *The Lost World*. However, critics who had not reacted favorably to Jarrell's plain style, his Freudian world view, and his sympathetic identification with the world's victims in his earlier poetry—the style was "flat," the world view simplistic, and the identification "sentimental"—were no more disposed to be impressed by these later poems than the earlier ones.

Consequently, criticism of Jarrell has been largely devoted to exploring the nuances of his vision and the sophistication of his world view, with the ulterior motive of justifying a style that leaves even his admirers at times uncomfortable. That his critics arrive at persuasive and thoughtful conclusions, this collection bears witness. Although I have represented some of the negative criticism, the work included is primarily partisan in Jarrell's favor as it stakes out Jarrell's "place" in twentieth-century letters.

REVIEWS

One is struck by how well Jarrell's work was reviewed—not how favorably, but how thoughtfully. Each book after *Blood for a Stranger* was given notice in virtually all the national journals: the *New York Times*, the *Herald Tribune*, the *New Republic*, the *Nation*, the *Saturday Review*, the *Christian Science Monitor*, and often the *Spectator* and the *Times Literary Supplement* as well. The reviewers were often themselves poets: Berryman, Philip Booth, Hayden Carruth, James Dickey, W. S. Graham, Lowell, William Meredith, Nemerov, Ransom, Schwartz, Yvor Winters. Many of these are poets Jarrell reviewed in turn, both favorably and unfavorably; some are friends, others "enemies," but one gets little sense of log-rolling on one side or spite on the other. All, it appears, try to engage with what is essential in Jarrell's work and define it for themselves as well as for readers, whether they approve or disapprove.

In reviews of Jarrell's first two collections, John Crowe Ransom in *The Kenyon Review* and Ruth Lechlitner in *The New York Herald Tribune*[4] both remark his links with "modernism," which Jarrell himself precisely and not very approvingly described in the introduction to "The Rage for the Lost Penny," his contribution to *Five Young American Poets* (1940); both note his technical skill and the threat to his individualism posed by the modernist influence on his themes and attitudes (Lechlitner) and his style (Ransom). Schwartz brilliantly analyzes the effects of Jarrell's by then more independent style in his review of *Little Friend, Little Friend* (1945),[5] which approves Jarrell's "expressive syncopation . . . a passionate stammer" while it worries about the tendency toward "brandishing and flourishing" political ideas and the potential overshadowing of the poetry by the wit of the criticism.

W. S. Graham and Hayden Carruth draw the battle lines over Jarrell's aesthetic choices in their paired reviews of the next book, *Losses* (1948), which appeared as "A Controversy" in *Poetry*.[6] Where Graham deplores Jarrell's attention to "incidentals" rather than action and his "slackness" of language, Carruth (who was later to revise his opinion downward) defends Jarrell's right to his subject and sees him as elevating the objects of daily life by turning them into poetry. Robert Lowell, reviewing *The Seven-League Crutches* (1951), praises Jarrell's "finesse" and originality; M. L. Rosenthal sees in that volume the "romantic idealist" in Jarrell.[7]

The *Selected Poems* (1955) provided an opportunity for a retrospective treatment by Karl Shapiro, who sums up Jarrell's themes—childhood, war, and literature—and remarks his "obsessive return to the great childhood myths"[8] and his habitual opposition of the intellectual to the mysterious and the sentimental to the cruel. Shapiro points out the influence of Rilke, an influence stressed by John Logan in his review of *The Woman at the Washington Zoo* (1960).[9] William Meredith compares Jarrell's earlier and later treatments of the theme of aging in his review of *The Lost World* (1965), concluding that, increasingly for Jarrell, "dailiness has been seen as drama." Philip Booth also notes in *The Lost World* the sense of the sacramental in daily existence, emphasizing the influence of Frost, especially in Jarrell's "flattened" language.[10] Looking over the whole body of Jarrell's poetry in *The Complete Poems* (1969), Helen Vendler calls the dependence for subjects on history, folk tale, and art "risky" but basically approves the "guileless" style Jarrell uses to write of them.[11] She begins to explore the theme of the need for "mothering" that some later critics have treated in greater detail.

Vendler found the "talent" of Jarrell's poetry raised to "genius" in his criticism. In her review of *The Third Book of Criticism* (1970) she wrote that Jarrell "thought naturally in metaphor," had a "talent for suspense" and an "unhesitating belief that though books may not be life, it is life they are about."[12] She saw Jarrell as a "generous evangelist" of other poets, a description that finds affinities in earlier as well as later reviews of his criticism. In *Poetry and the Age* (1953), Berryman and Schwartz had praised Jarrell's exquisite taste in literature, and both responded with enthusiasm to Jarrell's essays on individual poets, though only Schwartz appreciated Jarrell's evaluations of the contemporary situation of poetry in the more general essays of that volume.[13] The reviews of *A Sad Heart at the Supermarket* (1962)[14] provided little that was new in descriptions or evaluations of Jarrell's criticism, but John Lucas, in a review of *Kipling, Auden & Co.* (1980) that is actually a finely tuned survey of Jarrell's whole critical work, summarizes as Jarrell's great gifts his fearlessness in judgment, his wit in description, and his having so often been exactly "right" in his choices of writers and works.[15]

It is probably significant that the reviews of Jarrell's fiction have been less substantial than those on the poetry and criticism, reflecting not only Jarrell's smaller output but his peculiar forms: a series of increasingly nontraditional children's books and "a mosaically constructed long dramatic poem in a prose which, by its allusive and metaphorical tone, demands the same close application and has the same gradually unfolding effect as poetry."[16] Contemporary reviews of *Pictures from an Institution* (1954) were for the most part superficial, although the novel did evoke rather strong emotions pro and con depending on whether the critics liked Jarrell's wit or deplored his "cruelty." John Metcalf, who praised the former, was dubious about the "fuzzy" plot that later writers take as a central critical problem.[17] P. L. Travers found *The Animal Family* (1965) a "paean to family life" and praised its "lyrical factuality,"[18] but Updike's review of *Fly by Night* (1976) uncovers hidden psychological implications in all the children's books, suggesting that Jarrell's "imagery seeks to touch . . . the forbidden actual" in *The Bat-Poet* (1964) and *The Animal Family* as well as *Fly by Night*.[19] Updike remarks also Jarrell's "mix of pluralism and isolation" in the portrayal of his main characters.

The earlier translations, reviewed with the books of poems in which they appeared, were mostly admired as translations and frequently recognized as being work thematically allied to Jarrell's own, while the later *Faust* and *Three Sisters*[20] translations had more mixed reviews, particularly *Faust*, which was criticized for some of the same characteristics found objectionable in Jarrell's own verse: too many colloquialisms, lack of stylistic distinction.

BOOKS AND ESSAYS

The first serious essays on Jarrell's work are in fact long, substantial reviews: Parker Tyler's of *The Seven-League Crutches*, published in *Poetry* in 1952; C. E. Maguire's of *Pictures* in *Renascence* in 1955; and James Dickey's of the *Selected Poems*, in *Sewanee Review* in 1956.[21] Tyler's, reprinted here, explores Jarrell's metamorphic theme by focusing on the word and concept "wood" and showing both its thematic and technical ramifications. Maguire seeks thematic relationships between the novel and the other writings and finds them in Jarrell's "skeptical humanism." Dickey, whose essay is reprinted in *Randall Jarrell, 1914-1965*,[22] is so split between admiration and rejection of Jarrell's aesthetic that he writes in dialogue form with himself, ultimately arguing more persuasively against Jarrell's inadequately poetic language and his "predictable" emotions than for his humaneness and commitment to ex-perienced reality.

The first scholarly study of the poetry was Sister M. Bernetta Quinn's long chapter on Jarrell in *The Metamorphic Tradition in Modern Poetry* (1955),[23] presented here in an abridged version. Sister Bernetta has been Jarrell's most prolific and sympathic critic in a series of articles: after "Randall Jarrell: His Metamorphoses" came "Randall Jarrell's Desert of the Heart" (1961); "Randall Jarrell: Landscapes of Life and LIFE" (1969); and "Warren and Jarrell: the Remembered Child" (1976). Her book, *Randall Jarrell* (1981), is thematically rather than chronologically organized, with chapters on the war poems, the poems on art, the poems on girls and women, and on the children's books, as well as more general chapters on Jarrell's life, his criticism and translations, and his teaching.

The other full-length books to appear on Jarrell so far are my own *The Poetry of Randall Jarrell* (1971), and Helen Hagenbüchle's *The Black Goddess: A Study of the Archetypal Feminine in the Poetry of Randall Jarrell* (1975).[24] The former is a chronological study of the poetry, isolating Jarrell's themes and technical developments as they occur in the course of his career, with glosses on difficult poems and an attempt to designate Jarrell's most significant works. Dr. Hagenbüchle's monograph, her dissertation at the University of Zürich, deals with various symbolic manifestations of the feminine archetype (Jungian) in Jarrell's verse: the "horrid nurse," the "blind mother," the murderess, the witch's house in the forest, mythic goddesses, birds "of death and night" (vulture and owl), and the "devouring" mother. In her essay written especially for *Critical Essays on Randall Jarrell*, Hagenbüchle summarizes her argu-ments from the earlier study, showing how the various female figures in Jarrell's work merge into the figure of the muse of poetry, the inspiration or spirit that both destroys the poet and enables him to create.

Of over fifteen dissertations on Jarrell completed from the late sixties through the seventies, only a few have seen even partial publication, and—of these—fewer still seem to be of great interest, although a number have dealt with interesting themes: children, women, dreams, the imagination, etc. Russell Fowler's essay, "Randall Jarrell's 'Eland': a Key to Motive and Technique in his Poetry" (1974), is adapted from his 1971 University of Minnesota dissertation, "Lost and Found: the Poetry of Randall Jarrell"; Charlotte Beck's 1972 University of Tennessee dissertation yielded "Unicorn to Eland: the Rilkean Spirit in the Poetry of Randall Jarrell" (1979); and Janet Sharistanian's "Powerless Victims in the Poetry of Randall Jarrell," her dissertation at Brown in 1975, investigates the influence of Spinozan metaphysics and Freudian psychology on his poetry, motifs she explores in her essay on the relation of Jarrell's world view to his criticism, "The Poet as Humanitarian: Randall Jarrell's Literary Criticism as Self-Revelation" (1977).[25]

Between 1955 and 1980 a number of survey essays on Jarrell's work appeared, frequently as part of a series or a collection devoted to a number of modern poets, and in one case as an introduction to an anthology. Walter Rideout's long essay, "To Change, to Change!: The Poetry of Randall Jarrell" in *Poets in Progress* (1962), is one of the most useful and touching of these, especially on the war poems. Robert Humphrey's "Randall Jarrell's Poetry" in *Themes and Directions in American Literature* (1969) assesses Jarrell's significance in terms of his themes—necessity and pain, dreams and hope—which Humphrey calls "compass points of twentieth century psychology." Perceptive introductions to Jarrell are provided by M. L. Rosenthal in *Randall Jarrell* (1972), and by F. J. Hoffman in his relatively brief but eloquent introduction to a short anthology, *The Achievement of Randall Jarrell* (1970).[26]

Important scholarly essays by Jerome Mazzaro appeared in 1969 ("Arnoldian Echoes in the Poetry of Randall Jarrell") and 1971 (the brilliant "Between Two Worlds: The Post-Modernism of Randall Jarrell"). The two are amalgamated in Mazzaro's recent book, *Postmodern American Poetry* (1980).[27]

In 1961 *Analects*, a new literary magazine at Woman's College (now the University of North Carolina, Greensboro), produced a special issue on Randall Jarrell edited by Mortimer Guiney and others.[28] In addition to the essays, reprinted here, by Michel Benamou, Richard Fein, and Ingo Seidler, the collection included critical work by Nathan Glick, Glauco Cambon, and Sister Bernetta Quinn. The other important collection of essays on Jarrell is the memorial volume edited by Robert Lowell, Peter Taylor, and Robert Penn Warren: *Randall Jarrell, 1914–1965* (1967). Of the thirty-odd pieces in the volume, most are appreciations and memoirs, some are reprinted reviews, and a few are critical essays: those by Brooks (based on his analysis of "Eighth Air Force" in *Understanding Poetry*), Dickey (the review-essay described above), Denis Donoghue, John Crowe Ransom (also in *The Southern Review* in 1967), Stanley Kunitz, Sister

Bernetta (a shortened and updated version of the *Metamorphic Tradition* essay), and Karl Shapiro (a long essay also published as a Library of Congress pamphlet in 1967). I have chosen not to reprint any of those essays here, as they are readily available in the original collection, which anyone interested in Jarrell will want to consult, as much for the photographs and memoirs as the criticism. Especially valuable there are the reminiscences by Peter and Eleanor Taylor and by Mary von Schrader Jarrell. Mrs. Jarrell's essay, "The Group of Two," and her other biographically oriented pieces, such as the one on Jarrell's *Faust* translation,[29] are very important sources for the critic, and her work in editing Jarrell's letters[30] is simply invaluable, particularly because Jarrell's objection to an official biography has so far influenced Mrs. Jarrell not to approve any extensive biographical projects. My biographical essay for the *Modern American Poets (to 1945)* volume of the *Dictionary of Literary Biography* is the most substantial, reliable source. Jeffrey Meyers' "The Death of Randall Jarrell" (1982), is error-ridden and untrustworthy.[31]

Bibliographical studies begun by Charles Adams in 1958 (*Randall Jarrell: A Bibliography*) and updated in 1961 and 1971 established the groundwork for Jarrell students.[32] A comprehensive descriptive bibliography of primary sources is currently being prepared by Stuart Wright. Dure Jo Gillikin's "A Checklist of Criticism on Randall Jarrell, 1941–1970," useful but incomplete and marred by frequent errors, was compiled in 1971 for the *Bulletin of the New York Public Library*,[33] on the occasion of the Library's acquiring a large number of Jarrell manuscripts for the Berg Collection. Janet Sharistanian is preparing an annotated bibliography of secondary material on Randall Jarrell; her aim is to be comprehensive so far as scholarly material published in the United States is concerned.

CRITICAL ESSAYS ON RANDALL JARRELL

In the present volume I try to present a range both broad and deep, or—to return to my original figure—a body that represents the major trends in Jarrell criticism. After a selection of substantial reviews I present a set of introductory essays, early and late; an abridged version of Sister Bernetta's pioneering essay; Mazzaro's important 1971 essay; a powerful new essay based on *The Black Goddess* by Helen Hagenbüchle; and a recent lively evaluative survey by William Pritchard. This section is followed by more specialized and mostly shorter essays on the poetry, the criticism, the fiction, and the translations, arranged by themes and techniques rather than strictly chronologically. From Parker Tyler's "The Dramatic Lyrism of Randall Jarrell" (noted above) we turn to Richard Fein's "Randall Jarrell's World of War,"[34] a significant early study (1961) that examines the problem of voice in the war poems and contains detailed analyses of "The Death of the Ball Turret Gunner" and "Eighth Air Force." Frances Ferguson's "Randall Jarrell and the Flotations of Voice"

(1974)[35] pursues the question of defining the tone and identity of Jarrell's speakers, whom she sees as "spokesmen for a collective effort by dual or multiple characters." Russell Fowler and Charlotte Beck[36] both consider the motif of the eland (in "Seele im Raum") as a key to typical Jarrell themes and techniques, but Fowler concentrates on the poems as "parables" that use concrete instances to investigate questions about the human condition, where Beck pursues the connections with Rilke—motifs of *Kindertod*; life's transience; isolation and captivity; and the like. Sister Bernetta's essay, "Landscapes of Life and LIFE,"[37] examines how Jarrell's treatment of landscape description reflects his poetic themes and also his interest in painting. A shortened version of Mary Kinzie's "The Man Who Painted Bulls" (1980)[38] probes Jarrell's significance for his time as an explorer of the "unknown, unwanted life." Notes on "The Death of the Ball Turret Gunner" by Leven Dawson and David Cornelius and on "The Woman at the Washington Zoo" by Michel Benamou round out this section.[39]

Besides Janet Sharistanian's treatment of the criticism as a gloss on the values Jarrell also expressed in his poems (cited earlier), Jarrell's criticism is surveyed by Keith Monroe, whose 1979 University of North Carolina at Greensboro dissertation provided the research and conclusions for "Principle and Practice in the Criticism of Randall Jarrell," written for this volume. Monroe's clear and well-documented summary of Jarrell's stylistic techniques in the criticism could well form the basis of stylistic studies of Jarrell's other work.

Sylvia Angus's sensitive review essay,[40] written on the reissue of *Pictures from an Institution* in 1962, initiates a section on Jarrell's fiction. In an article written for *Critical Essays on Randall Jarrell*, "To Benton with Love and Judgment," I draw upon Angus's articulation of the theme of "paradise lost" in the novel to investigate what I see as a dialectical structure manifesting a conflict between Jarrell's natural inclination to find fault with the world and his impulse to love it. Kathe Davis Finney, in "The Poet, Truth, and Other Fictions: Randall Jarrell as Storyteller," another essay prepared for this volume, looks not only at the novel but at the children's books through the perspective of recent theories of metafiction, in an attempt to discover how Jarrell sees the relation of art to reality in general and to human wishes and needs in particular.

Ingo Seidler's twenty-year-old essay on the translations,[41] originally in *Analects*, is paired with a new, more widely-ranging essay by Richard K. Cross that not only evaluates the translations but sees them in the whole context of Jarrell's work.

PROSPECTS

Because Jarrell submitted his manuscripts letter-perfect and took great care with proofs, there are no textual problems as such, although there are problems in using the works and some of the manuscript materials because of their arrangement. *The Complete Poems* retains the ordering of the *Selected Poems* and places that group of poems first, followed by poems from the two collections written after it, *The Woman at the Washington Zoo* and *The Lost World*, and some poems Jarrell had planned to use in a new book. The volume then picks up poems from the earlier collections that were not reprinted in *Selected Poems*, uncollected poems, and unpublished poems, the latter given with dates, when known. Although the arrangement puts Jarrell's own choices first, as he likely would have done in a "collected poems," it is inconvenient to use as a scholarly tool. Those without immediate access to the original volumes or to one of the several incomplete bibliographies cannot tell which poems in the *Selected Poems* section come from which earlier collections. Moreover, in cases where poems were revised between successive publications, only the later version is given. Ideally, one might wish for a variorum edition, but lacking that a chronological index to be used with the *Complete Poems*, listing sources for other published versions of individual poems, would expedite matters. So, too, would careful cataloging and labeling of each piece of manuscript material held by the Berg Collection and by UNC-Greensboro. The essays and reviews are also presented nonchronologically in the various collections, and some but not all of *A Sad Heart at the Supermarket* is now reprinted in *Kipling, Auden & Co.* (There are also some differences between English and American editions of some of the books.) It is to be hoped that Stuart Wright's forthcoming bibliography will fulfill the need for a single source in which all such information can be located and verified, saving students from pointless iteration of each others' labors.

The upcoming publication of the letters should spur further biographical and source studies and make it possible for Jarrell's commentators to fill in some of the gaps and soft spots in the critical structure. Attention to particular groups of poems, especially the very early and very late poems, may well yield some revisions in the way Jarrell is seen. Studies of his style based on the manuscripts and informed by current research in linguistics would be valuable in describing more precisely the subtle effects Jarrell achieves in "voice" and rhythm and in dispelling the mistaken apprehension of some critics that Jarrell's style is artless. Perhaps most significant of all would be more sustained and probing attempts to view Jarrell in relation to his contemporaries—Lowell, Berryman, Schwartz, the other poets of World War II—and to his American influences—Whitman, Williams, Frost, and especially the Fugitives.

What has already been done, however, is substantial. With this collection and with *Randall Jarrell, 1914–1965*, with Sister Bernetta's *Randall Jarrell* and my *The Poetry of Randall Jarrell*, and with some of the survey essays noted above but not reprinted because of space considerations, the reader is well guided in developing an appreciation of the achievement of Randall Jarrell: poet, critic, novelist, writer for children, translator—a man of letters in a very complete sense, a man for his time and for ours.

SUZANNE FERGUSON

Notes

1. Suzanne Ferguson, *The Poetry of Randall Jarrell* (Baton Rouge: Louisiana State Univ. Press, 1971).

2. Randall Jarrell, *Blood for a Stranger* (New York: Harcourt Brace & Co., 1942).

3. Randall Jarrell, "The Rage for the Lost Penny," *Five Young American Poets* (Norfolk, Conn.: New Directions, 1940), pp. 81–123.

4. John Crowe Ransom, "Constellation of Five Young Poets," *Kenyon Review*, 3 (1941), 377–79; Ruth Lechlitner, "Music of Despair," *New York Herald Tribune Books*, 29 November 1942, p. 22.

5. Randall Jarrell, *Little Friend, Little Friend* (New York: Dial Press, 1945); Delmore Schwartz, "The Dream from Which No One Wakes," *Nation*, 161 (December 1945), 590.

6. W. S. Graham and Hayden Carruth, "Jarrell's 'Losses': A Controversy," *Poetry*, 72 (1948), 302–11; Randall Jarrell, *Losses* (New York: Harcourt Brace, 1948).

7. Randall Jarrell, *The Seven-League Crutches* (New York: Harcourt Brace, 1951); Robert Lowell, "Randall Jarrell's Wild Dogmatism," *New York Times Book Review*, 7 October 1951, pp. 7, 41; M. L. Rosenthal, "Of Pity and Innocence," *New Republic*, 2 June 1952, p. 21.

8. Randall Jarrell, *Selected Poems* (New York: Alfred A. Knopf, 1955); Karl Shapiro, "In the Forests of the Little People," *New York Times Book Review*, 13 March 1955, p. 4.

9. Randall Jarrell, *The Woman at the Washington Zoo* (New York: Atheneum, 1960); John Logan, "The Rilkean Sense: Randall Jarrell, *The Woman at the Washington Zoo,*" *Saturday Review*, 28 January 1961, pp. 29–30.

10. Randall Jarrell, *The Lost World* (New York: Macmillan Co., 1965); William Meredith, "The Adventures of a Private Eye," *New York Herald Tribune Book World*, 14 March 1965, p. 4; Philip Booth, "The Poet Fulfills the Man," *Christian Science Monitor*, 11 March 1965, p. 11.

11. Randall Jarrell, *The Complete Poems* (New York: Farrar, Straus & Giroux, 1969); Helen Vendler, "The Complete Poems," *New York Times Book Review*, 29 February 1969, pp. 5, 42.

12. Randall Jarrell, *The Third Book of Criticism* (New York: Farrar, Straus & Giroux, 1969); Helen Vendler, "The Third Book of Criticism," *New York Times Book Review*, 4 January 1970, pp. 4–5.

13. Randall Jarrell, *Poetry and the Age* (New York: Alfred A. Knopf, 1953); John Berryman, "Matter and Manner: *Poetry and the* Age," *New Republic*, 2 November 1953, pp. 27–28; Delmore Schwartz, "Light on the Poet's Waste Land," *New York Times Book Review*, 16 August 1953, p. 1.

14. Randall Jarrell, *A Sad Heart at the Supermarket* (New York: Atheneum, 1962).

15. Randall Jarrell, *Kipling, Auden & Co.* (New York: Farrar, Straus & Giroux, 1980); John Lucas, "Arriving at Acceptance," *Times Literary Supplement*, 19 June 1981, pp. 703–04.

16. C. E. Maguire, "Shape of the Lightning: Randall Jarrell," *Renascence*, 7 (1955), 181.

17. Randall Jarrell, *Pictures from an Institution* (New York: Knopf, 1954); John Metcalf

"New Novels: *Pictures from an Institution,*" *Spectator*, 22 October 1954, p. 506; C. E. Maguire, "Shape of the Lightning: Randall Jarrell," *Renascence*, 7 (1955), 115–20, 181–86, 195; Sylvia Angus, "Randall Jarrell, Novelist: A Reconsideration," *Southern Review*, NS 2 (1966), 689–96; Kathe Davis Finney, "The Poet, Truth, and Other Fictions," *Critical Essays on Randall Jarrell* (Boston: G. K. Hall, 1983), pp. 284–97; Suzanne Ferguson, "To Benton, with Love and Judgment: *Pictures from an Institution,*" *Critical Essays on Randall Jarrell*, pp. 272–83.

18. Randall Jarrell, *The Animal Family* (New York: Pantheon, 1965); P. L. Travers, "A Kind of Visitation," *New York Times Book Review*, 21 November 1965, p. 56.

19. Randall Jarrell, *The Bat-Poet* (New York: Macmillan, 1964); *Fly by Night* (New York: Farrar, Straus & Giroux, 1976); John Updike, "Fly by Night," *New York Times Book Review*, 14 November 1976, pp. 25, 36.

20. Randall Jarrell, trans., *Goethe's Faust, Part One* (New York: Farrar, Straus & Giroux, 1976); Anton Chekhov, *The Three Sisters*, trans. Randall Jarrell (New York: Macmillan, 1969).

21. Parker Tyler, "The Dramatic Lyrism of Randall Jarrell," *Poetry*, 79 (1952), 335–46; C. E. Maguire, cited above, n. 17; James Dickey, "Some of All of It," *Sewanee Review*, 64 (1956), 339–48.

22. Robert Lowell, Peter Taylor, and Robert Penn Warren, eds., *Randall Jarrell, 1914–1965* (New York: Farrar, Straus & Giroux, 1967).

23. Sister M. Bernetta Quinn, "Randall Jarrell: His Metamorphoses, *The Metamorphic Tradition in Modern Poetry* (New Brunswick: Rutgers Univ. Press, 1955; New York: Gordian Press, 1966), pp. 168–206; "Randall Jarrell's Desert of the Heart," *Analects*, 1 (1961), 24–28; "Randall Jarrell: Landscapes of Life and LIFE," *Shenandoah*, 20 (1969), 49–78; "Warren and Jarrell: The Remembered Child," *Southern Literary Journal*, 8 (1976), 24–40; *Randall Jarrell* (Boston: Twayne Publishers, 1981).

24. Helen Hagenbüchle, *The Black Goddess: A Study of the Archetypal Feminine in the Poetry of Randall Jarrell,*" Schweitzer Anglistische Arbeiten, Vol. 79 (Bern: Francke, 1975).

25. Russell Fowler, "Randall Jarrell's 'Eland': a Key to Motive and Technique in His Poetry," *Iowa Review*, 5 (1974), 113–26; Charlotte Beck, "Unicorn to Eland: the Rilkean Spirit in the Poetry of Randall Jarrell," *Southern Literary Journal*, 12 (1979), 3–17; Janet Sharistanian, "The Poet as Humanitarian: Randall Jarrell's Literary Criticism as Self-Revelation," *South Carolina Review*, 10 (1977), 32–42.

26. Walter Rideout, "To Change, to Change!: The Poetry of Randall Jarrell," *Poets in Progress: Critical Prefaces to Ten Contemporary Americans*, ed. Edward B. Hungerford (Evanston: Northwestern Univ. Press, 1962), pp. 156–78; Robert Humphrey, "Randall Jarrell's Poetry," *Themes and Directions in American Literature*, ed. Ray B. Browne and Donald Pizer (Lafayette, Ind.: Purdue Univ. Press, 1969), pp. 220–33; M. L. Rosenthal, *Randall Jarrell* (Minneapolis: Univ. of Minnesota Press, 1972); F. J. Hoffman, *The Achievement of Randall Jarrell: A Comprehensive Selection of His Poems with a Critical Introduction* (Glenview, Ill.: Scott, Foresman, 1970).

27. Jerome Mazzaro, "Arnoldian Echoes in the Poetry of Randall Jarrell," *Western Humanities Review*, 23 (1969), 314–18; "Between Two Worlds: The Postmodernism of Randall Jarrell," *Salmagundi*, 17 (1971), 93–113, rpt. *Contemporary Poetry in America*, ed. Robert Boyers (New York: Schocken Books, 1974), pp. 78–98, and *Postmodern American Poetry*, by Jerome Mazzaro (Champaign, Ill.: Univ. of Illinois Press, 1980), pp. 32–58.

28. *Analects*, 1 (1961).

29. "Randall Jarrell at Work," *Columbia Forum*, 2 (1973), 24–30; reprinted as the afterword to Jarrell's translation of *Goethe's Faust, Part One*. See also "Reflections on Jerome," in *Jerome: The Biography of a Poem*, by Randall Jarrell (New York: Grossman, 1971), pp. 11–18; "Ideas and Poems," *Parnassus*, 5 (Fall-Winter, 1976), 213–30; "Peter and

Randall," *Shenandoah*, 28 (Winter, 1977), 28–34; and "Randall Jarrell: Letters to Vienna," *American Poetry Review*, July/August, 1977, pp. 11–17.

30. To be published by Houghton Mifflin in 1983.

31. Peter Quartermain, ed., *Modern American Poets (to 1945)*, *Dictionary of Literary Biography* (Detroit: Gale Research Co./Bruccoli Clark Research, 1983); Jeffrey Meyers, "The Death of Randall Jarrell," *Virginia Quarterly Review*, 58 (Summer, 1982), 450–67.

32. Charles Adams, *Randall Jarrell: A Bibliography* (Chapel Hill: Univ. of North Carolina Press, 1958); "A Supplement to Randall Jarrell: A Bibliography," *Analects*, 1 (1961), 49–56; "A Bibliographical Excursion with Some Biographical Footnotes on Randall Jarrell," *Bulletin of Bibliography*, 28 (1971), 79–81. See also Margaret Kisslinger, "A Bibliography of Randall Jarrell," *Bulletin of Bibliography*, 24 (1966), 243–47; Karl Shapiro, *Randall Jarrell* (Washington, D.C.: Library of Congress, 1967), pp. 25–47.

33. Dure Jo Gillikin, "A Checklist of Criticism on Randall Jarrell, 1941–1970: with an Introduction and a List of His Major Works," *Bulletin of the New York Public Library*, 75 (1971), 176–94.

34. Richard Fein, "Randall Jarrell's World of War," *Analects*, 1 (1961), 14–23.

35. Frances Ferguson, "Randall Jarrell and the Flotations of Voice," *Georgia Review*, 28 (1974), 423–39.

36. In the essays cited above, n. 25.

37. Cited above, n. 23.

38. Mary Kinzie, "The Man Who Painted Bulls," *Southern Review*, NS 16 (1980), 829–52.

39. Leven M. Dawson, "Jarrell's 'The Death of the Ball Turret Gunner,' " *Explicator*, 31 (1972), item 29; D. K. Cornelius, "Jarrell's 'The Death of the Ball Turret Gunner,' " *Explicator*, 35 (1977), 3; Michel Benamou, "The Woman at the Zoo's Fearful Symmetry," *Analects*, 1 (1961), 2–4.

40. Angus, cited above, n. 17.

41. Ingo Seidler, "Jarrell and the Art of Translation," *Analects*, 1 (1961), 37–48.

REVIEWS

[From "Constellation of Five Young Poets"]

John Crowe Ransom*

The serious publisher owes a great obligation to the new poets, and this one discharges it by publishing five in one volume. Each supplies a photograph, a short essay about his understanding of the art, and thirty pages or so of verse. It sounds like being regimented into the army, but there is no real indignity about it; they would have been undignified if they had sulked and refused. Going in, not hanging back, they make one of the most interesting and important books of poetry in some years. None of them had been published in an independent volume; they had had only periodical publication, a good deal of that. But each is clearly a poet of some distinction, and more promise, superior to "finished" dozens who have achieved the books but not had the promise. Though it sounds severe, I think this is perhaps enough publication for them at the moment, and I believe they will think so too—so much do I believe in the possibility that their futures will eclipse their presents.

. . . .

To bestow another superlative, I think Jarrell is quite the most brilliant of the five. But he too has a curious compunction or so. One prevents him not so much from offering meters as from realizing them. He has an angel's velocity and range with language, and drops dazzling textures of meaning done up in a phonetic raggedness so consistent that we know he must be nursing some infection of puritan principle. Nor is that his only inhibition. I must quote from his prose statement of "some of the qualities of typical modernist poetry":

> . . . very interesting language, a great emphasis on connotation, "texture"; extreme intensity, forced emotion—violence; a good deal of obscurity; emphasis on details, on the part rather than on the whole; experimental or novel qualities of some sort; a tendency toward external formlessness and internal disorganization—these are justified, generally, as the disorganization required to express a disorganized age, or alternatively, as newly-discovered and more complex types of organization; an

*Review of 5 Young American Poets: George Marion O'Donnell, Randall Jarrell, John Berryman, Mary Barnard, W. R. Moses. Reprinted from The Kenyon Review, 3 (1941), 377–79, by permission of the journal.

extremely personal style—*refine your singularities*: lack of restraint—all tendencies are forced to their limits; there is a good deal of emphasis on the unconscious, dream-structure, the thoroughly subjective; the poet's attitudes are usually anti-scientific, anti-commonsense, anti-public—he is, essentially, removed; poetry is primarily lyric, intensive—the few long poems are aggregations of lyric details; poems usually have, not a logical, but the more or less associational structure of dramatic monologue; and so on and so on.

In the prose conclusion, as in the poetic sequel, Jarrell forbids us to say yet that he is a post-modernist. But probably he will be. It is self-consciousness which stops the young poets from their own graces; too much of thinking about all the technical possibilities at once, as well as too much attention to changes in the fashion. I quote the latter part of "Love, in Its Separate Being," a poem which shows how love, the selfish brat, grows and wheedles the world into accepting him as tyrant:

> From the tamer, the crammer, the trainer,
> The torturers' shredding hours,
> Who would have dreamed for a minute
> That love and love's perfection flower?
>
> Where love moved, a home-sick stranger,
> By bare shires and foreign shores,
> Earth crackles with love's repeated look:
> The subject's glance, the heart each shares
>
> To be ignorant, to be innocent,
> Welcome the warships sent for the exile,
> Divine in his words the perfected world
> Of—grown giant, gracious—the exposed child;
>
> Yield the great keys, the graves, and the charter—
> In the bared head, over the soldiers' song,
> See sparkling, rising and murderous in their grace,
> The emblems of that butchered king;
>
> And up the choked mouth and closing way
> The doomed men cry: He is one of us.
> But necessary, triumphant, beautiful,
> Love laughs and is not magnanimous.

I find beautiful and characteristic uses here; if one has read Jarrell before he will not go far in this without saying, Jarrell again. An individual poet, then. But there is nothing so private about the absurd near-rhymes and coy changes of pace, nor about some of the extreme elliptical densities. These, as Jarrell has pointed out, are "qualities" of "typical modernist." I do not mean to overstress them. I point out that they do not express what is individual in himself.

Music of Despair: *Blood For a Stranger*, by Randall Jarrell

Ruth Lechlitner*

This is the first book of a poet who grew up in Tennessee and California, and is now teaching at the University of Texas. Yet readers of the poems in "Blood for a Stranger" might justifiably believe them the product of a public school, Oxford educated Englishman. Randall Jarrell, however, is not an isolated case in point. He belongs with those sometimes called modernists or intellectuals whose convergent interests, symbols and technique owe nothing to nationalism: to them, at least, there are no more islands. Some poetry lovers may lament the current lack of a feeling for native roots and tradition that unmistakably set apart, for example, Wordsworth from Whitman, Masefield from Sandburg or Frost. But those inter-related changes which during the last two decades have made the world small, are largely responsible for breaking down national viewpoint and expression in contemporary writing. It is this, rather than any desire, conscious or unconscious, to imitate each other that has produced a consanguinity in the work of the younger poets.

Randall Jarrell's poems, then, are typical, almost compositely so, of what most of these young British and American poets have been writing in recent years. By this I mean no discredit to Mr. Jarrell; nor do I mean to imply that he lacks individuality. But the fact is that, given a "blindfold" test, more than one reader might name "90 North," for instance, as Spender's (note the resemblance to the latter's "Polar Exploration"); or Jarrell's "Because of Me, Because of You," as Auden's. To a greater degree than his American contemporaries, Jarrell does have that self-confessional, self-analytical temperament characteristic of the English group. Like them he uses the dream as symbol, and shares their interest in Freudian analysis. He is fond of exposing states of neurosis. "A Story," the thoughts of a boy away at school and ill, painfully and almost unbearably reflects self-dramatization and self-flagellation; likewise "Christmas Roses," in which the "patient" is adult.

Whether he speaks in direct comment, through the dream symbol or the fable (with its sorcerers, ogres, ghosts and talking animals drawn from a child's universe) Jarrell is sharply critical of the contemporary world. His recurrent theme is that humanity walks in an inescapable maze of guilt. We are all part of the world's crime, or accessory to it, and the best that can happen to us is death. Approximating the nihilism of Jeffers, Jarrell sees modern civilization as a system of destruction:

*Review of *Blood for a Stranger*. Reprinted from the *New York Herald Tribune Books*, 29 November 1942, p. 22, by permission of the author.

> "Tomorrow we may be remembered
> As a technologist's nightmare, the megalomaniacs
> Who present to posterity as their justification
> The best armies that the world ever saw."
> Who made virtue and poetry and understanding
> The prohibited reserves of the expert, of workers
> Specialized as the ant-soldier; and who turned from their difficult
> Versions to the degenerate myth, the cruelties
> So incredible and habitual they seemed escapes.

His fable of "The Blind Sheep" is repeated in "The Long Vacation," which darkly portrays the sick of humankind, stitched up and convalescent, ready to be taken back into the maze from which they had found the "only exit."

The theme is variably extended in "For an Emigrant." When Jarrell breaks free from the affectation and the cerebration that mars some of his work, he writes with simple, genuine compassion of those made homeless by the crimes of war and invasion. He pictures such a one voyaging to a new world with the hope of freedom; but

> You escaped from nothing; the westering soul
> Finds Europe waiting for it over every sea.

He carries on his bitter comment: the world one must really escape from is the America where each can think still, "I am innocent." And "The Refugees" concludes with a passionate indictment of the tragedy of wasted life in our time:

> What else are their lives but a journey to the vacant
>   Satisfaction of death? And the mask
>   They wear tonight through their waste
> Is death's rehearsal. Is it really extravagant
>   To read in their faces: What is there that we possessed
>   That we were willing to trade for this?

Altogether "it's bad music; but it's what we hear." Whether the "bad music" of despair and negation, however honestly and brilliantly set down, constitutes major composition in poetry is debatable. Certainly Mr. Jarrell has as much warmth and understanding and greater technical skill than most of his contemporaries who cry out against the evils of this day.

The Dream from Which
No One Wakes

Delmore Schwartz*

It is an open secret, and a pity, that Randall Jarrell is known chiefly as the author of overwhelming wisecracks about other poets. Jarrell is not entirely innocent of responsibility for this reputation, nor is the reader: both are perhaps too eager to forget everything for the sake of a good laugh. But only the reader who forgets the jokes and remembers Jarrell's first two books will be prepared for the extraordinary growth in this new book. In his first two books many of the poems were weakened by a thinness and abstractness of texture and reference; it was as if the poet saw his subjects through opera glasses. One was forced to remember Eliot's observation that "the great poets give us real men, talking; set up before us real events, moving." For all the genuineness of the poems, the net result resembled the dim and ghastly negative which has to be held up to the light, and not the developed photograph full of daylight and defined objects. And it was impossible not to think of Jarrell's critical prose and to guess that if only the wit might be part of the verse, what a modernist Pope we might have.

The wit remains absent and the abstractness is not entirely dissolved. But in this new book Jarrell has a much closer, much more intimate grasp of his subject, perhaps because he has actually lived through the war with which his first poems were also concerned, but concerned in terms of intuition and premonition, not of the event and the aftermath. From the start Jarrell's sensibility has been avid, ravenous to know, to take in what really exists, to stay awake and to stare at the dark as well as the light. In "Little Friend, Little Friend" this quality of mind, this passion to be aware and awake and alive, comes up against the immense, international, and yet muffled, scattered, masked terror of war, precisely the kind of phenomenon to make such a mind most articulate, as Shakespearean heroes are most eloquent and full of insight when they are dying. Instead of general affirmation or rejection of the war, Jarrell takes the particular part of the dead. In poem after poem the dead soldier says, "*Why did I die?*" And that is the end of the poem. The bombers can't land in the fog, the child does not know why he is in the refugee ship, the prisoners load trucks like automata, the halfwit can accept his mother's death and the drafting of his sister, he can accept everything but that "They took my cat for the Army Corps," "And I cried, and I cried, I wanted to die." Indeed, the obsessive symbols of the cat, the child, and the dream emerge through most of the book, forced by the pressure of the emotions of hopelessness, helplessness, animal terror and animal

*Review of *Little Friend, Little Friend*. Reprinted from the *Nation*, 161 (1 December 1945), 590, by permission of the journal.

tenderness, senseless death, and shrieking over-all perplexity at the fact that men kill each other.

These emotions show their effect in the development of Jarrell's versification. His personal rhythm is now both clear and various. To the ignorant or inattentive reader, who looks in poetry only for the sensational imagery and obvious chanting, Jarrell's writing may seem slack and loose when it is exactly the contrary. By means of justified repetition, hurried anapests, and a caesura fixed by alliteration Jarrell gets a wonderfully expressive syncopation of movement, a tone which insists, like a passionate stammer, and reiterates nervously because the whole being is compelled by anxiety and guilt:

> They lived, they died. "I am what I am,"
> Someone heard Swift stammer: he was crazy.
> Beethoven, dying, learned to multiply.
> What does it mean? Why, nothing.
> Nothing? . . . How well we all die!

New defects occur also as a result of the poet's growth. In some poems he writes like a *nouveau riche* in ideas, crudely brandishing and flourishing Marxist ideas and permitting himself such a line as "But soon all the *chimneys* were hidden with *contracts*," a mixture of the visual and the abstract which tries to and cannot become a genuine—which is to say, *seen*—image. An effort is made to versify Marx baldly, to go from statements about trade and credit to a perception of mines and mills. Consequently the poem collapses. Twice, and strangely for an author like Jarrell, he permits his emotions about the war to become an anger against books and the university. The thesis of Archibald MacLeish is renewed when Jarrell attempts to say that if knowledge and scholarship were not actually the causes of war, they ought somehow to have been able to transform capitalist society and prevent war. This banal and sentimental view arrives at hideous absurdity in the poem in which the climax is the burning of the university. Two opposed quotations bear directly on this kind of hysteria: "The letter killeth but the spirit giveth life"; "The spirit killeth, but the letter giveth life." It ought to be possible to remember both of these maxims, for both were spoken with authority and both may be useful pieces of knowledge.

For the most part, however, the motives of honesty, courage, and inconsolable love of life are here submitted to the conditions of poetry and fulfilled in them. If, as one poem declares, this life is a dream from which no one wakes, the dreamer has refused to deceive himself, to let himself go, and to forget what he believes and loves.

Jarrell's *Losses*: A Controversy

W. S. Graham and Hayden Carruth*

"IT ALL COMES BACK TO ME NOW"

Mr. Randall Jarrell's name as a poet and critic is one which in England as in this country carries considerable prestige. One is at a loss therefore to account for the shocking betrayal of poetic responsibilites and, by implication, critical ones exemplified by his third collection of poems. One's perplexity grows when one finds the critics comparing it variously to the work of Browning, Auden and Tennyson, and included with the "great artificers" who "bring us into a world so painfully clarified that it seems there is nothing more to say." Rarely have I witnessed such a dividing gulf between reputation and achievement. The situation raises fundamental questions concerning poetic and critical standards.

Losses comprises a collection of poems which are mostly spun from what should be the involuntary incidentals of a poem, rather than the poems being made first for the poetic action. Ideally, it is the intensity of the poetic action which sets off and elevates into significance these surrounding incidental values—news, observation, narrative or fiction, etc., of any "subject" separable from the words and alive in its own right. Mr. Jarrell's notes at the end of *Losses* indicate an almost naive reliance upon such incidentals. For example, to explicate a slight, versified anecdote, *O My Name It Is Sam Hall*, Mr. Jarrell obligingly informs, "These men are three American prisoners and one American M.P., at a B-29 training base in Southern Arizona—Davis-Monthan Field, in fact." Or in explanation of a line of imagery in *Pilots, Man Your Planes*, ". . . *But on the tubes the raiders oscillate*: On the radar set, that is; the view plate looks like a cathode-ray oscillograph." The painstaking documentation of the poems in the notes suggests that Mr. Jarrell believes there is some helpful connection between the reporting of poetic experience and its verifiability in the "real" world.

Behind this dependence on objective documentation there would seem to be a fear of any formal, consciously "made" poetry. As an addition to his intended verisimilitude Mr. Jarrell sprinkles his poems full of little conversational phrases trailing off to dots which, as a device, have a loosening effect upon a poetic line which is, in the first place, conceived at too low-grade a tension. He also employs dashes liberally, although not consistently, sometimes to do the work of commas, other times of periods. The whole would seem to represent a revolt against the "poetic," an urge to deal with an honest, thorny reality. While the surface of Mr. Jarrell's

*Reprinted from *Poetry*, 72 (1948), 302–11, by permission of the editor of *Poetry*. Copyright © 1948 by the Modern Poetry Association.

poetry is self-consciously modern, with all the up-to-date objects of the contemporary war-world—gun-turrets, flak, Jills, Stalags, radar, carriers, hutment, prisoners-of-war, etc.—seeking to create a contemporary fiction, in reality the timbre of the prosodic voice is old-fashioned and laboriously clichéd. Mr. Jarrell talks of ". . . . the train's long mourning whistle / Wailed from the valley below," "the last cloud-girdled peak," the ward is "barred" with moonlight, "the squirrel gnaws mechanically." Always the texture of the poem is as loose and casual as possible, as though attempting to hide the fact that the words follow each other in an order chosen for any conscious poetic end. So we have a poem, *Money*, starting with (surely a handicap) the extraordinary, certainly-not-nymph-and-shepherd lines:

> I sit here eating milk-toast in my lap-robe—
> They've got my night-shirt starchier than I told 'em . . .
>   Huh! . . .
> I'll tell 'em . . .

The poem, a monologue in dialect which does not succeed in creating its speaker, ends with the banal confession (a banality which is not relieved even if one is conscious of its contrivance for a dramatic purpose):

> When my Ma died I boarded with a farmer
> In the next county; I used to think of her,
> And I looked round me, as I could,
> And I saw what it added up to: money.
> Now I'm dying—I can't call this living—
> I haven't any cause to change my mind.
> They say that money isn't everything: it isn't;
> Money don't help you none when you are sighing
> For something else in this wide world to buy . . .
> The first time I couldn't think of anything
> I didn't have, it shook me.
>   But giving does as well.

In descriptive passages, as for example in the poem *A Country Life*, he piles up the adjectives till the nouns are over-governed and the picture no longer substantially visual:

> Or why, for once, the lagging heron
> Flaps from the little creek's parched cresses
> Across the harsh-grassed, gullied meadow
> To the black, rowed evergreens below.

Because most of the poems in *Losses* deal with a war environment one expects them to contain the antithesis of life and death (that is, both as subjects objectified by the created poems as well as common subject, by implication, in all poems). Yet here they are embossed and studded with capitalized Lifes and Deaths throughout. The word "Life" and the word

"Death" are no more help in articulating some vision of life and death than the word "orange." In fact, they usually serve as an evasion of any valid comment. In one poem, *Burning the Letters*, which otherwise might have been successful, Mr. Jarrell hits the jackpot and litters his pages with the big verities. We have words and phrases like "his Life wells up from death, the death of Man," "The dying God, the eaten Life," "The Light flames," "The unsearchable / Death of the lives lies dark upon the life," "eternal life," "O death of all my life" (there are nine mentions of life in the poem) and "O grave." O what a deafening organ-peal of the pseudo-profound. The voice which might have led us nearer the mysteries of life and death is lost in the noise. I had supposed the snare of the old abstract poetic gear would be more cunningly handled by a poet of Mr. Jarrell's training. Here he allows the poem to dissolve into "vague immensities."

Where Mr. Jarrell is influenced by Robert Frost, a poet to whom he has paid critical tribute, his work reveals a simple, old-fashioned nostalgia and these poems work successfully at a humble magnitude. *The Breath of Night* falls into this category. It begins

> The moon rises. The red cubs rolling
> In the ferns by the rotten oak
> Stare over a marsh and a meadow
> To the farm's white wisp of smoke.

But, it should be noticed, the final stanza effects an overtly moral dimension similar to that in Hardy's *Satires of Circumstance*. For as a matter of fact, Mr. Jarrell is more obligated to Hardy's small dramatic framework of incident than he is to Browning's interest in character or Frost's effectively restrained sermonizing. Still, when he remembers the deceptively homely but polished verse of Frost, he can achieve a pleasant simplicity, as in *A Country Life*:

> A bird that I don't know,
> Hunched on his light-pole like a scarecrow,
> Looks sideways out into the wheat
> The wind waves under the waves of heat.
> The field is yellow as egg-bread dough
> Except where . . .

There is a less hysterical "realism" in the careful observation of these details than in the more violent war poems. Unfortunately, however, such observation gives way towards the poem's end to Mr. Jarrell's reliance upon the worn-out poetic diction of lines like:

> The shadows lengthen, and a dreaming hope
> Breathes, from the vague mound, *Life*;
> From the grove under the spire
> Stars shine, and a wandering light
> Is kindled for the mourner, man.

> The angel kneeling with the wreath
> Sees, in the moonlight, graves.

Perhaps the most successful poem in *Losses* is *A Camp in the Prussian Forest*. It is a quiet, slow-paced description of a death camp. The action or the scene behind the poem, the incidental news which is contained in the poem, is moving as a good newspaper report of horror is moving. But few words in the poem are positioned to create that flash of vision which in its quality incorporates the "news" of the poem, but which is so much more than just that. When this does happen, as in stanza six, the effect is liberating:

> I paint the star I sawed from yellow pine—
> And plant the sign
> In soil that does not yet refuse
> Its usual Jews.

Here it is the word "usual" which, in its proximity to "Jews" (the musical half-chime should be mentioned) adds a philosophical dimension to what, up to that point, has been a statement made at a level of personal compassion.

Losses represents a retreat from the small eminence achieved by Mr. Jarrell's second collection, *Little Friend, Little Friend*. If his "modernity" has led him into an over-strategic attempt to resuscitate certain discarded poetic modes and intentions in the ordering of contemporary experience, I can only point out that the job has been much better done by poets of World War I like Owen, Read, Grenfell and Rosenberg. If *Losses* were a book by an unknown young poet, one would not consider it worth reviewing. Keeping in mind the reputation of Randall Jarrell, I find it a disappointing and baffling experience.

W. S. Graham

MR. GRAHAM AND THE DEAD CIGAR

Here is another reviewer who tells us what is the stuff of poetry. It was tried before, I think, by Bruin of Colchester and, somewhat later, by Mgr. Polidore Flaquet.

Now it is time to question this kind of talk by Mr. Graham. It is time to challenge what Mr. Stephen Spender, a better-tempered Englishman who is also living at present in our monstrous country, recently deplored as "the denigration of American poetry as external by English writers."

For the subjects of poetry cannot be limited. The lesson taught to us by Mr. Ezra Pound, Dr. William Carlos Williams, and Mr. T. S. Eliot cannot be soon forgotten. Poetry will be what it must be, and it is not the critic's job to administer it or patronize it, but rather to investigate its methods and explore its meanings.

It is apparent from Mr. Graham's review of *Losses* that poetry is, in his opinion, only that thing which puffs itself up, like a certain tropical fish, whenever you touch it. It must be a living thing, swimming back and forth between the lines of print, ready to explode in your face at the slightest anxiety. It is not the words, it is not what they say; it is a small organism which slips skittishly among the periods and commas, eyeing the barnacle-encrusted words with dark distrust. What a pity Mr. Graham has never caught one of these creatures to show to the rest of us!

The fact of the matter is that what Mr. Graham calls "incidental values" can be turned into very good poetry indeed. Furthermore, whether we would or no, these values are hardly incidental. The world is full of motor cars, of machine guns, of money. These things have a considerable influence, sometimes good and sometimes bad, on our modern life. They can be treated as instruments by all of us, as statistics by sociologists, as subjects by artists. Many poets use them as symbols; many more (and I believe Mr. Randall Jarrell is, on the whole, one of these) choose to employ them in their own right as things to be noticed and questioned. They cannot be eliminated from poetry, nor can they be made incidental to it.

Two capacities are required for the composition of poetry: a talent for writing in our English language, and a sure intelligence. If any person possesses these qualities to a sufficient degree, he can create poetry. I would be the last to deny that learning, sensitivity, good taste, and understanding of the tradition may assist poetic endeavor, but these attainments, however they may lend assistance, are surely not the first qualities that a poet must possess. Emotional sensitivity, above the rest, is the quality most overrated since the time of the Romantics in England. Poetry results, not from the conjuncture of an object and a sensitive perception (which children enjoy to a greater degree than adults), but from the observation of an event, "internal" or "external," by a penetrating intelligence. And if that event involves the operation of objective phenomena as it very often must, then those objective phenomena will assume central value for the observing intelligence.

I suspect that Mr. Graham will set this down as another argument for "realism," which is the malapropism he has so blindly pinned to Mr. Jarrell's poetry. Of course, realism in its broadest meaning must be adjunctive to all art: art depends on life. But realism as a literary dogma has long since been cast aside by serious artists. Mr. Jarrell, to select only one example, has hardly been concerned with the presentation of an accurate report of the war. The world of war which he has created in his poetry is one of which, I dare say, he, as a participating soldier, was unaware. But working as a poet, he has constructed a world, and it is a true one because it is a logical metaphor spanning the desert of imagination between reality and ideality.

Mr. Graham pays considerable attention in his review to the notes which Mr. Jarrell appended to the poems in *Losses*, and he seems to deprecate author's notes generally. Yet I think he would not disagree with the modern editors of the *Divine Comedy* who feel obliged to include in their notes explanations of the medieval concept of celestial and infernal geography. Such information is helpful and often entirely necessary for the understanding of poetry written about things of which readers may be more or less ignorant. Mr. Graham seems to say that it is improper for poets to write on subjects which readers do not know. But many people enjoy reading the *Divine Comedy* and the topical satires of Pope, Chaucer, or even Juvenal, about which they know next to nothing from personal experience. In our departmentalized world, where the experiences of life have become less and less common to society, objective understanding necessarily precedes imaginative understanding. How can a poet today write of war for a civilian audience unless he is willing to describe the apparatus of warfare? Is a poet to be denied the expression of a genuine experience merely because it occurs when he is seated before the view plate of a radar set?

It would appear, then, that at least one of the criteria adopted by Mr. Graham is bound to invalidate his criticism, and certainly this is so in his review of *Losses*. The book contains war poems quite as good as any written in this century. *A Camp in the Prussian Forest, Eighth Air Force, Burning the Letters*—these and others are without question successful poems. Yet all of them deal with the "incidental values" dispraised by Mr. Graham. Part of their power accrues, in fact, from their imminent recognition of the dehumanization of conflict and of the giant metal wills which crash together in our robot warfare. However much ultimate motives derive from men, it is the fictions and objects, not the human beings, which get out of hand and cause the immediate, disastrous damages, and since these forces lumber through society with elephantine strength and come together here and there in tropical bursts of tumult, they can be treated validly by Mr. Jarrell as real mythic movements against which our smaller events may be cast. These same external forces act behind the poems which are not about war: *Loss, Lady Bates, A Country Life*.

I come around again to my starting point: the subjects of poetry cannot be limited. Poetry is good or bad in its methods, not in its materials. The poetry written within the *milieu* recommended by Mr. Graham is often exciting, and it is unseemly of him to denounce other media with partisan animosity. It seems to me that the varieties of poetry in western literature which can be read with plenary enjoyment by contemporary readers ought to convince Mr. Graham that he is puffing quite preposterously on a dead cigar. It is time for him and his dogmatic, parochial colleagues to give over their idle wrath and ask themselves why a poem is worth reading, instead of why the poet sees different things than they want him to see.

Hayden Carruth

Randall Jarrell's Wild Dogmatism

Robert Lowell*

Randall Jarrell is our most talented poet under 40, and one whose wit, pathos and grace remind us more of Pope or Matthew Arnold than of any of his contemporaries. I don't know whether Jarrell is unappreciated or not—it's hard to imagine anyone taking him lightly. He is almost brutally serious about literature and so bewilderingly gifted that it is impossible to comment on him without the humiliating thought that he himself could do it better.

He is a man of letters in the European sense, with real verve, imagination and uniqueness. Even his dogmatism is more wild and personal than we are accustomed to, completely unspoiled by the hedging "equanimity" that weakens the style and temperament of so many of our serious writers. His murderous intuitive phrases are famous; but at the same time his mind is essentially conservative and takes as much joy in rescuing the reputation of a sleeping good writer as in chloroforming a mediocre one.

Jarrell's prose intelligence—he seems to know *everything*—gives his poetry an extraordinary advantage over, for instance, a thunderbolt like Dylan Thomas, in dealing with the present; Jarrell is able to see our whole scientific, political and spiritual situation directly and on its own terms. He is a tireless discoverer of new themes and resources, and a master technician, who moves easily from the little to the grand. Monstrously knowing and monstrously innocent—one does not know just where to find him . . . a Wordsworth with the obsessions of Lewis Carroll.

"The Seven-League Crutches" should best be read with Jarrell's three earlier volumes. "Blood for a Stranger" (1942) is a Parnassian tour-de-force in the manner of Auden; nevertheless, it has several fine poems, the beginnings of better, and enough of the author's personality for John Crowe Ransom to write in ironic astonishment that Jarrell had "the velocity of an angel." "Little Friend, Little Friend" (1945), however, contains some of the best poems on modern war, better, I think, and far more professional than those of Wilfred Owen, which, though they seem pathetically eternal to us now, are sometimes amateurish and unfinished. The determined, passive, sacrificial lives of the pilots, inwardly so harmless and outwardly so destructive, are ideal subjects for Jarrell. In "Losses" (1948) and more rangingly in "Seven-League Crutches," new subjects appear. Using himself, children, characters from fairy stories, history and painting, he is still able to find beings that are determined, passive and sacrificial, but the experience is quiet, more complex and probably more universal. It's an odd universe, where a bruised joy or a

*Review of *The Seven-League Crutches*. Reprinted by permission from the *New York Times Book Review*, 7 October 1951, pp. 7, 41. Copyright 1951 by the New York Times Company.

bruised sorrow is forever commenting on itself with the gruff animal common sense and sophistication of Fontaine. Jarrell has gone far enough to be compared with his peers, the best lyric poets of the past: he has the same finesse and originality that they have, and his faults, a certain idiosyncratic willfulness and eclectic timidity, are only faults in this context.

Among the new poems, "Orient Express," a sequel, I think, to "Dover Beach," is a brilliantly expert combination of regular and irregular lines, buried rhymes, and sestina-like repeated rhymes, in which shifts in tone and rhythm are played off against the deadening roll of the train. "A Game at Salzburg" has the broken, charmed motion of someone thinking out loud. Both, in their different ways, are as skillful and lovely as any short poem I know of. "The Knight, Death, and the Devil" is a careful translation of Dürer's engraving. The description is dense; the generalizations are profound. It is one of the most remarkable word-pictures in English verse or prose, and comparable to Auden's "Musée de Beaux Arts."

"The Contrary Poet" is an absolutely literal translation from Corbière. The original is as clearly there as in the French, and it is also a great English poem. "The Night Before the Night Before Christmas" is long; it is also, perhaps, the best, most mannered, the most unforgettable and the most irritating poem in the book. Some of Jarrell's monologues are Robert Frost for "the man who reads Hamlet," or rather for a Hamlet who had been tutored by Jarrell. In "Seele im Raum," he masters Frost's methods and manages to make a simple half-mad woman speak in character, and yet with his own humor and terror.

My favorite is "A Girl in a Library," an apotheosis of the American girl, an immortal character piece, and the poem in which Jarrell perhaps best uses both his own qualities and his sense of popular culture. The girl is a college student, blonde and athletic.

. . . .

I quote the ending:
> *Sit and dream.*
> *One comes, a finger's width beneath your skin,*
> *To the braided maidens singing as they spin;*
> *There sound the shepherd's pipe, the watchman's rattle*
> *Across the short dark distance of the years.*
> *I am a thought of yours: and yet, you do not think . . .*
> *The firelight of a long, blind, dreaming story*
> *Lingers upon your lips; and I have seen*
> *Firm, fixed forever in your closing eyes,*
> *The Corn King beckoning to his Spring Queen.*

"Belinda" was once drawn with something of the same hesitating satire and sympathy.

Of Pity and Innocence

M. L. Rosenthal*

Randall Jarrell's verse has the "tears of things" in it. It has been linked to Wilfred Owen's poetry of pity, though Owen was simpler and more direct in his nonconformist-pacifist idealism. Jarrell concerns himself less with systematic, patterned injustice in nature or society than with the vulnerable and helpless sensibility of innocence. His best poems often interpret the tragic confusions of children and soldiers in traumatic crises as instances of an unbridgeable contradiction between the operations of the human mind and those of the strange outer world. Myth, hallucination and "realistic" observation converge in these examples to produce a heightened awareness under shocking-pressure of the impersonal cruelty of that world, an unoriented awareness that

> Behind everything there is always
> The unknown unwanted life.

On an earlier poem, "The Death of the Ball Turret Gunner," this fusion of subjective responses produced an almost unbearably poignant emotional precision. The reader had no choice: his secret mind was deeply troubled and not directed toward itself, and the recognitions that followed were almost physical ones. So too, in the present volume, the fantasy life and dream imagery of children seek to absorb the painful facts of experience:

> When the swans turned my sister into a swan
> I would go to the lake, at night, from milking:
> The sun would look out through the reeds like a swan,
> A swan's red beak; and the beak would open
> And inside there was darkness, the stars and the moon.

or:

> All the graves of the forest
> Are opened, the scaling face
> Of a woman—the dead mother—
> Is square in the steam of a yard. . . .

Still, Jarrell does try to push past the sense of strangeness, to arrive at meaning in the more objective sense of the term. When he does so, he is not as successful as in the more opaque, self-contained monologues of innocence. His bravest effort outward, "Hohensalzburg: Variations on a Theme of Romantic Character," employs romantic whimsy and imagination in combination with supernatural linkings of love and death to get at a tenuous religious-metaphysical truth behind the strangeness. As in "A

*Review of *The Seven-League Crutches*. Reprinted from the *New Republic*, 2 June 1952, p. 21, by permission of the journal.

Conversation with the Devil" and other poems, the "argument" here is facile, sentimental, and somehow uncommitted and the poem is saved from disaster by and with emotional subtlety; they, and not the motivations of the poem, establish its values. Jarrell is a romantic idealist, but the fact is not decisive; the convention is, I think, the only one he has so far found usable to rationalize the ungloved sympathy with vulnerability that is the real key to his finest work. (It is interesting that in a recent essay on Whitman he has disregarded the rhetorical and political associations by which the latter transcends the contradictions of will and fate and has stressed his concrete sense of the strangeness of things, the "magic" way in which he is "faithful to the feel of things, to reality as it seems." The essential difference between the two poets' outlooks may nevertheless be pinned down by comparing Jarrell's lovely, unworldly "A Soul" with Whitman's lusty, affirming "I believe in you, my soul.")

Despite all qualifications, however, this volume is Jarrell's most solid achievement; there is more full-bodied poetry in it than in the earlier books, and he takes more chances. The translations and adaptations from Corbière and Rilke reveal an outward movement more in accordance with his genius than are the poems that "argue" explicitly. Corbière's "Le Poète Contumace," somewhat softened by Jarrell's italics and idiomatic phrasings, gives a wider range of reference to the concern with isolated, suffering sensibility; his "Rondels pour Après" come through with their heart-breaking "acceptance" heightened, their irony just reduced. In Rilke's, "The Olive Garden," Jarrell has responded to Christ as a lonely one, the type of man's need for a miracle, the German poet's identification of the sign that does not come.

This craftwork has produced in Jarrell a new mastery that allows him to use a wide variety of forms, from the oddly humorous "Nollekens" to the intense essay in humility called "Jonah." *The Seven-League Crutches* is one of the finest books of poems printed in a very fine year.

In the Forests of the Little People

Karl Shapiro*

The subtitle of this extraordinary fine book of poems might be "Hansel and Gretel in America." For one who looks at literature as a history, it is a work of very great importance. For one who reads poetry as just poetry, and is willing to be backed into a corner by it, this volume is quite as important. Randall Jarrell puts the reader into a corner he may never escape.

*Review of *Selected Poems*. Reprinted by permission from the *New York Times Book Review*, 13 March 1955, p. 4. Copyright 1955 by the New York Times Company.

His recurrent themes are childhood, war and literature. The world of the child is his chief area of symbolism—Jarrell is practically the only living poet who insists on this world—and his almost obsessive return to the great childhood myths is sometimes as painful as a psychoanalysis. The *Märchen*, the tales, the fables, the dreams, as well as the American girl drowsing in her college library, and the little English boy deranged by death and air raids: these materializations come at us with a relentlessness which is just short of unbearable. We bear them because we instinctively recognize the situations and because the poetry is so good we cannot turn away. The technique, or perhaps the pathology, of the language goes to the reader's heart like a scalpel.

Many of the war poems date from Jarrell's period of soldiering, but they are not "dated" poems. Here, too, the landscape drifts to Germany, the dark forest, the sleeping beauty, the dreamer and the modern war. The soldier is also a kind of Hansel, an American in Germany. His colloquies with the spirits of the ageless country across the Rhine are sometimes in the nature of a courtship, sometimes in the nature of a tour of duty of an M. P. of the Occupation. But Germany is and is not a place in this poetry: it is a facet of human nature and of the soul.

The poet whom Jarrell is closest to is the great modern Rainer Maria Rilke. And, like Rilke, he is on both sides of the Rhine at once. The literary theme in Jarrell, and the one he has the most fun with, is the eternal battle of the Rhine, across which an Enlightenment attacks Nature, or vice versa. Intellectually, Jarrell is on the "French" side: by natural disposition, however, he is more at home in the forests of the Little People. Rilke frequently used the device of "as if" in order to bring himself closer to the inanimate and the inarticulate. Jarrell uses the device of "and yet" in order to bridge the great distances between the actual and the possible. The humor, not only in this phase of his poetry, but throughout his work, is not to be equaled by any other American poet of our time.

In some of Jarrell's writing, criticism and fiction as well as poetry, there is a tendency toward sentimentality and cruelty, but in the major part—and the major part is certainly the poetry—there is a breadth of spirit which is wholly admirable and exemplary. This is a book which should certainly influence our poetry for the better. It should become a point of reference, not only for younger poets, but for all readers of twentieth-century poetry.

The Rilkean Sense

John Logan*

It's an extraordinary thing when you find a couple of poems in a volume to reread. A distinction of Randall Jarrell's "The Woman at the Washington Zoo," his sixth collection of verse, is that one can return to every poem. Indeed it hardly seems to matter that more than a third of the poems are translations (as the subtitle indicates) for these present themselves as good English poems too. The traductions are from Rilke, Radauskas, Mörike, and Goethe, whose "Faust" Jarrell expects to bring out in English version.

It is Rilke whose feeling, even outside the poems bearing his name, seems most closely to underlie Jarrell's creative intuitions: thus the brilliant final poem, "The Bronze David of Donatello," brings to mind the kind of response Rilke formed in the presence of Rodin's statues (and wrote about in what must surely be the most exciting "criticism" of sculpture one can discover).

Jarrell's equally splendid title poem, "The Woman at the Washington Zoo," shows the Rilkean sense for those emotional configurations animals set up in the minds of men, their artists catching in "bestiaries"—a favorite genre of modern poets as of ancient—so many projected fragments of their own caged, inner life. "The world goes by my cage and never sees me," keens The Woman. Jarrell's poem ends wishfully with the same theme that concludes Rilke's "An Archaic Torso of Apollo": *Du muss dein Leben andern* ("You must change your life"). "Change me, change me," implores The Lady at the Washington Zoo, of the creatures she beholds. In both Rilke's and Jarrell's poems it is ultimately the wilder, more deeply feeling, more hidden and more alive part of the speaker himself which intimidates him (her) into the yearning for change (as a good poem itself intimidates the reader). But in Rilke it is an art work—the archaic torso—which serves as the essential, reflecting catalyst, whereas in Jarrell it is an animal at the zoo. Is this not another way of putting the old saw that "both art and nature are an inspiration to man"? For man sees his lacked heart opened in anything outside himself whose life suits (as his does not) its shape, and this is as true of the mountain as of the jerboa.

Besides "The Bronze David" and "The Woman" (one poem started by art, the other by nature) the pieces that open us to ourselves most effectively are the remarkable "Nestus Gurley" (a vendor perceived as a god) and the long, viable, continually inventive myth in verse, "The End of the Rainbow."

The poems as a group carry forward artistically Jarrell's known

*Review of *The Woman at the Washington Zoo*. Reprinted by permission from *Saturday Review*, 28 January 1961, pp. 29–30. Copyright © 1961 by *Saturday Review*. All rights reserved.

devotion to dream and fairy tale technic, which he writes about so lucidly in his introduction to "The Anchor Book of Short Stories." Thus interested, Jarrell shows himself one of the "most contemporary" critics. I am not sure whether or not it is ironical that he is also a poet who, more than any other American easily brought to mind, assumes supremely well a central responsibility of art: the conjuring of spirits.

The Poet Fulfills the Man

Philip Booth*

Admitting himself to a fine dramatic monologue in his great new book, Randall Jarrell says, almost as if in a casual aside: "But I identify myself, as always, / With something that there's something wrong with, / With something human."

Stressed by his own speech patterns, these charged lines come from a poem called "The One Who Was Different." In the book of which that poem is a part, *The Lost World*, Jarrell (that always "different" poet) has finally found the open language and flexible rhythms which make humanly one the world of his poems and the world these poems now speak to.

The titles of Jarrell's earlier collections of essays, *Poetry and the Age* and *A Sad Heart at the Supermarket*, implicitly define his concern for, and his reaction to, the mid-century America he knows that poetry (now, if ever) must reach to redeem. As the most human critic of his age, and even as the cheaply tagged "war poet" of such famous poems as "The Death of the Ball Turret Gunner" and "Good-bye, Wendover; Good-bye, Mountain Home," Jarrell has constantly stretched himself to find a language commensurate with his affectionate sadness for the human condition, and his reserved belief in human joy. His imagination has, from the beginning, been flawless; but his full concern for speaking no less than the truth has sometimes (almost prosaically) flattened his lines, and (because the truth was ever complex) his poems have sometimes seemed confused in their always dramatic structure.

Now, not altogether newly, but in a clearly new depth, Jarrell dramatizes his sense of humanity with an absolute precision. Humanity may still be "what there's something wrong with," but these human poems are, in themselves, close to holy: they make painfully lovely sense of a world we've much confused but just might, because of poems like these, finally survive.

*Review of *The Lost World*. Reprinted by permission from the *Christian Science Monitor*, 11 March 1965, p. 11. Copyright © 1965 The Christian Science Publishing Society. All rights reserved.

The fashion, momentarily, in "modern" poetry, is confessional: to make of one's appendectomy or psychoanalysis a narcissistic (and perhaps masochistic) first-person-singular poem. As his first six books of poetry generously attest, Jarrell can speak for his own losses as well as the next man. But even in this book, rightfully called *The Lost World*, Jarrell continues to refuse the selfish mode of programmatic despair. Because his poetry understands that pain is a universal experience, Jarrell can identify with people beyond himself: in finding a language which dramatizes how people hurt, want, and try to define themselves, he peoples his poetry with those human beings who are, for him, what the great poem of the world is primarily about.

Frost did something of this in *North of Boston*. As Frost's most illuminating critic, Jarrell must surely have learned from Frost how speech stress, cutting across meters, can make a poetry of how people speak. But even Frost was less flexible than Jarrell in finding, shaping, and informing the various rhythms of individual experience.

Jarrell not only speaks for himself (recovering, perfectly, the "impotent omnipotence" of "The Lost World" of boyhood); he can write as Everyman in that singular poem called "Woman"; he can speak as a mother to "The Lost Children," and be wife to supermarkets in the poem called "Next Day." In all of these, there is an emotional precision comparable to that in Frost's "A Servant to Servants": there is compassion which lends its redemptive perspective to how (on the world's bare stage) people short of stardom walk on to speak for themselves.

The twenty-two poems of *The Lost World* would seem few were they not so full. Most of them are long by contemporary standards, yet none is padded; each explores its meanings with such a quiet flexibility that even the careful rhymes of the title poem seem natural. Within such technical brilliance (never greater than in "The Old and the New Masters," which reconstitutes, and then turns the theme of Auden's "Musée des Beaux Arts"), the final value of Jarrell's new poetry lies in its seemingly casual wisdom. Jarrell has always been "bright" (witness the shining wit of his academic novel, *Pictures from an Institution*); yet where some of his previous effects seemed merely to ornament knowledge, what's lapidary in *The Lost World* feels almost self-surprising, so wisely (in context) is it earned.

Randall Jarrell's new book is so surely wise, so demonstrably honest, and so purely human, that it's tempting to play Jarrell the critic: to name the names of sustaining poems, to praise them with grateful adjectives. But these new poems deserve the better thanks of the words that Jarrell himself once wrote to honor Frost: ". . . to have this whole range of being treated with so much humor and sadness and composure, with such plain truth; to see that a man can still include, connect, and make humanly understandable . . . so *much*—this is one of the freshest and oldest joys, a joy strong enough to make us forget the limitations and excesses and baseness that these days seem unforgettable, a joy strong enough to make us say, with the Greek poet, that many things in this world are wonderful, but of all these the most wonderful is man."

The Adventures of a Private Eye

William Meredith*

The vision of a serious artist is a very individual matter. Perhaps the most important thing he has to learn is, what am I clairvoyant about, what do I see *into* that other people simply see? The minor artist is, by comparison, a beachcomber. He lives off the discovery of novel beauties and horrors; he sees them *first*, but he sees them with the flat eyes of just anybody. Novelty in this sense is nothing to the serious artist, or worse than nothing—a temptation to desert his individual vision. We can't imagine Wallace Stevens trying to penetrate the complacencies of an oven bird, or Frost the complacencies of a peignoir. Artists like that know who they are and what they can see into.

Randall Jarrell's progress, volume by volume, seems to be toward greater awareness of what he can call his own. For 20 years he has been one of our best poets, in the company of Wilbur, Berryman, Roethke, almost of Lowell, but he hasn't been perfectly sure what to do with his restless gift. He's written a number of brittle, chilly poems that detach themselves from life with an irresponsible irony—poems like "The State," "Sears Roebuck" and "Variations"—which may be all right as poems but never seem to be quite Jarrell. At the same time he was consistently producing marvelous, deep-running dramatic poems that from the first were stamped with his voice and his eye for subjective imagery.

The recognition of his special vision, which can be accounted complete with this fine book, involved two things, though perhaps they were a single act: abandoning a timid, mechanical skepticism and embracing a wide human involvement. The accomplishment of these seems to have confirmed another fact: his gift is essentially dramatic, like Browning's.

Comparing poems that span a number of years we can see his dramatic talent grow brighter as though controlled by a rheostat. He returns to characters, images, even to lines. "A Hunt in the Black Forest" opens with the same lines that opened, 17 years ago, "The Child of Courts." And the returns to apparently autobiographical events of childhood are even more striking. There are things a man goes over and over until he gets them right.

Take a character that Jarrell finds in many guises—the woman

*Review of *The Lost World*. Reprinted from *New York Herald Tribune Book Week*, 14 March 1965, p. 4. By permission of the author.

whose growing old is an inexplicable and brutal mystery to her. Three poems on this theme, spaced over a number of years, conclude as follows:

> *But it's not right*
> *If just living can do this,*
> *Living is more dangerous than anything:*
>
> *It is terrible to be alive.*
>
> ("The Face")

> *Vulture,*
> *When you come for the white rat that the foxes left,*
> *Take off the red helmet of your head, the black*
> *Wings that have shadowed me, and step to me as a man:*
> *The wild brother at whose feet the white wolves fawn,*
> *To whose hand of power the great lioness*
> *Stalks, purring . . . .*
> *You know what I was,*
> *You see what I am: change me, change me!*
>
> ("The Woman at the Washington Zoo")

> *I am afraid, this morning, of my face.*
> *It looks at me*
> *From the rear-view mirror, with the eyes I hate,*
> *The smile I hate. Its plain, lined look*
> *Of gray discovery*
> *Repeats to me: "You're old." That's all, I'm old.*
>
> *And yet I'm afraid, as I was at the funeral*
> *I went to yesterday.*
> *My friend's cold made-up face, granite among its flowers,*
> *Her undressed, operated-on, dressed body*
> *Were my face and body.*
> *As I think of her I hear her telling me*
>
> *How young I seem; I am exceptional;*
> *I think of all I have.*
> *But really no one is exceptional,*
> *No one has anything, I'm anbody,*
> *I stand beside my grave*
> *Confused with my life, that is commonplace and solitary.*
>
> ("Next Day")

Granted that some of the differences come from the subjects' differences: the woman in "The Face" seems to have an aristocratic beauty, and her epigraph identifies her with the Marschallin in *Der Rosenkavalier*; the woman at the zoo seems to be an unmarried office worker; the woman in the final passage, the conclusion of the opening poem in *The Lost World*, is a suburban wife. But the final passage is, in the first place, free of the glamour of violence. It makes its point, it involves us, without a Marschallin on the one hand or a vulture on the other. Dailiness has been seen as its drama. And the attitude of the poet seems therefore a great deal more compassionate. Instead of crying, *beauty! horror!*, he seems to be saying, *life, life*, with a vision that elevates that remark to wisdom—that is to say, with a kind of wondering acceptance. He says this explicitly in the poem called "Well Water":

> *What a girl called "the dailiness of life"*
> *(Adding an errand to your errand. Saying*
> *"Since you're up . . ." Making you a means to*
> *A means to a means to) is well water*
> *Pumped from an old well at the bottom of the world.*
> *The pump you pump the water from is rusty*
> *And hard to move and absurd, a squirrel-wheel*
> *A sick squirrel turns slowly, through the sunny*
> *Inexorable hours. And yet sometimes*
> *The wheel turns of its own weight, the rusty*
> *Pump pumps over your sweating face the clear*
> *Water, cold, so cold! you cup your hands*
> *And gulp from them the dailiness of life.*

"Well Water" shows in small the insight which in large has yielded in *The Lost World* many astonishing, luminous poems. "Field and Forest" is a masterpiece of illumination: we pan in on a man whose ordinariness would seem unassailable and step by step, through the imagery Jarrell casts over us like a net, we *become* that man. The title poem, almost 300 lines of skillful, unobtrusive *terza rima*, along with "Hope," joins the totally successful dramatic poems named above. "The Old and the New Masters" shows the new, or authentic, Jarrell treading humbly near one of the dark mysteries where he was wont to roar like a liberal.

Three of the prettiest lyrics come from his children's book, *The Bat-Poet*. A poem called "Three Bills" may have been thrown in to see if anyone remembered when this seer was just a sharp-eyed beachboy.

The Complete Poems

Helen Vendler*

"We have lost for good," Randall Jarrell once wrote, "the poems that would have been written by the modern equivalent of Henry VIII or Bishop King or Samuel Johnson; born novelists, born theologians, born princes." We might add, born critics: because Jarrell, who was 51 when

*Reprinted by permission from the *New York Times Book Review*, 29 February 1969, pp. 5, 42. Copyright © 1969 by the New York Times Company.

he died in 1965, can be said to have put his genius into his criticism and his talent into his poetry.

That talent, in the course of his life, grew considerably, and the editors of those posthumous "Complete Poems" may have been right to put the better poems first: the "Selected Poems" of 1955 are followed by the collections of 1960 and 1965, and only after these groups are we permitted to see the lesser rest (composed from 1940 through 1965). If we reconstruct, from this fanciful arrangement, the boy Jarrell growing into the man Jarrell, we can see the progress of his peculiarly double nature, one side of it charming and comic, the other vulnerable and melancholy.

The poems Jarrell wrote before World War II—roughly before he was 30—are on the whole forgettable, but they foreshadow his continual risky dependence on history, folk tale and art: many of the later poems are retellings (of history or biography), redescriptions (of a Dürer etching, a Botticelli canvas, the Augsburg Adoration), or reworkings of a myth. That dependency in Jarrell never died; he was, nobody more so, the eager audience to any book or piece of music that captured his wayward interest; his poems in which the scene is a library are hymns to those places where we can "live by trading another's sorrow for our own."

His first steady original poems date from his experience in the Air Force, when the pity that was his tutelary emotion, the pity that was to link him so irrevocably to Rilke, found a universal scope:

> *We died like aunts or pets or foreigners.*
> *(When we left high school nothing else had died*
> *For us to figure we had died like.) . . .*
> *In bombers named for girls, we burned*
> *The cities we had learned about in school.*

Jarrell brings us his adolescent soldiers with their pitiful reality of high school—high school!—as the only notching-stick of experience; he brings us the veteran "stumbling to the toilet on one clever leg of leather, wire, and willow," with the pity all in the *faute-de-mieux* weird boastfulness of "clever"; he brings us the bodiless lost voices in the air—"can't you hear me? over, over—"; and, for all its triteness now, he brings us the death of the ball turret gunner.

The secret of his war poems is that in the soldiers he found children; what is the ball turret gunner but a baby who has lost his mother? The luckier baby who has a mother, as Jarrell tells us in "Bats," "clings to her long fur / by his thumbs and toes and teeth . . . / Her baby hangs on underneath. . . . / All the bright day, as the mother sleeps, / She folds her wings about her sleeping child." So much for Jarrell's dream of maternity; but the ball turret gunner has a different fate: "From my mother's sleep I fell into the State, / And I hunched in its belly till my wet fur froze."

Jarrell has often been taken to task for his sentimentality, but the fiction, recurrent in his work, of a wholly nonsexual tenderness, though it can be unnerving in some of the marriage poems, is indispensable in his long, tearfully elated recollections of childhood. The child who was never mothered enough, the mother who wants to keep her children forever, these are the inhabitants of the lost world, where the perfect filial symbiosis continues forever. The nostalgia for childhood even lies behind Jarrell's aging monologists—the Marschallin, the woman at the Washington Zoo, the woman in the supermarket—and gives them at once their poignancy and their abstraction.

For all his wish to be a writer of dramatic monologues, Jarrell could only speak in his own alternately frightened and consolatory voice, as he alternately played child and mother. It has been charged that Jarrell's poetry of the war shows no friends, only, in James Dickey's words, "killable puppets"—but Jarrell's soldiers are of course not his friends because they are his babies, his lambs to the slaughter—he broods over them. In his final psychic victory over his parents, they too become his babies as he, perfectly, in this ideal world of recovery memory, remains *their* baby:

> Here are Mother and Father in a photograph,
> Father's holding me. . . . They both look so *young.*
> I'm so much older than they are. Look at them,
> Two babies with their baby.

His students are his children too, and the sleeping girl in the library at Greensboro receives his indulgent parental solicitude:

> As I look, the world contracts around you:
> I see Brünnhilde had brown braids and glasses
> She used for studying.

The student—"poor senseless life"—is nevertheless finally the pure and instinctual ideal:

> I have seen
> Firm, fixed forever in your closing eyes,
> The Corn King beckoning to his Spring Queen.

This guileless taste requires a guileless style, and Jarrell found it late, in the gossipy, confidential and intimate manners of "The Lost World," his recollections of a childhood year in Hollywood:

> On my way home I pass a cameraman
> On a platform on the bumper of a car
> Inside which, rolling and plunging, a comedian
> Is working; on one white lot I see a star
> Stumble to her igloo through the howling gale
> Of the wind machines. On Melrose a dinosaur
> And pterodactyl with their immense pale
> Papier-mâché smiles, look over the fence
> Of The Lost World.

That childlike interest—in the cameraman, the artificial igloo and the cartoon monsters—was the primitive form of Jarrell's later immensely attractive enthusiasm for all the pets he kept in his private menagerie. Nobody loved poets more or better than Randall Jarrell—and irony, indifference or superciliousness in the presence of the remarkable seemed to him capital sins. In one of his last poems, "The Old and the New Masters," he takes issue with Auden, arguing that in any number of paintings the remarkable sufferer or redeemer is not tangential but is rather the focus of the whole:

> . . . everything
> That was or will be in the world is fixed
> On its small, helpless, human center.

Those lines could be the epigraph to these collected poems; and yet there are dimensions of Jarrell that we could wish for more of. One of his talents is to rewrite, in a grim way, nursery tales, so that we see Cinderella finally preferring the cozy female gossip of the fireside to life with the prince, or we see Jack, post-beanstalk, sitting in a psychotic daze by his rotting cottage, "bound in some terrible wooden charm . . . rigid and aghast." Another, and perhaps truer, Jarrell writes a disarming poem of pure pleasure ("Deutsch Durch Freud") on why he never wants really to know German; it's so much nicer only to know it halfway, via Rilke and lieder:

> It is by Trust, and Love, and reading Rilke
> Without ein Wörterbuch, that man learns German . . .
> And Heine! at the ninety-sixth mir träumte
> I sigh as a poet, but dimple as ein Schuler . . .
> And my heart lightens at each Sorge, each Angst . . .
> Till the day I die I'll be in love with German
> —If only I don't learn German . . .

In lines like these, all of Jarrell's playful wit is coming to surface, that wit which dazzled us from the pages of his energetic criticism, but which often falters under the (very Germanic) melancholy of "The Complete Poems." The refugees, children, recluses, soldiers and aging women who inhabit his verse might have left more room in it for their satiric and resilient creator, but Jarrell kept his two sides very distinct. "One finds it unbearable," he once remarked in an essay, "that poetry should be so hard to write," and he added that poets suffer their poetry as helplessly as anything else. He cannot be said, as a poet, to have invented new forms, a new style, or new subjects, in any grand way; but he made himself memorable as a singular man, at his most exceptional in denying his own rarity:

> How young I seem; I am exceptional;
> I think of all I have.

> *But really no one is exceptional.*
> *No one has anything, I'm anybody,*
> *I stand beside my grave*
> *Confused with my life, that is commonplace and solitary.*

So one late poem says, but it had begun, in a flash of the boyish Jarrell *brio*, with a woman in a supermarket "Moving from Cheer to Joy, from Joy to All." Zest, down to a zest for the names of detergents, stayed mixed, to the very last, with the tears of things.

Light on the Poet's Waste Land

Delmore Schwartz*

It has been clear for some time that Randall Jarrell is one of the most gifted poets and critics of his generation. The present volume, his first collection of criticism, should do much to confirm and strengthen his reputation. In it he discusses inimitably such poets as Whitman, Frost, Wallace Stevens, John Crowe Ransom, Williams, Walter de la Mare, Robert Lowell, and a good many others. And the book is made a whole instead of a collection of periodical pieces, by two important essays on the obscurity of modern poetry and on the overcultivation of criticism in contemporary writing. Thus it is perhaps the most comprehensive and certainly the most detailed of all studies of modern poetry.

It is a good deal more than that. In his essays on Whitman and Robert Frost, Jarrell moves forward to what may very well be the beginning of a new evaluation of poetry and of what poetry has been, what it is, and what it can be. Jarrell goes beyond the standards and the discriminations of T. S. Eliot, which have dominated the criticism of poetry for the past twenty-five years, and he does so by including and assimilating Eliot's views, rather than by the characteristic rejection and exclusion that almost always marks and cripples new movements and new points of view in criticism.

Eliot himself is an example of this kind of one-sidedness: he found it necessary to condemn Wordsworth and Keats in order to praise Dryden and Marvell. Jarrell has achieved—and with great richness and fullness of perception—a point of view from which it is possible to admire all these poets and to admire Whitman and Frost as well as Donne and Mallarmé. The same kind of justice and the same catholic love characterize his essays on Wallace Stevens and Marianne Moore.

Moreover, Jarrell writes in a prose style that possesses some of the best traits of both prose and poetry. He succeeds in being joyous, angry,

*Review of *Poetry and the Age*. Reprinted by permission from the *New York Times Book Review*, 16 August 1953, p. 1. Copyright 1953 by the New York Times Company.

contemptuous, and gay as well as lucid, direct, and colloquial with complete genuineness and ease. And when he is amusing, as he often is, he is at the same time and unerringly illuminating. Thus, when he says: "To expect Tate's and Warren's poems to be much influenced by Ransom's is like expecting two nightmares to be influenced by a daydream," his formulation may seem at first glance to be merely a piece of wit; but it is, in fact, an exact description and insight.

Behind the witty, passionate intensity of Jarrell's style there is always a huge, half-rhetorical, half-shocked question: How can any human being in his right mind disregard the power and the glory of poetry? It is as if someone asked: How can you disregard the Atlantic Ocean, the Grand Canyon, and Niagara Falls? Poetry has the overwhelming reality of these natural phenomena, and it is certainly far more interesting. Hence Jarrell is always speaking to the reader as a dedicated, possessed poet. But at times he is speaking only as a poet and purely as a poet. Poetry is one of the most important things in the world to him, as it should be; but at times it is the *most* important thing in the world, which is surely too close to poetry as the *only* important thing in the world.

The result is a certain narrowness of perspective. In his most eloquent and powerful essay, the one on obscurity of modern poetry, Jarrell describes the prevailing modern attitude toward poetry very well. He remarks that almost none of those who accuse modern poetry of obscurity are devoted and habitual readers of the presumably lucid poetry of the past. Indeed, for the most part, there is no reason to believe that they read any poetry whatever, at least to the extent of finding the works of the great poets a necessary part of their lives.

"Most people," he writes, "know about the modern poet only that he is *obscure—i.e.*, that he is *difficult, i.e.*, that he is *neglected*—they naturally make a causal connection between the two meanings of the word, and decide that he is unread because he is difficult." "And yet it is not just modern poetry, but poetry, that is today obscure. *Paradise Lost* is what it was; but the ordinary reader no longer makes the mistake of trying to read it—instead, he glances at it, weighs it in his hand, shudders, and suddenly, his eyes shining, puts it on his list of the ten dullest books he has ever read, along with *Moby Dick*, *War and Peace*, *Faust*, and Boswell's *Life of Johnson*. But I am doing this ordinary reader an injustice: it was not the Public, nodding over its lunch-pail, but the educated reader, the reader the universities have trained, who a few weeks ago, to the Public's sympathetic delight, put together this list of the world's dullest books."

Later, he notes that "one of our universities recently made a survey of the reading habits of the American public; it decided that forty-eight percent of all Americans read, during a year, no book at all. I picture to myself that reader—non-reader, rather; one man out of every two—and I reflect, with shame: 'Our poems are too hard for him.' But so, too, are

Treasure Island, Peter Rabbit, pornographic novels—any book whatso-ever. . . . A sort of dream-situation often occurs to me in which I call to this imaginary figure, 'Why don't you read books?'—and he always answers, after looking at me steadily for a long time: 'Huh?' "

This is in itself a perfect statement. It expresses the anguish of one who does not feel superior but lonely; and the dismay of one who does not want to be cut off from other human beings by his love of literature. But Jarrell writes as if this situation were an arbitrary fact, as if the reading public were merely self-indulgent and irrational in neglecting most poetry and disregarding most serious literature. He is so close to poetry, so involved with the art as such, that the causes of the situation, which are social, cultural, and spiritual, remain quite distant and entirely unexamined.

The same pure and professional concentration upon poetry as poetry circumscribes several other essays, particularly the one on Whitman. But this is Jarrell's first book of criticism; he has just begun to write; and he has written a book that will bring every reader closer to a knowledge of poetry and of experience.

Matter and Manner

John Berryman*

This is, I believe, the most original and best book on its subject since *The Double Agent* by R. P. Blackmur and *Primitivism and Decadence* by Yvor Winters. Since the other ablest American critic of modern poetry in the generation now about forty, Delmore Schwartz, has not collected his essays, we may be specially glad that Jarrell has begun to, and the book is overdue. It does not, indeed, contain his most plunging criticism so far, which will be found in his articles and reviews and lectures on Auden, whose mind Jarrell understands better than anyone ought to be allowed to understand anyone else's, especially anyone so pleasant and destructive as Jarrell; these will make another volume. But it exhibits fully the qualities that made Jarrell the most powerful reviewer of poetry active in this country for the last decade; and in its chief triumphs, the second essay on Frost and the first review of Lowell (I mean the first of the two here pre-served) it exhibits more.

William Empson I suppose was Jarrell's master. An early piece on Housman, not reprinted, seems to prove this, and there are several hand-some references here. His prose is not so manly as Empson's; it giggles on occasion, and nervous overemphasis abounds; but it sounds always like a

*Review of *Poetry and the Age*. Reprinted from the *New Republic*, 2 November 1953, pp. 27–28, by permission of the journal.

human being talking to somebody—differing in this from nine-tenths of what other working American critics manufacture. It is cruel and amusing, undeniably well known for these qualities, which it developed so far beyond Empson's traces that that critic presents in comparison an icon of deadpan charity. But what really matter in Jarrell are a rare attention, devotion to and respect for poetry. These, with a natural taste in poetry hardly inferior to Tate's, restless incessant self-training, strong general intelligence, make up an equipment that would seem to be minimal but in fact is unique.

The second essay on Frost is nothing much but thirty pages of quoted poems and passages, with detailed comment. To see how astonishing it is, you ought first to read through a pallid assemblage called *Recognition of Robert Frost*, to the authors of which (except Edward Garnett and Mark Van Doren) the Frost that Jarrell displays would be a horrifying stranger. Perhaps nothing of this vivid sort has ever surpassed the page on "Provide, Provide," unless it is the pages following on "Design."

Lord Weary's Castle was one of the stiffest books to review that has ever appeared. I have reason to know: Jarrell's was not only superior—far—to my own attempt: it is probably the most masterly initial review of an important poetic work, either here or in England, of this century so far. You have to compare it with wider-ranging reviews, like Eliot's of Grierson, or Dr. Johnson's of Soame Jenyns to feel its narrower but harder learning, its similar but submissive strength.

The studies of Ransom, Stevens, Marianne Moore (again especially the second piece on her), more conventional than those on Frost and Lowell, are nearly as good. A fine citation of Whitman, wittier even than usual, seems better now under a new, more modest title than it did originally, because it does not examine, as Jarrell usually does, substance or method or (save for a few remarks) style. This attention equally in him to matter and manner constitutes a development from what is called the New Criticism.

His general essays, on Obscurity and the Age of Criticism, which strike me as diffuse and making points rather familiar, will undoubtedly help many readers. At least the points made are right. A salient truth about Jarrell, for the present reader, is that he is seldom wrong. About William Carlos Williams's poetry, some of which I love too, he does, I think, exaggerate, and these papers are his weakest; even here he says much that is true, gay, and useful. One of his shrewdest, most characteristic remarks is apropos of a poet one might suppose he would not appreciate at all, the author of the beautiful "Song of the Mad Prince": "It is easy to complain that de la Mare writes about unreality; but how *can* anybody write about unreality?" One cannot but remark the healthy breadth of Jarrell's taste. Behind the writers here treated, perhaps his strongest obvious admirations are for Hardy, Rilke, and of course

Eliot, and I hope he will treat them; and Proust, and I wish he dealt more with prose.

On the other hand, his neglect to theorize about poetry, and to theorize above all about criticism, is one of the most agreeable features of a prepossessing and engaging book. Criticism of criticism—at best a languid affair, as Irving Babbitt observed in the preface to one of his books about criticism—is probably best left to very young men and older men. The point is to deal with the stuff itself, and Jarrell does, nobody better. Everybody interested in modern poetry ought to be grateful to him.

The Third Book of Criticism

Helen Vendler*

Randall Jarrell once wrote that his heart, confronted by the super-market offerings of public media, was sad; but that same sad heart, offered a good book, reacted with an almost disorderly passion of gratitude, and these posthumous essays and reviews (all previously published) breathe on every page the pleasure of suspended deprivation, as if the child with his nose pressed to the sweetshop window (Yeats's phrase about Keats) had suddenly been given a cake.

The relish of a starved palate accounts for the energy of Jarrell's recommendations, and the hunger he awakens in his readers is an envy of that relish and a wish to taste with that strenuous tongue. Since taste is personal, Jarrell can occasionally disappoint; we may follow him to a book and find it less good than his account of it. But generally he incarnates his own definition of a critic in his first book of criticism, "Poetry and the Age" (1953), as "an extremely good reader—one who has learned to show to others what he saw in what he read."

The limits of this definition are also Jarrell's limits: he was, for better or worse, a member of no school of criticism; he was no theorist; he felt happier writing about the 19th and 20th centuries than about earlier periods where what you see in what you read depends radically on historical information; he wrote always to "show to others" and not to muse to himself. He was not, in short, a Frye, an Auerbach, a Blackmur, an Auden.

On the other hand, his mind was anything but simple. No reader of poetry, however devoted, could fail to learn in generous amounts from his superlative essays on modern poetry (represented here by a "close

*Reprinted by permission from the *New York Times Book Review*, 4 January 1970, pp. 4–5.

reading" of Frost's "Home Burial" and a bewitching overview of Auden's whole career). It would be impossible for anyone, no matter how committed to theory or to historical scholarship, to condescend to the man who wrote these essays, or, to go back in time, to the man who could be so just, in "Poetry and the Age," to Whitman and Marianne Moore at once. Jarrell is a generous evangelist of books, forever metaphorically lending us his most recent favorite, as in fact in life he recklessly lent his own library. He says endearingly that of the people he lent his "Crime and Punishment" to "every fourth or fifth borrower returns it unfinished": fourth or fifth out of 20? out of 40? Which of us has ever lent a book out even five times?

Jarrell's gratitude to his authors can sometimes seem indiscriminate. Why should he use such superlatives about Graves, we wonder; but somewhere the balance of things is always restored: "When you compare Graves with Wordsworth or Rilke, you are comparing a rearrangement of the room with a subsidence of continents." Jarrell sensibly says about his enthusiasm for writers less than the greatest, "You can write better stories than Kipling's, but not better Kipling stories." Minor writers, in short, can be loved as purely as major ones, and sometimes more easily.

Jarrell, in his criticism, had three special talents. He thought naturally in metaphor (a source of charm and jokes as well as a source of truth); he wrote, in almost every account, an implicit suspense story; and he saw books constantly as stories about human beings. In his flashes of likeness, William Carlos Williams's lines "move as jerkily and intently as a bird"; Wallace Stevens, if he were an animal, would be "that rational, magnanimous, voluminous animal, the elephant"; Theodore Roethke is "a powerful Donatello baby who has love affairs, and whose marshlike unconscious is continually celebrating its marriage with the whole wet dark underside of things"; the beatniks operate on "iron spontaneity"; Marianne Moore's poems have "the lacy, mathematical extravagance of snowflakes"; T. S. Eliot is "a sort of combination of Lord Byron and Dr. Johnson."

These telling accuracies are the blackberries in Jarrell's wood, and one can go wandering through his pages for these felicities alone, sometimes so perfect that they are like little poems in themselves, reminding us that Jarrell was, in his own mind, first and foremost a poet, and wrote his metaphorical criticism with the same pen that wrote his metaphorical poetry.

His talent for suspense is more difficult to illustrate, since it governs entire essays, but two examples may serve. Jarrell's famous powers of persuasion are set to make us believe, through a description of "The Death of Ivan Ilych," that the most significant thing in the world is death, that death, in Tolstoy's words, "ruins all you work for . . . life for oneself can have no meaning." After Jarrell, with his harrowing sympathy, has forced us to a desolate acquiescence, he turns round and announces that

Chekhov, in "Ward No. 6," "detailedly contradicts this Tolstoyan analysis," and we are off, with relief breathing freely once again, hoping that after all "the pure immediacy of pleasure or pain, good or evil," is, or can be, "something ultimate."

The same suspense rules Jarrell's account, in this collection, of Auden's career. With Jarrell, we see Auden synthesizing "more or less as the digestive organs synthesize enzymes" his own order out of Marx, Freud, Groddeck, folk tales, science, and so on—a tale of a literary double helix. What will Auden do next? Tune into the next essay. What Auden did next (he turned godly) infuriated Jarrell, and the two essays on Auden in this collection, in their prejudicial view of Auden's "decline," may seem unfair. Nevertheless, there is no more brilliant short account to be found of Auden's matter and manner: Jarrell, even hostile, was hardly ever inaccurate.

His final virtue, and his most winning trait, was his unhesitating belief that though books may not be life, it is life that they are about. His own taste went unashamedly to the literature in which the connection of books and life is most explicit, and some of his flaws in judgment (like his unduly harsh dismissal of some late Stevens poems as "transcendental études") stemmed from his distrust, visible also in his rejection of late Auden, of abstraction in literature. But his appetite for event was inexhaustible. His list of topics in Kipling shows how humanely he absorbed a book of short stories (and who, after reading the list, would not hunger for the stories?): "A drugged, lovesick and consumptive pharmacist; an elderly cook and her lover's cancer; a providential murder committed by a brook; a middle-aged woman watching a wounded German pilot die in the underbrush" and so on. Kipling, he says, can make a list more interesting than the ordinary writer's murder; so can Jarrell.

The only theory that can be said to underlie Jarrell's fiercely sympathetic retelling of human predicaments is the Freudian one, significantly a theory of life rather than a theory of art. But the feeling that underlies all his writing is clear in what he said of one favorite volume, one of the many books with which, hour by hour, he assuaged his spiritual hunger, thirst and pain: "I cannot look at my bound copy without a surge of warmth and delight: if I knew a monk I would get him to illuminate it." Readers of this collection may feel that a writer illuminated by Jarrell has no need of monks.

Arriving at Acceptance

John Lucas*

Robert Lowell famously remarked that "Eulogy was the glory" of Randall Jarrell's criticism and it is so. Yet he is equally remarkable for his way with absolutely telling quotation and with the remarks that precede or follow it. This means that his critical judgments feel unerring and final. And this is the more remarkable when you realize that most of his criticism is concerned with contemporary writing. You have only to think of the standard names of English literary criticism of this century—of, shall we say, F. R. Leavis, Kenneth Burke, T. S. Eliot, I. A. Richards, R. P. Blackmur, Yvor Winters, William Empson—to realize the comparatively small amount of time they gave to writing about their contemporaries. As a reviewer and literary journalist, Jarrell was constantly called upon to write about first books by unknown writers and new books by the famous. The wonder is how right he nearly always proved to be. It is almost impossible to catch him out. To be sure, there are individual statements with which we might want to quarrel, but they count for very little compared with the marvellous, swift and untroubled certainty of his critical judgments.

Jarrell was not bothered by reputations. When he reviewed E. E. Cummings's *Poems 1924–1954*, he said, among other things, "What I like least about Cummings's poems is their pride in Cummings and their contempt for most other people; the difference between the *I* and *you* of the poems, and other people, is the poems' favourite subject." We might all think that nowadays, but who else would have thought or dared to say it in 1954? And who else, a year later, would have said of Stephen Spender's *Collected Poems*:

> When the muse first came to Mr. Spender he looked so sincere that her heart failed her, and she said: "Ask anything and I will give it to you," and he said: "Make me sincere."
>
> If you look at the world with parted lips and a pure heart, and will the good, won't that make a true and beautiful poem? One's heart tells one that it will; and one's heart is wrong.

There are countless other examples that one could give of the truthful clarity and wit that one loves and honours Jarrell for. It is impossible to imagine him being taken in by the fake, or the tawdry. In 1945 he reviewed a collection of *Five Young American Poets*, one of whom was Tennessee Williams, and about him Jarrell wrote that Williams "must be one of those hoaxes people make up to embarrass *Poetry* or *Angry Penguins*: no real person—no fictional one except Humpty Dumpty—would say about poets, 'For others, I know, the Army has offered a haven.' (That

*Review of *Kipling, Auden & Co*. Reprinted from the *Times Literary Supplement*, 19 June 1981, pp. 703–04, by permission of John Lucas and Times Newspapers Ltd.

haven, Dachau)." Yet in the same review Jarrell remarked of Lowell's *Land of Unlikeness* that Lowell "is a promising poet in this specific sense: some of the best poems of the next years ought to be written by him". And ten years later he wrote of Elizabeth Bishop that "the people of the future . . . will read her just as they will read Dickinson or Whitman or Stevens. . . ."

Jarrell was not only invariably right, he was quite fearless. How else would he have dared to say of a collection of poems by William Carlos Williams that his "limitations are neither technical nor moral but intellectual"? Or remark *à propos* of *The Age of Anxiety* that "The man who, during the thirties, was one of the five or six best poets in the world has gradually turned into a rhetorical mill grinding away at the bottom of Limbo, into an automaton that keeps making little jokes, little plays on words, little rhetorical engines, as compulsively and unendingly and uneasily as a neurotic washes his hands." Now one might, of course, argue that *Scrutiny* said something very similar about Auden, or would have done if any of its contributors had possessed a shred of Jarrell's wit; but then no contributor to *Scrutiny* was capable of seeing and explaining why Auden had been one of the five or six best poets in the world, and none of them was able to speak with a proper generosity and understanding of *The Shield of Achilles*, where Jarrell could remark of Auden's technical mastery that when another poet confronts it he "is likely to feel, 'Well back to my greeting cards.' " And how impossible it is to imagine the Scrutineers—or anyone else, for that matter—saying of Wallace Stevens's *Collected Poems* that "One might as well find fault with the Evening Star as find fault with so much wit and grace and intelligence. . . ."

It is proper to bring in *Scrutiny* and the New Critics here because they did, after all, promise to survey the field of contemporary literature and pass judgment on what was fit for human consumption. In fact, they managed comparatively little in this respect and their few judgments have not worn well. Jarrell, on the other hand, did a great deal. He is a marvellous close critic, quite at home in the world of the New Criticism, as anyone who has read his analysis of Frost's "Home Burial" will agree. (I take it that Jarrell's championing of Frost was of great importance for that poet's reputation and who but Jarrell could have wanted to preserve Frost from his admirers on the grounds that "they like his best poems almost as much as they like his worst"?) In a typically mordant essay, "Poets, Critics and Readers," he remarked that "Unless you are one critic in a hundred thousand, the future will quote you only as an example of the normal error of the past, what everybody was foolish enough to believe then. Critics are discarded like calendars. . . ."

It is true, they are. But not Jarrell. And this is not merely a matter of how well his judgments have worn. It also has to do with that extraordinary wit, which allowed him to tell the truth in the most unforgettable of ways, so that he could describe a book by Oscar Williams as giving the impression "of having been written on a typewriter by a typewriter," or suggest that "The people who live in a Golden Age usually go around complaining how yellow everything looks," or say of Matthew Arnold that, far from his age missing out on great literature, he "didn't know what he was having." Anyone who has read Jarrell will be in a position to supply his own dozen or so favourites. Often they come in the form of similes: for Jarrell was a master of the unexpected, truthful, simile. Who, having read it, can ever forget his remark about how a collection of critics would be unlikely to show any interest in Wordsworth's views of his own poetry? "In the same way, if a pig wandered up to you during a bacon-judging contest, you would say impatiently, 'Go away, pig! What do you know about bacon?' "

A wonderful critic, then. And yet he has his limitations, hateful though it is to admit to the fact. What did Jarrell actually *want* of literature? When you ask this question you find that you come up with a very odd, old-fashioned answer: that he wanted it to be like or about "life." In *Poetry and the Age* he has an account of Richard Wilbur's poem "The Death of a Toad," in which he says of the opening lines that "you stop to shudder at the raw being of the world . . . *that* toad is real, all right. But when you read on, you think with a surge of irritation and dismay, so it was all only an excuse for some Poetry." Jarrell takes it for granted that poetry should possess imitative form (no wonder he was so caustically witty about Yvor Winters). In a review of Roy Campbell's *Selected Poems* he says that "when I looked for the life in Campbell's poems all I could find was literature". There are many other such moments scattered through Jarrell's critical writing, and as is perhaps inevitable the word "life" seems vaguer the more you look at it, or try to understand what he might mean by it. (Much as it does, of course, in *Scrutiny*, where writers are regularly commended for being "on the side of life": but "What is life?" as Shelley's poet cried.) Perhaps the nearest one can come to understanding what Jarrell had in mind is by way of his disappointing essay, "On Preparing to Read Kipling." For there he quotes with absolute approval some words of William James's:

> "The lunatic's visions of horror are all drawn from the material of daily fact. Our civilization is founded on the shambles, and each individual existence goes out in a lonely spasm of helpless agony. If you protest, my friend, wait till you arrive there yourself!"

"A lonely spasm of helpless agony": the phrase is so Jarrell-like that it might almost have been written by him. In the same essay, trying to define what it was he thought Kipling lacked, he pointed to Turgenev and Chekhov and remarked that beside them Kipling reveals "a lack of dispassionate moral understanding, perhaps— . . . the ability both to understand things and to understand that there is nothing to do about them."

Such a statement might on the face of it seem grandly stoic, a re-phrasing of Spinoza's granite-like pessimism; and yet reading Jarrell in bulk, his poetry as well as his criticism, you realize that he doesn't have the massive, assured calm of Spinoza. I don't doubt that Spinoza would have appealed to Jarrell, much as he appealed to Matthew Arnold; but in the end Jarrell is more like Arnold in that he accepts the eternal sadness of things, and too swiftly arrives at the position of a helpless, wry dismissiveness about his world; he assents to being a sad heart at the supermarket. Indeed, there are occasions when Jarrell positively luxuriates in his melancholy, and this can infect even his best poems. The line between luxuriating and an energizing verve is a difficult one to draw but is vital; sometimes Jarrell falls on one side, sometimes on the other. The fine, late poem "Well Water" is a case in point:

> What a girl called "the dailiness of life"
> (Adding an errand to your errand. Saying,
> "Since you're up . . ." Making you a means to
> A means to a means to) is well water
> Pumped from an old well at the bottom of the world.
> The pump you pump the water from is rusty
> And hard to move and absurd, a squirrel-wheel
> A sick squirrel turns slowly, through the sunny
> Inexorable hours. And yet sometimes
> The wheel turns of its own weight, the rusty
> Pump pumps over your sweating face the clear
> Water, cold, so cold! you cup your hands
> And gulp from them the dailiness of life.

It's a lovely and lovable poem. And yet as you register that typical Jarrell run-on line, "the sunny / Inexorable hours," you feel that it's surely too much the planned surprise, too much in the nature of a wished-for Chekhovian irony. *Why* inexorable? (One way of answering that question is simply to recall the story of Jarrell and Lowell meeting and discussing contemporary English poets by whom they'd been impressed: Lowell said he liked Hughes, Gunn and Larkin: Jarrell replied that his favourites were Larkin, Larkin and Larkin.) And then you notice that for Jarrell it is inevitable that people are a means to; that they should be caught up in ways that typically require them not so much to act as to be acted upon. It would be wrong to assume that this can claim kinship with Spinoza's laconic agreement to conspire with necessity. Jarrell's sense of people being the helpless agents of fate is a softer thing. He lacks what he beautifully identifies in the Psalms as the "almost physiological dialectic of suffering, with its opposites struggling into a final reconciled, accepting ecstasy." His sadness is more enervate, more to do with a compassion that only just avoids sentimentality.

That is why, I think, he was obsessed by the Second World War—and obsession is not too strong a word. It comes out not only in the many poems he wrote about soldiers and airmen, but also in his critical writing. For example, he has an unusually severe note on Marianne Moore's war poem "In Distrust of Merits"—though it is typical of Jarrell that he should have been an early and acute admirer of her work—in which he says that she does not remember "that most of the people in a war never fight for even a minute—though they bear for years and die forever. They do not fight, but only starve, only suffer, only die: the sum of all this passive misery is that great activity, War." Also included in the present volume is an extraordinary elegy for the war correspondent Ernie Pyle, where you sense such empathy between Jarrell and his subject that it is as though he is saying, "I was the man, I suffered, I was there." (Jarrell did not in fact get overseas during the war.) Thus he remarks that because of Pyle's despatches "most people of a country *felt*, in the fullest moral and emotional sense, something that had never happened to them, that they could never have imagined without it—a war." And he adds that Pyle's writing, "like his life, is a victory of the deepest moral feeling, of sympathy and understanding and affection, over circumstances as terrible as any men have created and endured." It is impossible to avoid the feeling that at such moments Jarrell is projecting something deeply near the heart of himself into his account of the war correspondent. The result is that he succeeds in making Pyle sound like his version of Chekhov and Turgenev; more, he makes him sound like his own poetry. "For Pyle, to the end, killing was murder: but he saw the murderers die themselves." I do not see how you can read that sentence and not immediately think of Jarrell's own poem, "Eighth Air Force."

> If, in an odd angle of the hutment,
> A puppy laps the water from a can
> Of flowers, and the drunk sergeant shaving
> Whistles *O Paradiso!*—shall I say that man
> Is not as men have said: a wolf to man?
>
> The other murderers troop in yawning:
> Three of them play Pitch, one sleeps, and one
> Lies counting missions, lies there sweating
> Till even his heart beats: One; One; One.
> *O murderers!* . . . Still, this is how it's done!
>
> This is a war. . . .

The helpless agents of fate: it was a perception that could produce marvellous poems, as in "The Death of the Ball-Turret Gunner," and a handful of others; but it may also help to explain why, in an otherwise unaccountable lapse, Jarrell found nothing of worth in the poetry of Isaac Rosenberg. For Rosenberg's best poetry has precisely that sardonic quality which would make Jarrell acutely uncomfortable. He would not be able to call it heartbreaking (one of his most over-used, and most revealing, terms of critical approval). By comparison he found it easy to praise

Owen because his poetry "has shown to us one of those worlds which, after we have been shown it, we call the real world." And Owen's world is, of course, one of above all "pity," of the "eternal reciprocity of tears." It is guaranteed to appeal to Jarrell.

In a fine moment in *A Room with A View* E. M. Forster describes Lucy Honeychurch playing the piano so that "the sadness of the incomplete" throbs through her phrases—"the sadness that is often life but which should never be Art." There is that in Jarrell which is solidly in favour of the incomplete. Karl Shapiro was probably right when he said that "Jarrell is the one poet of my generation who made an art out of American speech as it is, who advanced beyond Frost in using not only a contemporary idiom . . . but the actual rhythm of our speech. Here Jarrell is unique and technically radical. No other poet of our time has embalmed the common dialogue of Americans with such mastery . . . . He listened like a novelist. . . ." This is true to the extent that Jarrell often uses the stumbling, cliché-strewn inadequacies of speech to convey important truths about the speakers of many of his poems. (It is notable that his warmest praise for W. C. Williams was reserved for Book One of *Paterson*, and that he singled out for especial mention the passage about the two girls gathering willow twigs, one of whom says to the other "ain't they beautiful." Jarrell comments, "How could words show better than these last three the touching half-success, half-failure of their language?"). The novelist in Jarrell is less importantly represented by the strung-together jokes of *Pictures from an Institution* than by a large number of poetic monologues. But the trouble with these monologues is that although different people may speak, they all seem to be variations of one person, and that one person—whether it is in "The Woman at the Washington Zoo" or "The Lost Children"—has a sad heart which isn't necessarily the fault of the supermarket so much as of, well, *life*. And it is that, every bit as much as Jarrell's lack of concinnity, of the canorous, which prevents him from being a major poet, though he is certainly a very fine minor one.

Several of the essays in the present collection were first published in *A Sad Heart at the Supermarket*, and the justification for re-printing them here is that that book is out of print. Why not re-print all of them? I imagine the answer is that the English and American editions are different, so that to include all the essays from both versions would take an unwarrantable amount of space. But this is to point to the fact that the state of Jarrell's published criticism is in something of a muddle—as is the *Complete Poems* for that matter. I hope that someday someone will straighten these muddles out: the whole of Jarrell ought to be made properly available. In the meantime, *Kipling, Auden & Co.* contains much of the best work of a critic who is essential reading for anyone that takes to heart the rhetorical questions he threw out to his fellow-critics: "Criticism *does* exist, doesn't it, for the sake of the plays and stories and poems it criticises? . . . Brothers, *do* we want to sound like the *Publications of the Modern Language Association*, only worse?"

[From "New Novels"]

John Metcalf*

The first novel of Mr. Jarrell, poet, is the most exciting book out of America this year. Poet needs emphasising; for this is more—and less—than the usual American intellectual's novel, all construction, Connecticut and conversation; this is a coruscating, cruel, corrosive firecracker of a book where wit substitutes for plot, intuition for the cunning development of character and irony for Adler.

Pictures from an Institution describes the Assyrian descent of a Mary McCarthy-like novelist on the fold of the snobbishly, smugly liberal women's college of Benton. Her brief course on Creative Writing is used as a string on which to hang beads of character-studies, shrivelled heads that glitter with malice, diamonds of trope, jade grotesques, even—here and there—lambent, inevitable truths of pearls.

At first sight Mr. Jarrell's writing is as casual as a literate Bing Crosby's. The guts of the book anyway were written fast and hot, and read that way. But the final words have been polished as though by a Gautier; and one realises that the pace arises from his use of poetic prose; no, not incantatory, more a post-Pound version of the eighteenth-century metaphysical (in the Eliot-Leavis sense), a condensed and concentrated prose tending continually towards the epigram.

Here for example, is Mr. Jarrell pinning his first butterfly to the board:

> His voice not only took you into his confidence, it laid out a fire for you and put your slippers by it and then went into the next room to get into something more comfortable.

Or he describes the peculiar gift of mimicry of Benton's Composer in Residence:

> It was never the individual sounds of a language but the melodies behind them that Dr. Rosenbaum imitated. . . . To hear him speak French if you didn't try to understand what he was saying, was as good as attending *Phèdre*: he seemed a cloud that had divorced a text-book of geometry to marry Guillaume Appollinaire—when you replied, weakly, *yes*, it was in the accents of Matthew Arnold appreciating Rachel.

*Review of *Pictures from an Institution*. Reprinted from the *Spectator*, 22 October 1954, p. 506, by permission of the paper.

Or clumsy Flo Whittaker the good, good wife of Benton's Professor of Anthropology:

> She was a sketch for a statue of Honesty putting its foot in its mouth. . . . After you had been with Flo . . . honesty and sincerity began to seem to you a dreadful thing, and you even said to yourself like a Greek philosopher having a nervous breakdown: 'Is it right to be good?'

President Robbins and Mrs. Robbins, the Rosenbaums, the Whittakers, Miss Batterson, Constance, Gertrude and Sidney, even Miss Rasmussen and Mr. Daudier—marginal characters—all are alive and alone; and lovingly re-created by Mr. Jarrell.

Pictures from an Institution is Donne out of Groucho Marx, Rochester out of Robert Benchley, Woolcott—putting it the other way round—with culture and without cant.

As you can see, Mr. Jarrell's trope is catching; and of course, as a whole, there's a lot wrong with the book. The relationship between Constance and the Rosenbaums drops on the wrong side of sentimentality. The fugue-like outline given to the interplay of characters is both pretentious and fuzzy. And, at times, the cleverness becomes strident, the jokes inbred, the language clipped and mannered; yes, at times Mr. Jarrell strains too hard at the gnat of effect and forgets what he's been meaning to say (and which one wants to hear) about someone. But, all this accepted, here's a book that's broken through, that's witty and exhilarating and right, right in the inevitable way of a book you're not going to forget. So let's be excited about it. *Pictures from an Institution* marks the arrival of (if he can spare the time from his verse) a new American novelist of high importance. Above all it means, I should have thought, that Mr. Jarrell has convinced himself that he can write a longish book in consecutive prose. Happy us; happy Faber (and Faber); and even happy Book Society, whose—bless them—recommendation this is.

A Kind of Visitation

P. L. Travers*

Occasionally, very rarely—like the spirit of delight—comes a book that is not so much a book as a kind of visitation. I had not known that I was waiting for "The Animal Family" but when it came it was as though I had long been expecting it. This is what happens when one encounters poetry. "Never seek to tell thy love," or "Fear no more the heat of the sun," or "Out of the cradle endlessly rocking" the voices cry and between

---

*Review of *The Animal Family*. Reprinted by permission from the *New York Times Book Review*, 21 November 1965, p. 56. Copyright © 1965 by the New York Times Company.

the reader and the poem there is an immediate recognition—as though one's own thoughts, till now mute, unknown, unquickened, leapt to life at the announcement.

Nothing could be simpler than this story, if indeed one can call it a story. A lonely hunter finds a mermaid, takes her to live in his hut and with her adopts successively a bear-cub, a lynx kitten and a boy from a drifting lifeboat. That is all—and yet, reading it, one is convinced that this all is everything, each happening inevitable, essential, right. The secret lies, of course less in the plot than in the telling. The author lingers over the facts with the absorption, the inner delight of the true storyteller, letting them play and range as they will; he listens to what they say, he notes down every informing detail, above all he takes his time.

Taking time takes one into timelessness. And thus the story, like the traditional fairy tale, seems to be without beginning and without end in the sense that one is aware of it existing long before the flyleaf and long after the back page. Was, is now and ever shall be is the meaning both of Once Upon a Time and Happy Ever After; and this is the world the book inhabits.

All good stories have this feeling of continuity, of going on and never ending. Moreover, the good story never explains. The courtship of the hunter and the mermaid is taken as a matter of course much as it is in the old Scottish ballads where, after all, mermaids who wive with humans are two-a-penny. There is nothing here of Hans Andersen's mawkish portentousness and nostalgia, no longing for an immortal soul, no craving for a pair of legs. *Our* mermaid accepts herself as she is, a sea-creature in love with the land, eager to understand its language, willing to submit to its limitations. She toils happily, if awkwardly, over the meadows, propelling herself by her own tail, lives on a diet of raw fish and when she takes up her abode in the hut proves to be an indifferent housewife. But there is more to homekeeping than sweeping floors or stirring the stew; it is relationship that matters. And here every domestic detail of their mutual life throws light upon the characters of the hunter and the mermaid and the affinity between them. "They were so different from each other that it seemed to them, finally, that they were exactly alike; and they lived together and were happy."

The book, indeed, is a paean to family life and its long unending thread. The reciting of its small, factual, intimate daily round constitutes, as it were, an epic in reverse. The reader is made party to all its lights and shadows, its souvenirs, heirlooms, problems; one grieves with the hunter when he dreams of his dead parents, is concerned for him in his moments of masculine uncertainty in front of the mermaid's feminine sureness, rejoices with them both when with the advent of the first child—the bear-cub—two and one make three. The animal children are beautifully drawn and juxtaposed; the clumsy, slow-witted bumbling bear and the quick lithe lynx—each becomes more truly himself when placed beside the other. After two such fully realized characters the author could artistically go no further in the world of beasts. The third child *had* to be a boy and with him the family is complete—at peace, with the charm wound up.

The story is a medley of lyrical factuality. Never once does its sentiment decline into sentimentality—"the bear's table manners were bad, but so were the mermaid's"—nor our belief into skepticism. There is the truth of fact and the truth of truth, as D. H. Lawrence said, and any child reading this book would know to which category "The Animal Family" belonged.

Is it a book for children? I would say Yes because for me *all* books are books for children. There is no such thing as a children's book. There are simply books of many kinds and some of them children read. I would deny, however, that it was written *for* children. But is any book that these creatures love really invented for them? "I write to please myself," said Beatrix Potter, all her natural modesty and arrogance gathered into the noble phrase. Indeed, whom else, one could rightly ask. And this book bears the same hallmark. Someone, in love with an idea, has lovingly elaborated it simply to please himself—no ax to grind, making no requirements, just putting a pinch of salt on its tail—as one would with a poem—and setting it down in words. How, therefore, could a child—and children come in all ages, remember—fail to read and enjoy it?

Fly by Night

John Updike*

In the few years before his sudden death in 1965, the poet and critic Randall Jarrell devoted surprisingly much of his energy to the creation of children's books. Translations from the German of the Brothers Grimm were followed by "The Gingerbread Rabbit" and "The Bat-Poet" in 1964 and the Newbery-Honor-winning "The Animal Family" in 1965. Now, after a delay longer than its 30 spacy pages would seem to require, the final and slimmest entry in the Jarrell juvenile canon arrives, entitled "Fly by Night." It is illustrated, as were the previous two, by Maurice Sendak; the illustrations are intense and loving and uneasymaking, in tune with the prose they illumine.

The hero of "Fly by Night" is a boy named David, who lives alone, with none save animals for friends, and who at night evidently lifts up out of his bed and skims through the moonlit air in the nude. The nudity is unspecified in the text but looms specific in Sendak's illustrations, one of

*Reprinted by permission from the *New York Times Book Review*, 14 November 1976, pp. 25, 36. Copyright © 1976 by the New York Times Company.

which shows a prepubescent penis and another a rather inviting derrière. Most little boys that I have lived with have been rather severe and shy about nakedness and slept with pajamas on, sometimes with underpants under the pajamas. But David's dreaming subconscious, and nòt his sleeping body, is presumably represented, which accounts also for the visually disturbing manner in which the boy's figure is out of scale with the other figures (mice, sheep, an owl's frown) in the finely hatched pen-and-ink drawings.

Flying of course is a euphemism in more than one language for sexual activity, and a man can recall those disorienting intimations of potency that visited him in bed at about the age David seems to be. The sensations of the blankets' weight, the illusions of changing direction and inert voyage, prepare the onanistic mystery; launched, the child glides with criminal stealth into his parents' room. His father is a substantial lump in the bed, with his head out; his mother however, has placed her head beneath a pillow. Mother, as she was for Oedipus, is unrecognizable. David invades their dreams, and sees himself in process of replacing his father: "his father, looking very small, is running back and forth with David on his back, only David is as big as ever. His father is panting." His mother's dreams, like her head, are eclipsed by feathers. These feathers, outdoors, become the face of a mother owl, "with its big round brown eyes: each of them has a feathery white ring around it, and then a brown one, and then a white one, and then a brown one, till the rings come together and make big brown and white rings around its whole head." This concentric vaginal apparition holds in its claws a "big silvery fish." David thinks to himself, "I didn't know owls could catch *fish*."

Himself a fish in air, he swims after the owl, and watches her feed her young, and listens as she recites to her owlets a long bedtime poem, about a lost owl making its way back to the nest. Floating back into his bed, David gropes after who the owl's gaze reminds him of, wakes to his own mother's gaze, and after a moment of confusion perceives by sunlight that "his mother looks at him like his mother." Finis. The storyteller should be commended for the tact of his language and the depth at which his imagery seeks to touch, amid its feathery circles gripping big silvery somethings, the forbidden actual. All of Jarrell's children's tales have a sinister stir about them, the breath of true forlornness felt by children. But the stir tends to remain unsettled, unresolved by the clarifying power adulthood promises. All successful children's literature has a conspiratorial element; but the conspiracy is not among equals, one side is pretending. With Jarrell there is little pretense; he shares with his young readers as one child shares with others a guilty secret, and imparts his own unease.

The poems he includes in "The Bat-Poet" and "Fly by Night" are not as good as they should be. They aspire to a tender sharpness achieved elsewhere, by his contemporary Theodore Roethke, whose animal poems catch Nature's flip cruelty in a line (in "The Heron": "He jerks a frog across his bony lip") or brood with the grief of a helpless god:

> *Where has he gone, my meadow mouse,*
> *My thumb of a child that nuzzled in my palm?—*
> *To run under the hawk's wing.*
> *Under the eye of the great owl watching from the elm-tree,*
> *To live by courtesy of the shrike, the snake, the tom-cat.*

By comparison Jarrell's own owls are symbolic menaces: "The ear that listens to the owl believes / In death." If he was no Roethke, he was no A. A. Milne either; his poems do not address themselves to children, exclusively and positively, but are included, with disturbing *double-entendre*, in his collections of "serious" poetry as well. As they appear in the children's books, they seem stuck-on, and a bit stuck-up. What is most poetic about the bat-poet is the author's prose description of him, "the color of coffee with cream in it," as he sleeps among his fellow-bats, the wriggling of one forcing a wriggling of all, so that "it looked as if a fur wave went over them."

Jarrell saw a strangeness in the daylight, and loved inhuman nature. The longest and best of his children's books, "The Animal Family," holds no formal poetry, but most intensely presents his habitual themes of individual lostness, of estrangement within a family, of the magic of language, of the wild beauty beyond our habitations. A hunter living alone in the forest makes his way to the shore and begins to converse with a creature of the sea, called a "mermaid" but in fact a female seal. He appears to marry her, she certainly shares his bed and does his housework, though Maurice Sendak, who decorates the book with landscapes, was not called upon to depict her dragging her flippers through these connubial duties. It's a disquieting match, as if Jarrell has taken literally Roethke's lovely erotic line, "She'd more sides than a seal." As in "Fly by Night," the mother's role is flooded with strangeness, and a male child's egotism is grotesquely served. The hunter/seal couple adopt first, a bear, then a lynx and finally a little boy found alive in a rowboat with his dead mother. With the acquiescence of his four-footed siblings, the human child takes over the prime place in the animal family, and is told by his adopted mother, in her liquid accent, that he has been with them always. With this lie, the book ends. To Jarrell's vision of bliss adoption by members of another species seems intrinsic. His first book for children, "The Gingerbread Rabbit," deviated from its gingerbread-man model in the cookie's adoption by a childless pair of real rabbits, while the human mother who had concocted the hero of pastry fabricated a substitute of cloth and thread, bringing yet another texture into the patchwork of fur, skin and dough.

The writing in "The Animal Family" is exquisite, and all of Jarrell's little juveniles are a cut above the run in intelligence and unfaked feeling.

The feeling, however, remains somewhat locked behind the combinative oddness, the mix of pluralism and isolation and warping transposition: these tales of boys active at night and bats active in day bend, as it were, around an unseen center. They are surreal as not even "Alice" is surreal, for the anfractuosities of Carroll's nightmare wind back to the sunny riverbank, while Jarrell's leave us in mists, in an owl's twilight, without that sense of *emergence* of winning through and clearing up, intrinsic to children's classics from "Cinderella" to "Charlotte's Web."

. . . .

ESSAYS

General Essays

[From "Randall Jarrell: His Metamorphoses"]

Sister M. Bernetta Quinn*

. . . .

Randall Jarrell has clearly been influenced by Germanic popular stories, as he himself acknowledges in *Mid-Century American Poets*, an anthology edited by John Ciardi, where he lists them as furnishing subjects for some of his poems. . . . In his collection entitled *Losses*, "The Märchen" appears, with "Grimm's Tales" as a subtitle; again in "Deutsch durch Freud" he pictures himself as sitting on a sofa reading Grimm. In the first poem allusions occur to many of the best-known tales, such as "Hänsel and Gretel" in which Hänsel is startlingly identified with Christ; as a matter of fact the Hänsel story figures conspicuously in two other Jarrell poems, "The Night before the Night before Christmas" and "A Quilt-Pattern." Other tales referred to in "The Märchen" include "The Peasant and the Devil," "The Valiant Little Tailor," "The Mouse, the Bird, and the Sausage," "Little Snow-White," "The Louse and the Flea," "Godfather Death," and "The Blue Light." Metaphor rather than metamorphosis dominates the introduction of the poem, the forest pictured as a sea which stands for life as a whole, considered as the kingdom of Necessity. But in the final lines Jarrell sums up the metamorphic lesson we ought to have learned from the *Märchen*:

> Had you not learned—have we not learned from tales
> Neither of beasts nor kingdoms nor their Lord,
> But of our own hearts, the realm of death—
> Neither to rule nor die? to change, to change! (85)[1]

Again, in "The Island," he mentions German folk literature—"the dawn's out-speaking smile / Curled through my lashes, felled the Märchen's wood"—in order to show how daylight destroys this modern Robinson Crusoe's dream in his desert solitude, a further linking of dream and folk tale. In still another poem, "The Carnegie Library, Juvenile Division," from an earlier book, *Little Friend, Little Friend*, Jarrell

*Excerpted from *The Metamorphic Tradition in Modern Poetry* (New Brunswick: Rutgers Univ. Press, 1955; rpt. Staten Island: Gordian Press, 1966), pp. 171–206. Reprinted by permission of Gordian Press and Sister M. Bernetta Quinn.

63

describes the child's world of make-believe, "where the beasts loom in the green / Firred darkness of the märchen," alluding in the same stanza to Aladdin, of all transformers perhaps the most famous. This lyric concludes on a note less optimistic than the finish of "The Märchen"; the speaker says that he and his contemporaries have learned many things from these children's books in the Carnegie Library; they have learned how to understand their lives, but they have not found here the will to put this knowledge into action: "We learned from you to understand, but not to change."

. . . .

Imagery from the fairy tales helps too in an explanation of the poetic process as Jarrell sees it. In discussing *What Are Years* by one of his favorite writers, Marianne Moore, he makes the following comparison, reminiscent of Grimm's "Rumpelstiltskin":

> She not only can, but has to, make poetry out of everything and anything:
> she is like Midas, or Mozart purposely choosing unpromising themes, or
> the princess whom a wizard forces to manufacture sheets out of nettles—if
> the princess were herself the wizard. (*The Kenyon Review*, iv, 408.)

Any examination of his own use of colloquial material, both in his verse and as illustration in his critical prose, reveals that Jarrell too possesses this magic power of conversion.

The most ambitious and complete handling by Jarrell of the metamorphosis theme as it appears in popular tales is "Hohensalzburg: Fantastic Variations on a Theme of Romantic Character." All during the summer of 1948 Jarrell lived under the shadow of this famous castle, supposed to be haunted by ghosts who, like the wizards of folklore, have power to change whomever they meet into something else. This belief, frequent in the *Märchen*, is summarized in the section about the chandelier with china roses, the swan floating beside its shepherd, the star set in the antlers of an iron deer, all of which were once human—a passage reminiscent of Grimm's Fundevogel tale, in which a woodman rescues a little boy from a bird of prey, only to leave him in the charge of a cruel old cook who plans to boil him alive but is prevented from doing so by the magic of the woodman's daughter Lina. Lina changes Fundevogel to a rosebush and herself to the rose upon it; when this trick is discovered, she turns the boy to a church, with herself as the chandelier in it; finally, in order to escape the enraged cook, who has penetrated their disguises, Lina transforms Fundevogel to a fishpond and herself to the duck upon it. The last metamorphosis (the stars in the antlers of the iron deer) has no antecedent in the *Märchen*, but rather refers to an actual iron deer with gilt stars in its antlers (an emblem frequently seen in Austrian decoration) which stood at the entrance to the park of Leopoldschloss where Jarrell stayed during the time that he taught at the Salzburg Institute.

Jarrell sets the Hohensalzburg scene carefully: the little people singing from the river, moving from the wood, calling from the rushes; the ancient woman spinning; the offer of a wish to be granted; the Briar Rose story from Grimm. In sketching the background of the ghost whose visit forms the heart of the poem Jarrell touches delicately on one form of metamorphosis of great anthropological interest, petrifaction. He represents a stone maid who was once a young girl of exceptional loveliness, now sunk in the waters of the earth and whispering to the child who has run all evening on the beach. Transformation into stone is as catholic a belief as that into animal shape. Here the stone maid symbolizes the skeletal future of man. The child's wish for invisibility which immediately follows the allusion to petrifaction is of course a reference to another variety of metamorphosis and is a skillful foreshadowing of the final passage in the poem.

Waking at night in a house near the castle, the protagonist is first aware of a strange visitor by a touch, swallow-light, on his hand. Next, he hears her speak. At first he sees only the moonlight, but she assures him that she is behind the moonlight. From moonlight, the "ghost" changes, at least in the way he talks about her, into the enchanted princess of the Grimm story, lying asleep "in the last, least room"; this passage has echoes of "The Garden of Eden" in Andersen's fairy tales. The Briar Rose story, a favorite with Jarrell, appears in at least five of his other poems: "La Belle au Bois Dormant," "When You and I Were All," "Head of Wisdom," "For an Emigrant," and "The Sleeping Beauty: Variation of the Prince." The protagonist here is merely one drop of Sleeping Beauty's blood, one drop of the immense quantities that death has sucked. Then follows a most effective creation of suspense, fright; in a breathless dialogue, the princess describes to her victim how, some day, she will come to him and

> I shall take you and . . .
>   *Tell me.*
> No, no, I shall never.
>   *Tell me.*
> You must not know.
>   *Tell me.*
> I—I shall kiss your throat.
> *My throat?*
> There, it is only a dream.
> I shall not so—I shall never so. (88–89)

Then, even as he kisses her, she takes on the taste of the lime tree, flower and fruit, and finally—horrible fulfillment of her prophecy—turns to a vampire who fixes her teeth into his throat and sucks all his blood into herself. The victim's dreadful predicament is dramatized through a crucifixion image; the moonlight pierces his extended arms as if with nails. Just as Christ's Body and Blood are separated on Calvary, so are the speaker's here:

> *When I saw that it was my blood,*
> *I used my last strength and, slowly,*
> *Slowly, opened my eyes*
> *And pushed my arms out, that the moonlight*
>   *pierced and held—*

The terror recedes, and his guest is a girl again. The speaker, too, grows backwards until he reaches his own childhood. In a passage included in the *Poetry* first publication of the poem but omitted in *The Seven-League Crutches*, the whole meaning of the experience is now clarified: "The past is a child that sucks our blood / Back into the earth." Here the man grows tender toward his "Little Sister," for he sees that she is really his life; somberly, she adds to his voicing of this truth that she is also his death.

Economically, Jarrell has selected effective fragments from the vast body of vampire superstition current in Europe until very recently (and probably not yet entirely vanished), a superstition allied to the belief in werewolves. The idea that by stealing blood the dead can sap the strength of the living is an ancient one, and even now not obsolete, one manifestation of a primitive conviction that the dead savagely hate the living. (Theda Kenyon, *Witches Still Live*, 56.)

This theme of the living mortal as having turned into a ghost after being bitten by a vampire has been anticipated in the protagonist's speech to the girl:

> *Before I was a ghost*
> *I was only a—*
>   *a ghost wants blood . . .* (89)

Towards the conclusion of the poem it is explicitly stated, by the spectral visitor herself:

> *Many a star*
> *Has fallen, many a ghost*
> *Has met, at the path to the wood, a ghost*
> *That has changed at last, in love, to a ghost.* (90)

Towards the end of "Hohensalzburg," Jarrell speaks again of the "harsh clumsy things"—no longer ghosts but now villagers and farmers in tunics, quite possibly wearing *Lederhosen* and with badges stuck in their Tyrolese hats—who when they find him without his blood, will search for the "child" all night, for the ghost whose identity is much more complicated than that of the famous composite one in the *Quartets*; the poet has the pursuers invoke God in order to trap the girl, the "dweller of the Earth," as he now calls her.

. . . .

It would seem as if this stratified interpretation of death were rich enough, without further deepening. Yet to understand Jarrell's lyric, one

must take under examination a final metamorphosis. The moonlight >
princess > vampire > girl ("Little Sister") > life > death becomes next a
star. Foreshadowing of this last change has occurred in the line "Your
cold flesh, faint with star-light"; the process is again suggested in the
earlier version of the poem by "as all my blood / Flows from your starry
limbs into your heart—"; it is at the end defined thus:

> We shall change; we shall change; but at last, their stars,
> We shall rest in the branches of the antlers
> Of the iron deer. (90)

German ghosts, one remembers from earlier in the poem, have power to
enchant. The fact of decay, a familiar theme of literature, was next
described in the *Poetry* version as the turning of the "great limbs" of the
protagonist and his murderess to lime trees, though Jarrell has seen fit to
omit this mutation in revising for book publication.

The poem closes with a declaration that there is something more,
something unexplained in the above account of reality, something best
represented by the Christian concept of the Word. All these things which
appear to be so different—"at the last, all these are one, / We also are
forever one: / A dweller of the Earth, invisible." In these lines the two
chief characters in the poems become one and achieve invisibility, the
metamorphosis which is the consummation of the girl's childhood wish.

. . . .

Jung and his theories have influenced many modern poets. And if
they believe, as Jung believes, that a layer of the collective unconscious
forms the foundation of the personal unconscious in every mind and is approximately the same in all Western men, then for them the myths and
later the fairy tales (both of which are after all only the recorded thought
of the race) codify the basic images of the collective unconscious. Myths
thus represent the nature of the psyche, not an allegorization of nature;
dreams take over the same archetypal symbols to voice the deepest needs
of the ego.

A poetic way of voicing these needs—and here is the truly exciting
feature of dream-imagery as used by Jarrell—is through a new language,
one composed not of words but of pictures. These pictures, however, are
not purely personal; they recur from dreamer to dreamer. What words
figure in them have lost their character as conventional symbols and have
become, like the name of Rumpelstiltskin, inseparable from their
referents ("Deutsch Durch Freud"). Jarrell has noted this traumatic approach in W. H. Auden, a writer who exerted tremendous influence upon
the younger poet's first book of verse:

> They [the early poems] gain an uncommon plausibility from the terse
> understated matter-of-factness of their treatment, the insistence (such as
> that found in the speech of children, in Mother Goose, in folk or savage

verse, in dreams) upon the thingness of the words themselves. (*Partisan Review*, xii, 438).

In "Hohensalzburg" the two types of images, dream and folklore, are combined. As a matter of fact, no image, not even that of blood or of ghosts, is more integral to Jarrell's work than that of the dream, which appears in more than half of the lyrics published by him thus far in book form.

In the folk tale, the worlds of fantasy and of dream unite, a fact now generally recognized. Lightning metamorphoses in dreams are part of the experience of the ordinary person as well as the stuff that fairy-lore is made of. According to modern psychology, the heroes, heroines, and villains of both *Märchen* and myth serve to concretize the life of the psyche which goes on uninhibited during the time of dreaming. Outside space, time, and causality, the dream-elements give a picture of the individual unconscious, which Jung and others view as a microcosm of the collective unconscious. A more traditional interpretation, rooted in the fact that human nature remains always and everywhere the same, would account for the latter purely as the expected resemblance between one mind and another.

Borrowing from Saint Augustine, Jung refers to the recurrent symbols of dreams as archetypes, somewhat like Plato's ideas, except that they embody the imperfect as well as the perfect:

> Today we can hazard the formula that the *archetypes appear in myths and fairy-tales just as they do in dreams and in the products of psychotic fantasy*. The medium in which they are embedded is, in the former case, an ordered and for the most part immediately understandable context, but in the latter case a generally unintelligible, irrational, not to say delirious sequence of images which nonetheless does not lack a certain hidden coherence. (*Essays on a Science of Mythology*, 100.)

On the preceding page in this essay, Jung points out how standard motifs, the same all over the world and from age to age, run through the structure of dreams:

> In the dream, as in the products of psychoses, there are numberless combinations to which one can find parallels only in mythological associations of ideas (or perhaps in certain poetic creations which are often characterized by a borrowing, not always conscious, from myths).

Jarrell mentions Jung's archetypal images in his discussion of Auden's poetry quoted above, a circumstance which suggests that he is conscious of their pertinence to the poet's problems.

Appositely, Randall Jarrell in his poetry almost always identifies death with dreaming. The most extensive expression of this identification, "The Night before the Night before Christmas," is a poignant case-history of adolescent heartbreak. It begins with the simplicity and generality of a fairy tale, one set in an apartment house significantly called the Arden Apartment. Throughout its twelve pages, the principal character is referred to only as "the girl"; her mother has been dead for two years and she lives with her father, her invalid brother, and an aunt. Jarrell supplies obliquely the dreary intercourse of her daily life: her transferred love for the new high school teacher; the chapped hands with bitten nails, pressed together in a middy blouse; the unselfish efforts to amuse her brother with dominoes or books; the Christmas presents which she wraps, each one a gauge of her regard of the recipient; the bedroom with its babyish decorations; the Marxian propaganda she reads, straining to illuminate its abstractions by the various light of her imagination; the clanking radiator, like the voice of Martha in the dark; her pet squirrel, a "clawed / Dead rat with an Angora tail," symbol for her of all the injustice in the world, injustice which she cannot reconcile with the thought of God.

The girl's first dream, upon falling asleep the night before the night before Christmas, is a grotesque scene in which a big squirrel teaches lines from *Romeo and Juliet* to six others with radiator-steam-valve voices, an application of the Communist panacea of education which will at last destroy all evil. Then: "She whispers: 'I'm awake. / No, I'm not dreaming, I'm awake.' " The girl thinks of the vertiginous expanse of the universe; from her window she stares at the evergreens, stars, trees, the bushes covered with snow that stand like Hänsel and Gretel, sparkling as brightly as Lot's wife after her metamorphosis to salt. She sees herself and her brother look at the squirrel dead in the snow:

> *She and her brother float up from the snow—*
> *The last crumbs of their tears*
> *Are caught by the birds that are falling*
> *To strew their leaves on the snow*
> *That is covering, that has covered*
> *The play-mound under the snow . . .*
> *The leaves are the snow, the birds are the snow,*
> *The boy and girl in the leaves of their grave*
> *Are the wings of the bird of the snow.*
> *But her wings are mixed in her head with the Way*
> *That streams from their shoulders, stars like snow:*
> *They spread, at last, their great starry wings*
> *And her brother sings, "I am dying." (50)*

The passage just following conveys in a brief dialogue, partly through manipulation of tenses, the children's bewilderment at this mixture of fantasy and truth. Then the dream goes on:

> *They are flying.*
>
> *They look down over the earth.*
> *There is not one crumb.*

> *The rays of the stars of their wings*
> *Strike the boughs of the wood, and the shadows*
> *Are caught up into the night. . . . (50–51)*

The leaves and the birds—a skillful use of motor imagery—have become the snow; the boy and girl, buried in their graves of snow, are radiantly transformed to the wings of the bird of the snow. Such a mutation is grounded in primitive belief: "To the natural mind the soul is a bird, and at certain rare moments, when the issue of life or death hangs in the balance, or when the rational habit of the mind is humbled by the presence of death, the vision of a bird at the window touches a chord in the heart which will not be silenced by all our scientific scepticism." (H. G. Baynes, *Mythology of the Soul*, 707). In *The Tree of Mythology, Its Growth and Fruitage*, the folklorist Charles De B. Mills points out another basis for Jarrell's image: "The comparison of snow-flakes to feathers is an ancient one, and is found in Greek history. Herodotos says the Scythians declared the regions north of them inaccessible, because they were filled with feathers" (123).

The snow-birds increase in magnificence in the poem till their great starry wings spread like the Milky Way itself. As in "Hohensalzburg" and in the fifteenth book of Ovid, where Caesar is made a constellation, they have been changed after death into stars. Looking back to earth, both of the children whisper of the time when they were alive. The motto hanging in their father's office—*To Travel Hopefully Is a Better Thing Than to Arrive*—becomes *To End Hopefully Is a Better Thing—A Far, Far Better Thing*, the girl's memory of Sidney Carton from her English book. The motherless girl's crying, with which the poem ends, belongs not to the world of death and dream which she had created but to the problems that Christmas Eve will bring.

This poem, then, represents a retreat from reality into the glittering world of dreams; it is focused upon the normal way of escape from unpleasantness, but at the same time it serves as a parallel of the abnormal method of fleeing from the difficult. Freud has shown this symbolic connection in his *New Introductory Lectures on Psycho-Analysis*:

> The state of sleep represents a turning away from the real external world, and thus provides a necessary condition for the development of a psychosis. The most penetrating study of serious cases of psychosis will reveal no characteristic which is more typical of these pathological conditions. In psychosis, however, the turning away from reality is brought about in two ways; either because the repressed unconscious is too strong, so that it overwhelms the conscious which tries to cling on to reality, or because reality has become so unbearably painful that the threatened ego, in a despairing gesture of opposition, throws itself into the arms of the unconscious impulses. (27)

What for the girl is only a brief respite, a tranquil and shimmering interlude, is for the psychotic a permanent if diseased release from suffering.

"The Black Swan" is another child's attempt to understand death by way of the hallucinatory imagination; its title is the name usually given to a *pas de deux* extracted from Tchaikowsky's ballet, *Swan Lake*. Instead of facing the fact that her sister is dead, the little girl in the poem makes up a fairy tale about her: the swans have turned her into a swan. At sunset, when chores are done, the girl goes in search of her transformed sister, down to the lake across which even the sun has become a swan with a red beak huge enough to contain the night:

> *When the swans turned my sister into a swan*
> *I would go to the lake, at night, from milking:*
> *The sun would look out through the reeds like a swan,*
> *A swan's red beak; and the beak would open*
> *And inside there was darkness, the stars and the moon.* (54)

Jarrell understands the why and how of children's make-believe; he uses it to its fullest poetic possibilities. The reeds by the edge of the lake are not reeds, but clusters of little voices whispering an incantation intended to metamorphose the living girl into the same form as her dead sister:

> *Out on the lake a girl would laugh.*
> *"Sister, here is your porridge, sister,"*
> *I would call; and the reeds would whisper,*
> *"Go to sleep, go to sleep, little swan."*
> *My legs were all hard and webbed, and the silky*
>
> *Hairs of my wings sank away like stars*
> *In the ripples that ran in and out of the reeds:*
> *I heard through the lap and hiss of water*
> *Someone's "Sister . . . sister," far away on the shore,*
> *And then as I opened my beak to answer*
>
> *I heard my harsh laugh go out to the shore*
> *And saw—saw at last, swimming up from the green*
> *Low mounds of the lake, the white stone swans:*
> *The white, named swans . . .*

The pathetic child leaves her own body waiting with the bowl of porridge on the shore and finds herself a swan, at the center of the lake, where the laugh had come from: through the intensity of her longing and loneliness she becomes her sister. Across the lapping water—the very waves hissing like swans—comes her own voice, faintly calling; and now, from the other side of death, she learns the impossibility of any reconciliation. It is as if the white tombstones of the cemetery where they had laid her sister come swimming up from the lake's bottom—the low green mounds, the named white stones.

But all this hasn't happened, no, not really happened; in her dreams, the little girl has created even the trip to the lake; actually, she is home in bed, though the moon, stars, frogs, waves, swans are all about her in the darkness as her dead sister soothes her to rest (or calls her to death):

> *"It is all a dream,"*
> *I whispered, and reached from the down of the pallet*
>
> *To the lap and hiss of the floor.*
>   *And "Sleep, little sister," the swans all sang*
> *From the moon and stars and frogs of the floor.*
>   *But the swan my sister called, "Sleep at last, little sister,"*
> *And stroked all night, with a black wing, my wings.* (54)

There is a great tenderness here, and a willingness to present emotion without apology, unique among poets writing today. Sentimentality is avoided by the union of dream and fantasy, both of which refuse to be bound by the precepts of waking, practical life.

The concept informing "The Black Swan"—a girl's transformation into a swan—is part of an old and very extensive body of folklore centering around swan-maidens, folk-stories which perhaps originated as dramatization of white fleecy clouds swimming through a sea of sky, even as in the beginning the werewolf may have been the night-wind. (John Fiske, *Myths and Myth-Makers: Old Tales and Superstitions*, 102.) Traditionally these swan-maidens have been thought of as summoning mortals to their home in a far-away land, thus figuratively as beautiful omens of death.

The ballet upon which this lyric is based, Tschaikowsky's *Swan Lake*, is thoroughly in the metamorphic tradition. In the second act, Prince Siegfried and his followers come upon a crowned swan floating toward the shore of a moonlit lake. She is no ordinary bird, but a victim of sorcery:

> This is the hour when Odette—a Queen who has incurred the enmity of the enchanter Von Rothbart—may for a brief time resume the human form of which she has been deprived by her enemy's magic act. . . . With the arrival of dawn Odette and her ladies must change their human forms and again become swans. (Grace Robert, *The Borzoi Book of Ballets*, 314.)

Through the offer of the Prince to share Odette's doom, she and her companions are freed of the spell. To parallel this, Jarrell has the live sister share the enchanted fate of her swan-sister, though the poet permits no happy dénouement at sunrise to the girl of "The Black Swan."

Another metamorphic ballet used by Jarrell in his series of poems giving dream experiences is *Giselle*, by Jean Coralli. The plot is a graceful and melancholy fantasy: Giselle, gone mad, kills herself when she discovers deception in her fiance, Loys, and after death is transformed into one of the Wilis, maidens enchanted by a fairy queen, Myrtha, who by night dance through the moonlit shadows of the wood.

. . . .

Randall Jarrell might have written a dramatic monologue on this theme, as he did, for instance, in "The Island," wherein Robinson Crusoe speaks. He prefers to present Giselle, however, at one more remove from the real world, and therefore calls his poem "The Girl Dreams that She Is Giselle."

. . . .

An examination of [its] verbs and verbals . . . reveals in how remarkable a manner Jarrell has caught the exquisite nuances of faeryland, the glimmering motion and uncertain light of the realm of magic. In the end, Giselle is figuratively ignited by the white fire that flickers out to her from the Queen. As she dances, one might visualize a flame, leaping high and wildly under the supernal excitement.

. . . .

The girl who dreams she is Giselle, then, is perhaps using her subconscious imagination to transform the undesirable in her waking life.

"A Rhapsody on Irish Themes" begins with a half-dream, half-waking experience in which the poet's great-grandmother appears at the porthole of his ship waiting to set sail from Ireland. In mocking rhetoric he shows her, even as she holds out to him a handkerchief made by the Little People, undergoing metamorphosis:

> Then you turned into the greatest of gulls
> That brood on the seasaw green
> Swells of the nest of the harbor of Cóbh. (74)

Later in the poem he playfully refers to the old woman as "old Circe," enchantress who will detain him on her island of Faith, lulled by the musical speech of her countrymen. "Great-grandmother, I've dreamed of you till I'm hoarse," he exclaims, but in the end the cold practical world conquers the dream.

In "The Venetian Blind" Jarrell again works the difficulty of separating dream from reality and again discovers that the true nightmare is the wide-awake one. Here also he utilizes the technique of metamorphosis. The person waking has the illusion that he is in Eden on the first day of the world. Falling in the shape of bars of a musical staff, the sunlight becomes his face. Then: "His dream / Has changed into this day, this dream. . . ." He cannot remember where he is—a common enough experience—and imagines that his limbs are curled about space:

> He thinks that he is younger
> Than anything has ever been.
> He thinks that he is the world.

> *But his soul and his body*
> *Call, as the bird calls, their one word—*
> *And he remembers.*

> *He is lost in himself forever.* (55)

The implications of this attitude, as they affect the question of personal identity, are echoed in many of Jarrell's lyrics.

Another type of effect in dream-analysis is obtained in the final lines of "King's Hunt," wherein a child dreams a complete fairy story, one in which a tyrannical king is poisoned by a deaf-mute whose tongue has been cut out by a royal order; after the crime, the mute and a dwarf who has led the king to the trap prepared for him gaze through the window at the corpse until their two faces merge into the face of a child (the one dreaming the story) who knows that something is dreadfully wrong without understanding precisely what and is all the more fascinated on that account: "Their blurred faces, caught up in one wish, / Are blurred into one face: a child's set face." The murder by the mute and the dwarf in the dream represents the child's passionate wish to destroy some part of the grown-up world that oppresses him. About this type of dream Freud says:

> Very often pictures and situations appear in the manifest content of the dream which remind one of well-known themes from fairy stories, legends and myths. The interpretation of such dreams throws light on the original motives which created these themes, though naturally we must not forget the change of meaning which this material has undergone during the passage of time. (*New Introductory Lectures on Psycho-Analysis*, 39.)

"A Quilt-Pattern" is another dream of an unhappy child, an invalid whose subconsciousness tries to compensate for the agonies of his conscious life. The title is drawn from the actual quilt on his sick-bed; on it is blocked out the Tree of Life, gray as the light fades. On seven-league crutches the boy travels into the "oldest tale of all," sleep.

In his dream he sees his mother dead and transformed into a house; her "scaling face" is "square in the steam of a yard." He hates her demanding, possessive love that pursues him every moment of his waking life; only by such a stratagem can he evade it. At first the boy (divided into two selves, one good and one bad) is confined in the cages near the house, the cages for

> *All small furry things*
> *That are hurt, but that never cry at all—*
> *That are skinned, but that never die at all.* (57)

Through the wire of the cages "Good me, bad me" gather black-berries, their only food. It is very likely that one may be the boy himself, the other an imaginary companion such as small children commonly construct. The house itself is deep in the forest, "here in the wood of the dream."

At this point, Jarrell makes it unmistakable that he is using, in a Freudian way, the Hänsel and Gretel tale (probably read by the child during the tedious day) as a basis for the boy's dream:

> *Here a thousand stones*
> *Of the trail home shine from their strings*
> *Like just-brushed, just-lost teeth.*
> *All the birds of the forest*
> *Sit brooding, stuffed with crumbs* (57–58)

He combines the two trips of the children into the forest, adding modern touches—the extracted teeth on strings, agleam from recent polishing. The lies little Hänsel told to his mother to account for his backward glances are united in "His white cat eats up his white pigeon." It seems as if no deceit is strong enough to conquer the powers of evil working against him.

The next stanza divides the child again into separate selves, existing in the boy's mind, though actually they are only one, who "Sits wrapped in his coat of rabbit-skin—" But this coat is more than coat:

> *—good me*
> *Sits twitching the rabbit's fur of his ears*
> *And says to himself, "My mother is basting*
> *Bad me in the bath-tub—"* (58)

Back in the Hänsel and Gretel framework, the boy looks into the house, which has a mouth, not a door, and hopes he will find what he needs, but "there is nothing." Psychoanalysis commonly interprets the house in dreams as a symbol for woman. In hunger, he breaks off one of his mother's fingers, and when the house asks who is eating her he replies with her remembered pet name for him, "It is a mouse." Just as his mother is accustomed to singing around the house (the first reference to her is to "the humming stare / Of the woman—the good mother—") the house of bread "Calls to him in its slow singing voice" to ask if he is fat, demanding that he hold out his finger; instead, he extends the bone of her own finger, which moves. She tells him that he hasn't eaten enough to *know*, and one thinks of the Tree of Life in Eden, which brought knowledge of death into the world. Even in dreams, the little boy will not face the fact that the house is the mother whom he has desired dead.

The dream itself, personified and blending into the house, whispers:

> *"You are full now, mouse—*
> *Look, I have warmed the oven, kneaded the dough:*
> *Creep in—ah, ah, it is warm!—*
> *Quick, we can slip the bread in now. . . ."* (59)

The house, up to this point apparently representing the dead mother, is now clearly and horribly identified with the witch of Grimm's fairy story, scolding at the boy who complains that he doesn't know how to slip the bread into the oven and bending over to show him. (It is hardly coincidental that when Hänsel and Gretel return after the witch has been killed they find their mother dead.)

As the witch screams in the hot oven, Hänsel and Gretel (the two sides of the child) look at each other and smile. The mouse (the small boy) has escaped roasting; certainly what burns in the oven is nothing dear to him. But his guilt, even in sleep, prompts him to explain: "It was the Other," that part of him rebellious to parental approval and to his own better judgment. In the end of the poem, he cannot bear to give up his dream-world and face the mother who tiptoes to the invalid's door and whom he intensely and silently wishes away. Even his nightmare is preferable to waking and meeting her synthetic and paralyzing affection.

Death itself, the mystery at the heart of "King's Hunt" and "A Quilt-Pattern," has lost its reality in these days of abstraction, where the targets of the bombardiers are only names learned in geography classes. In "A Conversation with the Devil" Lucifer himself is appalled by modern man's attitude toward death:

> I disliked each life, I assure you, for its own sake.
> —But to deal indifferently in life and death;
> To sell, wholesale, piecemeal, annihilation;
> To—I will not go into particulars—
> This beats me. (32)

Indeed, Mephistopheles is a changed devil, an anachronism whose occupation is gone. Contemporary warfare has removed from man his freedom of choice, leaving no room for a devil's operations. And death, which used to have dignity, ritual, cannot be believed in; we only dream that we die. Thus the flier in "Losses," horrified at the contrast between actuality and the stereotyped war reports, blends dreaming and dying: "It was not dying—no, not ever dying; / But the night I died I dreamed that I was dead."

The life-as-a-dream motif so unusual in Jarrell's poetry finds one of its best articulations in "The Dream of Waking," the first two stanzas of which represent what goes through the mind of a wounded soldier in a hospital as he dreams he is a child waking; he is back home again—the water around the drifting boat from which he was picked up changes into light, then into laughter, then into a blend of himself, his room, and the tree outside the window. In that earlier day, his sun is gold mixed with air, is his own life. Then he really wakes, remembering back to the boat, to the origin of his present plaster cast brown with dried blood, the boat where his friend died in spite of his own frenzied begging. The reality he wakes to now is gruesomely different from the childish reality he woke to

in the dream and once used to wake to in life. The interpenetration of self
with environment continues throughout the last stanza:

> . . . *the boat is bodies*
> *And the body broken in his broken arms*
> *And the voice, the old voice:* Please don't die—
> *His life and their death: oh morning, morning.* (396)

The situation described so movingly here is very much like that in "A
Field Hospital," where the patient thinks that he is dreaming after he has
awakened—the "old mistake."

In "Absent with Official Leave," the soldier escapes to life through
sleep, escapes to civilian lands where death is not organized; where roads
hop aimlessly instead of leading to objectives; where hunters sprawl for
birds, not men; where fires are lit not to burn down cities but to dry "His
charmed limbs, all endearing from the tub." Near the end of the poem
Jarrell's devotion to Grimm finds voice in "He moans like a bear in his enchanted sleep," with its overtones of the Snow-White and Rose-Red story.
The soldier wakes from the spell not to a princess but only to the night, its
silence broken by the sighs and breathing of his co-sufferers.

The dreams in these poems speak to their protagonists through images, not through the verbal counters debilitated by waking usage. What
they communicate extends as far as the human race extends, and even
beyond, since man is the world in miniature; they correspond to prophecy
and religious vision; as Joseph Campbell says, they express truths which
are eternal and immutable:

> Therefore, in sum: The "monstrous, irrational and unnatural" motifs of
> folk tale and myth are derived from the reservoirs of dream and vision.
> On the dream level such images represent the total state of the individual
> dreaming psyche. But clarified of personal distortions and pro-
> pounded—by poets, prophets, visionaries—, they become symbolic of the
> spiritual norm for Man the Microcosm. They are thus phrases from an
> image-language, expressive of metaphysical, psychological, and sociolog-
> ical truth. (Folkloric Commentary, in *The Complete Grimms' Fairy
> Tales*, 1944, 1971, 861.)

. . . .

Besides these two major uses of the metamorphosis concept (*Märchen*
and dreams), Jarrell utilizes the changes wrought by friendship and connubial love, both traditionally accredited with effecting the union or exchange of souls. This idea is carried out in "Burning the Letters." Here
Jarrell puts into the mouth of a war widow an account of the mutation
undergone after the death of her aviator-husband:

> *The poor labored answers, still unaswering;*
> *The faded questions—questioning so much,*

> *I thought then—questioning so little;*
> *Grew younger, younger, as my eyes grew old,*
> *As that dreamed-out and wept-for wife,*
> *Your last unchanging country, changed*
> *Out of your own rejecting life—a part*
> *Of accusation and of loss, a child's eternally—*
> *Into my troubled separate being.* (158)

The pilot's life was that of a child—resentful of what reality was doing, forced to give up that wonderful never-never land which his wife was to him as he dreamed about her waking in the hostile airways over the Pacific or sleeping in the doubtful shelter of an island camp; their beings were somehow one in those days, but now she is herself again, *troubled* and *separate*. Out of his death will rise her life, if she wants it:

> *The mourning slaves*
> *In their dark secrecy, come burying*
> *The slave bound in another's flesh, the slave*
> *Freed once, forever, by another's flesh.* (159)

She has lost all faith in religious dogma—the headnote tells us that she was once a Christian, a Protestant—especially in that supreme Metamorphosis, the Holy Eucharist, which now seems to her a nightmare from which she awakens. Her husband is described in lines suggestive of Hart Crane as being beyond change; burning his letters symbolizes the end of their togetherness, the beginning of her own life and the world of her life.

Some Jarrell lyrics use transformation as a primary device; in others it is incidental. "The Emancipators" is addressed to such scientists as Galileo, asking them whether they guessed to what fearful uses their discoveries would be put. What for them was a formula has resulted first in the Industrial Revolution, then in the wars of the present century, since today: "The equations metamorphose into use." The prose-poem, "1914," reminiscent of Auden as is much of Jarrell's earlier work, represents the first World War thus:

> *Now the forts of Antwerp, broken into blocks,*
> *slide into a moat as bergs break off into the sea;*
> *the blocks, metamorphosed into the dead, sprawl*
> *naked as grave-mounds in the stalky fields.* (202)

It reiterates the life-is-a-dream motif discussed above by picturing minutely a photograph of a dead soldier and then pointing up the significance in these words: "Underneath his picture there is written, about his life, his death, or his war: *Es war ein Traum.*" Jarrell goes on to say, fusing the opposites life and death with their meeting place, war: "It is the dream from which no one wakes." This conclusion, however, is not as negativistic as one might think without reading the body of Jarrell's work. Delmore Schwartz, reviewing a book of his verse, says: "If, as one poem declares, this life is a dream from which no one wakes, the dreamer has refused to deceive himself, to let himself go, and to forget what he believes and loves." (*The Nation*, CLXI, 592.)

. . . .

A further example of mutation caused by war is in the lyric called "The Metamorphoses" (194). . . . Between the first and the second stanzas peace has been converted into war. The peace was a degenerate, not a healthy one: surplus commodities were being destroyed as an artificial way of keeping up prices (the oranges thrown into the harbor, the burning coffee); idle ships were riding the waters; the protagonist too was idle. Once war breaks out, with its acceleration of the country's economic life, the scene springs to action: oil-tankers dot the bay, crated bombers cover the wharves, the unemployed "I" works all day in the rush caused by war needs. The significance of the title is underlined in the final quatrain. In a ghastly perversion of the prince-flounder idea in Grimm's "The Fisherman and his Wife," the speaker has been changed into a fish—Jarrell's way of describing a swollen corpse, floating upon the "oil-black bay," with wounds in his sides which gape like gills. The "rust of the freighters" has been replaced by the "blood of the transports"; however, whereas the rust blended into the tide, the blood remains separate with a frightful distinctness.

The whole poem emphasizes an idea which permeates several of Jarrell's pieces: war metamorphoses men into things. "The Lines" develops this thought, pursuing it up through the time of discharge from service, when the "things" are changed back into men again. "After the naked things, told they are men, / Have lined once more for papers, pensions. . . ." The horror of regimentation over, the things are free, human beings once again.

The way in which war changes men into things suggests the punitive aspect of metamorphosis, usually present in classical treatments, such as the tales of Ovid and Apuleius (cf. Ovid's account of Actaeon, Io, Narcissus, Lycaon, etc., or Homer's telling of the Circe myth). Jarrell puts but little stress upon metamorphosis as a means of punishment, although there is a suggestion of this in "The Wide Prospect," where he says of native laborers in colonies: "Their lives, enchanted to a thousand forms, / Are piled in holds for Europe." Changed to new vegetables, tobacco, gold, the lives of the natives are transported in galleons to Europe while their bones go on working the mines and fields. The poem concludes with the "Hohensalzburg" image of the banquet of human flesh: Man, the grisly abstraction, feeds upon the individual men who people the earth.

. . . .' . . . .

World War II brought into the focus of popular attention the truth that a man is at least two persons: the soldier but also the civilian of the past who still exists in the minds of those back home and in dreams. Herman Fränkel classifies one of Ovid's intentions as the split-in-the-ego, so much discussed today: "Furthermore, the theme gave ample scope for displaying the phenomena of insecure and fleeting identity, of a self divided in itself or spilling over into another self. . . . Separation from the self means normally death, but not in a metamorphosis." (*Ovid: A Poet between Two Worlds*, 99.) In the days of old Rome, personal identity was not so fleeting a thing as it is today, after Berkeley's idealism, Locke's sensism, James's flux, Bergson's intuitionism, Sartre's extistentialism, and all the other attempts to break down the notion of an abiding self.

. . . .

With the self-consciousness of the artist, Jarrell approaches this problem of identity, subjects it to poetic examination. One of his favorite symbols in so doing is the mirror. *Die alte Frau, die alte Marschallin* in "The Face" (a character borrowed from *Der Rosenkavalier*) repudiates what she sees in the looking glass, reflecting that: "It is terrible to be alive," when what you are and what you appear to be are so different; this creature in the mirror cannot be she. The protagonist in "A Ghost, A Real Ghost" thought that he could never survive looking in the mirror and finding the room empty; yet this happens and he keeps on existing. Someone in "An Old Song" speaks of "the mirror's lamentable change." The speaker goes on to wonder, looking into a grave, if the soul might be deceived into thinking it could escape punishment or praise in such depths, where it "might endure / The altering ages in that altered shape." The princess who wakes in the wood, in still another poem, does not know who she is, though she feels that she is identical with the universe. "The Venetian Blind," already mentioned in connection with dreams, reveals a man groping frantically for his identity, for his niche in the cosmos; for that inexplicable *something* which is his true self, left out in every account of the world:

> And the Angel he makes from the sunlight
> Says in mocking tenderness:
> "Poor stateless one, wert thou the world?

. . . .

> And yet something calls, as it has called:
> "But where am I? But where am I? (56)

The italicizing of the personal pronoun shows upon which facet of the mental agony Jarrell wishes accent to fall.

That Randall Jarrell is concerned with philosophical explanations of inner and external reality is further evident in "The Place of Death," which portrays a student walking, his Spinoza in hand, among the tombstones of a cemetery which is reminiscent of Robert Lowell's Quaker graveyard in Nantucket:

> He has felt the boundaries of being fade,
> These long-outmoded, mounded, dewy modes

Lapse to the seeding and inhuman Substance
Whose infinite, unchanging, and eternal thought
Is here extended in a thousand graves. (138)

Essence, substance (defined as that which makes a thing what it is, regardless of accidents) having been rejected by certain modern philosophers in favor of "A thing is what it seems to me or what I think it is," the conversion of one thing into another is no longer exclusively an imaginative account of origins designed to provide courtly entertainment as in Ovid, or even a poetic representation of the verities of daily conscious and subconscious experience, as in the folklore collected by nineteenth-century scholars. It is an attempt to go back to that principle of change, natural to the child and common in dreams, in order to live more adequately our mortal measure of years. It is one of Randall Jarrell's ways of voicing that unfathomable disillusion which informs his poetry, and at the same time of reaching a wisdom beyond that proffered by science, a wisdom which may yet successfully oppose those forces seeking the blood of Man.

Note

1. In the original version of this essay, the poems were cited only in acknowledgments to the individual volumes in which the poems appeared. For this reprinting page references to *The Complete Poems* (New York: Farrar, Straus & Giroux, 1969) are given.

Between Two Worlds: The Post-Modernism of Randall Jarrell

Jerome Mazzaro*

In his lifetime, Randall Jarrell found his poetry consistently praised in reviews yet excluded from the powerful Oscar Williams anthologies and ignored by all but a National Book Awards committee in 1961. As a result, it never quite succeeded into popular acceptance or acclaim. The occasional recognition it did get from the *Southern Review* or *Sewanee Review*, the Guggenheim Foundation or *Poetry* merely reinforced the image of a poet with an intense but narrow audience. The presence of *The Complete Poems* (1969) provides a basis for discussions of why this image occurred as well as for discussions of Jarrell's proper place among the poets of his generation. The view that Karl Shapiro expressed in 1966, shortly after Jarrell's death, that he had outpaced all of his contemporaries, seems already overgenerous. Nor does the opinion of Helen Vendler seem more lasting. Her review of the volume leaned heavily on Oscar Wilde to assert that Jarrell "put his genius into his criticism and his talent into his poetry." Jarrell's own sense in *A Sad Heart at the Supermarket* (1962) that all poetic audiences were falling before "the habitual readers of Instant Literature" indicates how he might have explained the neglect, but one has the sense, too, in essays like "The End of the Line" (1942), of his "wandering between two worlds, one dead, / The other powerless to be born." Most accurate, it seems, is the metaphor which Jarrell used about Wallace Stevens: "In a lifetime of standing out in thunderstorms," Jarrell managed to be "struck by lightning" enough times to secure himself a notable but not paramount place among those poets who came into their own during and after World War II. Given Jarrell's own need to excel, to go on living life to the fullest, highest reaches and aims of man, this last may seem a harsh judgment, but it is one which in his lifetime Jarrell was willing to make of others and which in his last volume he seems to have understood of his own poetry.

*Reprinted from *Salmagundi*, 17 (Fall, 1971), 93–113; also reprinted in *Contemporary Poetry in America*, ed. Robert Boyers (New York: Schocken Books, 1974), pp. 78–98. An expanded version appeared in Mazzaro's *Postmodern American Poetry* (Champaign: Univ. of Illinois Press, 1980), pp. 32–58. Published here by permission of the author and the University of Illinois Press.

More than any of his contemporaries, Jarrell took seriously Matthew Arnold's hope that a writer should see the world " 'with a plainness as near, as flashing' as that with which Moses and Rebekah and the Argonauts saw it" as well as Arnold's statement in "The Study of Poetry" (1880) that "more and more . . . mankind will have to turn to poetry to interpret life." Most of what his age considered religion and philosophy, Arnold contended, would be replaced by poetry. Without poetry, even science would appear incomplete. Poetry's attachment of emotion to the idea—its refusal to materialize itself in the fact—would allow it to realize for Jarrell the post-Modernist's equivalent to an id's attachment to the superego and the reality of an ego's workaday world. In fact, one difference which Jarrell seems to have from William Carlos Williams and the poets of the previous generation is an uncritical acceptance of Freud's view of the psyche. "The English in England" (1963) hypothesizes of Rudyard Kipling's late stories: "If the reality principle has pruned and clipped them into plausibility, it is the pleasure principle out of which they first rankly and satisfyingly flowered." Similarly, "Stories" (1958) establishes: "the writer is, and is writing for, a doubly- or triply-natured creature, whose needs, understandings and ideals—whether they are called id, ego, and superego, or body, mind, and soul—contradict one another." In the same essay Jarrell asserts: "Reading stories, we cannot help remembering Groddeck's 'We have to reckon with what exists, and dreams, daydreams too, are also fact; if anyone really wants to investigate realities, he cannot do better than to start with such as these. If he neglects them, he will learn little or nothing of the world of life.' " This familiarity with Freud and Georg Groddeck, Jarrell may owe to his attachment to the early poetry of W. H. Auden and Auden's sense of the pair. More even than Arnold's, their visions help to explain Jarrell's own considered "factitiousness" in light of his often unresolved notions of literature as "the union of a wish and a truth" or a "wish modified by a truth."

The previous generation's rejection or neglect of Freud frequently left it without a means for handling the discrepancies between inner and outer experiences except through the terminologies of philosophy and religion and with no language to speak of to handle the area of the age's tendencies toward self-consciousness. Stevens accordingly had erred for Jarrell by "thinking of particulars as primarily illustrations of general truths, or else as aesthetic, abstracted objects, simply there to be contemplated"; he had often treated things or lives so that they seemed "no more than generalizations of an unprecedented low order." Jarrell goes on to insist that "a poet *has* to treat the concrete as primary, as something far more than an instance, a hue to be sensed, a member of a laudable category." In "From the Kingdom of Necessity" (1946), he praises Robert Lowell's "detailed factuality" and "the contrary, persisting, and singular thinginess of every being in the world" which set themselves against the elevation and rhetoric "of much earlier English poetry." Yet, Williams, who does treat particulars as primary in his early poetry, errs by under-emphasizing the "organization, logic, narrative, generalization" of poetry, thinking it enough to present merely "data brought back alive." Kipling's description of his writing suffers from a comparable failure in that he, according to Jarrell, "was a professional, but a professional possessed by both the Daemon he tells you about, who writes some of the stories for him, and the demons he doesn't tell you about, who write others." "Nowadays," he continues, reverting to psychoanalytic terminology, "we've learned to call part of the conscious *it* or *id*; Kipling had not, but he called this Personal Daemon of his *it*."

For Jarrell the expression of all art involved a balance between emotion and idea or id and superego along lines similar to those which Arnold and Freud drew and carrying in their mediation residues of both extremes. "The Age of the Chimpanzee" (1957), for example, presents the hands of a figure in Georges de la Tour's *St. Sebastian Mourned by St. Irene* as resembling "(as so much art resembles) the symptomatic gestures of psychoanalysis, half the expression of a wish and half the defence against the wish," and Jarrell's few comments on music suggest a corresponding emphasis. Jarrell may even have believed that art was a kind of medium to make the forces of the id acceptable to the superego and that, in literature, language worked as wit or dream works in Freud to allow passage through an ontogenetic censor of what Jarrell consistently depicts as dark and phylogenetic feelings. Certainly wit and dream form several of his main stresses when dealing with poetic language. His review of Walter McElroy's translation of Tristan Corbière (1947), for instance, makes "puns, mocking half-dead metaphors, parodied clichés, antitheses, and paradoxes, idioms exploited on every level . . . the seven-league crutches on which . . . poems bound wildly forward," and, as if to emphasize the connection, Jarrell entitles his own next volume *The Seven-League Crutches* (1951) and includes in it his own version of Corbière's "Le Poète contumace" and four "Rondels pour Après."

Likewise, as early as "Poetry in War and Peace" (1945), Jarrell was investing the previous generation's poetry with Freudian equivalents, dividing it along conscious and unconscious lines, and indicating of Williams that "the tough responsible doctor-half that says and does" and "the violent and delicate free-Freudian half that feels and senses" contribute to one of the "great mythological attitudes" of the country—"the truck-driver looking shyly at the flower." In "The Situation of a Poet" (1952), he notes further of Williams that "he speaks for the Resistance or Underground inside each of us" and of Walter de La Mare (1946) that "from his children and ghosts one learns little about children and nothing about ghosts, but one learns a great deal of the reality of which both his ghosts and his children are projections, of the wishes and lacks and love that have produced their 'unreality.' " Much of the discussion of his "Robert

Frost's 'Home Burial' " (1962) is given over to distinguishing the characters' rational and compulsive behavior, and, in "Changes of Attitude and Rhetoric in Auden's Poetry" (1941), he cites the pre-human forms which lurk always behind Auden's individuals in the early poems and concludes: "Many of the early poems seem produced by Auden's whole being, as much unconscious as conscious, necessarily made just as they are; the best of them have shapes (just as driftwood or pebbles do) that seem the direct representation of the forces that produced them." He then generalizes on poetry that it "represents the unconscious (or whatever you want to call it) as well as the conscious, our lives as well as our thoughts; and . . . has its true source in the first and not the second."

The unique character of the ontogenetic half-self assures Jarrell that its presence in the language of art without any additional mannerisms will make that art human and individual. He lauds Frost for "a verse that uses, sometimes with absolute mastery, the rhythms of actual speech." In reviews of Auden's later work, Jarrell sees increased mannerisms subverting the unconscious. "Poetry in a Dry Season" (1940) says of *Another Time*: "Auden at the beginning was oracular (obscure, original), bad at organization, neglectful of logic, full of astonishing or magical language, intent on his own world and his own forms; he has changed continuously toward organization, plainness, accessibility, objectivity, social responsibility. . . . Now, in too many of the poems, we see not the will, but the understanding, trying to do the work of the imagination." Jarrell dismisses the volumes as "moral, rational, manufactured, written by the top of the head for the top of the head." He repeats the complaint a year later in a review of *The Double Man*: "Auden's ideas once had an arbitrary *effective* quality, a personality value, almost like the ideas in Lawrence or Ezra Pound. They seem today less colorful but far more correct—and they are derived from or are conscious of, elements over most of the range of contemporary thought." Thus, it seems that, given a situation where the "thought" of Arnold's overt moral view of art conflicts with an honest resolution of life's "realities," Jarrell chooses Freud and Groddeck, and one gets the first suggestion of the two worlds which his art would wander between.

Later, when Jarrell returns to praise Auden for *The Shield of Achilles*, he does so in *The Yale Review* (1955) with statements that indicate his impatience at Auden's letting art's morality conflict with life: "In many of these last poems the Conscious and Moral Auden is, quite consciously and immorally, coming to terms with the Unconscious Auden by going along with it, letting it have its way—and not just in life, where we can do and gloss over anything, but in poems, which are held against us by us and everyone else." "Perhaps," Jarrell asserts in an effort to keep art moral, "Auden had always made such impossible exacting moral demands on himself and everybody else partly because it kept him from having to worry about more ordinary, moderate demands; perhaps he had preached so loudly, made such extraordinarily sweeping gestures, in order to hide himself from himself in the commotion. But he seems, finally, to have got tired of the whole affair, to have become willing to look at himself *without doing anything about it*, not even shutting his eyes or turning his head away." In *Harper's*, writing of the same volume, Jarrell repeats his reluctance to abandon his belief that moral and artistic senses lie very close together. He attributes their separation in Auden's writing to a lack of Arnoldian high seriousness: "A few of the poems are good, and all of them are brilliant, self-indulgent, marvelously individual: if Auden sometimes loses faith with something as frivolous as poetry, he never loses it in anything as serious as Auden." This last is an allusion to *The Age of Anxiety* (1947), which Jarrell had reviewed, complaining: "One understands what Auden meant when he said, in a recent review, that all art is so essentially frivolous that he prefers it to embody beliefs he thinks false, since its frivolity would degrade those he thinks true. What sounds like an indictment is a confession, and 'The Age of Anxiety' is the evidence that substantiates the confession."

Conversely, "The Age of the Chimpanzee" indicates Jarrell's opposition to a complete submergence of art into the unconscious half-self where it would have at no time the redeeming factors of individuality, Freudian reality, or Arnoldian morality. "Abstract-Expressionism," he writes, "has kept one part [the unconscious] of this process, but has rejected as completely as it could the other part and all the relations that depend on the existence of this other part; it has substituted for a heterogeneous, polyphonic process a homogeneous, homophonic process." This opposition to unconscious art is expanded to include such notions of man as his being an objective, uncensoring recorder. In a review of *Paterson* (1951), Jarrell complains of Williams that he should not have left so much of Book II "real letters from a real woman": "What has been done to them," he asks, "to make them part of the poem *Paterson*? I can think of no answer except: 'They have been copied out on the typewriter.' " Trite and unexamined language come in for similar condemnation. "These Are Not Psalms" (1945) objects that the work of A. M. Klein "has none of the exact immediacy, the particular reality of the language of a successful poem; it has instead the voluntary repetition of the typical mannerisms of poetry in general—mannerisms that become a generalized, lifeless, and magical ritual without the spirit of which they were once the peculiar expression." The redemption of language into this spirit prompts Jarrell to fall back on Goethe's statements concerning technical facility and risk. "Poetry, Unlimited" (1950) asserts: "Goethe said that the worst thing in art is technical facility accompanied by triteness. Many an artist, like God, has never needed to think twice about anything." In "The Profession of Poetry" (1950) Jarrell complains of Howard Nemerov's timidity: "He knows very well that the poet, as Goethe says, is someone who takes risks (and today most intellectuals take no risks at all—are, from the cradle, critics); but he thinks romantic and old-fashioned, couldn't believe, or hasn't heard of something else Goethe said: that the poet is essentially naive."

This sense of naiveté, which would allow a dark-world layer into the poem, provides the basis on which Jarrell would merge Freud and Arnold so that poetry might outlast religion and philosophy. As he explains in "Ernie Pyle" (1945), "What he cared about was the facts. But the facts are only facts as we see them, as we feel them; and he knew to what a degree experience . . . is 'seeing only faintly and not wanting to see at all.' The exactly incongruous, the crazily prosaic, the finally convincing fact—that must be true because no one could have made it up . . . was his technical obsession." This stress on naiveté—the individually unreflective as opposed to the overly worked—may have led him, as John Berryman's "Randall Jarrell" (1967) would have it, to overvalue Williams considerably. "I'm very fond of Bill Williams' poetry," Berryman writes, "but not as fond as Jarrell was." Moreover, the view would ally Jarrell with John Ruskin, who had written in *Modern Painters* (1855) of the soul's need "to see something and tell what it saw in a plain way" as "poetry, prophecy, and religion,—all in one." Jarrell's preface to *The Best Short Stories of Rudyard Kipling* (1961) refers to Ruskin's stand on perfectibility in art: "They [Kipling's stories] are not at all the perfect work of art we want—so perhaps Ruskin was right when he said that the person who wants perfection knows nothing about art." A precise lack of naiveté in the overly worked, lifeless perfection of Richard Wilbur's poetry turns Jarrell against it. In "A View of Three Poets" (1952), he accuses Wilbur of being "too poetic," of letting life become an excuse for poetry, and, as Ruskin would have it in the opening volume of *Modern Painters* (1843), of letting art "sink to a mere ornament" and "minister to morbid sensibilities, ticklers and fanners of the soul's sleep."

The strongest indication of the role of language as a mediator between one's senses of art and life and the descending priorities which Jarrell attaches to it as its impulses moved progressively outward come in a review of Rolfe Humphries's *Forbid Thy Ravens* (1948): "What Mr. Humphries's poems say is agreeable, feeling common sense, necessarily a little too easy and superficial, since it has neither the depth of the unconscious, nor that of profound thought, nor that of profound emotion, nor that of the last arbitrary abyss of fact." Under such conditions, poetry in its inmost and purest state would work as Groddeck's It or a Hegelian Geist so that a sequence of its manifestations would provide proof of that motivating inner force adumbrated by psychoanalysis or a history of the highest and noblest thoughts of man similar to the imperfect picture of God that results from a Hegelian survey of history. Jarrell's view in "The Profession of Poetry" that "a poet in the true sense of the word [is] someone who has shown to us one of those worlds which, after we have been shown it, we call the real world" substantiates such a hypothesis.

Jarrell proposes what critics typically hold for psychoanalysis. For them, Freud "thought of the artist as an obdurate neurotic who, by his creative work, kept himself from a crack-up but also from any real cure." The artist fashioned his fantasies into a "new kind of reality" that men conceded "justification as valuable reflections of actual life." The context of Jarrell's view which in its desirability embraces Hegelian "highest and noblest thoughts" is the German poet Rainer Maria Rilke: "Rilke, in his wonderful 'Archaic Statue of Apollo,' ends his description of the statue, the poem itself, by saying without transition or explanation: *You must change your life*. He needs no explanation. We know from many experiences that this is what the work of art does: its life—in which we have shared the alien existences both of this world and of that different world to which the work of art alone gives us access—unwillingly accuses our lives."

Jarrell's view also coincides with the starting point of Existential philosophy, that existence precedes essence and that man knows his essence by reflection. As early as "The Dramatic Lyrism of Randall Jarrell" (1952), Parker Tyler hinted at a connection when he framed Jarrell's view of existence and knowledge to echo Jean-Paul Sartre's famous pronunciamento. Tyler wrote, "*Existence* comes before *knowledge* because it retains, even after knowledge has arrived, the unknowable that is so often unpredictable." The Sartrean position which has moved beyond Groddeck has led to the development of an Existential psychoanalysis. As Rollo May's *Existence* (1960) maintains, this psychoanalysis asserts that "what an individual seeks to *become* determines what he remembers of his *has been*. In this sense, the future determines the past"; but the future does so in order to change the present by making the pattern of life it deduces the instrument for one's handling the domains of the past and present. As Hendrik M. Ruitenbeek writes in his introduction to *Psychoanalysis and Existential Philosophy* (1962), "Unlike Freudian analysis, which deals with the *Umwelt* and the *Mitwelt*, the biological and social worlds, but almost ignores the *Eigenwelt*, existential analysis stresses the self and the mode of the patient's relationship to that self." What Existential psychoanalysis offers to the patient is the future directness and choice that the Rilke poem suggests, but its Dasein—unlike Hegel's Geist and Groddeck's It—shows a conscious and willful shaping force which, like his reliance on naiveté rather than consciousness, a need for metaphysical mystery will not let Jarrell accept. As he formulates the present's relation to the future in "A Sad Heart at the Supermarket" (1960), Hegel and Arnold seem most influential: "An artist's work and life presuppose continuing standards, values extended over centuries and millennia, a future that is the continuation and modification of the past, not its contradiction or irrelevant replacement. He is working for the time that wants the best that he can do; the present, he hopes—but if not that, the future."

Upon the sequence of the changes brought about by one's reactions to art, the present world shapes its future along with an evolving new poetry, conceived of for such purposes and, as Arnold believes, in terms "worthily and more highly than it has been the custom to conceive it" and "capable of higher uses, and called to higher destinies, than those which in general men have assigned to it hitherto." Thus, there is a second, more practical disjunction between future and present that arises from Jarrell's efforts to fuse psychoanalysis and Arnold and that his refusal to accept the consciousness of Existential psychoanalysis prevents a resolution of. Throughout his criticism, Jarrell can complain, on the one hand, of living in a time that is worse than Arnold's or Goethe's and, on the other, admit that he is "old-fashioned" enough to believe, like Goethe, in Progress—"the progress I see and the progress I wish for and do not see." The blindness and optimism of this progress—since for Jarrell only the future can judge the best of the past and that by what it has knowingly incorporated—raises certain questions about the purposefulness of the present which repeatedly, as Arnold before him, Jarrell tries to solve but which, unlike Auden, he is not willing to dismiss by disowning the seriousness of art.

The failure to collapse these visions into one suggests a schematicization of the world—an inner lens—through which one is to see darkly the darkling plain with the "plainness near and flashing" that Arnold called for. Moreover, the failure seems to be built into the vision for as Moses and Rebekah and the Argonauts had cosmic views against which to measure their daily experiences and which never dissolved into an atmosphere of complete immediacy, so, too, in Arnold and Jarrell forces outside their work dictate the selection of words. Goethe's view that the poet must be naive is at least to the extent negated: the "ignorant armies," for instance, which end Arnold's "Dover Beach" are ignorant not because of anything in the poem but because of the world view out of which the poem springs. The same may be said of the emotive language of many Jarrell poems. Delmore Schwartz registers such a complaint in "The Dream from Which No One Wakes" (1945): "In his first two books many of the poems were weakened by a thinness and abstractness of texture and reference; it was as if the poet saw his subjects through opera glasses. . . . For all the genuineness of the poems, the net result resembled the dim and ghastly negative which has to be held up to the light, and not the developed photograph full of daylight and defined objects."

Jarrell's various positions on Auden demonstrate, in addition, an unwillingness to resolve the matter of these disjunctions by focusing necessarily on one persona or about the writings of a single man. This suggests another kind of disjunction hinted at by Shapiro: a yearning for and an opposition to Authority. Shapiro writes of Jarrell's opposition: "It became necessary for everyone my age to attack Auden, as sculptors must attack Mount Rushmore. Nevertheless Auden and Mount Rushmore still stand and probably always will." Nor was Williams a more suitable subject. Jarrell notes of him: "He is a *very* good but *very* limited poet, particularly in vertical range." He adds, "he keeps too much to that tenth of the iceberg that is above water, perhaps." Jarrell is more generous toward Frost: "Frost is that rare thing, a complete or representative poet, and not one of the brilliant partial poets who do justice, far more than justice, to a portion of reality, and leave the rest of things forlorn." And Jarrell says of Whitman, "Of all modern poets he has, quantitatively speaking, 'the most comprehensive soul'—and, qualitatively, a most comprehensive and comprehending one, with charities and concessions and qualifications that are rare in any time." But he reduces his praise of Frost by adding, "if we compare this wisdom with, say, that of the last of the Old Ones, Goethe, we are saddened and frightened at how much the poet's scope has narrowed, at how difficult and partial and idiosyncratic the application of his intelligence has become, at what terrible sacrifices he has had to make in order to avoid making others still more terrible."

As an alternative to shaping his views into a single voice, Jarrell seems at times to suggest multiple personae. He champions, for example, anthologies as an ideal critical expression and exposition of an age's taste and laments the fact that Arnold's touchstones "never evolved into an anthology." He also praises individual poets like Williams, Whitman, and Frost for their abilities to get out of themselves, to suggest other voices than their own in their poetry, and he complains of Robert Lowell in "A View of Three Poets" that "you can't tell David from Bathsheba without a program; they both (like the majority of Mr. Lowell's characters) talk just like Mr. Lowell." A decade earlier, "Poets: Old, New, and Aging" (1940) had noted the same of Pound: "Everything is seen through a glass darkly, the glass being Mr. Pound: 1766 B.C. talks exactly like 1735 A.D., and both exactly like Ezra Pound. To the old complaint, 'All Chinamen look alike,' Mr. Pound makes one add, 'And talk alike, and act alike—and always did.' " Jarrell repeatedly insists on dramatic monologue as the poetic vehicle, though, at times, as in the case of Elizabeth Bishop, he is willing to grant morality to description and landscape as had Ruskin.

All three suggestions—anthologies, flexible voices, and the dramatic monologue technique—seem part of a philosophical relativism which Jarrell betrays in statements like "Williams had a real and unusual dislike of, distrust in, Authority; and the Father-surrogate of the average work of art has been banished from his Eden. His ability to rest (or at least to thrash happily about) in contradictions, doubts, and general guesswork, without ever climbing aboard any of the monumental certainties that go perpetually by, perpetually on time—this ability may seem the opposite of Whitman's gift for boarding every certainty and riding off into every infinite, but the spirit behind them is the same." His enlisting of readers to join him on every journey recalls Oswald Spengler's position in *The Decline of the West* (1918). Spengler branded this philosophical relativism the modern counterpart to Classical skepticism which was ahistorical and denied outright. The new skepticism which "is obliged to be historical through and through" gets its solutions "by treating everything as relative, as a historical phenomenon, and its procedure is psychological." It leads to a voice in Jarrell's poetry that is consciously nonauthoritative or whose authoritative tone is undermined by the poem's context in the volume or by other tones within it. Only in his criticism was Jarrell willing to become authoritative, and this may have prompted Helen Vendler's remark that his poetry had talent but his real genius was criticism.

Jarrell's treatment of the childhoods of Auden and Kipling and poems like "A Story" (1939) indicate that there may be added, personal reasons behind his dislike of Authority. The accounts in these works strangely blend into each other and, one suspects, Jarrell's own boyhood. "Freud to Paul: The Stages of Auden's Ideology" (1945) says of Auden's childhood and its part in the creation of "the wicked Uncle": "It is no surprise to learn, in *Letters from Iceland* and other places, that Auden's parents were unusually good ones, very much venerated by the child: Auden moralizes interminably, cannot question or reject Authority except under the aegis of this pathetically invented opposing authority, because the superego (or whatever term we wish to use for the mechanism of conscience and authority) is exceptionally strong in him." Jarrell then cites a statement by Abraham Kardiner that "the superego is based on affection, not hatred." Of Kipling's boyhood, Jarrell notes, "For the first six years of his life the child lived in Paradise, the inordinately loved and reasonably spoiled son of the best of parents; after that he lived in the Hell in which the best of parents put him, and paid to have him kept." After six years, they rescued the boy "and for the rest of their lives they continued to be the best and most loving of parents, blamed by Kipling for nothing, adored by Kipling for everything." Jarrell goes on to conclude: "It is *this* that made Kipling what he was: if they had been the worst of parents, even fairly bad parents, even ordinary parents, it would have all made sense, Kipling himself could have made sense out of it. As it was, his world had been torn in two and he himself torn in two: for under the part of him that extenuated everything, blamed for nothing, there was certainly a part that extenuated nothing, blamed for everything—a part whose existence he never admitted, most especially not to himself."

"A Story" details the same emotions in the son of "the best of parents." The lad eventually extenuates everything and blames his parents for nothing while at the same time he extenuates nothing and blames them for everything. He arrives at the "Hell" of a boarding school whose emptiness is juxtaposed to the "good" mother's concern—even to the point of using the "right" language: "Remember to change your stockings every day— / Socks, I mean." Recollection of the concern changes to resentment as the boy's "mail-box is still empty, / Because they've all forgotten me, they love their / New friends better." The boy plots to punish his parents by disappearing. The same "concern" and "indictment" fill late poems like "Windows" (1954), where the parents who have been accused by their son of being "indifferent" show their concern in noting "you have not slept." For Jarrell, whose parents were divorced, these "parents" are often his paternal grandparents with whom he lived for a while in Hollywood. Significantly the movement in these later poems is ever away from indictment to forgiveness. "In Those Days" (1953) recalls: "How poor and miserable we were. / How seldom together! / And yet after so long one thinks: / In those days everything was better." The sentiment extends to both "The Lost World" and "Thinking of the Lost World" (1963), which concludes that, having spent most of his life learning to forgive his parents for having damaged him, he is left with "nothing" as his reward. The mechanisms by which one's self has been defined, once withered away by forgiveness, leave one nothing by which to define self—a fear implicit in any real skepticism and here expressed "in happiness." Jarrell had come to a similar conclusion twenty-three years before in "For an Emigrant" (1940), and the despair of nothingness, so much complained of by reviewers, runs through the early books. In one of his last poems, "A Man Meets a Woman in the Street" (1967), the narrator gives up identity and the human drive of imagination and contents himself with the wish of the birds' that "this day / Be the same day, the day of my life."

Faced with these various disjunctions, Jarrell's advice in "The Obscurity of the Poet" (1951) is "there is nothing to do different from what we already do: if poets write poems and readers read them, each as best they can—if they try to live not as soldiers or voters or intellectuals or economic men, but as human beings—they are doing all that can be done." Here he falls back on the thesis of Groddeck's *The Book of the It* (1923) that at man's inception he incurs a force that shapes his destiny, and things like breathing which have much to do with the It have little to do with the will. Man may, as Jarrell indicates in "To Fill a Wilderness" (1951), find that the world imaged by poetry is "our nation's life as Yeats saw his own—as a preparation for something that never happened." "A Girl in a Library" (1951), the opening selection of *The Complete Poems*, depicts such conditions. Centering on a girl, a "student of Home Economics and Physical Education, who has fallen asleep in the library of a Southern College," it evolves into a colloquy between the poem's speaker (the present) and Tatyana Larina (the past), who materializes out of Aleksander Pushkin's *Eugen Onegin* (1833). Tatyana wonders at the value of sleep where "the soul has no assignments, neither cooks / Nor referees; it wastes its time." Without ideas against which to shape the present, a person is no more than a "machine-part"; dream and reality are one and homogeneous like the homogeneous Abstract-Expressionism attacked in "The Age of the Chimpanzee." Indulgent with this "machine-part," as often Jarrell's speakers are not, the narrator responds that, since "the ways we miss our lives are life," it is better at death "to squawk like a chicken" and meet Death's challenge "with a last firm strange / Uncomprehending smile" and, then, to see the "blind date that you stood up: your life," than to be aware of the failure beforehand.

Incorporated in this response is Jarrell's somewhat inconsistent view that, whatever the innate or obscure and expanding reaches of excellence, like Rebekah and the Argonauts, people are somehow accountable to strive after them. As with Groddeck's patients, this striving may take the form of a self-examination to make one adjust to the It, but no amount of will can shape an It that is not there. Here knowledge by way of Tatyana emphasizes literature as the source of reform. Jarrell repeats this stress in "The Intellectual in America" (1955) where he speaks of the writer again as "the man who will make us see what we haven't seen, feel what we haven't felt, understand what we haven't understood—he *is* our friend." The student's failure like the failures of the children of "Lady Bates" (1948) and "The Black Swan" (1951) and of the pilot of "The Dead Wingman" (1945) relegates her to the unearned oblivion of "everlasting sleep." In contrast, the "saved"—those whose visions help shape the future—become part of a hovering Spirit which "Burning the Letters" (1945) shows inspiring the present. But even there it must be finally abandoned in order to let new life evolve. In time, as "The Memoirs of Glückel of Hameln" (1942) asserts, "We take your place as our place will be taken." In both instances, "The Knight, Death, and the Devil" (1951) maintains, man achieves his judgment not by any human design but by doing what he must. Under such nontraditional terms, "The Night before the Night before Christmas" (1949) indicates that "to use God's name" (that is, to imagine him) is "to misuse His name," for what can be imagined, as "In the Ward: The Sacred Wood" (1946) makes clear, can also be unmade. "A Sick Child" (1949) depicts God as "all that I never thought of," and "Eighth Air Force" (1947) shows Christ not as divine but as a "just man" without fault, whom the speaker has tried to imitate. This imitation causes "suffering" and a final self-image as Pontius Pilate, and, in "Seele im Raum" (1950), it produces the "eland," that imaginary creature of the mind which gives life to the soul and humanity to the "machine" and which in German translates as "wretched" (*elend*).

The human designs which result from this wretchedness—often dictated in terms of daydream, wish, fairy tale, make-believe, dream, myth, miracle, and masterwork—are the products, Jarrell insists, only of children and men, and men only insofar as they are childish. In no case are they as idiosyncratic as Heideggerian Daseins. Girls have them until they marry and become women. Then, as "Woman" (1964) states, they become "realists; or a realist might say, / Naturalists," for it is "woman's nature / to want the best, and to be careless how it comes." "Cinderella" (1954) records a coy but significant conversation between a daydreaming girl and her daydream godmother (the Virgin Mary) in the absence of Prince Charming and Christ, who are out childishly imagining. It ends with God's Mother inviting the girl to await inside the return of their men, which might be soon or never. "Mary" herself has taken on the aspects of the Devil's grandmother in Grimm's "The Devil with the Three Golden Hairs." In the light of man's inability to imagine correctly Divine Will, the "wisdom" of their position is obvious, for what they do realize by becoming mothers is a role in Jarrell's almost Darwinian evolution and divinely willed preservation of the species. Here, however the individual may be disregarded, the form or species will be cherished. Yet, as Jarrell seems to say in variations of the "Cinderella" situation such as "The End of the Rainbow" (1954), "Seele im Raum," and "The Woman at the Washington Zoo" (1959), becoming a woman is not very easy. The women of these poems are looked on by their worlds as machine-parts. Only in their imaginations do they preserve their humanity, often by dreaming of fairy-tale and animal creatures in whom to invest their love.

As in Arnold, the cherishing of this species takes the form of the perfection of the state—"the nation in its collective and corporate character"—rather than of the individual. Many of the essays in *A Sad Heart at the Supermarket* are directed toward this end which critics of Jarrell's early poetry mistook for Marxism. Such essays as "The Taste of the Age" (1958), for example, even image Jarrell as a latter-day Arnold or Arnold's favorite, Goethe. The essay opens with a negative reaction to the age: "When we look at the age in which we live—no matter what age it happens to be—it is hard for us not to be depressed by it." Jarrell then goes on to note: "We can see that Goethe's and Arnold's ages weren't as bad as Goethe and Arnold thought them: after all, they produced Goethe and Arnold." The rest of the essay unfolds as an attack on popular culture and an appeal for continuing to upgrade culture, as Arnold had thought to do, through education. Similarly in recommending the second book of Wordsworth's "The Excursion" in *The New York Times*'s "Speaking of Books" column (1955), Jarrell writes: "I feel Matthew Arnold's approving breath at my shoulder, and see out before me, smiling bewitchingly, the nations of the not-yet-born." The state thus conceived becomes organic, and war in "The Range in the Desert" (1947) is looked upon as the pitting of one state against another in a struggle for survival much as the lizard of the poem survives by devouring "the shattered membranes of the fly." Caught in a movement from greater to lesser imperfection similar to man's, the state at no time is perfect and incapable of change. Yet, as "The Night before the Night before Christmas" indicates, only a just state may triumph, for the triumph of an unjust state is an indication of an unjust God. The view of this relationship between the state and God is explicitly pronounced in "Kafka's Tragi-Comedy" (1941): "God is the trust, the state, all over again at the next higher level. God's justice and the world's contradict each other; and yet what is God's justice but the world's, raised to the next power, but retaining all the qualities of its original?"

Rather than legally centered upon the protection of the many, the justice of this "just" state is built upon "poetic justice"—the good receiving rewards and the bad, punishments. This central wellspring of art adds a vein of aestheticism which is not obvious in Arnold but which is consistent with nineteenth-century philosophy. It frequently held that the act of poetic creation was closest to the nature of God. Such pieces as "A Sad Heart at the Supermarket" are willing to admit the aestheticism: "To say that Nature imitates Art . . . is literally true. . . . Which of us hasn't found a similar refuge in the 'real,' created world of Cézanne or Goethe or Verdi?" But the aestheticism which Existential psychoanalysis relegates to the past and present by the creation of the Dasein is negated in part by Jarrell's drive toward the future. While granting, as had Wilde, "that the self-conscious aim of Life is to find expression, and that Art offers it certain beautiful forms through which it may realize that energy," Jarrell's location of the real force of art in the realm of the spirit—the phylogenetic or Groddeck's It—gives it a timelessness which transcends, as he supposed Freudian analysis might, the otherwise past-directedness of the recollected childhood.

"The State" (1945) tries to make acceptable through it a state's having killed a child's mother and drafted his sister and cat. Although the acts lead finally to the child's wish to die, they may in the realm of spirit be ultimately right. The deranged nature of the speaker prevents any clear assurance, but Jarrell's concluding remarks in "Auden's Ideology," published in the same year, indicate a willingness to put up with some inconveniences to direct his efforts toward a larger enemy. One senses this "larger enemy" is fears like those expressed in Arthur Miller's *Situation Normal* (1944). Miller defined World War II as a struggle to maintain "the right of each individual to determine his freedom" against "the tyrannic corporate control of the minds and wills of men." A later Jarrell poem, "A Well-to-do Invalid" (1965), tells of a self-interested nurse (the individual?) who tends a self-indulgent invalid (the state?) taking to herself his care so that she feels her justification and her hope of his inheritance in his not being able to get along without her. She dies, and the poem's speaker sees the invalid "well with grief," realizing in the act how easily her vacancy will be filled. The premise of the poem echoes Jarrell's comments on Alex Comfort. Recognizing "that the states themselves are at present the main danger their citizens face," Jarrell adds reluctantly (1945): "It is we who wither away, not the state."

Jarrell comes to these views slowly, and even more slowly is a reader able to put them together. Some are already formed by *The Rage for the Lost Penny* (1940) but their presence is obscured in a more conspicuous admixture of Audenesque phrases. These include "efficiently as a new virus," "the star's distention," and "the actuaries end." They later disappear but their presence here affirms Jarrell's statement in the preface that "Auden is the only poet who has been influential very recently; and this is because, very partially and uncertainly, and often very mechanically, he represents new tendencies, a departure from modernist romanticism." One tendency was the dream poem and its mediation of subconscious and conscious levels, typified by the second poem in Auden's first collection. The poem, which was dropped in subsequent reprintings, forms one reason why Jarrell always cited the 1930 edition of *Poems*, though for convenience he tended to quote from the 1934 edition. A second tendency was Auden's millennialism rooted in "Darwin, Marx, Freud and Co., . . . all characteristically 'scientific' or 'modern' thinkers" about whom the previous generation had "concluded, regretfully: 'If they had not existed, it would not have been necessary to ignore them' (or deplore them)." A third was the power of women to motivate history, as typified by the mothers of Auden's *Paid on Both Sides*. These women keep the feud between their families alive and bloody, and their power, which is present quite often in the backgrounds of these early poems, becomes more apparent as women move into the foreground of Jarrell's poetry with *Losses* (1948).

In *The Rage for the Lost Penny* are located a number of poems which belong to the child's singsong world and whose half-lines and themes occasionally foreshadow lines and themes in Theodore Roethke's *The Lost Son* (1949). The narrator of "A Little Poem" (1940) speaks to his yet-to-be-conceived younger brother in the womb with such Roethkean expressions as "My brother was a fish" and reference to the world as "this sink of time." The opening lines of "The Ways and the Peoples" (1939) add: "What does the storm say? What the trees wish" and "I am the king of the dead." This last assertion finds itself repeated in Berryman's *The Dispossessed* (1948), at the end of the second and psychologically based "Nervous Songs" ("The Song of the Demented Priest"). Jarrell's introduction to *The Golden Bird and Other Fairy Tales* (1962) makes the connection between these poems and Freud apparent: "Reading *Grimm's Tales* tells someone what we're like, inside, just as reading Freud tells him. *The Fisherman and His Wife*—which is one of the best stories anyone ever told, it seems to me—is as truthful and troubling as any newspaper headlines about the new larger sized H-bomb and the new antimissile missile: a country is never satisfied either, but wants to be like the good Lord." Earlier Jarrell's essay on Kafka had described *Amerika* as "a charming and often extremely funny story, as a sort of *Candide* à la Hans Christian Andersen, with extraordinary overtones": "This world is hardly *judged* at all; its cruelties and barbarities elicit only the blankly anthropological interest we extend to the vagaries of savages or children. The conscientious naiveté, the more-than-scientific suspension or tentativeness of judgment of the later books, are already surprisingly well developed in *Amerika*. In its capacity for generating ambiguity and irony (reinforced in the later books by the similar possibilities of allegory), the attitude resembles that of Socrates, that of the scientist making minimal assumptions, or that of the 'humble observer': child, fairy-tale simpleton or third son, fool."

In addition, Jarrell knows enough about the Arnoldian future of his poetry to begin *The Rage for the Lost Penny* with "On the Railway Platform" (1939). Like the later "A Girl in a Library," it has as its theme the ideas that man travels "by the world's one way" and that his "journeys end in / No destination we meant." What man leaves, he leaves forever. "When You and I Were All" (1939) continues the Arnoldian cast with the lines: "What kiss could wake / whose world and sleep were one embrace?" The influence reappears as well in the telling question of "The Refugees" (1940): "What else are their lives but a journey to the vacant / Satisfaction of death?" "For the Madrid Road" (1940) adds the prospect of people who die to preserve their ideals and who ask continually, "But when were lives men's own? . . . Men die / . . . that men may miss / The essential ills." Malcolm Cowley's review of *Blood for a Stranger* (1942) lists the further echoes of Wilfred Owen's "The Show" in "The Automaton" (1937) and of Allen Tate's "Ode to the Confederate Dead" in "A Description of Some Confederate Soldiers" (1936). But the reader's task has been formed: he must reject the surface and work backward from the language of Jarrell's writing not to influences but to the conscious and unconscious impulses which fashioned the work.

Moreover, the views translate into an overall sense of a poetry which, in striving after the noblest thoughts of men and a style which might serve the higher destinies to which poetry has been called, consistently appears unreal and valueless. Often the unreality is necessary, for, by believing that imagination must precede change, Jarrell must stress moments of imagination—daydream, fairy tale, and wish—and minimize the fact. In this, he faces a problem similar to that faced by Dante and Gerard Manley Hopkins: weighing the sensuous beauty of the world which attracts the artist against the idealism which leads him to reject that world for the idea. In reviewing, Jarrell faced the problem by beginning his reviews with his most adverse statements, reversing the usual order of reviewers and prompting Berryman's statement that "Jarrell's reviews did go beyond the limit; they were unbelievably cruel." But their cruelty was often the way Jarrell had for forcing readers out of their complacency into realms where the imagination might function. Since the highest and noblest thoughts of men exclude the ugly, Jarrell tended to exclude it from his poetry or redeem it by means of sentimentalism and romanticism. In a war situation like that opening "Transient Barracks" (1949), the ugly may intrude and allow a sense of life to emerge, but this is rare, and one suspects the additional influence of Pyle. Miller's analysis of Pyle here proves relevant: "Ernie Pyle's thought *was* in his columns. His thought is people. His thought is details about people. War is about people, not ideas. You cannot see ideas bleeding."

More common are the moments in Jarrell's last volume where man is located amid a gross commercialism which hawks its panaceas of Cheer and Joy and All and things are stripped plain. At those moments, as ever where the fact and idea clash, Jarrell's wit intrudes to work, as Freud indicates all wit works, to overcome the valuelessness by letting an unaltered or nonsensical ambiguity of words and multiplicity of thought-relations appear to the consciousness at the same time senseful and admissible as jest. In "A Man Meets a Woman in the Street," Jarrell is willing to forgo such ambiguity by accepting the factitiousness of the world, but the willingness is itself indication that the fact has not occurred. These instants when idea and fact clash are most often the occasions where the purposelessness of the present fades into the brilliance of Jarrell's lines as the concerted direction of his life lay always obscured by the veneer of an incessant instinct of expansion and a refined sensibility. This sensibility, for all its stress on modernism, loved sports cars, bucolic atmospheres, traditional art, good music, poetry, technological advances, and the Russian ballet. Lowell's "Randall Jarrell" (1967) recalls: "His mind, unearthly in its quickness, was a little boyish, disembodied, and brittle. His body was a little ghostly in its immunity to soil, entanglements, and rebellion. As one sat with him in obvious absorption at the campus bar, sucking a fifteen-cent chocolate milk shake and talking eternal things, one felt, beside him, too corrupt and companionable. He had the harsh luminosity of Shelley—like Shelley, every inch a poet, and like Shelley, imperiled perhaps by an arid, abstracting precocity."

Only the imaginary portrait of the poet—akin to the Imaginary Portraits of fin-de-siècle writers—shifting among Goethe, Arnold, and Auden, and formed early by Jarrell—offered him something worldly and static and positive against which to shape his life. That portrait is sketched in the allusions to these writers, the self-comparisons with them, and the appropriations of their tastes that run through all of Jarrell's work. These appropriations go hand in hand with an attack on idiosyncratic individualism which he associated in "The End of the Line" with modernism. This sense led early to a growing drift from the personal that was not reversed until *The Woman at the Washington Zoo* (1960) and *The Lost World* (1965). Here, as M. L. Rosenthal's *The New Poets* (1967) observes, "a change had begun to take place, heralded by three poems in the former book: 'In Those Days,' 'The Elementary Scene,' and 'Windows.' These are poems of private memory—of a time in the past that seemed, often was, 'poor and miserable' (and yet 'everything was better'); of the sadness of what appears, in 'The Elementary Scene,' to have been an unsatisfactory childhood, with a last ironic allusion to the speaker's adult condition ('I, I, the future that mends everything'); and of the impossibility of recovering the dead, simple past of parents who 'have known nothing of today.' " This reversal which brings Jarrell into the Confessional School so much a part of the age was roundly applauded by reviewers who, like Philip Booth, tended to refer to *The Lost World* as a "great new book."

In fact, one might chart the progress of *The Complete Poems* as a succession of efforts by Jarrell to get rid of the "aloneness" which he felt without resorting to the condemnations of his parents which he associates with both Kipling and Auden. Repeatedly one senses what in *The Divided Self* (1960) R. D. Laing calls "ontological insecurity": "The individual in the ordinary circumstances of living may feel more unreal than real; in a literal sense, more dead than alive; precariously differentiated from the rest of the world, so that his identity and autonomy are always in question." Jarrell's personae are always involved with efforts to escape engulfment, implosion, and petrification, by demanding that they somehow be miraculously changed by life and art into people whose ontologies are psychically secure. The changes may allow them then to drop the mechanism by which in their relations they preserve themselves and to feel gratification in relatedness. Laing, who indirectly cites Kafka as a prime example of a writer of ontological insecurity, strikes close to Jarrell's own sensibility. There is something there that along with Rilke's Apollo or Norman O. Brown's *Love's Body* (1966) announces: "Meaning is not in things but in between; in the iridescence, the interplay; in the interconnections; at the intersection, at the crossroads."

For a person with less skill, such purposelessness and militating against the fact might be enough to make his life and poetry unwelcome. Without Williams's rhythms of descent or a comparable instrument of sacramentalization to bridge inner and outer existences, Jarrell's world remains disparate, and he must rely on language as his major means for keeping it together. There is such a reliance running explicitly through much of his criticism and implicit in his poetry; yet, as he perceived in "The Taste of the Age," even language was failing him: "The more words there are, the simpler the words get. The professional users of words process their product as if it were baby food and we babies: all we have to do is open our mouths and swallow." Without a complex language, a language capable of multiplicity, of the ambiguity necessary to wed conscious and unconscious realms, successful poetry would become impossible. Nevertheless, a thingy liveliness might be preserved and, because the future always holds something better, hope as well. Like Arnold who never realized his dream of someday supplanting Tennyson and Browning as the poet of the mid-nineteenth century because of the self-defeating nature of his momentary stays against the confusion of the world, Jarrell seems destined because of his overwhelming reliance on the translucency of language for a secondary role. Readers should not be discouraged, however, from discovering the excellences or the abundances of wisdom, hope, humanity, and despair which the in-betweens of Jarrell's poetry contain, nor from a recognition of his role in bringing psychological concepts to the techniques of American poetry. If, as Shapiro senses, he fails in that role, all the same, he succeeded in making others aware of the course poetry must take. One expects that, as Arnold, Jarrell—though perhaps not as highly ranked as others of his generation—will live as long as any of them.

Blood for the Muse:
A Study of the Poetic Process in
Randall Jarrell's Poetry

Helen Hagenbüchle*

As critics have variously noticed, much of Jarrell's poetry springs from the conflict between intellect and imagination. His remarkable genius for articulate form is felt to be struggling with the desire to yield to an upsurge of unconscious images and dreams. This tension between consciousness and the perilous realm of the unconscious—central to Jarrell's oeuvre—is not unrelated to the poet's lifelong concern with psychology and strongly colors his use of images and symbols. In fact, many poems directly enact this tension through the device of contrasting pairs like darkness/light, sea/island, forest/clearings, sleep/waking. The beginning of "The Märchen" is a case in point.

> Listening, listening; it is never still.
> This is the forest: long ago the lives
> Edged armed into its tides (the axes were its stone
> Lashed with the skins of dwellers to its boughs);
> We felled our islands there, at last, with iron.
> The sunlight fell to them, according to our wish,
> And we believed, till nightfall, in that wish;
> And we believed, till nightfall, in our lives.[1]

The reader quickly notices the structural opposition between forest, sea, and night on the one hand, and clearing, island, and sunlight on the other. The two groups of images (interchangeable in each set) clearly represent the underlying antithesis of the conscious and the unconscious. While the reference to the history of tools used by primitive man alludes to the phylogenetic evolution of the human mind, the ontogenetic development is implied as well: each individual clears his own space in the forest ("We felled our islands there") encouraged by the illusory belief in the permanence of his achievement. However, at the end of day (both in terms of individual life and of human history) original darkness will once more prevail. In Jarrell's work, correlative pairs of this type always betray a latent instability; light, island, clearing, and their variants precariously maintain their existence against overwhelming odds.[2] To Randall Jarrell

*This essay was written specifically for this book and appears by permission of the author.

the conflict between consciousness (form) and the unconscious (energy) is the very essence of the poetic process. In the act of writing the poet bravely attempts to win archetypal images from the dark source of the unconscious: ". . . well water / Pumped from an old well at the bottom of the world. / The pump you pump the water from is rusty / And hard to move . . ." (300). The poet appears as a mythmaker, and his creative act as a ceaseless struggle between unconscious drives and the conscious control of form.

It has often been observed that Jarrell's poetry abounds with motifs from myths and fairly tales, as well as with psychoanalytic casebook studies and dreams. Like C. G. Jung, Jarrell regards myths, fairy-tales, and individual dreams as revelatory of the nature of the human psyche in general and of the creative act in particular. In this essay I shall examine some pervasive psychological and mythic motifs and demonstrate how Jarrell uses them to express his preoccupation with the poetic process.

The archetype most expressive of human creativity has always been the Great Mother figure with its cluster of mythical associations, both negative and positive. Just because the artist is still open to and in touch with the powerful reservoir of the unconscious, the Great Mother archetype remains dominant with him, while its importance for the noncreative person appears to diminish in the course of individuation. According to Jung, archetypal images tend to be more easily accessible when the mind is in a state of reduced intensity of consciousness as in dreams, drunkenness, or early childhood. The fact that Jarrell has written a considerable number of poems in which dreamers, sick people, or children express their obsession with a mother figure calls for a closer examination of the archetype and its psychological and literary significance.

In confronting these poems the reader is struck by the frequent recurrence of the motif of a devouring mother. In "Variations" the nurse who takes the place of the lost mother—"My mother was dead and my nurse was horrid" (122)—frightens the child by saying: " 'I'll stew your ears all day, little hare, / Just as God ate your mother, for you are bad, / Are bad, are bad—' " (122). In the poem "A Quilt-Pattern," which is based on the fairy tale *Hansel and Gretel*, the witch—the negative aspect of the mother figure—threatens to cook and eat the little boy. In a letter to Sister Bernetta Quinn, Jarrell declared that the "Quilt Pattern" was "the most carefully Freudian, best worked-out child's dream" he had ever done. According to this letter the poem is

> the child's redreaming of *Hansel and Gretel* in terms of his mother and himself. . . . The mother is the house (a common symbol for women in dreams, all psychoanalysts say) and the witch too. . . . The fact that the house is the mother who used to nurse him is alluded to in *house of bread*, the finger he sucks at, and *the taste of honey / Is the taste of his*—he won't admit this to himself even in the dream, but it thinks "No, I don't know." (Later, very unexplicitly—I wanted to have it far under the surface) there

is a sort of sexual symbolism, since the child does at first conceive of sexual things in terms of his mother, and this mother has made this child her whole emotional life.[3]

The dream fantasy ends with the boy vindictively pushing the witch into the oven, because he cannot face his Oedipal guilt-feelings toward his mother.[4]

The reader wonders how much of this material might be autobiographical, the more so, as Jarrell's poems always present this fundamental relationship as a troubled one. In his poetic world no child can rely on maternal help in a moment of distress or danger, for the mother is invariably depicted as either absent, dead, fainting, crazy, or thoroughly hostile.[5] Throughout his life Jarrell was painfully aware that his character had largely been determined by his childhood experiences, in particular by the unbringing he received from his mother. Since his father left the family when Randall was still a little boy, his mother became his chief influence. And yet, the biographical evidence is not sufficient to explain the predominance of the mother figure in Jarrell's work. Although he repeatedly asserts that man cannot escape his own mother, whose image he carries forever with him,[6] it is clear that the poetic significance of the mother figure far transcends that of any individual woman: "Back far enough, down deep enough, one comes to the Mothers" (310).

The poem "A Rhapsody on Irish Themes" contains a further instance of a potentially devouring mother figure. The persona addresses an "old woman, met in sleep," whom he calls his "Great-grandmother," when he exclaims: "Old sow, old Circe, I'm not your farrow. / Yet ah, to be eaten!" (75). Jarrell is alluding to an Irish myth which was suggested to him by Robert Graves's book *The White Goddess*.[7] Graves repeatedly points out that Cerridwen, the great Goddess and Muse, is often represented as the Sow-goddess. In his essay on that book, Jarrell quotes the following passage: "A woman should 'either be a silent Muse' or 'she should be the Muse in a complete sense; she should be in turn Arianrhod, Blodenwedd and the Old Sow of Maenawr Penarrd who eats her farrow.' For the poet 'there is no other woman but Cerridwen and he desires one thing above all else in the world: her love. As Blodenwedd, she will gladly give him her love, but at only one price: his life.' "[8] Every artist must wish "to be eaten" by the Mother-Muse, for her love is the prerequisite for creative activity. The myth suggests that the poet's crucial problem is the precarious balance between the conscious realm of linguistic expression and the wordless unconscious, the dreamlike source of his poetic ideas, associations, and images. Despite the risks involved, the poet must open himself up to the potentialities of the unconscious in order to be creative. That the poetic process is indeed central to this poem may be gathered from the fact that Jarrell himself called it "a parody of the Odyssey." The persona plays the role of Ulysses while the old woman metamorphoses into a goddess and then into a prophetess warning him: " 'There's no rest for you, grandson, till you've reached the land / Where, walking the roads with an adding-machine on your shoulder, / You meet no one who knows it' " (75). This oracle seems to be a caricature of Tiresias telling Ulysses in Hades that he must sacrifice to Poseidon in a place where salt is unknown and an oar is mistaken for a winnowing fan. The goddess's prophecy to the poet indicates that authentic poetic expression can be gained only at the price of abandoning the "adding-machine" which, like Coleridge's "Fancy," would merely allow for the accumulation of isolated details stored in the memory; the true poet, however, plunges deeper using the imaginative faculty lodged in his unconscious to fuse those details into poetry.[9] But the treasures of the unconscious are—as many myths illustrate—guarded by dragons that threaten to devour the intrepid intruder.

Before we can continue our exploration of Jarrell's use of mythic mother figures, we must briefly review the way Jungian psychology interprets this archetype. The Great Mother stands for the mainspring of being in the most universal sense, as well as for that unknown and dark unconscious which brings forth and engulfs both individual and historic consciousness. In *The Origins and History of Consciousness* Erich Neumann remarks: "With the emancipation of consciousness and the increasing tension between it and the unconscious, ego development leads to a stage in which the Great Mother no longer appears as friendly and good, but becomes the ego's enemy, the Terrible Mother. The devouring side of the *uroboros* is experienced as the tendency of the unconscious to destroy consciousness. This is identical with the basic fact that ego-consciousness has to wrest libido from the unconscious to preserve its own existence, for, unless it does so, its specific achievement falls back into the unconscious, in other words is 'devoured.' "[10] In plumbing the depths of his own creativity the poet runs a similar risk. Devouring and engulfing are variants of "the archetype of surrender which can be active or passive, positive or negative, and rules the ego's relation to the self in the various stages of development."[11]

Jarrell's prophetic "Great-grandmother" and the "old sow who eats her farrow" in "A Rhapsody on Irish Themes" arguably have a symbolical significance similar to Jung's archetype of the *magna mater*. As the devouring Blodenwedd this Janus-faced Muse represents the Terrible Mother; as the bountiful Cerridwen, however, she resembles the Good Mother, to use Jung's terminology. That Jarrell was not only an adherent of Freudian psychology but also a willing borrower of Jung's insights can be concluded both from his interest in Robert Graves's mythopoeic concepts and from his own use of symbols connected with the Jungian mother archetype. On the reverse side of a work sheet for the poem "Woman" we find the following list: "water cave arch house cup veil / bud eye hull or shell mussel clam / bush dolphin earth sea / moon suck smell pocket fidget gig wetness filth."[12] The majority of these terms refer to the creative or protective aspect of the *magna mater*, but symbols like "earth, wood, night, the dark sea," evoking her destructive side, are just as frequent in Jarrell's work.[13] The complex configurations of his poems remind us that moral distinctions—such as "creative" and "destructive"—exist only in the human mind and that apparent opposites may "objectively" be one and the same thing. One of his poems bears the characteristic title "In Nature There Is Neither Right nor Left nor Wrong." A symbol may simultaneously suggest life and death, the conscious and the unconscious, the self and the loss of self. The house, for example, which Jarrell himself explained as a mother symbol in his exegesis of "A Quilt-Pattern," is protective as well as threatening, signifying both life and death. This ambiguity is, of course, a basic property of every archetype.

An especially fascinating example of a paradoxical symbol with clear archetypal and mythopoeic overtones is the vulture in "The Woman at the Washington Zoo." The protagonist's wishing to be eaten by this bird represents a case of suicidal lack of ego stability. Beyond being a mere cogwheel in the social machinery of her world, the woman feels trapped in the prison of her consciousness. She sees her body reflected,

> small, far-off, shining
> In the eyes of animals, these beings trapped
> As I am trapped but not, themselves, the trap,
> Aging, but without knowledge of their age,
> Kept safe here, knowing not of death, for death—
> Oh, bars of my own body, open, open! (215)

In her "manless, childless, fleshless existence"[14] she identifies herself with the unwanted "white rat that the foxes left" (215) and longingly cries out to the vulture to "change" her. The rat's whiteness is contrasted to the "red helmet" and the "black wings" of the bird from which the woman expects the beneficial change. Since red is commonly regarded as symbolic of life and love, while black stands for death, the two colors of the vulture refer to contradictory spheres. The ambiguity of the beast is further increased when it is expected to "step" to the woman "as man." The vulture thus combines features from the animal world of instinct with those of man's rational superiority over nature. The expression "wild brother" synthesizes the two aspects. The woman's longing for the vulture is, therefore, expressive of two antithetical desires: the wish for love and the wish for death. Love would redeem her from her social as well as from her inner isolation, while death might break up the bars of her existential prison of consciousness.

To clarify why the vulture here symbolizes both sexuality and death, let us briefly consider the mythopsychological implications of this bird. We may understand the vulture as an archetypal image of the Great Mother. In *Leonardo da Vinci*, Freud pointed out that in old Egypt "the vulture goddess Mut, identical with Nekhbet, was often represented phallically. . . . The androgynous Great Mother Goddess, i.e., equipped with a phallus and sometimes a beard, is a universally distributed archetype symbolizing the unity of the creative in the primordial creatrix, the 'parthenogenetic' matriarchal Mother Goddess of the beginning."[15] The totality of life and death, *eros* and *thanatos*, consciousness and the unconscious, male and female as symbolized by the vulture is obviously what fascinates the woman at the Washington Zoo. She herself is rigid, lifeless, pallid, uncreative, and empty. By accepting the dreaded vulture, however, she seems prepared to accept her own death and with it the personal "I" instead of an impersonal "One," to use Heidegger's terms. This new attitude might enable her for the first time to live an authentic life in which each moment would stand out as a fulfilled present instead of an unactualized fragment within linear time. It is significant that Jarrell uses the vulture or mother archetype to symbolize this creative change. Only forces from the unconscious can make our lives creative, thereby filling the void in us. They alone endow the present with that eternity which man needs in order "to make" (234). The woman's yearning for the archetypal deathbird can therefore be understood as an allegory of the poet's own longing for creative existence.

In his interpretations of "A Quilt-Pattern" and "The Woman at the Washington Zoo" Jarrell makes explicit use of Freud's insight into the connection between food and sex. However, Jung's transpersonal analysis is critically even more rewarding. The motif of devouring, which occurs in many fairy-tales, myths, and fertility rites, can be linked with incest or castration and represents the threat of self-loss to the immature ego. In this postadolescent phase of man's development (both in an ontogenetic and phylogenetic sense), masculinity and ego are often symbolized by "the higher phallus" or "higher masculinity," that is, "the head, symbol of consciousness, with the eye for its ruling organ."[16] According to Erich Neumann, beheading and blinding may legitimately be interpreted as forms of higher castration[17] representing the ego's surrender to the self. While devouring belongs to the adolescent stage of consciousness, blinding and beheading form part of adult consciousness. It is for this reason that in Jarrell's poetry the symbolism of devouring usually appears with the personae of children, whereas that of beheading invariably occurs in connection with grown-ups.

The frequency of themes like death by devouring and, as we shall see, by beheading at the hands of a mother figure, indicates the poet's preoccupation with the processes in his own mind. The fact that his poems may often be understood as allegories of the creative act associates him with a major concern of romanticism—makes him, in effect, a post-romantic poet. For Jarrell, poetic creation involves an act of self-sacrifice on the part of the artist, whose surrender is not unlike that of a priest or victim in a fertility rite, with the Muse as his inexorable Goddess. Yet, mythopoeic representations of the creative process are often complicated by the figure of the shadow or *Doppelgänger*. In *The White Goddess*, Graves claims that "all true poetry . . . celebrates some incident or scene" from "the antique story," whose theme is

> the birth, life, death and resurrection of the God of the Waxing Year; the central chapters concern the God's losing battle with the God of the Waning Year for the love of the capricious and all-powerful Threefold Goddess, their mother, bride and layer-out. The poet identifies himself with the God of the Waxing Year and his Muse with the Goddess; the rival is his blood-brother, his other self, his weird. . . . The weird, or rival, often appears in nightmares as the tall, lean, dark-faced bedside spectre, or Prince of the Air, who tries to drag the dreamer out through the window, so that he looks back and sees his body still lying rigid in bed; but he takes countless other malevolent or diabolic or serpent-like forms.[18]

We are, indeed, startled at the close resemblance between what Graves calls the theme of all poetry and a recurrent subject of a large part of Jarrell's work. Not only does his treatment of the mother archetype closely correspond with Graves's analysis of the ambiguous nature of the Great Mother, but the frequent occurrence of split personae is also strongly reminiscent of Graves's notion of the *Doppelgänger*. The poem "A Hunt in the Black Forest" comes to mind, where the red dwarf's double, the mute, poisons the Hunter-King in a hut in the forest and then lifts up the red dwarf to watch the scene through the window (319–21). One may also think of "A Quilt-Pattern" in which the boy, after having pushed the witch into the oven, holds his breath: "Bad me, good me / Stare into each other's eyes, and timidly / Smile at each other: it was the Other" (59). Every reader of "The House in the Wood" will remember the persona staring at his own weird self, lying on the bed "like a cut-off limb, the stump the limb has left" (323), before all ego-consciousness is blacked out and the unconscious regains control: "Here at the bottom of the world, what was before the world / And will be after, holds me to its black / Breasts and rocks me: the oven is cold, the cage is empty, / In the House in the Wood, the witch and her child sleep" (323).

Jarrell's reaction to Graves's poetry demonstrates his awareness of the psychic forces lying behind this kind of poetic mythology: "One does not need much of a psychoanalytical or anthropological background to see that Graves's world picture is a projection upon the universe of his own unconscious, of the compulsively repeated situation in which, alone, it is able to find satisfaction; or to see that this world picture is one familiar, in structure and in much detail, in the fantasies of children and neurotics, in dreams, in fairy-tales, and, of course, in the myths and symbols of savages and of earlier cultures."[19] In view of Jarrell's intimate understanding of this psychological process, we feel justified to apply his observations to his work and to interpret his reliance on dreams, fairy-tales, myths, and symbols as a projection of the relationship between his ego and the unconscious in the act of writing. As we have noticed before, the ego appears frail and relatively powerless when confronted with the unconscious; the Terrible Mother—be it as darkness, forest, or sea—inevitably prevails in the end.

This disproportion can readily be traced in Jarrell's poetry on women.[20] It can hardly be denied that Jarrell's poems were often inspired by real women, such as his own wife or his mother; yet the individual portraits tend to merge with the image of the archetypal Mother. As a result, the poet's concept of woman takes on a deeper significance. At the end of the poem "Woman," there is an impressive passage revealing the numinous power of the female:

> But you should gush out over being like a spring
> The drinker sighs to lift his mouth from: a dark source
> That brims over, with its shining, every cup
> That is brought to it in shadow, filled there, broken there.
> You look at us out of sunlight and of shade,
> Dappled, inexorable, the last human power.
> All earth is the labyrinth along whose ways
> You walk mirrored: rosy-fingered, many-breasted
> As Diana of the Ephesians, strewing garments
> Before the world's eyes narrowed in desire.
> Now, naked on my doorstep, in the sun
> Gold-armed, white-breasted, pink-cheeked, and black-furred.
> You call to me, "Come"; and when I come say, "Go,"
> Smiling your soft contrary smile . . .
> > He who has these
> Is secure from the other sorrows of the world. (328–29)

Although the verbs "come" and "go" may refer to the poet's actual wife or to women in general, the element of female self-sufficiency strongly reminds us of the willful Goddess in whose service the poet sacrifices his existence. Her ambiguous nature is exposed in the double aspect of the spring which is one of her attributes: a life-giving well on the one hand and a "dark source" on the other. Graves's Threefold Goddess, "the Mother, Bride, and Layer-out," reappears in this triple description: the motherly breast "the drinker sighs to lift his mouth from," the fulfillment when the cup is brimming over, and the shadowy end when the vessel is finally "broken there." The earth is seen as a labyrinth of glass in which the Goddess is mirrored. The display of nature's variety and the evolution of life are presented as a colossal striptease of the many-breasted Goddess.[21] Finally, the Goddess-Muse approaches the poet, abiding naked on his very doorstep. Graves explains that "the poet's inner communion with the White Goddess [is] regarded as the source of truth. Truth has been represented by poets as a naked woman: a woman divested of all garments or ornaments that will commit her to any particular position in time and space."[22] Henceforth the poet will be at her beck and call, depending on her "contrary smile" for his inspiration. His service to the Muse consumes all his energy, so that he is indeed "secure from the other sorrows of the world." Or, in Emily Dickinson's words: "The Missing All—prevented Me / From missing minor Things."[23]

Although a man has no chance of ever finding "his ideal, / The Good Whore who reminds him of his mother" (326), he cannot escape Her thraldom when confronted with a woman:

> When he looks upon your nakedness he is blinded.
> Your breasts and belly are one incandescence
> Like the belly of an idol: How can a man go in that fire
> And come out living? (327)

Words like "incandescence" or "idol" clearly point to underlying archetypal associations. At an earlier stage of the poem, the word "incandescence" referred to the Mosaical bush that burned but was not consumed. The poet then transferred the idea of incandescence to the face of Zipporah, the wife of Moses:

> (When Moses came down from Sinai he had seen
> God's back parts, but his face he had not seen.)
> But when Zipporah the wife
> Of Moses came down from whatever mount
> It was she mounted, the skin of her face shone,
> It was with far other tablets, not of stone,
> That she commanded him. He put a veil on her face.[24]

Right below this typed passage Jarrell wrote by hand:

> overwhelming
> infantile
> primordial
> UR-
> UNCONSCIOUS

Moses, the spokesman of the Eternal, may here be understood as the poet in his function of "unacknowledged legislator of the world," who, however, cannot bear to see God's face directly; he perceives His bright "incandescence" only as reflection on the face of Zipporah, the archetypal Woman or Muse. But the vision of her unveiled face is nonetheless "overwhelming"; it reduces the poet to a state of "infantile" dependence, for it is the "primordial UR-UNCONSCIOUS" itself which is shining through her. The veil is therefore a necessary protection from her deadly power.

Characteristically, in "Orestes at Tauris" the hero can see the unveiled beauty of the priestess only when she is about to put him to death.

> Gold hung from her arms, dark gold clasped round
> Her haggard face; what beasts worked red with gold
> Twisted their antlers past her tangled hair?
> Rays like a fan's shrivelling ribs

> Curved from her lips to color her burnt cheeks;
> Her lips were dyed; and through dyed lashes peered
> Eyes with a bird's pitiless and gloomy stare.
> So she looked: and yet in all that press
> At Argos or Mycenae, or in all the isles
> You never saw her like: a face so fair! (412)

All the details of this description aim at making her numinous and more than human. Although her beauty is unparalleled, it fills the observer with terror. There is no hint of a feminine softness that Orestes could woo or appeal to. Her real face cannot be seen, for her skin is tattooed, her lips and lashes dyed. Her true nature, death, must be guessed from eyes which "peer" with a "pitiless and gloomy stare." The terrifying aspect of her appearance is further stressed by the ornaments in her hair. She wears an antlerlike crown in the shape of "twisted beasts" or snakes, which likens her to the deadly Medusa. Graves remarks that the Syrian Moon-goddess was represented with a snake headdress to remind the devotee that she was death in disguise.[25] Absolute beauty is awe-inspiring because it invariably involves death. Or, as Rilke put it: "the beautiful is nothing / but the beginning of the terrible."[26]

Although the numinous female is dangerous, the male protagonists of Jarrell's poems resolutely seek her deadly fascination. In Jung's psychology the quest-motif not only symbolizes the struggle between ego-consciousness and the unconscious, but also describes the poetic process as a descent into the creative unconscious, the dangerous realm of the Great Mother. In "Orestes at Tauris," his most extensive treatment of a classical hero myth, Jarrell uses a mythical quester as his poet-persona.

"Orestes at Tauris" is based on the well-known Greek myth, but differs from its original in that the sister/priestess, Iphigenia, sacrifices Orestes instead of assisting him in his endeavor to steal the statue of the Goddess. It may therefore be legitimate to ask if the death of Orestes was meant to represent the fate of the poet slain by and for the Muse. According to Bachofen, Aeschylus's *Oresteia* is "a symbolic representation of a last fight between the maternal goddesses and the victorious paternal gods."[27] This interpretation offers a clue as to why the myth of Orestes has been chosen as a symbol of the poetic quest. From mythology we learn that Clytemnestra killed her husband, Agamemnon, so as not to lose her lover, Aegisthus. Orestes avenged his father's death by killing both his mother and her lover. The Erinyes, representatives of the old matriarchal principle, persecuted Orestes and demanded his punishment, while Apollo and Athena (the latter not born from woman but sprung from the head of Zeus!), as representatives of the new patriarchal religion, took Orestes' side. Bachofen's argument centers on the antagonism between the old matriarchal and the new patriarchal order. In a matriarchal world the tie between mother and child is sacred; matricide, therefore, appears as the ultimate crime, beyond the hope of pardon. By the same token,

Clytemnestra's murder of her husband is considered a minor fault, since she was not related by blood to the man whom she killed. As a result, her act does not arouse the Erinyes. From a patriarchal point of view, however, the son's love and respect for his own father is an inviolable duty, and parricide becomes the paramount crime. To the Olympian gods, Orestes' murder of Clytemnestra is no crime, since it is carried out in revenge of Agamemnon's death. In Aeschylus' *Oresteia* Orestes is acquitted, but this victory of the patriarchal principle is somewhat diminished by a compromise with the defeated goddesses. They agree to accept the new order and content themselves with minor roles, as deities of the earth and of fertility. In terms of Bachofen's theory, Jarrell's version of the myth implies a countervictory of the matriarchal world. This is quite consistent with the poet's vision of the powerful Female and the Muse as the "many-breasted" Diana of the Ephesians. It strengthens the argument that Orestes' quest in fact symbolizes the poet's quest, for, as Jungian psychology maintains, the artist's dependence on the Great Mother as a wellspring of inspiration is so strong that he is never capable of the "matricide" necessary for the liberation of the anima and its differentiation from the mother archetype.[28]

In "Orestes," however, Jarrell introduces a man who has committed matricide and is, therefore, subject to the revenge of the Mother Goddess. His murder could be interpreted as the attempt of ego-consciousness to free itself from its bondage to the unconscious. And indeed, Orestes' initial sense of restlessness and estrangement as he is sailing to Tauris may well portray a frustrated poet whose source of inspiration has dried up:

> Days, hung at the wind's aging breast—
> The sail had no shade, the place of the sun
> No shape to tell you where he rode. (406)

Presently, Orestes' ship runs aground and begins to decay. The stranded ship, which is stuck and begins to "rot and scale," is symbolic of the poet's flagging imagination.

> And as each wave burst, the plunging spray
> Broke round you and clustered on you in such clouds
> You looked like men whom darkness overtakes
> In harshest winter, when snow falls so thick
> They look like ghosts among the silent flakes
> And hardly speak. So you stood mute
> With hanging head. . . . (407–08)

The similarity to Coleridge's "The Ancient Mariner" lends support to the conjecture that this passage is a description of the poet's uncreative or "wintry" state. The crimes of the Ancient Mariner and Orestes may be understood as deeds that disrupt man's harmony with his deeper self. What is even more important, both poems are about the poet's search for a voice.

In this desperate situation Jarrell's Orestes suddenly discovers Iphigenia. Her song disperses the mist, and for the first time Orestes beholds the glittering shore that he has been seeking for so long. The vision of the priestess is, however, accompanied by the unleashing of matriarchal and unconscious forces in the form of the Furies, which begin to threaten the persona:

> Then from the sea-depth voices groaned,
> And you looked down, shrieked out to see
> The black ship breaking, half-sucked-down.
> Stripped off the mantle! flung down the sword!
> Diving into the whirlpool. . . . (408)

Although terrified at being sucked up by the whirlpool, the hero decides to accept his fate by diving into the vortex. Having given up his sword—the symbol of masculine power and of analytical consciousness—he is saved by Iphigenia, but only to be made prisoner of the priestess, the representative of Artemis.

After a painful journey inland, Orestes finds himself before the statue of the deity for whose sake he ventured on his perilous voyage. While he is being prepared for immolation, he is finally allowed to see her; in death the veil of ignorance is commonly supposed to be withdrawn from the eyes of man; yet, what an anticlimax:

> You looked astonished at the image there
> That crouched like a hunted and misshapen thing,
> Swathed with the hides of horses, fox furs, and the skins
> Of some long-horned, long-furred, and long-tailed beast,
> A fleece with its knotted and dragging fringe. (410)

Nothing of the expected overawing beauty or terror resides in the dismal statue that looks rather like an effigy of man's own forlornness. The epiphany for which poets have sacrificed their lives turns out to be a fake, at least to a postromantic like Jarrell. The fleece is no longer golden, but "knotted" with dirt. The only reality that remains of the romantic quest is death, as the heads of the previous victims vividly manifest.

Throughout the preparation for the sacrifice Orestes scarcely speaks at all. He only moans "unpitied words—and no more known as words;" and again, "with a wordless shriek, [his] head lolled back." His utmost anguish takes the form of a nightmare in which the dreamer frantically but uselessly tries to utter words in order to gain distance from the terror of the dream. Orestes is described as "lashed like a sail upon a pole," waiting for the wind, the inspiration, to move him. His belated recognition that the Goddess is a hoax—that the essential truth, which poetry has always been said to explore, is wishful thinking and a figment of the imagination—cannot save him now. He watches himself vainly straining for a voice to express at least his desperate insight that poetry has lost its power to signify. Swathed in furs, he observes the ritual dance which initiates his own death:

> . . . and strange it was to see
> The dancers with their masks and swords and leaves,
> And hear no music, no, nor sound except
> Their feet against the turf and their intaken breath
> Or your own moans and painful gasping breath. . . . (412)

It is, indeed, "strange" to watch the dancers lift their feet and arms rhythmically without hearing a single sound. Poetic expression is shown to be a painful and absurd ordeal. Robert Graves described it in much the same way in *The White Goddess* (1947), which influenced the composition of "Orestes," itself originally a part of *Losses* (1948). The resemblance is unmistakable: "Poetry began in the matriarchal age. . . . No poet can hope to understand the nature of poetry unless he has had a vision of the Naked King crucified to the lopped oak, and watched the dancers, red-eyed from the acrid smoke of the sacrificial fires, stamping out the measure of the dance, their bodies bent uncouthly forward; with a monotonous chant of 'Kill! kill! kill!' and 'Blood! blood! blood!' "[29]

After revealing the spuriousness of the romantic concept of poetic truth by debunking the Goddess, the poet describes the execution of Orestes at the hands of his sister, the priestess. If poetry itself can offer no absolute or transcendent insight, is there at least some knowledge to be gained from the poet's descent to the dark threshold where consciousness is about to be engulfed by the unconscious at the moment of decapitation?

> . . . when between you and her face
> The sword's line came—what did you see then, Orestes?
>
> The head sprang up, spun once, and fell. (413)

The poem cannot do more than dramatize human ignorance. There is here no hint of an epiphany. The vital question is answered graphically by a gap between the lines.

At this point we note an interesting change of perspective. The omniscient observer who has been addressing an internalized Orestes is now replaced by the priestess who stands with the victim's head in her outstretched hand, pondering if she has lived "all to that end!"

> How strange to stand like a child, and tremble
> At a headless body[30]—one more head
> To stuff and smoke and set on an empty stake;
> And if in the long nights of the long winter
> It still stares at you with its aching smile,
> And when you name it, and lean to it longingly,
> Its eyes seem to cloud in the firelight
> And it turns from you, slowly, in the stinging smoke—

> What is it but one more head? If it seems to you
> The whole world and the way to a world
> Lost in one instant, under the plunging sword—
> Now once more your fingers shine with blood.
> The maidens lift their jars, pour through your hands
> Water that falls past stained; and after strew
> Bright shells and sea-sand on that sodden ground. (414)

The ritual death of Orestes appears to be totally empty of significance. His head is going to rot and soon it will be only one among many others impaled on stakes—all victimized poets and their books.[31] Indeed, all works of art are ultimately bound to disintegrate in the merciless wind of time:

> On poles around, their long hair stirring in the wind,
> Some heads stood drying. One had rotted there so long
> Shreds of its face hung fluttering like a beard. . . . (411)

Even the poet himself tries in vain to recover the experience which catalyzed his writing in the first place ("when you name it . . . it runs from you"). The composition seems to lose its original meaning and the artifact is just one more poem, but not the desired living symbol which might "call the hair up on another age" (385).[32] Jarrell deeply deplores that the original vision which once had seemed "the whole world and the way to a world" is "lost in one instant"—at the moment of expression—"under the plunging sword." However, as he affirms in "Esthetic Theories," "the poets thrive on bleeding" (364); they go on creating poems, killing visions: "once more your fingers shine with blood." To the modern writer the unconscious, the realm of the Great Mother, is as alluring as it was to the first artist. The image of the Taurian Artemis is still with us: "Naked and grim among her worshippers" (415).

"Orestes at Tauris" concludes with a bitter attack on the indifference of the American audience. The death ritual of Orestes takes place far away from the eyes of men in a remote country to which "the traveller might have come, but no man came" (415). The artist is always alone. Here, as well as in essays like "The Obscurity of the Poet" and "The Age of Criticism," or more indirectly in *The Bat-Poet*, Jarrell complains that the public is incapable or unwilling to follow the artist on his desperate quest to regain meaning for what is to all appearances an absurd existence. The transformation of experience into form and back into the reader's experience has broken down at every point. Art, in Jarrell's eyes, is always bought at the price of life, not only the poet's life, but also at the cost of the "winged life" of experience which is inevitably destroyed when it is transformed into language.

Jarrell's desperate view is based on the insight that life and art spring from a common "crazy womb," the womb of the Great Mother who produces images in much the same way that she brings forth life in "blind strength" (400), bleeding it to death. In "Esthetic Theories: Art as Expression" he asserts that poetry and life are indistinguishable in their source and that both "start surprisingly, like blood in bones" (384). The creative act is compared to the bleeding of a hemophiliac. Poets are like "unlucky" bleeders because the slightest "cut" of inspiration results in a profuse "bloodshed" of expression. But their bleeding is not terminal: "poets thrive on it, as if the muses / . . . / Found bleeding adequate for anything; / Becoming in time, almost, autonomous" (384). What then is the disease which the muses cure by bleeding the poet? Again, Jarrell's essay on Graves provides a clue. Graves characterizes poetry as "a personal cathartic for the poet's suffering from some inner conflict, and then as a cathartic for readers in a similar conflict."[33] Jarrell explains this conflict as "the antagonism of the rational and emotional sides in Graves" and emphasizes the therapeutic value of poetry and myth in Graves's case. Yet, although he accepts writing as a cure for the split consciousness of the modern poet, his remarks on the artist's "distilled" life-blood are disheartening indeed:

> Dried, or preserved in jars, and certified
> By experts of some bureau of the State,
> It would be found invaluable, like pots,
> To show all sorts of things about an age:
> What the people worshipped, whom they ate.
> For centuries the reconstructed cultures
> That festered uncertainly in someone's heart
> Would pale and warp among the glances
> And desiccation of a gallery
> Where children in sterile coveralls would falter:
> 'The diseases glitter darkly, like a jewel.'
> One sees *der Uebermensch* endow
> A Chair of Paleohaemolysis. (384)

The metaphor is, of course, a conventional one. Milton, for instance, wrote in *Areopagitica*: "Books . . . do preserve as in a vial the purest efficacy and extraction of that living intellect that bred them." Jarrell takes a bleaker view. He stresses the disproportion between the unbearable pain of the artist and the fate of his work. The blood cultures "pale and warp" in the gallery. It remains doubtful if the bottling of the poet's life-blood, the transformation of experience into form, can be successfully accomplished, because the medium is an impure one; the jars are said to hold "diseases." Furthermore, the conversion of art into experience is made difficult by the "desiccation" of the gallery, that modern climate so totally uncongenial to the poet's work. People seem to be afraid of the power of art, as if it were some contagious disease which might threaten the dull routine of their complacent lives; that is also why children have to wear "sterile coveralls" when contemplating the "jars." It is precisely our academic attitude toward art which brings about this "desiccation."

Critics and historians misuse the poems to study the civilization which has produced them. Mocking the self-promoting critical activity of the all-too-typical professor of literature, Jarrell calls him *"der Uebermensch"* endowing "A Chair of Paleohaemolysis," a professorship devoted to the analytical breaking down of blood into its components.

In the felicitous if bitter title *Blood for a Stranger* (where "Esthetic Theories" first appeared) Randall Jarrell summarizes his despair concerning art, artist, and reader alike. For him there is no healing vision, no comforting message, no prophecy of a redeeming future to proclaim. Although the painful dichotomy between the self-conscious ego and the vague apprehension of something greater beyond drives the poet to probe into the deepest reaches of his experience, he cannot come up with a satisfactory find. The reason lies in what we have found to be both a central insight and a pervasive theme of his poetry: the immense difficulty and even impossibility of gaining wisdom through converting experience into form. There will always be an unbridgeable gap between the conscious and the unconscious; at the most, language can give oblique expression to that process which translates dimly perceived intimations into palpable forms. In Jarrell's poetic world, the katabasis to the Great Mother, the search for meaning, always ends in pain and darkness. In "90 North" he sums up this conviction in the memorable lines:

> I see at last that all the knowledge
>
> I wrung from the darkness—that the darkness flung me—
> Is worthless as ignorance: nothing comes from nothing,
> The darkness from the darkness. Pain comes from the darkness
> And we call it wisdom. It is pain. (114)

Notes

1. Randall Jarrell, *The Complete Poems* (New York: Farrar, Straus and Giroux, 1969), p. 82; hereafter cited by page number in the text.

2. For further examples see n. 13.

3. Letter to Sister Bernetta Quinn (15 December 1951), New York Public Library, Berg Collection.

4. The punning title of the poem, "A Quilt-Pattern," hints at the classic development of this type of "guilt."

5. For a detailed illustration of this statement see Helen Hagenbüchle, *The Black Goddess* (Bern: Francke Verlag, 1975), Ch. 1. Jarrell's poems on this motif are "Hope" (pp. 305–12), "A Street off Sunset" (pp. 289–93), "Thinking of the Lost World" (pp. 336–38), "The State" (p. 189), "The Prince" (p. 97), "A Hunt in the Black Forest" (pp. 319–21), "London" (p. 360), "Protocols" (p. 193), "Variations III" (p. 122), "The Night before the Night before Christmas" (pp. 40–51), "Mother, Said the Child" (p. 396), and "The Player Piano" (pp. 354–55). If we interpret unreachable airfields or destroyed carriers as metaphors for mothers out of touch with their children, then this theme of a "deadly parental-child relationship" can be extended to much of Jarrell's war poetry. See Richard Fein's brilliant essay "Randall Jarrell's World of War" (*Analects*, 1, No. 2 [Spring 1961]).

6. Cf.

> Just as, within the breast of Everyman,
> Something keeps scolding in his mother's voice,
> Just so, within each woman, an Old Woman
> Rocks, rocks, impatient for her kingdom. (310)

> Possessed by that prehistoric unforgettable
> Other One, who never again is equaled
> By anyone, he searches for his ideal,
> The Good Whore who reminds him of his mother. (326)

7. Actually, Jarrell blends several originally separate myths. The Attis cult with the swine-figure of the Great Mother and the myth of Circe are amplified through the use of the Irish myth of Blodenwedd. For detailed information on this myth see Robert Graves, *The White Goddess* (1948; rpt. New York: Farrar, Straus and Giroux, 1970), p. 448. Jarrell may even have thought of James Joyce's *Ulysses*, where Ireland is called an old sow that eats her farrow.

8. Randall Jarrell, *The Third Book of Criticism* (New York: Farrar, Straus and Giroux, 1969), p. 98.

9. In *The Bat-Poet* Jarrell expresses the same thought by contrasting the Mockingbird symbol of the mimetic poet, with the Bat that stands for the true imaginative poet.

10. Erich Neumann, *The Origins and History of Consciousness* (Princeton: Princeton University Press, 1970), p. 299.

11. Neumann, pp. 53–54.

12. See Jarrell's worksheets of the poem "Woman," Berg Collection. See C. G. Jung, *Von den Wurzeln des Bewusstseins*, p. 97. See also Neumann, p. 14: "Anything deep—abyss, valley, ground, also the sea and the bottom of the sea, fountains, lakes and pools, the earth, the underworld, the cave, the house, and the city—all are parts of this archetype," i.e., the mother archetype.

13. The following examples serve to substantiate the claim that "wood," "sea," "darkness," and "earth" are consistently used as symbols of the destructive aspect of the mother archetype.

"The wood" as archetypal symbol occurs in poems that use a fairy-tale structure. The wood is the locale of the tale as well as a symbol of the dream state of the protagonist. Examples are "A Quilt-Pattern" (p. 57), "A Hunt in the Black Forest" (p. 319), and "The House in the Wood" (p. 322). For a detailed analysis of "The House in the Wood" see my *The Black Goddess*, pp. 46–60. "The wood" as a symbol of the pit of being as well as of the unconscious occurs, for instance, in "The Märchen" (p. 82), where Jarrell explicitly speaks of "the Necessity / Men spring from, die under: the unbroken wood" (p. 83). A similar extended use of the forest symbol can be found in "Field and Forest" (p. 334).

"The sea," symbol of death and the unconscious, often occurs in conjunction with "the island," symbol of consciousness and ego. In this context the poem "The Island" is of great interest. For an analysis of this poem see *The Black Goddess*, pp. 79–80. At the beginning of "The Märchen," the symbolisms of wood/clearing, sea/island, and darkness/light are combined. In "The Difficult Resolution," Jarrell makes extensive use of the sea as symbol of the unconscious and of the negative mother archetype: "the night's dead . . . escape. . . . To the dreams along whose beaches laps / The owned and amniotic sea" (p. 398); "Wet still with the tides that formed us, with the blind / Determiners of that blind mother" (p. 400). Another hint at the deeper significance of this symbol is found in the poem "The Iceberg," which closes with the rather explicit lines: "The conscious and witty evil of the air, / The witless and helpless evil of the sea" (p. 366). For further passages of interest see pp. 103, 154, 159, 197, 204, 387, 390.

An extended use of the "darkness/light" symbolism is found in "The Venetian Blind," which I have analyzed at length in *The Black Goddess*, pp. 72–77. The "devouring" night as symbol of death in the shape of the murderous owl appears in "The Bird of Night" (p. 313) and in "The Breath of Night" (p. 134). Of special interest is also the poem "Jerome," since the night is here combined with yet another mother symbol, the dragon. In "A Quilt-Pattern," the boy falls "Through darkness, the leagues of space / Into the oldest tale of all" (p. 57). Further examples are pp. 65, 159, 357, 177–78, 391.

The symbolic use of "earth" appears in other related forms like "the grave," "the pit," or "the abyss." Two especially intriguing examples may here be cited: "he [the devil] bleats / The herd back to the pit of being" (p. 21); and "these blossoming alleys of the maze / That lead, through a thousand leaves, to the beginning / Or that lead at last into—dark, leaved—a door" (p. 110), i.e., ultimately back to the Great Mother, origin of life and death alike.

14. See Randall Jarrell's account of the composition of "The Woman at the Washington Zoo," in *Understanding Poetry*, by Cleanth Brooks and Robert Penn Warren (New York: Holt, Rinehart and Winston, 1960), pp. 531–39, or rpt. in *A Sad Heart at the Supermarket*, pp. 160–73.

15. Neumann, pp. 11–12.

16. Neumann, p. 158.

17. Neumann, p. 159.

18. Graves, p. 24.

19. Randall Jarrell, "Graves and the White Goddess," in *The Third Book of Criticism*, p. 106.

20. "Hope" (pp. 305 ff.), "In Nature There Is Neither Right nor Left nor Wrong" (p. 331), "Cinderella" (p. 217), "Woman" (p. 324).

21. In view of the following interpretation of "Orestes at Tauris," it should be noted that Diana of Ephesus was a representation of the same goddess that occurs in the Orestes myth as Taurian Artemis. Diana is the Latin name of Artemis.

22. Graves, p. 448.

23. Emily Dickinson, Poem no. 985, *The Complete Poems* (Boston: Little Brown, 1960), p. 459.

24. From the manuscript of "Woman" in the Berg Collection.

25. Graves, p. 448.

26. Rainer Maria Rilke, "Erste Duineser Elegie," in *Sämtliche Werke*, Vol. 1 (Frankfurt: Insel Verlag, 1955), p. 685: "Denn das Schöne ist nichts / als des Schrecklichen Anfang."

27. The following summary of Bachofen's theory is adapted from Erich Fromm, *The Forgotten Language*, pp. 206–ff. If Bachofen's description of matriarchy is understood psychologically rather than sociologically, his discoveries have a lasting value.

28. Cf. Jarrell's reference to this essay of Jung's in "Graves and the White Goddess," in *The Third Book of Criticism*, p. 107.

29. Graves, p. 448.

30. This nightmarish vision of a woman holding a bleeding head in her hand has its biographical source in a childhood experience of the poet, which is described in "A Street off Sunset" (p. 292): his grandmother is standing in the garden with a chicken's head in her hand, while young Randall—identifying with the chicken—looks on in horror.

31. Jarrell uses the same quaint metaphor in *Pictures from an Institution* (New York: Alfred A. Knopf, 1954), p. 35, where he remarks that Gertrude, the novelist, "was never polite to anything but material: when she patted someone on the head you could be sure that the head was about to appear, smoked, in her next novel."

32. This criterion of good poetry, mentioned at the end of "Esthetic Theories," is a Jar-

rellian adaptation of A. E. Housman, whose test, according to Graves, was "simple and practical: does it make the hairs of one's chin bristle if one repeats it silently while shaving?" (quoted in Graves, *The White Goddess*, p. 21).

33. Randall Jarrell, "Graves and the White Goddess," in *The Third Book of Criticism*, p. 107.

Randall Jarrell: Poet-Critic

William H. Pritchard*

After Randall Jarrell's sudden death in the fall of 1965 his publisher brought out a group of tributes to him: essays and reviews of his poetry and criticism; personal recollections and appreciations of his character as a man.[1] One expects a good deal of admiration in such a memorial volume, but is particularly struck here by the unfailingly interesting quality of these testimonies to his genius—I think the term is not too strong—from the pens of such different literary and cultural warriors as Hannah Arendt, Alfred Kazin, Leslie Fiedler, John Crowe Ransom, Karl Shapiro, and others. It is as if each rose to the occasion, knowing that they'd been asked to write about a marvel; somehow the marvel lifted them up, and even veteran ax grinders like Fiedler or Shapiro sound relatively free of their obsessions. Most of the contributors take on the challenge of saying why Jarrell was different, in a class by himself, somehow beyond the reach of ordinary men in his writings and his life. On the superlative side there is Hannah Arendt: "Whatever I know of English poetry, and perhaps of the genius of the language, I owe to him" (4). Or, more ruefully, there is Karl Shapiro describing what it felt like to have been unfavorably reviewed by him: "I felt as if I had been run over but not hurt" (199). Looking up Jarrell's review (a 1948 one of *Trial of a Poet*) we find that the title poem is described as "a sort of bobby-soxer's *Mauberley*,"[2] and it's possible that after Shapiro picked himself up off the ground, he might have been so pleased with the ingenuity, even accuracy, of the epithet, that it hardly hurt at all.

More testimony. There is John Berryman telling of a time when Jarrell visited him in Princeton and claimed to have a hangover. Nothing odd for a poet to have a hangover, except that, as Berryman tells us, Jarrell didn't drink: "He's the only poet that I've ever known in the universe who simply did not drink. So how did he get the hangover? Well, he'd been to a cocktail party the day before in New York and had eaten a poisoned canapé. So here's Jarrell walking up and down in my living room, miser-

*A shorter version of this essay appears in *The American Scholar*, 52 (Winter 1982–83), pp. 67–77. Copyright © by the United Chapters of Phi Beta Kappa. Reprinted by permission of the journal.

able and witty" (15). Robert Lowell had also been invited to dinner, so Jarrell proceeded to make up and recite a typical Lowell poem, amusing everyone in the room but Lowell. Eventually, Berryman says, they quieted him down, gave him a book of pictures of the ballet to look at, and while the rest of them ate dinner Jarrell sat on the couch, making witty remarks about ballet. Another contributor to the volume verifies the fact that not only did Jarrell not drink, he didn't smoke, nor did he use profanity, nor did he like jokes about sex or even conversation about sex. Or there is Robert Fitzgerald, recalling a moment when he and Jarrell went swimming in a quarry, during the summer of 1952 when they were both at the Indiana School of Letters. Jarrell, in the midst of discovering the pleasures of Robert Frost's poetry, "hanging on a floating log in the quarry pool . . . began one day to quote aloud from the poem 'Provide, Provide,' and to his growing astonishment and delight succeeded in going straight through it from memory. 'Why, *I* didn't know I had memorized *that!*' Randall is one of the few men I have known who chortled. He really did. 'Baby doll!' he would cry, and his voice simply rose and broke in joy" (71). Only a poet who never drank, a reviewer who ran you over but didn't hurt you, could quote "Provide, Provide" while hanging on a log in an Indiana quarry pool, then proceed to do something called "chortle." Baby doll, indeed!

To bring this introductory portrait of a marvel to its close, some sentences near the end of Robert Lowell's eulogy evoke the larger-than-life many-sidedness of the man, or myth, who was sensitive to everything:

> Poor modern-minded exile from the forests of Grimm, I see him unbearded, slightly South-American looking, then later bearded. . . . Then unbearded again. I see the bright, petty, pretty sacred objects he accumulated for his joy and solace: Vermeer's red-hatted girl, the Piero and Donatello reproductions, the photographs of his bruised, merciful heroes: Chekhov, Rilke, Marcel Proust. I see the white sporting Mercedes-Benz, the ever better cut and more deliberately jaunty clothes, the television with its long afternoons of professional football, those matches he thought miraculously more graceful than college football. . . . Now that he is gone, I see clearly that the spark from heaven really struck and irradiated the lines and being of my dear old friend—his noble, difficult, and beautiful soul. (111)

Even for Lowell, who perhaps found it easy to rise to eulogistic heights for too many poets, this is a peak of something which one doesn't read without being moved. But after we get through being moved, after we have responded to the mythical Jarrell who imposed himself so powerfully and inspiritingly on the minds and souls of his contemporaries, we may need to bring him, for awhile, back from the heaven into which their hosannahs wafted him, to earth, to life, and to a fresh sense of why he mattered so much as a poet-critic.

I

Does he still matter so much as a critic? At a time when many professional students of literature, particularly younger ones, find themselves stimulated and guided by a recent book like Geoffrey Hartman's *Criticism in the Wilderness,* in which something called "the English tradition in criticism" is confidently tagged and disposed of as "sublimated chatter,"[3] what are the chances of Jarrell's criticism still mattering? For surely Hartman's waggish patronizing is a clever way to name a habit of proceeding which, typically, had this to say about Richard Wilbur's second book of poems:

> An unusually reflective halfback told me that as a run develops there is sometimes a moment when you can "settle for six or eight yards, or else take a chance and get stopped cold, or, if you're lucky, go the whole way." Mr. Wilbur almost always settles for six or eight yards; and so many reviewers have praised him for this that in his second book he takes fewer risks than in his first. (He is like one of those Southern girls to whom everybody north of Baltimore has said, "Whatever you do, *don't* lose that lovely Southern accent of yours"; after a few years they sound like Amos and Andy.)[4]

Whether or not this comment, with its very American allusions to football and radio, is strictly in what Hartman calls "the English tradition," it's certainly chatter; and if its homely illustrations make it less than sublimated, try instead another typical Jarrellian passage, his response to the clutch of lines from Whitman which conclude with "I was the man, I suffered, I was there":

> In the last lines of this quotation Whitman has reached—as great writers always reach—a point at which criticism seems not only unnecessary but absurd: these lines are so good that even admiration feels like insolence, and one is ashamed of anything that one can find to say about them. How anyone can dismiss or accept patronizingly the man who wrote them, I do not understand.[5]

It would be a pretty bold or extremely small-minded reader of that piece of sublimation (indeed of the sublime, as they say at Yale) who could raise his voice to disagree or even to qualify the claim.

These examples may serve to identify two recurrent and essential habits in Jarrell's critical procedure, so thoroughly internalized as to seem natural as breathing. First the use of wit, wisecrack, sarcasm, and the brilliant one-liner, as a devastatingly compressed response to a poet, worth more than a thousand words; second, the large-souled testimony to a poet's overwhelming fineness which leaves the critic, after his testimony, wordless. It's not just, or even mainly, that Whitman's lines are so great as to abide no critical questioning; rather that Jarrell keeps working to place himself in situations where he can say the equivalent of—"Look, you and I are readers, and I've been (I admit it) turning out this piece on the man's poetry, but really he's too large for my writing, for my categories, for *mere* 'criticism.' I'm almost ashamed of what I've said; on the other hand I'm large enough—not just a mere critic—to recognize and salute the size of his achievement. What about it, reader? Wouldn't you rather throw up your hands and marvel along with me at the gap between art and words about art, than keep plugging away at your pious close analysis? *Ars longa, vita brevis*, baby doll!"

This attempt to write criticism which would not be mere "criticism," which would be always conscious of (to use his own words about Whitman) the "point at which criticism seems not only unnecessary but absurd," is, consciously or not, a method of disarming the reader, inviting him to feel capacious and free-wheeling rather than constricted and pedantic. If you are having trouble reading Whitman, if you keep breaking down in *Leaves of Grass*, appalled by this or that piece of rhodomontade—

> Americanos! conquerors! marches humanitarian!
> Foremost! century marches! Libertad! masses!
> For you a programme [with two *m*'s] of chants

—don't think that you've seen through anything Jarrell has not seen through, then seen through his seeing of it: "I have said so little about Whitman's faults because they are so plain: baby critics who have barely learned to complain of the lack of ambiguity in *Peter Rabbit* can tell you all that is wrong with *Leaves of Grass*."[6] So much for Whitman's faults: go ahead and point them out if you aspire to being a baby critic, and how unnecessary and absurd you will show yourself to be. Or consider a two-line poem of Frost's titled "An Answer":

> But Islands of the Blessèd, bless you son,
> I never came upon a blessèd one.

Have you taken the full measure of "An Answer"? Not if you don't see that "this strange little joke" has undergone a sea change "so that it becomes worthy of Prospero himself, all nacreous with lyric, tender, amused acceptance and understanding and regret. If you haven't or can't feel this—you *are* a Convention of Sociologists."[7] What could be more degrading than to be *that*, gasps the reader, resolved to take the little couplet altogether more richly than he had managed to previously.

It takes a stubborn, not to say an ungracious, reader to resist this disarmament and hold back from going all the way from Frost to Prospero, or from "Americanos!" to Whitman's faults not mattering except to pedants. In Jarrell's first essay on Wallace Stevens he does a skillful dance by way of discussing Stevens's sense of the isolation of the poet in twentieth-century, businesslike America. He quotes (from *Harmonium*) "Disillusionment at Ten O'Clock," which laments that life lacks color, that all the houses are haunted by white nightgowns—"none of them strange," and says that in the town

> People are not going
> To dream of baboons and periwinkles.
> Only, here and there, an old sailor,
> Drunk and asleep in his boots,
> Catches tigers
> In red weather.

Jarrell begins his commentary on the poem breezily, admitting that "Any schoolboy (of the superior Macaulayish breed) more or less feels what [it] means," then selects various details which he presses into a little allegory about how, in this prim, colorless world where everybody goes to bed at ten, the only color and poetry lie in a

> drunken and disreputable *old sailor* [who] still lives in the original reality (he doesn't dream of catching, he *catches*): *sailor* to bring in old-fashioned Europe, old-fashioned Asia, the old-fashioned ocean; *old* to bring in the past, to make him a dying survival. What indictment of the Present has ever compared, for flat finality, with "People are not going / To dream of baboons and periwinkles"? Yet isn't this poem ordinarily considered a rather nonsensical and Learish poem?[8]

As so often in his criticism, Jarrell writes as if a question like the last one, rhetorical and casually turned, is the perfect touch to make the scales fall, once more, from our eyes, now able as we are to see the profundity of what we mistook for a trifle of a poem. So it's worth making the effort to answer one of these unanswerable questions. "What indictment of the Present has ever compared, for flat finality, with those baboons and periwinkles?" Well for one, try

> Any my poor fool is hang'd! No, no, no life!
> Why should a dog, a horse, a rat, have life,
> And thou no breath at all? Thou'lt come no more,
> Never, never, never, never never!

Or try these lines from Wordsworth:

> My former thoughts returned, the fear that kills
> And hope that is unwilling to be fed;
> Cold, pain and labor, and all fleshly ills
> And mighty poets in their misery dead.

You may then find that Stevens's fanciful fooling around with baboons and periwinkles doesn't really rate very high on the flat-finality scale; indeed you may find, after all, that Stevens's poem is more like Edward than King Lear. But chances are that rather than engaging in such a questioning of Jarrell's claim for the Stevens poem, you will instead be carried along by the convincing strength and ease of his tone. Isn't it pedantic to make a fuss over what he says about one little poem, since the flow of his rhetoric is so persuasive, the act such a pleasure to observe?

In one of his Frost essays he quoted what Sarah Bernhardt said about Nijinsky: "I fear, I greatly fear, that I have just seen the greatest actor in the world." Jarrell imagines Yeats saying it about Frost; but I think any witness of this critic's own performance, in the essays collected in *Poetry and the Age*, *The Third Book of Criticism*, and now in *Kipling, Auden and Co.*, would find it has a reflexive application. Our original response to these essays is surely to how much fun they are; later we reread with delight, noticing how—except for an allusion here or there reminding us he's read more than we have—how free they are from the snags that meet us on any page of a really difficult critic like Empson or Blackmur, to say nothing of more recent agonizings in literary theory. They are essays which invite reading aloud—particularly the ones on general subjects like "The Obscurity of the Poet" (given originally as a lecture) or "The Age of Criticism"—which feel as if they were designed for the purpose, above all else, of keeping the reader awake and entertained. Of course it is exactly this high-stepping confidence, one joke or clever saying after another, which has caused some to feel that the procedure is too clever to be true, that an essay like "The Age of Criticism" is mainly an exercise in showing off how much Jarrell has read that the others haven't: long on witty complaint; short on helpful analysis and diagnosis.

However justified such complaints might be about, in particular, "The Age of Criticism," they are less interesting to consider than what that essay reveals of Jarrell's central critical identity. In his posthumous tribute, Fiedler made the acute suggestion that Jarrell was "not *quite* a critic finally, but rather a 'real reader' joined in a single body to a compulsive talker" (64). Although I'd prefer to call him *quite* a critic rather than not quite a one, Fiedler is right to emphasize the "real reader" aspect, and not in quotation marks either. The most striking moment from "The Age of Criticism" comes when Jarrell launches into the list of books that, if you wanted to talk about them with somebody at a party, you were out of luck. If you wanted to talk about *Ulysses* or *The Castle* or *The Brothers Karamazov* or *The Great Gatsby* you were in luck:

> But if you wanted to talk about Turgenev's novelettes, or THE HOUSE OF THE DEAD, or LAVENGRO, or LIFE ON THE MISSISSIPPI, or THE OLD WIVES' TALE, or THE GOLOVLYOV FAMILY, or Cunningham-Grahame's stories, or Saint-Simon's memoirs, or LOST ILLUSIONS, or THE BEGGAR'S OPERA, or EUGEN ONEGIN, or LITTLE DORRIT, or THE BURNT NJAL SAGA, or PERSUASION, or THE INSPECTOR GENERAL, or OBLOMOV, or PEER GYNT, or FAR FROM THE MADDING CROWD, or OUT OF AFRICA, or the PARALLEL LIVES, or A DREARY STORY, or DEBITS AND CREDITS, or ARABIA DESERTA, or ELECTIVE AFFINITIES, or SCHWEIK, or—or any of a thousand good or interesting but Unimportant books, you couldn't expect a very ready knowledge or sympathy from most of the readers there.[9]

You may recall your individual experience as a reader of this passage: how guilty it did or didn't make you feel about how many of the titles you could, then or now, put together a few sentences of possible interest and conviction. As one who has always liked going to parties, I used to imagine a less superficial society of readers than hung out at the ones Jarrell attended and didn't drink at; I and my like-minded friends would, at these ideal parties, exchange fine insights about books, and not just about the approved ones either. (I was cured of this fantasy when I began to read Wyndham Lewis and found that not even my best friends and colleagues wanted to talk to me about at a party, or even wanted to read, *Tarr* or *The Revenge for Love* or *Snooty Baronet*.) Think of how the other readers at Jarrell's imaginary party must have felt about him: here comes that guy who never drinks and is always asking me what I think of Cunningham-Grahame's stories; or, there he is again, and I still haven't touched *Electric Affinities*! The more you think about it the stranger it seems, and one begins to appreciate another remark of Fiedler's about how the roots of Jarrell's taste were closer to madness than to method: which I translate to mean that he couldn't help himself, that he was the servant of his own brilliant gift.

"It is his reading that we judge a critic by, not his writing," he says in "The Age of Criticism."[10] The caveat is directed against cultivating a style for its own literary effects, rather than "responding to the true nature and qualities of a work of art" and being able to distinguish good writing from bad. But the essay's force as a whole is in insisting that to be a really interesting critic you've got to be extensive and daring in the books you read. This is going to take up a lot of time, since you must make room for both Cunningham-Grahame and Goethe; indeed, the reason why those other, unreal readers at the parties Jarrell imagines, couldn't talk about very many books of the highbrow top ten list, was that they tended to go to parties; nowadays instead they are going to films three nights a week. This isn't to say that the critic as Heroic Reader has passed from the scene. There is George Steiner for one, who is known to have cast his eyes over everything ever in print, and not just novels and poems. The difference is, I think, that as with the discovery in the quarry that he could recite "Provide, Provide," Jarrell always seems to be discovering something for himself, as if for the first time and right before our eyes; while Steiner, or perhaps Frank Kermode, write as if they had taken it all in at an early age, effortlessly. Jarrell's prose cultivates surprise, sudden glory, wildness: as a description of the kind of reader he wants to encourage, he reaches instinctively for the word "wild," which Emerson and Frost had used previously to indicate the quality of the poetry they cared about. Vowing his love of "wild air," Emerson looking into a new issue of *The Dial* could tell in a moment "which is the wild poetry, and which the tame," and could see also that "one wild line out of a private heart saves the whole book." Frost's tribute in "The Figure a Poem Makes" is similar:

"If it is a wild tune it is a poem." Jarrell laments that too many tame critics act as if, really, they'd rather do anything than read: "Good Lord, you don't think I *like* to read, do you" he imagines them saying to someone insufficiently impressed with what a serious business it all is. By contrast, "Readers, real readers, are almost as wild a species as writers."[11]

If, by dint of sufficient imagination and heroic labor, one manages to become a real reader in this Age of Criticism, one will also be a real critic, not one of your domesticated or institutionalized sort. Jarrell makes the point to which all of us give lip service: "We do not become good critics by reading criticism and, secondarily, the 'data' or 'raw material' of criticism: that is poems and stories. We become good critics by reading poems and stories and by living."[12] How many times has one wanted to say that to the student who, even after writing three papers in the course and coming in dutifully to talk about what he or she "did wrong" in each, still hasn't got the knack. It's a bold teacher who would say, "Well really you've just got to read, oh, and also live a good deal more"—probably best to leave that unspoken. But I think Jarrell's emphasis on "living" here is an important element in his wildness as a writer; really what he is saying to the puzzled student is, in the words of his favorite poet, "You must change your life." "Real criticism demands of human beings an almost inhuman disinterestedness"; or "Criticism demands of the critic a terrible nakedness: a real critic has no one but himself to depend on. He can never forget that all he has to go by, finally, is his own response, the self that makes and is made up of such responses."[13]

We have perhaps become all too domesticated to such utterances, and D. H. Lawrence said it all before at least as eloquently; still that word "finally" in Jarrell's description of the real critic—"all he has to go by, finally, is his own response"—deserves looking at. Jarrell's "finally" came a good deal nearer the beginning of his dealings with a poem than at the end of it. His absolute reliance on taste, on what he hears in the poem and whether what he hears is worth hearing, reminds me of no other recent critic of literature so much as it does of B. H. Haggin, two of whose volumes of music criticism Jarrell reviewed handsomely. For years Haggin gave a lecture titled, uncompromisingly, "The Approach to Music," which approach was through no more no less than what one *heard* in the performance. (Once a student asked him tentatively, at the close of this lecture, whether there might not be other "approaches"—like the musicological one—which could also, perhaps, at times, be of some use. The answer was, unequivocally, no.) Haggin's own "finally" was really there all along—"a real critic has no one but himself to depend on," as Jarrell put it. But Jarrell's actual practice is less severe and exclusive than Haggin's, and part of the reason for this is suggested in the final paragraph of "The Age of Criticism" where he puts on a sincere face and tells us the kind of essay against current criticism he *should* have written: "An article like this ought, surely, to avoid satire; it ought to be documented and persuasive and sympathetic, much in sorrow and hardly at all in anger."[14] It's hard to know whether he realized quite the length of his own ingenuousness here which says, in effect, "Sorry if I've been a bad boy and fooled around, but you'll forgive me, I trust; next time I'll promise to be more sober and objective." In fact he never tried to "avoid satire" but went out of his way to look for it and usually found it, often with consequences so amusing that they frustrate any attempt to follow and assess, agree or disagree with an "argument" about, say, the age of criticism.

One example of such satire will have to do, the charming passage from "The Age of Criticism" about the pig and the bacon. Jarrell is complaining about the patronizing superiority affected by critics toward the writers they criticize, and he tells of attending a meeting where critics were discussing Wordsworth's theories of poetry. Their patronizing tone toward Wordsworth was similar to what a novelist-friend of his had detected at a writers conference where the novelist went to the critics' lectures but they didn't to his—as if he weren't really literary enough for them. It is as if, Jarrell says, "*they* knew how poems and novels are put together, and Wordsworth and my friend didn't, but had just put them together. In the same way, if a pig wandered up to you during a bacon-judging contest, you would say impatiently, 'Go away, pig! What do you know about bacon?' "[15] This is of course irresistible, so much so that for years I never questioned its perfect appropriateness as a rebuke to critical hubris. Yet when considered it seems less than final; after all, if you were judging bacon and a pig wandered up to you, distracted your attention from the critical task at hand, wouldn't you be tempted to respond impatiently to him? What in fact *does* the pig know about bacon? One might even say that bacon is just what the pig can't know about, is no concern of his, except insofar as he's likely to be made into it, and that such an eventuality is not a matter for sensitive discrimination. Or we might consider that whatever Jarrell's friend the novelist knew about his own work, Wordsworth liked all of his poems more or less equally well, treated them all with the highest degree of reverence, couldn't tell which was bacon and which was ham.

My point is not to defend the critics, who were probably a grim enough lot, but to show how fertile was Jarrell's analogy-bank and how he was perfectly willing to raid it and let the analogy carry him away, with "In the same way" doing very loose work indeed as a connector of poets and pigs. This passage is I suppose an example of the sort of satire he apologizes for later on in the essay, says he really shouldn't have practiced; but its deepest point may be not that critics are blind, but that anything—criticism, discrimination, words *about* the thing—pales when the thing itself, like a pig or a Wordsworth, wanders up to you. And satire is good because it helps us become freshly aware of this wondrous fact and of our limitations in front of it: "Art matters not merely because it is the most magnificent ornament and the most nearly unfailing occupation of our lives, but because it is life itself," he says in "The Obscurity of the Poet," the other "topic" essay from *Poetry and the Age*.[16] And if you're going to criticize "life itself," how can you possibly do so without revealing yourself to be, in comparison, small-minded or at any rate a good deal less than magnificent?

This was the challenge Jarrell took on in criticizing the poetry of Frost, Stevens, Ransom, Graves, Marianne Moore, William Carlos Williams, Auden, Lowell, Elizabeth Bishop, and others. Almost all of this criticism, except for the first Auden essay, appeared in the postwar years and ceased around 1955. In American criticism of poetry, certainly of modern poetry, its only rival is the series of essays published in the 1930s by R. P. Blackmur in *The Double Agent* and *The Expense of Greatness*. It is hardly surprising to find that Blackmur on a poem is often deeper and subtler than Jarrell, since he was deeper and subtler than anyone. Recalling the breezy assurance with which Jarrell handled Steven's "Disillusionment at Ten O'Clock," as if it were clearly "about" life, "an indictment of the Present" rather than Learish or nonsensical, we might recall also that it was Blackmur who years before had said of the poem, after quoting the same lines about baboons, periwinkles, and the drunk old sailor—"Every part of the poem makes literal sense. Yet the combination makes a nonsense, and a nonsense much more convincing than the separate sensible statements."[17] He went on to speak of Stevens's language having "a persuasive force out of all relation to the sense of the words": "The simpler the words are the more impressive and certain is the ambiguity. Half our sleeping knowledge is in nonsense; and when put in the poem it wakes." But if Blackmur is subtle and deep, he is also murky and pretentious, humorless in the main, longwinded. Art is a serious business, much more hieratic and formal than "life itself." Blackmur would never have been so bold or amateurish as to make up a list of favorite poems, as Jarrell does for each poet he writes about; the latter's reliance on taste inclines him more toward evaluation. And of course compared to Blackmur he seems freer of the Pound-Eliot modernist poetic; there are lots of other ways to be interesting and attractive in poems—Frost's or Graves's or Ransom's.

Jarrell liked to evaluate and rank, which practice should make him anathema to advanced literary study these days, since one of its dirtiest words is to "valorize," to fix a high price on this or that poem. Let us consider one instance of Jarrell's valorizing, noticing how the power of his rhetoric establishes a poem as marvelous without fully clarifying it. In "To the Laodiceans" he takes up "Provide, Provide," as the second of his chosen "big five" less well-known poems of Frost, and after quoting it writes as follows:

> For many readers this poem will need no comment at all, and for others it
> will need rather more than I could ever give. The poem is—to put it as
> crudely as possible—an immortal masterpiece; and if we murmur some-

thing about its crudities and provincialisms, History will smile tenderly at us and lay us in the corner beside those cultivated people from Oxford and Cambridge who thought Shakespeare a Hollywood scenario-writer.[18]

Abruptly we are launched, with the suggestion first that commentary is in one way or the other superfluous; that to call the poem "an immortal masterpiece" is not putting it crudely at all, since this authoritative unillusioned critical voice can use seriously and get away with them, terms which in the mouths of the rest of us would be mere cant. Then a kind of Raymond Chandler tough guy hit at those Oxbridge types, and Frost is pleasantly established as Shakespearean. Jarrell continues:

> Since I can't write five or six pages about the poem, it might be better to say only that it is full of the deepest and most touching, moral wisdom—and it is full, too, of the life we have to try to be wise about and moral in (the sixth stanza is almost unbearably actual). The Wisdom of this World and the wisdom that comes we know not whence exist together in the poem, not side by side but one inside the other; yet the whole poem exists for, lives around, the fifth stanza and its *others on being simply true*—was restraint ever more moving?[19]

As Jarrell reads the poem, its effectiveness consists in "the Wisdom of this World" demonstrating to us that the Wisdom of this World isn't enough: "The poem puts, so to speak, the minimal case for morality, and then makes the minimal recommendation of it (what worked for them might work for you); but this has a beauty and conclusiveness that aren't minimal."

As with the pig-bacon analogy, such commentary sounds convincing until you begin to fuss with it. What it seems unaware of or unbothered by, is the strange sequence, or lack of discernible sequence, in stanzas 4 through 6 of the poem:

> Make the whole stock exchange your own!
> If need be occupy a throne,
> Where nobody can call you crone.
>
> Some have relied on what they knew;
> Others on being simply true.
> What worked for them might work for you.
>
> No memory of having starred
> Atones for later disregard
> Or keeps the end from being hard.

Jarrell says that "the whole poem exists for, lives around" that middle fifth stanza with its minimal case for morality. But how difficult it is to identify the tone and impulse of "What worked for them might work for you." Elusive, off there somewhere, madly suggestive, not to be depended on by a reader anxious to know where he is and what exactly to feel. And then, without any shift of gears, we move into the final two stanzas with their advice about how one should "provide" for the hard end to come. Immortal masterpiece or not, the poem is stranger and less comprehensible than Jarrell makes it in his brilliant commentary, and I'd argue that more often than not this is the case with his treatment of individual poems. The dazzling, enthusiastic, impressionistic flights make one aware of the poem in question more intensely than one had been before, but don't provide a wholly trustworthy guide to it—especially to its sequential unfolding. It was Jarrell who I suspect called the attention of a lot of people to Frost's poem "Design," and the three pages he wrote about it—one of his longest flights on an individual poem—are absolutely memorable; yet I wonder whether any others, as I do, remember most from that commentary his discussion of the phrase "a flower like froth" and how, when he tried to elicit from a class some sense of the horror of that line, asking them what it reminded them of, he was told by the young woman into whose blue eyes he was desperately looking—"Fudge. It reminds me of making fudge."[20]

If this sounds as though I, a professional critic of modest stature, am seeing through the poet-critic for his instabilities, indulgences, or eccentricities with respect to individual poems, be assured that the procedures of Eliot or Pound or Yeats or Coleridge could be just as easily seen through, with no consequent diminishment of their great value to us. Jarrell differs from those critics—and perhaps we must call him a postmodern poet-critic—in that the catholicity of his admiration (Frost *and* Eliot, Stevens *and* Williams) exists in relation to a comparative lack of egoism in his own poetry. "Style is the way the man takes himself," said Frost, and Jarrell did not take himself as a great poet, as a heroic poet, as a wonder—the way his contemporary Robert Lowell very much took himself. Lowell admired everybody, not just his predecessors but his contemporaries; and yet, without demeaning him by saying it, I have always felt something forced, willed, *occasional*, in his screwing himself up for one more moving tribute to Williams or Crane or Plath or Jarrell himself. Lowell was always somehow in competition with them; whereas one might read Jarrell's critical appreciations endlessly and never think to turn to his own poetry.

II

I now propose to turn to that poetry, making an attempt at Jarrellian characterization and appreciation. For not dwelling more on fine particular moments from the critical essays, I excuse myself by assuming that you have your own favorites and that the more sweeping, impressionistic sense of it I've given is appropriate to the kind of critic (or as Fiedler would say, not-quite-critic) he was. As for his reputation as a poet, he has surely won a place in the anthologies, yet I want to claim for him more

than that, allowing for the possibility that my "estimate" (in the Arnoldian sense) may be less a "real" one (seeing the object as in itself it really is)
than a personal one. For even though the number of fully achieved poems
is small, and the amount of dross in the *Collected Poems* substantial, he is,
along with Lowell, the American poet from the later part of this century I
return to most often, and with continuing rewards, new discoveries.
Berryman, Roethke, Nemerov, the admirable Bishop and Wilbur and
Merrill—all in their different ways can be admired as creators of more
finished, concentrated, even verbally distinctive poems; yet Jarrell has
something more, and to be as embarrassing as possible I will claim that
what he has more of in his poetry is life.

The word "life" certainly occurs often enough in those poems, as in
this passage from the long meditation "Woman," published in *The Lost
World*, where the poet muses on how quickly "the bride's veils evaporate"
and she turns into a wife:

> A girl hesitates a moment in mid-air
> And settles to the ground a wife, a mother.
> Each evening a tired spirit visits
> Her full house; wiping his feet upon a mat
> Marked *Women and Children First*, the husband looks
> At this grown woman. She stands there in slacks
> Among the real world's appliances,
> Women, and children; kisses him hello
> Just as, that morning, she kissed him goodbye,
> And he sits down, till dinner, with the paper.
> This home of theirs is haunted by a girl's
> Ghost. At sunset a woodpecker knocks
> At a tree by the window, asking their opinion
> Of life. The husband answers, "Life is life,"
> And when his wife calls to him from the kitchen
> He tells her who it was, and what he wanted.
> Beating the whites of seven eggs, the beater
> Asks her her own opinion; she says, "Life
> Is life." "See how it sounds to say it isn't,"
> The beater tempts her. "Life is not life,"
> She says. It sounds the same. Putting her cake
> Into the oven, she is satisfied
> Or else dissatisfied: it sounds the same.[21]

Readers of Jarrell's earlier poems will find nothing surprising about the
notion these lines play with—that the yearnings and dissatisfactions
which occur to us as we go about our lives aren't amenable to formulaic
understanding; that to think of yourself as satisfied or dissatisfied may not
make very much difference—"it sounds the same"—insofar as you keep
on doing what you're doing. In one of the best of those earlier poems, "A
Girl in a Library," the college girl has fallen asleep instead of studying her

Home Ec. and Phys. Ed. textbooks, and the poet encourages her to "let them go" as he dreams her into something richer than the ordinary world. Eventually she receives a visitation from Pushkin's Tatyana Larina (from *Eugen Onegin*) to whom the poet laments the girls' unshakeable innocence, even when "in the last light sleep of dawn" the messenger comes with his message":

> Oh, Tatyana,
> The Angel comes: better to squawk like a chicken
> Than to say with truth, "But I'm a *good* girl,"
> And Meet his Challenge with a last firm strange
> Uncomprehending smile; and—then, then!—see
> The blind date that has stood you up: your life.
> (For all this, if it isn't, perhaps, life,
> Has yet, at least, a language of its own
> Different from the books'; worse than the books'.)
> And yet, the ways we miss our lives are life.
> Yet . . . yet . . .
> to have one's life add up to *yet*! (18)

The girl will turn into the woman, beating those eggs into a cake, and being teased by the beater into momentary rebelliousness, into saying "life is not life." Yet "the ways we miss our lives are life," a further truth to which the only response is "Yet . . . yet . . . to have one's life add up to *yet*!"

In the long perspective we see that Jarrell's aim as a poet was importantly similar to his practice as a critic, since he attempted—and succeeded, mainly in the poems from his last book—to work himself into situations where he stood before "life." Such life might be exhibited in a poem by Frost or Whitman; in the poetry it is more often than not embodied in the figure of a woman at the stove or a girl in a library. Confronted with life, the poet finds that words fail him, almost; he comes to the limits of his language, of mere poetry, and yet. . . . And yet this condition of awe, admiration, sadness, speechlessness, is achieved only after and through intensely playful sequences like the lovely description of the husband ("a tired spirit") coming home at close of day and wiping his feet on the mat marked Women and Children First; or like the physical education major in the library whose spiritual innocence has a good deal of physical and vocal ballast:

> This is a waist the spirit breaks its arm on.
> The gods themselves, against you, struggle in vain.
> The broad low strong-boned brow; these heavy eyes;
> These calves, grown muscular with certainties;
> This nose, three medium-sized pink strawberries
> —But I exaggerate. In a little you will leave:
> I'll hear, half squeal, half shriek, your laugh of greeting—

> Then, *decrescendo*, bars of that strange speech
> In which each sound sets out to seek each other,
> Murders its own father, marries its own mother,
> And ends as one grand transcendental vowel. (15)

Remembering that Jarrell the critic once spoke of Wallace Stevens's poems as transcendental, all too transcendental études, one hears once more, in the crack about the vowels of the girl's speech, the clever epigrammatist. But in his poetry Jarrell learned to control that ready wit, or rather to direct it into verbal play where the effect was one of strangeness, of opening up into something hitherto undisclosed, discovered at a dramatic moment in the poem—instead of closing down the hatches with a killer line.

An effect of this sort is what distinguishes a poem short enough to quote entirely and perhaps providing a test case for separating those whose admiration for his poetry is extreme, and those less enthusiastic. Here is "Aging":

> I wake, but before I know it it is done,
> The day, I sleep. And of days like these the years,
> A life is made. I nod, consenting to my life.
> . . . But who can live in these quick-passing hours?
> I need to find again, to make a life,
> A child's Sunday afternoon, the Pleasure Drive
> Where everything went by but time; the Study Hour
> Spent at a desk, with folded hands, in waiting.
>
> In those I could make. Did I not make in them
> Myself? The Grown One whose time shortens,
> Breath quickens, heart beats faster, till at last
> It catches, skips. . . . Yet those hours that seemed, were endless
> Were still not long enough to have remade
> My childish heart: the heart that must have, always
> To make anything of anything, not time,
> Not time but—
>   but, alas! eternity. (234)

The sad joke on which this poem turns is of course the notion, in its double sense, of "making a life." A life is made, alas, by living, by opening the oven door once more and putting in the cake. But "to find again, to make a life" is something else again, a matter for eternity rather than time. In this poem, the Pleasure Drive, the Study Hour, are just capitalized stabs at such a making, though they suggest how strong the current of nostalgia ran in Jarrell's sensibility. One remembers the final stanza from a little poem titled aptly, "In Those Days":

> How poor and miserable we were,
> How seldom together!

> And yet after so long one thinks:
> In those days everything was better. (230)

Everything was better, everything seemed, *was* endless, in places like the pleasure drive or study hall, because they so irrevocably belong to those days and are so indisputably not these days here now, through which the Grown One too-quickly passes.

Jarrell's nostalgia I see not as a debilitating limitation, an "immaturity," but as his special gift or curse, a unique way of making a life. There is a beautiful instance of such making in the poem "The Lost Children" in which a woman watches her grown-up daughter show the daughter's husband pictures of her childhood from the photograph album the woman has kept:

> He enjoys them
> And makes fun of them. I look too
> And I realize the girl in the matching blue
> Mother-and-daughter dress, the fair one carrying
> The tin lunch box with the half-pint thermos bottle
> Or training her pet duck to go down the slide
> Is lost just as the dark one, who is dead, is lost.
> But the world in which the two wear their flared coats
> And the hats that match, exists so uncannily
> That, after I've seen its pictures for an hour,
> I believe in it: the bandage coming loose
> One has in the picture of the other's birthday,
> The castles they are building, at the beach for asthma.
> I look at them and all the old sure knowledge
> Floods over me, when I put the album down
> I keep saying inside: "I *did* know those children.
> I braided those braids. I was driving the car
> The day that she stepped in the can of grease
> We were taking to the butcher for our ration points.
> I *know* those children. I know all about them.
> Where are they?" (302)

As "all the old sure knowledge" floods over her, she rises to passionate insistence: in those days everything was better, even if the thing was a can of grease and a trip to the butcher's, because of the intensity with which it can now be known, held absolutely in imagination.

This is the nostalgic's reward, and Jarrell's poetry often plays with the way in which it does and doesn't constitute a reward. In the final poem from *The Lost World* volume, the fifty-year-old bearded poet, revisiting Los Angeles where he grew up, finds that "Back in Los Angeles, we missed / Los Angeles," finds that he can't find the bow and arrows he used to wield, or his crystal set, or his mother's dark blue Buick—all those things that made up what he calls "The Gay Twenties": "But it's all right: they *were* gay, / O so gay! A certain number of years after, Any time is

Gay. . . ." Finally the rememberer of things past contemplates his own present condition:

> When my hand drops to the wheel,
> It is brown and spotted, and its nails are ridged
> Like Mama's. Where's my own hand? My smooth
> White bitten-fingernailed one? I seem to see
> A shape in tennis shoes and khaki riding-pants
> Standing there empty-handed; I reach out to it
> Empty-handed, my hand comes back empty,
> And yet my emptiness is traded for its emptiness,
> I have found that Lost World in the Lost and Found
> Columns whose gray illegible advertisements
> My soul has memorized world after world:
> LOST—NOTHING. STRAYED FROM NOWHERE. NO REWARD
> I hold in my own hands, in happiness,
> Nothing: the nothing for which there's no reward. (338)

It is the wit which saves this touching passage from mawkishness, but a more gently rueful wit than is usually encountered in the sharp edges of his criticism.

The interesting thing about this poem—"Thinking of the Lost World"—and what gives it the distinctive Jarrell accent, is the way it insists on ending in happiness, in the sense of loss made radiant and serene. From its beginnings the notion of loss had informed his poetry; an earlier 1948 book was titled *Losses*; the war poems, whose excellence and rareness only become apparent after repeated exposure to them—are full of it. His last volume, *The Lost World*, has as its opening poem the unforgettable "Next Day" in which a middle-aged woman confronts what she has become. As the shopboy puts her groceries in the car, she notices that he does not notice her, and she realizes that

> Now I am good.
> The last mistaken,
> Ecstatic, accidental bliss, the blind
>
> Happiness that, bursting, leaves upon the palm
> Some soap and water—
> It was so long ago, back in some Gay
> Twenties, Nineties, I don't know . . . Today I miss
> My lovely daughter
> Away at school, my sons away at school,
>
> My husband away at work—I wish for them.

People tell her she is fortunate, still young-seeming, exceptional, and she admits it:

> I *am* exceptional;
> I think of all I have.

> But really no one is exceptional,
> No one has anything, I'm anybody,
> I stand beside my grave
> Confused with my life, that is commonplace and solitary.
>
> (280)

Again the standing before life; the revelation (in Stevens's words) of "Nothing that is not there and the nothing that is" is given fresh truth by Jarrell's chilling line "No one has anything, I'm anybody," and the final descent into silence as the poem ends. Although superficially "Next Day" ends in an unhappy manner, unlike the final "Thinking of the Lost World" where the speaker holds in his own hands, "in happiness / Nothing," the poems are alike fortifying and consolatory in their effect. After reading a poem by Lowell or Berryman one may say, what an impressive performance, what a daring improvisation. With Jarrell (and here he is more like Bishop at her best) the figure the poem makes is less interesting (think how typographically nondescript and formless Jarrell's poems usually look on the page) than the illusion of life it creates and illuminates.

In this sense Jarrell is an old-fashioned poet, for all the originality with which he uses ordinary American language, and in this sense he resembles the Frost about whom he wrote so brilliantly. The Frost Jarrell most admired—although he paid tribute to many sorts of Frostian poems—was the one present in the dramatic narratives and dialogues of *North of Boston*, and occasionally thereafter in *Mountain Interval* and *New Hampshire*. He was particularly fascinated, even obsessed, by "Home Burial," "A Servant to Servants," "The Witch of Coös"—poems in which long-hidden secrets finally get expressed in order that life can be confronted in the full lostness of its losses. In a long and rich interview with the poet in 1959, he keeps pushing Frost to talk about these narratives, about the fact that their speakers are frequently women, and what difference that makes to the whole experience. At one point Frost says it may have something to do with his sense that "the woman always loses" and "the man comes out on top." But then Frost goes on, as if a further thought had struck him, by saying that "She loses in a strange way—she pulls the whole thing down with her." Maybe something like this happens in "Home Burial"; but in Jarrell's own poetry possessing or being possessed by the lost world is, finally, what "the whole thing"—what life—amounts to.

In a somewhat confusing earlier poem of his, "Seele im Raum" (about a woman who for years had imagined an eland at her dinner, taking its meals with her, her husband and children), the woman, when eventually the eland is no longer there, comes to ask the ultimate question about herself:

> Is my voice the voice
> Of that skin of being—of what owns, is owned

> In honor or dishonor, that is borne and bears—
> Or of that raw thing, the being inside it
> That has neither a wife, a husband, nor a child
> But goes at last as naked from this world
> As it was born into it—

And she is granted, at the end of the poem, the answer from within which says

> in a voice
> Rich with a kind of longing satisfaction:
> "To own an eland! That's what I call life!" (39)

Jarrell's own madness, his "nervous breakdown" for which he was hospitalized for three months, came in February of 1965, the final year of his life. Just before it happened, according to Mary Jarrell his wife, "he was granted a few magic weeks of Lisztian virtuosity when nothing in his lectures or readings was veiled to him any longer. Everything his heart desired seemed possible to him." She says that "poems flew at him," "until just words beat at his head like many wings." Other magical things happened; a devotee of pro football, he finally met and talked to Johnny Unitas. Then came the ordeal, then a seeming recovering, as he resumed teaching in the fall, then the sudden death in October, struck down by a car. But I like to think that sometime in that last year he was granted, in extreme vision or on the manic side of breakdown, a sense of the oneness of poetry and life, too heady to be lived with for very long.

In the posthumously published poem, "A Man Meets a Woman in the Street," which I presume to have been written during that time, the focus or vehicle of this sense of oneness is a woman, followed by the narrator in a New York City street, and provoking him to meditation on things ranging from Proust's Swann, to Madame Schumann-Heink, to Strauss's *Elektra* and Shakespeare's *Midsummer Night's Dream*, to Proust's Bergotte, to Greta Garbo listening to a joke about McGillicuddy and McGillivray, finally to the birds he'd heard that morning, back home in the country, and how as the birds played their daily piece

> I wished as men wish: "May this day be different!"
> The birds were wishing, as birds wish—over and over,
> With a last firmness, intensity, reality—
> "May this day be the same!" (352)

But as the poem proceeds to its close, the man walks faster and reaches out to touch the woman, finding not "the nothing for which there's no reward" but something else, only attainable it seems on the threshold, at the last moment of a poetic career:

> Because, after all, it *is* my wife
> In a new dress from Bergdorf's, walking toward the park.
> She cries out, we kiss each other, and walk arm in arm

Through the sunlight that's much too good for New York,
The sunlight of our own house in the forest.
Still, though, the poor things need it . . . We've no need
To start out on Proust, to ask each other about Strauss.
We first helped each other, hurt each other, years ago.
After so many changes made and joys repeated,
Our first bewildered, transcending recognition
Is pure acceptance. We can't tell our life
From our wish. Really I began this day
Not with a man's wish: "May this day be different,"
But with the birds' wish: "May this day
Be the same day, the day of my life." (353)

Notes

1. Robert Lowell, Peter Taylor, and Robert Penn Warren, eds., *Randall Jarrell, 1914–1965* (New York: Farrar, Straus & Giroux, 1967), hereafter cited by page number in the text.

2. Randall Jarrell, *Kipling, Auden & Co.* (New York: Farrar, Straus & Giroux, 1980), p. 151.

3. Geoffrey Hartman, *Criticism in the Wilderness* (New Haven: Yale Univ. Press, 1980), p. 199.

4. Randall Jarrell, *Poetry and the Age* (New York: Vintage Books, 1955), pp. 229–30.

5. *Poetry and the Age*, p. 115.

6. *Poetry and the Age*, p. 119.

7. *Poetry and the Age*, p. 58.

8. *Poetry and the Age*, p. 125.

9. *Poetry and the Age*, pp. 71–72.

10. *Poetry and the Age*, p. 71.

11. *Poetry and the Age*, p. 73.

12. *Poetry and the Age*, p. 80.

13. *Poetry and the Age*, p. 82.

14. *Poetry and the Age*, p. 86.

15. *Poetry and the Age*, pp. 66–67.

16. *Poetry and the Age*, p. 21.

17. R. P. Blackmur, "Examples of Wallace Stevens," *Form and Value in Modern Poetry* (New York: Doubleday Anchor Books, 1957), p. 188.

18. *Poetry and the Age*, p. 41.

19. *Poetry and the Age*, p. 41.

20. *Poetry and the Age*, p. 43.

21. Randall Jarrell, *The Complete Poems* (New York: Farrar, Straus & Giroux, 1969), p. 328; hereafter cited by page number in the text.

The Poetry

The Dramatic Lyrism
of Randall Jarrell

Parker Tyler*

What psychology calls *projection* exists as *poetry* in Randall Jarrell to a high degree. When, in the very playful and charmingly offhand *Deutsch Durch Freud*, published in *Poetry* for December, 1950, but not included in his new book [*The Seven-League Crutches*], he says:

> . . . I am the log
> The fairies left one morning in my place,

it is, no less than a lyric, a dramatic, statement; it is no mere metaphoric analogy but the serious indication of a magical occurrence. Why? Because of the character of wood as a symbol given over and over in Mr. Jarrell's books. It is the substance of the forest which legend calls the Sacred Wood, famous in Frazer as the archetypal Nemi. The poem *In the Ward: The Sacred Wood* (from *Little Friend, Little Friend*) identifies it through the hallucination of a delirious soldier in the hospital: his imposed suffering is sacred; he is the anointed, sacrificed god. Of course, the soldier as the ritual sacrifice is a theme with which readers of Mr. Jarrell are very familiar, but this element of his poetic insight cannot be properly valued without considering the substance of the magic "log."

Alchemically—to be historical about it—this "log" contains the traditional metaphysical idea of the philosopher's stone which was supposed to transmute all elements to gold, and with Mr. Jarrell—to be simple about it—the log is the gold of poetry. It has in it, as we find in *The Märchen* (from *Losses*), awful "Necessity" itself. And the following two lines from that poem state the mythic-historic status of the Frazerian wood as though it were unalterable:

> Invulnerable to any power—the Necessity
> Men spring from, die under: the unbroken wood.

The Nemian wood, where the aspirant to Diana's priesthood broke off the "golden bough" to equip himself for mortal combat with the incumbent, is thus, in Mr. Jarrell's sight, an image of the world: it is the scene of all

*Reprinted from *Poetry*, 79 (1952). 335–46. Copyright 1952 by The Modern Poetry Association. Reprinted by permission of the editor of *Poetry*.

action and the essential meaning of the battlefield. It is where Mr. Jarrell soliloquizes and writes his poetry; it is a dramatic concept whose multiple-Hamlet he is, and which he is magically equipped to know because he is part of its substance: "the log the fairies left."

Assuredly, the log is also a sword, as the bough is a weapon of combat, and the bomb likewise. There is a Browning-motif in Mr. Jarrell's work: the "I" (whether literally or not in the first-person) that speaks in the poet's place. In this device we have the perspective of the magic substitution just mentioned. Mr. Jarrell the dramatic lyrist, as his books have continuously told us, possesses three chief personalities: the soldier, the child, and the fairy prince. How marvellously such poems as *The Child of Courts, Moving,* and *The Truth*—the first two from *Losses,* the last from the present book—prestidigitate a child's *within* to Mr. Jarrell's speech! According to the Sleeping-Beauty legend as found in *The Seven-League Crutches,* the prince is given a magic sword and in conquering the forest of thorns and arriving at the enchanted castle and its sleeping princess, he lays the sword between her and himself, and stretching himself beside her, becomes, rather than awaken her with a kiss, part of her lasting enchantment. It is Mr. Jarrell's princely "variation" with closely related legends, such as Tristram-and-Iseult, in mind. The poem is as lovely and fragile as the dust covering everything in the castle: its theme is explicitly the acceptance of death through a negation, or anticlimax, of the sword's mortal—and here sexual—power: the prince releases the original drop of blood poised on the princess finger into, as it were, final non-existence. And their divine union in endless time is unmistakeable:

> When the world ends—it will never end—
> The dust at last will fall from your eyes
> In judgment, and I shall whisper:
> "For hundreds of thousands of years I have slept
> Beside you, here in the last long world
> That you had found; that I have kept."

He has kept it because he is the poet, too. The wood is essentially the same enchanted one as that at Nemi, and the sword (in its numerous magic variations) is the Golden Bough of sacred office. In Mr. Jarrell's sight, as his books have told us, it is automatically put in every soldier's hand. And not wholly in irony, in *Eighth Air Force* (from *Losses*), did he project himself into a "Pilate" who unfalteringly exonerates his comrade "murderers."

To the poet, gold—the gold of utterance—is often dim because of the immeasurable distances through which he sees. One notes the connection between "the poor, bleak, guessing haze of dawn" from his earlier work and this from *Losses*:

> But at evening the poor light, far-off, fantastic—
> Sun of misers and of mermen, the last foolish gold
> Of soldiers wandering through the country with a
>   crutch—

Anent "mermen" we can go forward to the present book with its variation on the Ondine legend in *A Soul*, and anent "misers" we can go back, and inversely, to the ironic devastation of the first-person capitalist in *Money*, from *Losses*, and refer further to *The Märchen*, from which the above lines come, for a different image of the capitalist, "gorged Hänsel," the perpetual father who witnesses "How many ages boiled Christ's bark for soup!" One is likely, too, to stumble on these ritual versions of wood. The same poem has its way of telling us that the Ark as well as the Cross is part of Mr. Jarrell's philosopher's "wood." The substance, in its actual phases, is converted to many uses; for example, till metal contemporaneously replaced it, to make crutches: the mainstay of mutilated soldiers. Mr. Jarrell thinks of the victim, the scapegoat as the important actor in his wood, Hänsel *the son*, who in real life and in the mass is usually so passive. We witness the haunting pervasiveness of the scapegoat-image for Mr. Jarrell in that so distinctively moving poem—swept by the tragedy of the commonplace—*Burning the Letters*. The dead soldier's surviving wife thinks:

> The dying God, the eaten Life
> Are the nightmare I awaken from to night.

Thus, Mr. Jarrell projects himself not merely into his dying comrade, as so eloquently he has shown he could do, but also into that comrade's wife. Astoundingly, he is at the woman's center—which is, as we learn from the lines just given, the center of the Sacred Wood, where the dead, the "defeated," have a claim prior to the living, the "victorious."

Mr. Jarrell is always *at the center* in the way that the substance of the forest is the pivotal wood of the single tree. As it is the single tree that matters, the wood stands for *original substance*, and we find in Mr. Jarrell's poetry, brimmingly, that the substance matters much more than the magic implementation, the sword or the bough or the bomb, which hacks, bludgeons or dismembers. Metaphysically, the wood remains "unbroken" (see the above-quoted lines) because it is *the poetic or "sevenleague" faculty of the crutches*. And it remains, in *A Description of Some Confederate Soldiers*, realistically as the sentinel laurel trees even though Necessity has "instructed and destroyed an age."

Hänsel's devices to overcome the unknown labyrinth of the forest, the pebbles and the crumbs, availed him nothing. He was trapped, absorbed by the forest, and achieved his ordeal and escape with the help of his sister, Gretel. Maintaining the background of the Eucharist ritual, Mr. Jarrell's magic is to become, not Grimm's little hero, but a child who knows the story and who, as in *A Quilt-Pattern* from the present book, conceives it in terms of his own experience. In Grimm's child-flattering story, the little protagonists outwit the strategy of their parents and their parents' surrogate, the witch of the woods, and become—in the exemplary fable—the saviors of their own and their male parent's fortunes (that ethical scapegoat, the evil stepmother, obligingly having died). But notice Mr. Jarrell's pun: the poem is too a *guilt*-pattern, where "All the graves of the forest / Are opened," and an image of "the dead mother" appears. "Good me, bad me" speaks, and because the child listener or reader *always* imagines Hänsel actually roasting in the oven, the boy thinks of himself, washed by his mother in the tub, as "basted." The poem verifies, to a spectacular degree, many insights of Freud while emerging "unbroken" in its own intuition and formal achievement.

An attentive and thoroughgoing reader of Mr. Jarrell's four books may reach, it seems to me, but one conclusion: his transmuting or projective faculties carry with them much in tradition and much in the poetry of contemporaries without in the least suggesting these poems are not the poet's own. Some facet of another's work is constantly being caught by Mr. Jarrell's active light and, as it were, automatically registered: the poem, the course of the thought, remains integral. Mr. Jarrell has built the physique of his verse with help from, conspicuously, Hart Crane, T. S. Eliot, Allen Tate, and John Crowe Ransom. But a measure of his magic of transmutation lies in the beautiful, complete English manner of his version of Tristan Corbière's *The Contrary Poet*, included in the present book. Probably just because of the magic of his attitude, he learned to move fluently and expertly among what he found around him. The wand—the "seven-league" capacity of the crutches—is his, and we know it well from the webbiness of many poems, their structure as of a labyrinth of which only the poet can claim the organic secret. Such silken poems as *The Black Swan* and *The Sleeping Beauty: Variation of the Prince* (both in the new volume) seem made of spider's rope: their strength is in their bend and their minute, invisible links.

This fragility does not prevent Mr. Jarrell from being a poet of the chthonic depths, but on the contrary is a way of confirming that very situation of the poet-magician-soldier's *katabasis*: the journey that, even as Orpheus' archetypal journey, is reversed. The soldier returns; the poet returns; the child and the symbol return. If Mr. Jarrell's projection is a dramatic lyrism, if he makes up many poems and songs as on the lips of others and even disappears (as he could do in that dreadfully concise poem) with the final remains of a ball-turret gunner, still the curious connection between the speaker and the person identified with can be imperceptibly adjusted, in the reading, to the entirely private; somehow, but certainly, the poet does as Orpheus did: returns to *himself*. And suggestively the orientation of the new book is toward the subjective, a fact concretely illustrated by *A Soul*, where love becomes that of the body for its own soul. Or, most significantly, in *La Belle au Bois Dormant*, the hideous incident of a female corpse in an unclaimed trunk in a railway station becomes an unravelling of the person's inward depths. Mr. Jarrell teaches us not to overlook the *distant* gold of the bough. When the lines say of the corpse that "she coils breathlessly inside his wish," the unidentified third-person masculine becomes inseparably the speaker of the lines and the fairy prince; not merely because "the thorns clamber up her stone veins" (perhaps she is the statue of an Abstraction) but because she lies in a "trunk," which, owing to the possibility of a pun with tree-trunk, is of wood and therefore Mr. Jarrell's familiar magic. The poem's title tells us that the trunk is the enchanted wood, which here has at least three concentric layers: Mr. Jarrell is at the very center—he has projected himself *into* the trunk with its secret of the missing person. He desires what is there ("alas! not beautiful") if only because he knows it waits to be awakened. It is *her* wish and *his* wish. So the poem says. The second layer is therefore love of person for person. The third is the most enigmatic, but I, for one, sense it. Is it an abortion of Truth, Justice, or Freedom—some clairvoyant, ruined image in the blood of modern man?

The present book shows that Mr. Jarrell's themes tend to haunt him and he plays with them as he plays ambivalently with the mythified yet intimate figure of his great grandmother in *A Rhapsody on Irish Themes*. In *An English Garden in Austria*, Europe itself materializes out of the capital-R of "these ruins, your Ruin." And *Hohensalzburg: Fantastic Variations on a Theme of Romantic Character* blends the Sleeping-Beauty motif with what seems a contemporary amour set in the milieu of Fascist-tempered Europe. Mr. Jarrell's virtuoso form of the soliloquy, in which personality-shift is so smooth, even imperceptible, reflects his encyclopaedism as a modern poet: the reach from the personal and particular to the social and universal. But he returns to his individualism—to the innermost chambers of the spirit. Here there is no "escaping." Grimm's Hänsel escaped. The soldier often does not escape. Modern man does not escape the "guilt-pattern." Mr. Jarrell's Hänsel turns out to be one whose flesh is duly sacrificed. Certainly we are with Hänsel's chthonic internality when we come to the penultimate poem of the present book: *The Venetian Blind*. With his sly, dry wit in puns, Mr. Jarrell signifies the blind as the abiding wood whose abidingness affords light-flecked shade but which also "blinds": misleads, conceals, traps. In this poem

> It is the first day of the world
> Man wakes into: the bars of the blind
> And their key-signature, a leaf,
> Stream darkly to two warmths;
> One trembles, becomes his face. . .

But "He is lost in himself forever." The statement seems stark, irreparable. "The bars of the sunlight fall to his face." He is in the prison of the forest. The poem ends with what Mr. Jarrell has often embodied differently: the cry of the child lost in the woods:

"But where am *I*? But where am *I*?"

However, this cry becomes only *rhetorical* when the poet shows how he completes the *katabasis*. This is, however he goes, going *back* the way he came.

In *The Iceberg*, from Mr. Jarrell's first book, *Blood for a Stranger*, two levels or "depths" of evil were portrayed:

The diver (before he dies) can judge between
The conscious and witty evil of the air,
The witless and helpless evil of the sea.

The former evil is bombing, the latter inert "Necessity," which the poem has just invoked as "great Necessity / Stamped on the blinding faces of the sea." The diver is, of course, both the soldier and the poet. Both, for Mr. Jarrell, seem concerned with nature and necessity in direct symmetrical lines, for in *Siegfried*, from his second book, he spoke of war thus:

It is a dream . . .
It happens as it does because it does.
It is unnecessary to understand. . .

In Nature there is neither right nor left nor wrong.

Neither does the poet, imbedded in nature, escape or "understand." He ("Hänsel") also has his way of not knowing the left turning from the right. In *Deutsch Durch Freud*, Mr. Jarrell may lightly, cynically contrast the "unaesthetic" method of the clinic with the "aesthetic" method of the poem, but he knows very well, and manages to convey in the same poem, that Freud was an apostle of the chthonic depths no less than a doctor, an apostle of the curing light or upper air. It is Freud's late philosophy of the beyond-pleasure principle that Mr. Jarrell unquestionably cites in these lines from *London*, a poem in *Blood for a Stranger*:

. . . man, you must learn to live,
Though you want nothing but to die.

In death itself, as the "prince's variation" helps to tell us, lies a part of Mr. Jarrell's enchanted wood of Necessity. Thus he has designed a beautifully ambiguous irony quite justifying his projection into the killed and the killer, the friend and the enemy (the "stranger"). His basic mechanism for this is the structure invented by Freud: the Super-ego, the Ego, and the Id. Man's life-element and the glory of the poet, the *air*, becomes the sphere of a "conscious and witty evil." It is that of the Ego which invented proud wings and, using them against an enemy, abused the function of the Super-ego. Reinstatement of the latter is the ironic privilege of "the diver" who, by his vertical journey from the air, past the sea-surface, to the depths, may judge between the two evils of ambitious Ego and inert Id. Yet what is the soldier's Necessity, *killing*, what is man's Necessity, *dying*, is the poet's Freedom, *creation*.

Why is it the poet's freedom? Technically, it is because the poet understands *the magic* of the wood. And what *is* the magic of the wood in which killing and crippling reign? It is the symbolic conception of knowledge: all primal knowledge, asserts Mr. Jarrell in more than one way, is obtained through "the aesthetic method"—not conceptually or actually, but intuitively. Children who read, understand vaguely, and then dream or hallucinate their fancies (in *The Night Before the Night Before Christmas* and *A Quilt-Pattern*) say: "I don't know, I don't know, I don't know . . . I don't *know*." And the first poem of *The Seven-League Crutches, The Orient Express*, ends:

> Behind everything there is always
> The unknown unwanted life.

The two adjectives carry here the entire weight of the poet's aesthetic creed. As a motto, the lines account for the spontaneous air of fantasy which saturates so many of Mr. Jarrell's poems—an easy way of speaking metaphorically and colloquially at once—and which, as an insistent *leitmotif*, even invades so "statistical" a poem as *Transient Barracks* whose dormitory chatter is suddenly characterized: "These are. Are what? Are."

Existence comes before *knowledge* because it retains, even after knowledge has arrived, the unknowable that is so often the unpredictable. Everybody, if life is kind, grows old before dying. Yet in *The Face*, from the new book, the poet joins "*die alte Marschallin*" in projecting into the mirror's factual image a primal wonder:

> Here I am.
>   But it's not *right*.
> If just living can do this,
> Living is more dangerous than anything:
>
> It is terrible to be alive.

The simplicity is triumphant. It is the same simplicity with which Mr. Jarrell identified himself as the log and as the prisoner behind the Venetian blind. It is the ultimate *in*-sight of poetry. Therefore, despite the coherent, and certainly often conscious, symbolism of Mr. Jarrell, his poetry remains a "blind" or naively-seeing assertion of existence, whose transparency is altogether illusive. At the same time, we are aware of an abiding, manifest center, a glowing point of self-consciousness, which renders Mr. Jarrell's poetry one of the most mature and rewarding bodies of verse produced in our time. In effect, his is a personal mystery that halts at the outer margin of a complex device such as Orestes' sacrifice (in contradiction of the legend) by his priestess-sister in *Orestes at Tauris* and takes wing toward the unassailable, unorientable center of the wood. Here the chthonic poet reigns over his triune realm of Sleep-Dream-Death.

Though the wood appears in many forms, its mercuriality retains an alchemic secrecy. As the sacred image of Diana, goddess of the woods and the hunt, which Orestes (according to fable) brought back from Tauris, it seems closest to Mr. Jarrell's own myth: the flesh of an untouchable virgin. Yet we must not underrate the dramatic lyrism which is, rather than the complex symbolism, the more negotiable aspect of this poet's enchanted realm of personality. In his work, the forest appears over and over as the child's vision of loss and strangeness; it is, as in *New Georgia* from *Losses*, the conscious mirage of cell-bars derived from tree-branches; it is the actual material of crutches and of rabbit cages, and in this image from *Loss*, the poem-unit from the volume *Losses*, it is the evanescent stuff of metaphor:

> Bird of the spray, the tree of bones:

Nor should we forget that the forest implies the sun and the stars, the water, the animal, and the bird—that, in Mr. Jarrell's own poetry, Hänsel's "white cat eats up his white pigeon" and still is only the illusion made by moonlight on the chimney.

The final interpretation of Mr. Jarrell's dramatic lyrism is that the single tree projects itself into the forest and *is* the forest—in various particulars and in the mass—and is the ontology, the scene of all action, which I mentioned at the beginning. So the unique poetic substance attains the other (objective, social, general) half of its dupartite freedom: its *katabasis*. To communicate is to reach *through others* to the *self*. Sometimes, in the medium of prose, one encounters Mr. Jarrell, the ax-man, at work upon grown-up reputations. Then the wood has become the inimical "bough" of the fervid aspirant to the priesthood. That destructive implementation on which the poet has spent so much irony and so much pathos has triumphed in another symbolic form of knowledge: criticism. And thus we have the other "face" of the chthonic poet: the rational man whose encyclopaedic intelligence beats off rivals for the sacred office. The very substance, the intrinsic "wood," as precious indeed as gold, must always contain this *critic*, or Super-ego, which decides when and how and into whom the poetry (and the blade) shall be projected. Mr. Jarrell's poetic consciousness as Hänsel, the son and victim, is complemented by his poetic consciousness as Hänsel, the father and victor—and judge. The basic measure of his achievement as literary artist is that, whatever happens in the poems, he is also, incessantly and musically, the mere air moving in the branches. He knows, this user of the seven-league crutches, that *this* is poetry.

But the poet himself is flesh; and Hamlet was, too. In this flesh, *katabasis* is also *katharsis*. And there reëchoes in our awareness of Mr. Jarrell's body of work—the transparent alley of his arborealness—the ideal of the ancient Greek stage. Possibly no poet of all time has submitted himself more purely to the purge of the flesh's will and the flesh's guilt than Mr. Jarrell in the war experiences reflected by his three earlier books, *Blood for a Stranger; Little Friend, Little Friend*; and *Losses*. It is a performance at once infinitely modest and irrepressibly pyrotechnic. The bright shadow of the Aeschylean "Prometheus" hovers about such poems in the new book as *Jonah* and *The Island*, the latter a brilliantly handled monologue of Robinson Crusoe toward the end of his life. Both Robinson and Jonah had set out in (wooden) boats, and in Mr. Jarrell's poem Jonah holds his dialogue with God from inside a gourd in which dry leaves "rattle." It is the sacred sound—and to search in Mr. Jarrell's continuously gratifying pages for elements of the ritual rebirth and ritual resurrection in wood is to come out richly laden, even if it is to come out through *Terms*, in the latest book, with an amputee veteran whose arm and leg, literally having substituted wood for their first substance, have already begun to build his future coffin around the living man.

Randall Jarrell's World of War

Richard Fein*

I

War, in the poetry of Randall Jarrell, is a masquerade of experience in general, the catastrophes and disasters of war being violent and symbolic extensions of what it simply means to be alive. Constantly confronted by that maze of experience which is permanently threatening, his people are the common and helpless victims of war. And if they strive for awareness of their plight, they are usually left only with a frustrating self-knowledge. To the persons of Jarrell's world, experience is like a dream; the world is a place where they are lost like frightened children. It is this theme of entrapment, this perennial and wistful sense of unfulfillment, of being lost, which dominates the character of his poetry. The detachment of the individual experience of war from the public slogans and the isolation of the private suffering from what the state demands and history acknowledges produce for the persons of Jarrell's poetry an unrelenting and usually helpless exposure to the realities of war and enforce the awareness that the ragged activities of war are knitted to the soiled fabric of overall experience.

In such poems as "Siegfried," "Losses," "The Sick Nought," "Pilots, Man Your Planes" and "The Learners," Jarrell takes a soldier through wounds, fears, deaths, in order that the soldier will know that he has undergone some basic suffering because of which he can no longer deny not only the horrors and bitterness of war but the harshness of human personality and culture as well. No soldiers mature as quickly and as irreparably as do Jarrell's wounded Siegfrieds. Through their wounds they bleed their innocence. Yet it is a striking paradox of Jarrell's poetry, and probably an expression of his own ultimately sardonic conception of freedom and human effort, that despite those poems which persist in a confrontation of the realities, all that awareness comes up with in the end is the knowledge of its own ineffectuality, the knowledge that perceives the blind alley in which it gropes. This theme of ultimate frustration is most

*Reprinted from *Analects* 1, No. 2 (Spring 1961), 14–23, by permission of the author.

obviously dramatized in the poems about war prisoners and the war dead and suffuses those poems in which Jarrell expresses pity and sympathy for all the human flotsam and jetsam drenched in war.

Losses, which contains most of the poems about war prisoners and the war dead, is an immersion in compassion. The poems in *Losses* alone express pity and sympathy for American prisoners of war in Germany, American Army criminals, Jews in concentration camps (both in Germany and Cyprus), wounded American soldiers, dead American and Japanese soldiers, and the families of dead soldiers, Japanese as well as American. Darkness, death, prison-like experiences, the sense of entrapment—this is the atmosphere that pervades military life to the point that Jarrell's poetry about prisoners and the war dead and wounded is really about what it means to be alive. Jarrell conceives of imprisonment in some broad sense, as the touchstone of experience in general. Yet the pity for those who helplessly suffer in war, this compassion for what the poet sees as almost inevitable and unredeemed suffering, also threatens to become the beaten shape of its own awareness, which is unflinching and relentless in the grief it exposes.

It is not only that one wonders what good is it to break through old habits and standard perceptions if the result is only a recognition of one's helplessness in the face of experience. But, in his pity for the helplessness of men and their struggle to become aware—aware of that helplessness—Jarrell subverts the nature of awareness for the persons who speak in his poems and exploits his characters as objects of his own recurrent understanding of man's ineffectuality. And thus what occurs in the poems is a posturing, through the characters, of the plight of man according to the Jarrell view, which although not altogether irrelevant and never superficial, results not in the characters speaking for themselves but in their becoming attached to what Jarrell must force them to see, to what Jarrell obliges them to understand. He sometimes treats his characters as intelligences which must be forcefully directed toward self-understanding of helplessness.

Jarrell pushes into the mind of the hobbling "Siegfried":

> If, standing irresolute
> By the whitewashed courthouse, in the leafy street,
> You look at the people who look back at you, at home,
> And it is different, different—you have understood
> Your world at last: you have tasted your own blood.

He points a finger at the recuperating soldier in "The Sick Nought":

> Surely your one theory, to live,
> Is nonsense to the practice of the centuries
> What is demanded in the trade of states
> But lives, but lives?—the one commodity.
> To sell the lives we were too poor to use,

> To lose the lives we were too weak to keep—
> This was our peace, this was our war.

He scrutinizes the shot-down pilot in "Pilots, Man Your Planes:"

>   the pilot,
> Drugged in the blanket, straining up to gulp
> From the mug that scrapes like chalk against his mouth,
> Knows, knows at last; he yawns the chattering yawn
> Of effort and anguish, of hurt hating helplessness—
> Yawns sobbingly, his head falls back, he sleeps.

Is there not an apostrophizing in these lines, a nervous tendency to at-titudinize toward those who are suffering? The repetitions register Jarrell's intrusion on the turmoil of the persons in the poems. In this concentration on the sad, the pathetic, the painful, one feels, despite the relevance of Jarrell's observations to contemporary experiences and the depth of his orientation, an overindulgence, an immersion in suffering that seems extended beyond necessity. Ironically, Jarrell as writer finds his art restricted by his importunate sympathy no less than his characters are cornered by their experience.

"Burning the Letters" is one of the most intensive efforts in all of Jarrell's war poetry to break through the patterns that surround either the speaker or one whom the poet is thinking of. Once a Christian, the widow of a dead pilot must struggle to release herself from the memory of her husband; she prepares to burn his letters in the effort to repossess her life; she is the phoenix who must rise out of the ashes of his letters, her old identity. The woman in this poem is like the widow in Robert Lowell's "The Mills of the Kavanaughs" and the meditative lounger in Wallace Stevens' "Sunday Morning." In each case the woman is alone and must in-dividually work through the burdens of her experience and loss. In each of these poems religious experience is brought down to an almost personally pagan level. In their loss these women must find new religious meanings.

Jarrell tries to center "Burning the Letters" in the consciousness of this young widow, but the poem is also subject to Jarrell's "pushing" into the mind of the woman:

> In its savage figures—worn down, now, to death—
> Man's one life issues, neither out of earth
> Nor from the sea, the last dissolving sea,
> But out of death: by man came death
> And his life wells from death, the death of Man.
>
>   In the darkness—darker
> With the haunting after-images of light—
> The dying God, the eaten Life
> Are the nightmare I awaken from to night.
>   O death of all my life,

Because of you, because of you, I have not died,
By your death I have lived.
                                Here in my head
There is room for your black body in its shroud
The dog-tags welded to your breastbone, and the flame
That winds above your death and my own life
And the world of my life. The letters and the face
That stir still, sometimes, with your fiery breath—
Take them, O grave! Great grave of all my years,
The unliving universe in which all life is lost,
Make yours the memory of that accepting
And accepted life whose fragments I cast here.

Even though the religious declamations have a tendency to go beyond the situation of the poem (sometimes the widow seems to be reciting from Frazer), the reader can still be caught up in her struggle, her memory of the sinking ship, her looking at her husband's old picture, her returning to and now discarding the "poor labored answers," "the faded questions"—all these do pull us into the sphere of *her* suffering. Yet there is a disturbing tendency toward declaiming in all these passages, Jarrell tends to intrude his dogged awareness, his persistent knowledge, and to suffocate the particulars of this woman. We are involved in the woman's plight and are also forced to pursue Jarrell's understanding and perception of her dilemma. But while we know her situation through her words and her voice, sometimes nevertheless we have the impression they are imposed from above rather than coming from within the poem, from within the woman's consciousness. Of course in some sense, the poet always speaks through his character, but he must avoid expropriation of her consciousness. The problem is twofold. Technically, the voice of Jarrell tends to replace the voice of the woman. His understanding tends to replace or dominate the consciousness of the character who is thereby deprived, in some basic sense, of a will or life of her own. Jarrell is insistent, overly so, that his people, his characters, be equipped only with the understanding that Jarrell perceives, thereby limiting the ability of the characters who should have their own lives in the poem, even though it is the artist who constructs their consciousness in the first place. Thematically, or philosophically, what is the poet's justification for pushing his people into self-knowledge if time and time again the effort only leads to the knowledge that reads its own doom and defeat? Jarrell at one and the same time incites and defeats his characters. The woman who burns the letters makes a strenuous effort to surmount the pattern. Jarrell's sympathy and awareness are both engaging and frustrating. The technical problem of the poet's voice replacing the voice of the character in the poem has its origins in the burden of the poet's knowledge. And his persistent inclination to harness his characters to his bleak awareness is at one and the same time a kind of intellectual sentimentality and a significant understanding of the way individuals are cornered in the squares of their experience.

II

This sense of entrapment takes on complex and further forms in Jarrell's war poetry. The confusion in personal and historical direction, a basic theme in Jarrell's first volume, *Blood for a Stranger*, reappears in a distinct way in the war poetry that followed. That failure to find purposeful direction, expressed in the line "The maze where all of us are wandering" from the first volume's "For an Emigrant," is evoked in increasingly despairing and frustrating situations, and the line's image of experience is given further significant metaphorical expression in some of the war poems from Jarrell's second and third volumes. "The Metamorphoses," from *Little Friend, Little Friend*, shows the development of the first volume's basic metaphor—"The wharves were a maze of crated bombers."

The idea of frustrated movement is dramatized in one of the recurrent situations of disaster in Jarrell's war poetry, the flier's inability to return to the home base. Both "A Pilot from the Carrier" and "Pilots, Man Your Planes" are about pilots who are shot down and cannot return to their carrier, and in "A Front" the bomber crashes while trying to land at the fogbound airbase. This inability to return home takes on extended meaning in the poetry, as do other situations of the war.

In "A Pilot from the Carrier," the mother ship for the plane is, like the home base in "A Front," inaccessible, beyond the reach of the pilot and the plane. In "Pilots, Man Your Planes," the airplanes flying off, looking for another carrier to replace the one which has been destroyed, are like orphaned birds seeking a new nest, and the scene of the wounded or dying men in the water hanging on "to the lines / Lowered from the old life," the sinking carrier, further suggests that some fundamental haven or base of security has been destroyed. Certain basic imagery in Jarrell's war poetry begins to emerge, along with the themes it conveys.

The uniting of birth and death or childhood and death is also a motif basic to Jarrell's war poetry. In "Mother, Said the Child," the child dies in his mother's arms, and in "Protocols" the child dies in his mother's hug. These poems about deadly parental-child relationships are variations of the plight which is also symbolically expressed in "A Front," with the landing field out of reach of the plane, or in "A Pilot from the Carrier," with the parachuted pilot hanging helplessly over his carrier which cannot help him, or in "Pilots, Man Your Planes," with the carrier inadvertently shooting down its own pilot before it itself sinks. No matter what the situation is, in combat when the plane and base are out of touch, or in a family in which the mother cannot help or save the child, death is received from or cannot be averted by precisely the object or person looked to for support or security. The maze of *Blood for a Stranger* metamorphoses into the network of death and violence of the later war poetry. The war itself in Jarrell's poetry becomes the situation which speaks for the even larger plight of man helpless in this world, torn from any secure footing. The war becomes a violent extension of that maze through which we continually stumble.

The separation-from-mother theme or the mother's inability to protect the child is recurrent in Jarrell's war poetry. Of course this theme is also part of the world of frightening childhood which is familiar in modern literature (though by no means is it a world first introduced in twentieth century literature), and children throughout Jarrell's poetry are hunched in fear. Children in his war poetry not only confirm Jarrell's general poetic presentation of childhood, but they inhabit a world in which their inability to control or understand reflects how adults similarly feel in that same world, or as Auden (whom Jarrell resembles in a number of ways) describes adults in "September 1, 1939":

> Lest we should see where we are,
> Lost in a haunted wood
> Children afraid of the night
> Who have never been happy or good.

Both Jarrell and Auden in referring to children point up not only the fears of childhood but also the nightmare of experience in which adults feel like children. Adults themselves cannot control the world they inhabit, do not understand what is happening to them. This horror in childhood as a reflection of adult experience, in that adults are as frightened as children, makes for some distinction between the children of Jarrell and the children of Dickens. Similarly, Jarrell's world of children differs from Wordsworth's because it is a different world each poet sees himself inhabiting. To grasp the difference between the nature of childhood in Wordsworth's poetry and in Jarrell's poetry one only need compare "We Are Seven" with "The Black Swan." In Wordsworth's ballad the child of course does not count her buried brother and sister as dead. The innocent child does not conceive of death. In Jarrell's poem the child's thoughts, which at times are like nightmares, dwell in fantasies of the dead sister, who is recognized as gone, but whom the child tries to bring back or associate with through her imagination. Perhaps it could be said that the poems are alike in that in both cases the child tries to avoid recognition of death. Yet the bland disregard of the child of "We Are Seven" is in contrast to the frightening and introspective configurations of the mind of the child in "The Black Swan." The very titles connote different worlds. The open dialogue of Wordsworth's poem contrasts with the interior hallucinations of the child in Jarrell's poem.

Children and their nightmares are concerns not only of Jarrell's war poetry. In general, he has a way of bringing into his poetry fairy tales, dreams, and various aspects of children's fantasies. Childhood in Jarrell's poetry is not a particularly pleasant time. His book titles alone bare bizarre and frightening qualities which haunt fairy tales and childhood dreams: "The Rage for the Lost Penny"; *Blood for a Stranger*; *Little Friend, Little Friend*; *Losses*; *The Seven-League Crutches*. But it is perhaps his war poetry which most intensively portrays the horrors of childhood. The refugee poems from his first volume present the child as victim of international aggression and place him in the center of European violence. In some fundamental way for Jarrell, childhood and war (and all that war symbolizes in his poetry) are linked. Through descriptions of the mind of a child or child-like feelings that adults experience, Jarrell gives play to the sense of infinite loss felt by the average dreamy mind which finds itself near abandonment in a world beyond full human possession.

The poem that most compactly presents this theme and unites it with others I have been considering is the brief and final poem from *Little Friend, Little Friend*, "The Death of the Ball Turret Gunner":

> From my mother's sleep I fell into the State,
> And I hunched in its belly till my wet fur froze.
> Six miles from earth, loosed from its dream of life,
> I woke to black flak and the nightmare fighters.
> When I died they washed me out of the turret with
> a hose.

This poem of five lines touches on five themes found throughout Jarrell's war poetry: childhood; the individual manipulated by the State; animal and cold imagery which bears the heartlessness of war; dreams, especially nightmares; and finally, a combination of birth and death.

"The Death of the Ball Turret Gunner" is a compact verse supplement to Jarrell's prose criticism of Marianne Moore's "In Distrust of Merits," which he considers a mistaken notion of the heroism of war, war being less fighting than "passive misery." Actually, the basis of Jarrell's objections to Miss Moore's poem lies in the difference between one who sees war as simply suffering and not the purged way toward peace, and one who sees war as the difficult road toward peace, toward a rebirth of the finer qualities of man. These different reactions to the war are also evident in the poems' different styles, in Jarrell's letting the war demonstrate its own stupidity and cruelty, in Miss Moore's interpolating what the war can mean. What "saves" Miss Moore's poem in Jarrell's view, or at any rate what makes it most pertinent, is her humility, her selfless caring about how the world goes. But her "fighting, fighting, fighting" soldier contrasts with the passive ball turret gunner. While Miss Moore speaks of "those patient dyings" which are teaching the rest of us how to live, Jarrell only notes the stupid passivity of the soldier, whose ignorance of what is happening to him is as indicative of his peace, or that peace he is supposedly dying for, as it is of his war. Jarrell softly chided Miss Moore because "she should have distrusted the peace of which our war is only the extrapolation." Jarrell knows his war, Miss Moore her hopes. "The Death of the Ball Turret Gunner" and "In Distrust of Merits" are polar reactions to the war. Who doubts Jarrell's hold on reality? Who begrudges Miss Moore her hopes? Meanwhile, the ball turret gunner is washed out.

The poem makes its impact in the way it unifies physical death and psychic awakening in a compact combining of stages. There is an awakening to life at the very point of death, as if the very essence of life is to be facing death, particularly during war. In the poem's amalgamation of contrasting experiences, in the combination of death and consciousness, is the awakening and final recognition on the part of the gunner that he exists only to be a victim. The gunner wakes only to know that he was used to die. The compressed demarcation of stages of existence in the poem transforms the life of the ball turret gunner into an assembly line product. From the beginning he is moulded for only one purpose, and all that happens to him is for this public usefulness. His consumption by the war is a fate familiar in Jarrell's poetry where individuals are inevitably destroyed in the public maw.

The gunner's ending is almost literally his beginning. He is flushed out in his wastes on his going as on his entrance. He goes from nothing to nothing, or more accurately, from one blob to another. And the masculine hose accents the poem's striking and appropriate unity of beginning and ending. The poem seems to be bathed in amniotic fluid. In a note on the poem Jarrell remarks that the gunner in the turret "hunched upside down in his little sphere . . . looked like the foetus in the womb." The note confirms what the reader finds for himself.

There is a calmness, almost stolidity, to the poem. The scene, or what is happening, becomes more important than the consciousness that is describing the scene, even though of course it is the gunner who is talking. Yet it is not the careful perception of his experience that finally matters but the way that his mind spills it out, the way his mind reaffirms a line from Jarrell's "Siegfried"—"*It happens as it does because it does.*" Things happen to this hapless warrior, as the verbs indicate: he falls into the State; he is loosed from his dreams; he is awakened. Throughout the poem, forces operate on him. The voice of the poem advances the speaker as a helpless victim. He mumbles like a child. His sentences are short, his syntax simple. The sentences are strung together in an unsophisticated manner which reminds us of a child's speech. The speech increases our sense of the speaker as helpless before his experience. In addition, the gunner "hunched till my wet fur froze" is shaped in a dependent situation; he crouches in his fear like a frightened, defenseless animal. Children throughout Jarrell's poetry hunch and cower in the dark. "The Death of the Ball Turret Gunner" unobtrusively employs many of the motifs and themes common to Jarrell's poetry.

The helplessness of the speaker is clear; it is furthered by the appearances of his speaking from within a dream, or from within a haze. Even the gunner's slipping from a confining position only leads him into a darker and more ominous confinement as he falls out of the mother but into the State. What seems to be an escape is only a *cul-de-sac*. Awakening, or consciousness, is no redemption either. He is "loosed from its dream of life" only to be further immersed in a dream atmosphere where, "I woke to black flak and the nightmare fighters," with its shock effect and bare but aggressive imagery. Consciousness is nightmarish; nor does it advance control over one's own fate. No doubt the dream-like sensations result from the mind's indisposition to fully comprehend and acknowledge its own annihilation. But Jarrell is also referring to man's estrangement in an alien world, in a world he never entirely claims for himself, a world in which something men never understand hangs over their lives—"the black flak and the nightmare fighters."

The familiar theme of the disastrous mother also enters the poem. Here she is associated not only with the home base that cannot be reached alive, but she is also identified with the State, "its belly" referring back to both. Her pregnancy is an implicit death; she gives birth to a stillborn victim of the State. The sexual motif, so prevalent in recent war poetry, is partly explained by the poet's understanding of how creation and nourishment of life turn out to be merely a means for the military and public expenditure of that life. The imagery, throughout Jarrell's war poetry, projects his understanding that the nature of existence is a growing toward disaster, that men are like children hunched in the dark. How doomed and unprotected that gunner who looks like a foetus really is as he is wrapped in the penumbra of disaster! Jarrell's war poetry intends to be a significant measure of the world we inhabit.

"The Death of the Ball Turret Gunner" in itself summarizes and utilizes the major concerns and motifs of Jarrell's war poetry. But here awareness is not superimposed on the mind of the speaker, is not forced upon his consciousness. In some ultimately stupid way the gunner babbles out the nature of his narrow fate, his destiny as victim. And the reaching of this understanding is his attainment of the nature of his doom, which in Jarrell's world is the ironically farthest reach of self-awareness. People in Jarrell's poetry awake to the dark knowledge of their own death, their awareness of being caught in the grip of great forces. Though in some poems the entrapment is expressed in terms of an airbase that cannot be returned to, the essence of experience as frustration is also symbolized in the separation of mother from child, or in the role of mother as purveyor of death to the child. It is also expressed in the identification of the mother with the State, at which point the perverse sexual theme is employed. Jarrell's juxtaposition of sex and war is not thrust upon the reader, as one feels is often the case in modern war poetry. Indeed, passivity is at the center of "The Death of the Ball Turret Gunner" as it quietly utilizes the major themes and motifs of Jarrell's war poetry, as it achieves a blending of tone and idea.

In "The Death of the Ball Turret Gunner" we witness a consciousness that is not subject to the overt manipulations of Jarrell's overriding awareness. The very haze of the scene and the very shroud of the mind of that gunner sitting in the turret convince us of his helplessness without the need for the poet's admonishment to the gunner. The scene and the speaker's tone affirm the gunner's victimized state. "The Death of the Ball Turret Gunner" is at the center of Jarrell's concerns and art. But even in this poem Jarrell is not able to emerge from his persistent theme of entrapment; this he succeeds in doing only in "Eighth Air Force."

III

"Eighth Air Force" traces the effort of the poet to move from a full recognition of man in his act of destruction to the kind of acceptance of man that is difficult to reach and inspiring to see achieved precisely because it does not flinch from recognizing the unpleasant and aggressive qualities of war and human behavior. "Eighth Air Force" registers in full intensity the contradictory nature of man and the burden this imposes on the intelligent spectator who observes and comments on man.

About those who bombed the continent from England, the poem is an effort to redeem these men.

> If, in an odd angle of the hutment,
> A puppy laps the water from a can
> Of flowers and the drunk sergeant shaving
> Whistles O Paradiso!—shall I say that man
> Is not as men have said: a wolf to man?
>
> The other murderers troop in yawning;
> Three of them play Pitch, one sleeps, and one
> Lies counting missions, lies there sweating
> Till even his heart beats: One; One; One.
> O murderers! . . . Still, this is how it's done:
>
> This is a war. . . . But since these play, before they die,
> Like puppies with their puppy; since a man,
> I did as these have done, but did not die—
> I will content the people as I can
> And give up these to them: Behold the man!
>
> I have suffered, in a dream, because of him,
> Many things; for this last savior, man,

I have lied as I lie now. But what is lying?
Men wash their hands, in blood, as best they can:
I find no fault in this just man.

In the very first stanza the dual reference to animals is indicative of the conflict generated within the poem. If violent man is suddenly seen in a pose of peace, can he be forgiven for his bellicosity? But more than that, does he rescue himself from his own violence? This is the dilemma out of which the poem grows. The peacefulness of the first stanza is disarming to the critical intelligence. Even the act of shaving is a civilizing act in contrast with the hirsute beast. But as the first line indicates, this is not the usual scene. And the ancient knowledge that man is wolf to man (which also appears in Miss Moore's "In Distrust of Merits") looms in the mind that observes the unexpected peaceful scene.

As the poem proceeds, the other murderers also relax in unmilitary postures. They try to recover after the violence. The poet knows they are murderers, yet seeing them like this makes him understand how human these men are. He must struggle with what he knows these men have done and with the tenderness and human casualness of the scene before him. The rest of the poem is a moving outward from this dilemma of knowledge and forgiveness. The allusions to the New Testament support the reach toward forgiveness and intensify the medley of violence, suffering and pity which the poet must sort out in his consciousness.

The "I" is a mingling of the poet's voice and a voice (or voices) from the New Testament. In a note on the poem Jarrell says, "The phrases from Gospels compare such criminals and scapegoats as these with that earlier criminal and scapegoat about whom the Gospels were written." Yet analogies between the Gospels and the poem are not as limiting as the note might suggest. For in addition to the men being compared to Christ, and in addition to the poet's voice mingling with that of Peter's, "I did as these have done," and Pilate's "Behold the man," and Pilate's wife's, "I have suffered in a dream because of him," the speaker's tone of forgiveness also associates *him* with Christ. (Jarrell goes among these soldiers with that mixture of observation and pity that Whitman brought to his war poetry.) His identification with the men he sees before him, the men whose experience he is a part of, is a strong Christ-like quality in the poem. The speaker finds it necessary to forgive these men, as if it is his task to do so. One can almost see the poet viewing these men as the Christ of Rouault's painting looks at the Roman soldiers who torment him.

The association of the poet's voice with those of various personages from the New Testament advances his final acceptance of the men who, like himself, "wash their hands, in blood, as best they can." This acceptance is also evident in the way "man" and "can" serve as the principal and repeated rhyme in all the stanzas except the second. Man is accepted as he is and within the limits of his possibilities. As the last line's rephrasing of

Pilate's statement, "I find no fault in this just man," also indicates, the poet accepts man and his possibilities as he is, a doer of good as he can, "just" serving in the sense of only and as the first syllabic tendency toward justice. Yet in the acceptance the poet says he is lying. In a sense the acceptance necessitates a submerging or disregarding of the awareness of man's murderous activities. Yet the "I" accepts. Even though the recollection of passages from the Gospels makes him reflect on man with a measure of historical pity, what essentially enables the speaker to make the leap toward acceptance is perhaps finally undefinable. One, however, feels the poet's arrival at an acceptance even if the basis of that reconciliation cannot be pinpointed or defined. And one can trace the struggle that finds its release in the acceptance.

The structure of the poem is relevant to this ongoing struggle and final gesture of reconciliation. The questions of stanzas one and four finally resolve themselves into an acceptance:

> Shall I say that man
> Is not as men have said: a wolf to man?
> . . . .
> But since these play, before they die,
> Like puppies with their puppy;

and,

> But what is lying?
> Men wash their hands in blood, as best they can:
> I find no fault in this just man.

The dilemma of the poem often structures itself around colons, as if there is a weighing of alternative reactions and shades of feelings throughout the poem. Also the colons, as well as the dashes and ellipses, bridge references, allusions, thoughts—"*O Murderers!* . . . *Still, this is how it's done*"—and heighten the conflict of the poem, bring awareness to a recognition of the duality it is immersed in. The punctuation is suited to and dramatizes the conflict of the poem. The dashes, ellipses and colons, all rather abrupt means of pausing, make the consciousness halt and turn around on itself or jump in the opposite direction, and are therefore relevant to the dramatic resolution of the conflict. As parts of the poem turn upon themselves and question themselves, sudden, unexpected, newly forged shapes of consciousness appear. In the first stanza, the "If" of the introductory clause springs from the various sights to the basic question of the poem. And in the last stanza, after the final "But," after the final effort of the mind to weigh alternatives, the poet ends on a final note of acceptance, the soft, last and only line of eight syllables. Understanding springs out of hesitancies the way love surmounts its own doubts. The syntax and punctuation of the poem enforce the conclusion that after such knowledge—sudden and magnificent forgiveness.

In the casual aftermath of the bombing, in their playing, sleeping, dreaming, these fliers are redeeming themselves, recovering for themselves the saving human capacities for friendship and self-indulgence outside the murderous social obligations. They must escape from what they have done, for in their escape lies not only the risk of callousness (of "lying") but also recovery from their deed. Of course the recovery is not complete, for this is impossible, and it can only be possessed by a mind that is a moral vacuum. There is not even a recovery in terms of conscious capacities; the explicit ethical awareness and absolution is only in the mind of the observer, but his intense drama of awareness and forgiveness is a donated ritual through which the participants receive dispensation. Also in escaping the burden of consciousness, the victory is no less Jarrell's than that of the men he writes about. If there is a moral level beyond good and evil and if it can enter art, it must surely be a part of the struggle and resolution of the kind of pity and knowledge that inhere in "Eighth Air Force."

This is a poem of forgiveness for man as murderer, and forgiveness remakes the image of man (wolf is not mentioned after the first stanza) and succeeds in the attempt to place him above war. And this is done perhaps not so much because man deserves it as that he needs it and that the poet needs to purge himself of the filth of war. The poem is a catharsis, and in its immersion in pity it suitably occupies a page in *Losses*, that volume of compassion, whose meaning, as Dudley Fitts has said, "we shall neglect at our peril." The source of the poem is a profound need to be relieved of the guilt of murder in war. The necessary repentance and personal reintegration after killing one's own kind is basic to the poem, which is as much an outgrowth of the need to discover the peaceful self above the self of violence and destruction as is found in any post-war ritual of some tribe that has emerged from slaughter. And perhaps what primitive warriors do through some organized ritual in order to relieve themselves of guilt after war, and in recognition of their offense against other men, the poet does through his poetry, for himself and for others.

War is all that Jarrell has recorded in his other poetry, but it is also the sensitivity after or between violence that is "Eighth Air Force." In the concentration on the dilemma that confronted the speaker in the poem, and letting it, in a sense, work itself out, Jarrell avoids an over indulgent pathos or forced statements of knowledge. In "Eighth Air Force" he allows consciousness to emerge from within the scene and evolve towards its own understanding.

We cannot read "Eighth Air Force" without realizing that, as Jarrell has said in prose, "In war the contradictions of our world, latent or overt, are fantastically exaggerated. . . ." In the same essay in which these words appear, Jarrell explains that Ernie Pyle was an important observer of war because Pyle knew that killing was murder, but he also saw the murderers die themselves. It is this double and enlarged understanding that pervades "Eighth Air Force." No other poem from the war so dramatically presents the dilemma of man's moral duality and of the sensitive observer who is entangled in this awareness. War or no war, this is man's conflict. War poetry or peace poetry, the noun survives the adjective. Or to put matters with a particular justice to Jarrell, "Eighth Air Force" is about a kind of war of awareness which is as permanent as poetry.

"Eighth Air Force," like "The Death of the Ball Turret Gunner," is a poem that contains a number of themes prevalent in Jarrell's war poetry. But the themes take on a unique role in "Eighth Air Force," for here the men return to the airbase, here they seek and find some release in dreams, and here, even though it is clear that the men are the inevitable practitioners of the State's will, the poet neither expropriates their consciousness nor indulges in the theme of entrapment, nor unduly immerses himself in the bleakness of self-knowledge. Yet the poem is no less forthright in the dilemmas and burdens it perceives and dramatizes. In "Eighth Air Force" Jarrell has surmounted the persistent mournful sympathy that dominates his poetry.

Randall Jarrell and the Flotations of Voice

Frances C. Ferguson*

Even before Randall Jarrell's untimely death, it already seemed appropriate to talk about his untimeliness—the way in which he never quite seemed to fit the expectations of even his most sensitive contemporaries. Looking to the puzzlements of others in the memorial volume *Randall Jarrell: 1914-1965*, one almost feels criticism ricocheting off the sides of an extremely impenetrable substance as one reads confession after confession: none of us really knows quite what to do with him. James Dickey has to write a dialogue in an effort to suggest the mysterious nether region of Jarrell's literary power; Robert Lowell tries to choose the criticism over the poetry to solve the problem of decision; and each one of us who reads Jarrell returns to his naive wonderment: why did he have so many "characters" populating his poems? why so many women? why such a mixture of quiet eloquence, nostalgia, and stridency? One can only hope that the access of "relevance" which Jarrell's poems may seem to have acquired from our current awareness of the sorrows and the rights of women will not deaden our sense of the curious elusiveness of his work. For those perceptions of "relevance" may merely serve to reimport an obsession with Jarrell's themes and statements of position.

If we hope to avoid simple thematizing of Jarrell's work, and also to get beyond the respectable (and even appropriate) confusions of most readings, then a useful point of departure lies in Jarrell's own critical writings. His essay "Stories," perhaps the most interesting prose piece he ever wrote, is remarkable primarily for its unwillingness to yield to any of the dead-ended perplexities and simplifications that are ever-present dangers in the act of reading. "Stories," more a short story masquerading as a commentary on one man's anthology of great stories than a straightforward critical essay, serves to remind us that Jarrell was not a poet with his left hand, and a critic with his right; like all of Jarrell's best critical essays—the two on Frost and the later one on Wallace Stevens in particular—"Stories" eschews the two basic approaches that criticism on Jarrell has followed. For him, "talking about" literature involves neither

*Reprinted from the *Georgia Review*, 28 (Fall 1974), 423–39, by permission of the author and the journal.

163

theme-hunting nor the discovery of a "tone," a way in which these words might be spoken. Jarrell's celebrated "authority" as a critic begins, on a close examination of "Stories," to participate in the same concern for "voice" that his poems reveal.

In "Stories," we find a strange opening:

> Story, the dictionary tells one, is a short form of the word *history*, and stands for *a narrative, recital, or description of what has occurred*; just as it stands for *a fictitious narrative, imaginative tale; Colloq. a lie, a falsehood*.

Although Jacques Derrida's use of dictionary definitions and etymologies as epigraphs may have reaccustomed some modern readers to this general procedure, Jarrell's opening citation of the dictionary is nonetheless unusual. Were we to see Derrida's version, it would be an exact quotation of the most scholarly dictionary available, a gesture reminding us that there is resonance in even the stodgiest of our archival productions. The imaginary comparison may simply serve to remind us of the air of naiveté in Jarrell's citation. We wonder first about this dictionary: it is, one might say, conspicuously unscholarly—perhaps one of those abridged editions of Webster prescribed in high school courses, or maybe even one of the many bilingual editions which provide little bits of strangely symmetrical information about two languages at once. These are, of course, tongue-in-cheek hypotheses, little fictions about what we find in Jarrell's dictionary definition; but any sense of the need to construct such fictions may call to our attention the ways in which Jarrell's first paragraph does not feel like any dictionary to which one is accustomed. The story has begun already—both in the appearance of a definition so concise that it seems "foreign," and in the supplemental narrative which fleshes out the stringent asyndetons of our ordinary dictionary entry. And after such genial simplifications, Jarrell proceeds to a gloss on the definition. "A story, then, tells the truth or a lie—is a wish, or a truth, or a wish modified by a truth." For anyone who would ask, "But do we really *need* a gloss on that definition?" the gloss would seem to reply, "Precisely." "Definitions," etymologically speaking, are supposed to provide us with "boundaries"; and Jarrell has proceeded to convert the delimitations of his dictionary citation into a radical reduction—a reduction so radical, in fact, as to explode the boundaries that had apparently been invoked.

In Jarrell's narrative, *everything* suddenly seems to be a story. From the initial use of a dictionary definition as an *objet trouvé* to this gloss, the story about stories has expanded through reduction, so that the combination of logical-positivistic truth and aesthetic imitation which we all occasionally, primitively, appeal to appears instantly foolish. Stories, as Jarrell says, want to do as they please. And although he rehearses most of the traditional justifications for stories in terms of human needs, he keeps formulating his story as if stories had lives of their own. They are a part of us, but other. Even as Jarrell seems to ascribe the most simplistically biological causes possible to our love of stories, the story again becomes the elusive agent of the piece:

> A baby asleep but about to be waked by hunger sometimes makes little sucking motions: he is dreaming that he is being fed, and manages by virtue of the dream to stay asleep. He may even smile a little in satisfaction. But the smile cannot last for long—the dream fails, and he wakes. This is, in a sense, the first story; the child in his "impotent omnipotence" is like us readers, us writers, in ours.

Without invoking categories of poetic inspiration which make the poet or storyteller the passive vehicle of the imagination, this text provides us with a powerful myth of the story's voice. But the irony implicit in this straightforward little sketch is that the baby's version of the story, strictly speaking, has no voice; Jarrell has made the story a story, given voice to its voice by finding words for the pre-verbal, sleeping child.

Yet if the essay "Stories" reads somewhat like a chant of other people's stories, we must keep in mind the fact that there are at least two dialogues here—Jarrell's dialogue with the storytellers whose stories he recounts, and (probably more importantly) the dialogue which emerges as the divided consciousness of the text itself. This latter dialogue may reveal some of the difficulties attached to the whole notion of "voice" for Jarrell's poetry, in which the apparent utility of voice is in expressing a sudden shock of recognition. Because the temporal coordination of voice and self is at best precariously imaginable, let us construct two crude schemata—one in which self precedes and chooses voice, the other in which voice precedes and chooses self. The story of the sleeping baby temporarily appears to remove the problematic quality from this second schema; the voice seems, of necessity, to choose the self. Yet simultaneously we realize that we are getting a third-person/first-person account—a narrative in which the supplemental voice is primary. This is not merely "a story from all time which has found yet another vehicle" in entering the baby's unconscious, as our deterministic belief in the constancy of ideal forms would have it; it is, rather, an interpretation which has overwhelmed the mute sleeper's gestures which provoked it—a kind of covert assertion that a good reader is a good storyteller (perhaps sometimes a better one than the original storyteller). The boundaries between roles blur, as if identities were not clearly discernible.

Throughout "Stories" we encounter a similar conflation of third person and first person that makes it appear that the search for individual identity is somehow at issue. We start to wonder about a text which makes the Yeatsian concept of the "emotion of multitude" seem entirely reconcilable with distinct—even lonely—individuality. In this doubled version of things, the voice does not make the self present to itself; instead, the voice seems to be performing two functions at once. The movement from the first to the third person registers the unease with which the self continues to be just that—a self; self-recognition, the implication is, is always best when it seems like the recognition of others (or at worst, of ourselves along with others). But the counter-movement, from the third to the first person, demonstrates the appropriateness of Jarrell's story about a sleeping baby's story: interpretation, like the existence of other people, forces an individual to discern the fact that others force existence upon him—a perception of him exists for others even when he does not exist for himself.

Two passages from the essay may help to describe the motions of Jarrell's voice more carefully:

> There are all kinds of beings, and all kinds of things happen to them; and when you add to these what are as essential to the writer, the things that don't actually happen, the beings that don't actually exist, it is no wonder that stories are as varied as they are. But it seems to me that there are two extremes: stories in which nothing happens, and stories in which everything is a happening.

> The truths that he systematized, Freud said, had already been discovered in the poets; the tears of things, the truths of things, are there in their fictions. And yet, as he knew, the root of all stories is in Grimm, not in La Rochefoucauld; in dreams, not in cameras and tape recorders. Turgenev was right when he said, 'Truth alone, however powerful, is not art'—oxygen alone, however concentrated, is not water; and Freud was right, profoundly right, when he showed 'that the dream is a compromise between the expression of and the defence against the unconscious emotions; that in it the unconscious wish is represented as being fulfilled; that there are very definite mechanisms that control this expression; that the primary process controls the dream world just as it controls the entire unconscious life of the soul, and that myth and poetical productions come into being in the same way and have the same meaning. There is only one important difference: in the myths and in the works of poets the secondary elaboration is much further developed, so that a logical and coherent entity is created.'

One might say that the first passage attempts almost as little articulation as possible. We have no outlines here; rather, the distinctness of all objects of contemplation is obscured in the effort to talk about the "all" of things. Similarly, the individuality of the speaker never obtrudes itself upon the reader's consciousness when one reads "But it seems to me that there are two extremes: stories in which nothing happens, and stories in which everything is a happening." There can be precious little self-assertion in saying either the tautological or the obvious, and we feel only the traces of an individual voice that has become so thoroughly merged in the voice of collective wisdom that it seems supremely capable of saying also, "It seems to me that two plus two equals four."

But if the first passage appears to skirt articulation and any assertion of the individual speaker's voice, the second presents a more difficult case. Although the passage is essentially a montage made up of quotations from other writers, individuality seems more conspicuous here than in the first passage; perhaps the passage troubles us by reminding us that "truthfulness" is one of the least interesting traits we can ascribe to something. To say that Turgenev and Freud were "right," or even "profoundly right"—and to insist that "the root of all stories is in Grimm, not in La Rochefoucauld"—is to suggest a residue of individual selfhood which becomes, finally, more striking than the statements from the various authorities that are cited. Ideas, we know, are neither "right" nor "wrong" in themselves; they are merely consistent or inconsistent with themselves. It is people who seem right or wrong, whom one sides with or against. In fact, serious political thought may be said to be grounded on the effort (and the recognition of the absurdity of the effort) to reconcile these two related but discontinuous systems of authority. So why, we must ask, does Jarrell frame authority in the rhetoric of personalities, in the rhetoric of rhetoricians? An answer is probably needed less than an explanation. This passage, it seems to me, can be read as the inversion of the previous one. While the earlier passage seems authentically to represent a voice by saying what no one needs special information to say, this passage points simultaneously to the assertion of self and to the concomitant fear of losing oneself entirely. While something like "homespun wisdom" or the "voices of the elders" seems to dictate the earlier passage, so that others—or the world—seem both to recognize and to participate in this particular voice, this later passage seems almost to constitute a plea that the authorities choose a voice for him. Even if we were to grant special credence to the notion that the voice makes the self present, this citation of authorities depends upon our acceptance of a more remote notion: that *only* the voices of *others* make the self present to itself.

Yet precisely the most disturbing element in this second passage is that we are reminded rather glaringly of the metaphorical nature of this word "voice." We have been speaking as though it were somehow "natural" to say that the words on a printed page could have a voice. But the conspicuous feature of the second passage is that we are made aware of the physical remains of books by the text itself; particularly the long quotation from Freud looks like a skeleton of what Valéry called "verbal materialism," valuing "the words and the forms." Now there is nothing intrinsic to "verbal materialism" which precludes the metaphor of "voice." In fact, Valéry also provides us with an appropriately ambiguous and suggestive statement of the relationship between written text and voice:

> An epic poem is a poem that can be told.
> When one *tells* it, one has a bilingual text.

Paraphrasing, one could say that most of Jarrell's stories are stories that can be told—and that when one tells them, one has bilingual texts. But this second passage, even though it occurs in the midst of stories that could be told about stories that could be told, seems curiously at odds with them in so far as it seems book-bound and untellable. It is as though the text of Jarrell's essay temporarily warped itself, thus laying bare some of its organizing principles.

The explicit terms of the passage are "truth" and "art," and the argument seems to be a response to those who would see Freud as reductively dismissive of art. In sum, the truth is that art is truer than truth. But the terms "truth" and "art" begin to appear inadequate when we recall other parts of Jarrell's text—from the opening definition of "story" to the "artistic yet true" story of Hilda Kristle. ("A Sunday school teacher, mother of four children, shot to death her eight-year-old daughter as she slept today, state police reported. Hilda Kristle, 43, of Stony Run, told police that her youngest daughter, Suzanne, 'had a heavy heart and often went about the house sighing.' ") In fact, the dichotomy between "truth" and "art" seems to resolve itself primarily in terms of another age-old dichotomy—that between "form" and "content." The temporary appeal to authorities for the truthfulness of art represents an attachment to "content," yet this reductively totalizing gesture of privileging "content" over "form" points us back to the essay's primary interest in "form" as the only index to what we can think of as "content." For "content" suggests both substantial and spatial terms, while Jarrell's examples throughout "Stories" involve "formal" or "structural" principles, of which repetition is only the most striking. Besides the obvious fact that repetition is essentially a temporal rather than a spatial concept, the repetitions within and between Jarrell's examples of stories—along with the essay's initial declaration that it will rehearse what has oft been thought and just so well expressed—create within the text the illusion that it is multilingual—or at least bilingual. While writing has more temporal endurance simply because it can be reread, the mythology of "voice" rests upon what can be re-said. But as Jarrell elaborates his version of "voice," it is not a concept that ultimately reveals a unique, individual selfhood to the speaker. Rather, the speakers in Jarrell's work have almost no individual character at all, precisely because the (at least) bilingual nature of his texts generates speakers which seem the spokesmen for a collective effort by dual or multiple characters.

It is, however, important to distinguish between such dual and multiple selves within the texts of Jarrell's poems and essays, on the one hand, and "representative characters," on the other. For if, as I have hinted, the awareness of the multiplicity of speakers in a voice involves primarily a recognition of the repetitions in disjunct temporal experience, then the foreshortening that is potential in focussing on a "representative man" may jeopardize the very perceptions on which the construction of voice is based. As Kierkegaard suggested when he insisted that a concern for the future rather than the past was the essence of true repetition, patience—the cherishing of manifestations in time—becomes an appropriate mental frame for this expansive movement of voice. And it seems precisely such patience that poems of "representative men" refuse, in their eagerness to make equations between men rather than to follow the processes through which individual selves seem to overlap in oscillating patterns of force. As a poem like "The Death of the Ball Turret Gunner" indicates, a collective consciousness can be projected beyond the figure of the individual speaker, but, ultimately, all of the members of the collective consciousness are rather undemocratically equal:

> From my mother's sleep I fell into the State,
> And I hunched in its belly till my wet fur froze.
> Six miles from earth, loosed from its dream of life,
> I woke to black flak and the nightmare fighters.
> When I died they washed me out of the turret with a hose.

"The Death of the Ball Turret Gunner" has long been admired, and justly admired. Yet it does occupy a polar position in Jarrell's work, fixing the limit of omission. The poem so thoroughly manifests the lack of a middle between the gunner's birth and his death—in the life and in the brevity of the poetry—that the time between birth and death is lost. Because the poem presents a man who seems to have lived in order to die, we forget the fiction that he must have lived.

In this poem, Jarrell pays his shocked tribute to the indeterminate forces that produce mere circumstance, which in turn becomes a kind of grisly determinism as it overtakes the speaker, along with his counterparts, the nameless and faceless soldiers who died along with him. But the middling region between birth and death comes to occupy the central position in Jarrell's best and most characteristic poems—poems like "Eighth Air Force," "Cinderella," and "Jerome." In these poems, the initially individual speakers borrow from dream lives obliquely related to their own, and the speakers merge so thoroughly with their dream counterparts that they create new amplitude for themselves in the act of speaking. These Jarrell figures recognize their imaginary analogues primarily in terms of the limitations and burdens which they share: the woman in "Cinderella" reenacts a negative version of the Cinderella story by dreaming up an imaginary godmother as a companion for her in her sullen watch for her prince; the bomber pilot forms his speech from the casuistry of Pontius Pilate as he accommodates himself to the notion of murdering "just men"; and the psychiatrist Jerome sees himself in Saint Jerome's self-projection into the pains of a suffering lion. Even though the likenesses emerge from a sense of shared limitation, no grim determinism constricts the speeches of these texts. Their beginnings and endings—their births and deaths—become insignificant as the overlappings of different selves begin to override the individual's concern with his own birth, his own death.

How Jarrell insinuates the dream voices into the speech of the apparently individual characters is really the question of how any one of his poems establishes his particular version of voice. "Jerome," a fine but rather neglected poem from *The Woman at the Washington Zoo*, stands as one of the finest examples of Jarrell's process of depicting an individual by dissolving the boundaries of his individuality. . . . [In the original essay, Ferguson here quotes "Jerome" (*Complete Poems*, pp. 271–72).]

In keeping with Jarrell's definition of a story, "Jerome" "tells the truth or a lie—is a wish, or a truth, or a truth modified by a wish." Or rather, "Jerome" becomes one of the most oxymoronic poems possible as it freely shuffles conjunctions and disjunctions, until we no longer know where the boundaries can be drawn between Jerome a modern psychiatrist and Jerome the learned saint—or where the boundaries can be drawn between the psychiatrist and the lion.

The physical image of the mirror recurs with great frequency in Jarrell's poems. "The Face," "The Player Piano," and "Next Day" explicitly dwell on the image, that becomes a vehicle forcing the characters who see themselves mirrored to recognize suddenly that they have changed irreversibly and that movement toward death is their fixed condition. The physical mirror denies their dreams of youth and beauty, and sternly locates the reality that they cannot escape from the limitations of their lives. In "Jerome," however, the mirroring is linguistic—a process rather than an image; the repetition of phrases, the substitution of one figure's dream for another's reality, and the cyclical movement of the poem establish an interpenetration of figures so that they reflect mutually in a release from individuality. Where Ego was, there Id shall be.

The verbal mirror in which Jerome reflects Jerome and in which both reflect the lion appears to develop from Jarrell's interpretation of Freud's observations on language: uttering one word may seem an arbitrary choice, but the arbitrary word begins to operate as a causal caprice; as soon as it is committed to consciousness, it infects the words which surround it. In comparing Jerome with Jerome, the poet initially seems to be giving himself up to the randomness of linguistic similarity. (In the poem "Cinderella," there was at least the implicit story of a shoe-which-fits to connect the modern woman with her predecessor from the fairy tale.) Although the saint's epithet, *"Der heilige Hieronymus,"* immediately connects the psychiatrist with the saint by standing in the midst of the fairy-tale description of the psychiatrist's working day, the opening stanza associates words so freely that they seem more like interruptions than connections. As soon as the epithet points to a link between the psychiatrist and the saint, it gives way to a distinction between them: "His lion is at the zoo." Numerous hints of thoughts associate themselves in the speaker's mind, and linguistic contagion has overwhelmed ordinary logical distinctions: "As the sun sets, the last patient rises." Each phrase seems to call up a mirror phrase, but always with a difference; one never quite catches up with the meanings before they shift again in the process of association, so that a parallelism becomes a disappointed expectation: "Often to the lion, the saint said, *Son*. / To the man the saint says—but the man is gone." No ego remains in place long enough for it to be fully constituted.

However much the parallelisms refuse to hold—or insist upon holding in an unpredictable fashion, the lines of the parallels perhaps create their most surprising effect when they turn out not to be dead ends. For the poem arrives at an ending which seems as premature as the psychiatrist's arrival at the zoo, in which "The old man walks placidly / To the grocer's; walks on, under leaves, in light, / To a lynx, a leopard—he has come." The alliterative movement from "leaves" to "light" shamelessly displays itself, conscious of its artifice and arbitrariness; but the arbitrary sequence of sound merges with an alliterative pattern that hovers around the object of the search. The psychiatrist has been walking down the row of cages in reverse alphabetical order, and he comes to the unnamed lion in walking to the spot between the lynx and the leopard.

The sight may focus on the lion, but Jarrell's use of the lynx and the leopard in pointing to the lion diverts and blurs the focus. It is as if he could not individuate the lion, even in the act of moving toward him. And the reciprocal gestures of the psychiatrist and the lion at the ending ("The man holds out a lump of liver to the lion,/ And the lion licks the man's hand with his tongue") also avoid individuation even in the moment of recognition. The lion's motion perfectly fits with the man's, so perfectly that the two motions virtually constitute one continuous motion. In this unity, moreover, we return to the infinite regress of likenesses that shapes the earlier sections of the poem.

Because there are no precise boundaries to be drawn between individuals, the entire poem "Jerome" becomes a "middling" in which the beginning and the ending seem less to delimit the scope of the poem than to absorb themselves in infinitely self-repeating and self-extending association. Whereas "The Death of the Ball Turret Gunner" consists only of a beginning and an ending, "Jerome"—along with "Cinderella," "Eighth Air Force," and "Well Water"—erases its beginning and ending to put the entire poetic effort into the area of the included middle. Jarrell's "middling" becomes not only a process but a voice; it translates the determinism of the mediocre routines which Jarrell perceived in modern life into the possibility of escape from the term which can be limited, the self. As Jerome the saint, Jerome the psychiatrist, and the lion of their mutual unconscious merge into one another, the poem attaches less significance to the "I" than to the entreaty "Pass it on"—without defining and thus delimiting "it."

From looking at Jarrell's manuscripts of many of the poems, one begins to recognize that, for him, the language—even the very letters of the alphabet—seemed a supplemental consciousness, a partner in his enterprise of discovering the multiplicity of voice. Scratch sheets crawl with apparently random letters, traced over and over again until words came as the fuller form of the individual letter. And it is perhaps this gesture which demonstrates most clearly the insights which Jarrell had derived from Freud. Although "*Seele im Raum*," with its mad punning on eland-*elend*, and even nightmare poems like "A Story" and "The House in the Wood," most closely approach what seems like bare poetic Freudianism, Jarrell's letter plays in his work sheets more radically reveal the Jarrellian-Freudian willingness to impute—and therefore to receive—significance from the smallest traces of forms.

But if Jarrell's Freudian version of automatic writing, along with his repeatedly avowed enthusiasm for Freud's work, lead us back to Freud, we must ask which Freud was his Freud? The determinism implicit in "The Death of the Ball Turret Gunner," for instance, and the moral assertiveness that occasionally appears in Jarrell's poems would seem to imply a rather familiar Freud—a Freud for whom the seeming predictability of development (if one could only *know* the causes determining it) and the moralism of ego psychology are the message. Yet we have been arguing that the voice of some crucial Jarrell poems has abandoned the perception of the self as an individual entity, and moralism seems an inappropriate response to voices which are not seen as individual selves. What is morality if one is responsible for the morals of the consciousness which overlap with, and interpenetrate, one's own consciousness—particularly when these consciousnesses exist in different temporal spheres?

Although the concept of morality is, in some sense, the theme of "Eighth Air Force," one of Jarrell's most impressive war poems, the movement of the poem reveals that moral judgments have become inapplicable. The poem springs from the mouth of an initially unidentified casuist: "If . . . / A puppy laps the water from a can / Of flowers, and the drunk sergeant shaving / Whistles *O Paradiso!*—shall I say that man / Is not as men have said: a wolf to man?" The scene combines the roughness of military life with rather child-like attempts at comfortable domesticity; the place remains a "hutment," a ramshackle barracks into which the men have introduced a puppy and flowers to ameliorate the bleakness of the place—and if the puppy does not have a water dish and if he drinks from the can for the flowers, that is part of the men's game of "making do" as if this were a child's playhouse which tried to imitate the big world. The drunk sergeant means no harm to anyone: he whistles his tenor aria with abandon. And the whole scene appears to be so helplessly charming that the speaker's question sounds an ominously discordant note: "shall I say that man / Is not as men have said: a wolf to man?"

With the opening of the second stanza, the speaker begins taking the charge of man's cruelty seriously enough to call the airmen "murderers," but in the context of the first line of this stanza ("The other murderers troop in yawning"), the word feels almost comically misapplied. All of the men are accounted for, finally revealing the one that "lies there counting missions, lies there sweating / Till even his heart beats: One; One; One," the one who silently cries "*O murderers!*" to himself and to his comrades in a parallel to the earlier gaiety of "*O Paradiso!*" This airman, with his one mission left to fly before he leaves this routine of bombing the continent to return home, has been giving this casuistical account as both innocent spectator and implicated airman. Not even "Still, this is how it's done: / This is a war . . . ," emphasized as it is by the violent wrenching it bears in bridging two stanzas, can restore the sense of moral security which appeared implicit in the opening lines of the poem. In fact, this sentence has about it an air of "facing reality," as if the speaker were saying, "Have I forgotten where I am? This is a murderers' den." And the pragmatic apologetics of his words heighten the ominousness as well as the absurdity of the cry "O murderers!" by insisting that *this* is the fact—a painful necessity, but true nonetheless. Now the description of the men as "puppies with their puppy" cannot avoid a sinister suggestion of the kinship between puppies and wolves.

Because of the baleful implications that have been caught up in the dog-wolf imagery and because of the very vacillation of the moral argument from the "shall I say that man / Is not . . . a wolf to man"—a proposition waiting to be disclaimed—to the limp justification "Still, this is how it's done," one feels the logical security of the speech fall apart; the airman's arguments war with one another. But then, the airman's logic has been so colored by his sense of moral conflict that he makes explicit the tacit connection between his being a *pilot* and fulfilling the role of *Pilate*; he begins to appropriate Pilate's words from Matthew at this point. Although the logical form remains ("since, a man, / I did as these have done, but did not die"), the fact that the speaker is an innocent (like the other men in stanza one), a murderer (like them), and now a judge (like Pilate) erodes what once seemed like a logical appraisal into a moral limbo.

In his fear that he may be killed on his one last flight, the airman in his hopeful imagination puts himself in the place of power—dispensing an amnesty to "the man." The airman's suffering "in a dream" for "this last saviour, man" reveals both his fear of being murdered and his recurrent guilt at being a murderer. Remembering and using the lines from Matthew in which Pilate's wife sends him an account of her dream and says, "Have thou nothing to do with that just man" (Matthew 27:19), the airman playing Pilate rules on this saviour (man, himself): "I find no fault with this just man." In allowing the inevitable war to proceed, as the airman does in his fantasy, while pardoning "this just man," he rejects any resort to a tamer, Puritanical, or absolute morality: "But what is lying?" Only the lying enables him to pardon, to acquit "this just man" as just despite all his brutality.

Although forces like the "State" apparently hold grim control over some of Jarrell's war poems, the voice of the airman finally evades all control, as the initially locatable speech becomes a voice constructed by the multiple participants in this unpathetic tragedy. While the woman at the Washington Zoo pleads, "Oh, bars of my own body, open, open!" the airman's body becomes less and less present, so that transcendence or de-incarnation seems irrelevant. What remains is the voice of a choric criminal-victim-saviour-spectator, whose incorporation of all of the possible stationings toward pain into himself is so thorough that moral scruples seem beside the point. On the one hand, it is as if the man destroys only himself; on the other, it is as if all the world would have to be punished if moral judgments were invoked against the untold, interlocking processes of inflicting and suffering pain. And in this poem, the possibility of apocalypse itself appears to be annihilated. The temporal patterning of the merged, multiple voice projects a future of repetition out of the infiltration of the poem's present by the imagined past of Pilate's speech.

Finally, in the poem "The Bird of Night," originally included in *The Bat-Poet*, the traces of voice itself as a construct within the poem begin to dwindle away. If in "Jerome" and in "Eighth Air Force" the lion and the puppy-wolf emerge as unconscious consciousnesses overlapping with the human, in "The Bird of Night" all vestiges of human selfhood seem to have diminished nearly to nothingness. Voice becomes a register of the loss of all consciousness, all objects of consciousness and concern:

> The ear that listens to the owl believes
> In death. The bat beneath the eaves,
>
> The mouse beside the stone are still as death.
> The owl's air washes them like water.
>
> The owl goes back and forth inside the night,
> And the night holds its breath.

"Nothing goes down so deep as sound" in this countdown from the cries of the owl to the darkness and silence of the night holding its breath. A nature that might be "red in tooth and claw" overturns its terror in being traced out of all apparent existence. The blank nothingness of death has already been appropriated into the being of the creatures, so that the death-bearing owl is a confirmation rather than a disruption of their state.

We are left with only the residue—the poet's written inscription on the page to remind us of the voice which once was written into the text. And when Jarrell portrays the mockingbird as poet in *The Bat-Poet*, this remainder appears insistently to remind us of what has been abandoned. "Now, in the moonlight," the mockingbird "sits here and sings."

> A thrush is singing, then a thrasher, then a jay—
> Then, all at once, a cat begins meowing.
> A mockingbird can sound like anything.
> He imitates the world he drove away
> So well that for a minute, in the moonlight,
> Which one's the mockingbird? which one's the world?

Through the course of Jarrell's work, the voice figures less as the presence of an aid to self-recollection than as an evanescent movement. The merger of selves with selves dissolves the boundaries of individual identity, thus freeing "voice" to represent a fictional temporal infinitude. "Voice" becomes the principle of learning how little will suffice, so that finally the text into which voice was written begins to reveal the disappearance of the voice itself, imitating the world which it drove away.

Randall Jarrell's "Eland":
A Key to Motive and Technique
in His Poetry

Russell Fowler*

The growing critical interest in the work of Randall Jarrell reveals two things: his reputation as one of the most perceptive and helpful literary critics of the last three decades continues to flourish, while his own poetry remains the center of intense controversy. Judgments of its overall value and place alongside the work of contemporaries like Robert Lowell and Theodore Roethke vary radically, and even his admirers seem unable to relate his poetry conclusively to any of the major critical or methodological "schools" of this century. For friend and foe alike he is the most "idiosyncratic" of modern poets, for the one consistent element in the diverse collection of strategies and subjects found in the poems from "The Rage for the Lost Penny" (1940) to *The Lost World* (1965) is an insistence on unfettered improvisation, an absolute refusal to be systematic or provide a theoretical or symbolic paradigm for his own work. This attitude is also clearly operative in his criticism, and, ironically, is chiefly responsible for its fresh and innovative approaches to writers like Whitman and Frost. Nothing like Stevens' "Supreme Fiction," Frost's characteristic idioms and landscapes, or Pound's consistent use of private sources is available to the reader of Jarrell, for the core of his work, the announced *purpose* for its existence, is emotional and quasi-mystical rather than theoretical or aesthetic.

What unifies the poems modeled after German Märchen and dreams, the dramatic monologues on war and supermarkets, and the tortuous, syntactically dense considerations of life and death in the "Modern Age" is the attitude behind them, the belief that they all provide specific answers for the same vague question and sponsor recognition (not necessarily understanding) of the human condition in its primal form. Necessary manifestations of this belief in the poetry are an ongoing, painfully sympathetic tone and an overt hostility toward absolute definition of any kind or "that traumatic passion for Authority, any Authority at all, that is one of the most unpleasant things in our particular time and our particular culture."[1] Once one recognizes the fundamental character of

*Reprinted from *The Iowa Review*, 5, No. 2 (1974), 113–26, by permission of the journal.

Jarrell's sensibility and its insistence that poetry function as a "location" where the effects of experience are most dramatically presented, the common purpose behind much of Jarrell's experimentation with the dramatic monologue and the vital presentation of scenes of childhood, warfare, and modern culture becomes clearer. His characteristic use of syntactically complex stanzas, heavy with apposition and qualification, his love of paradox and his "muscular identification with his subject matter" (a phrase Jarrell used to explain his special admiration for Rilke's lyrics), are all designed to show the "real and difficult face" of human experience *and* to promote sympathy for those who suffer its effects.

Many critics have either failed to recognize the importance of this emotional nexus or dismissed it as sentimental and self-indulgent. The latter is an easy judgment often applied to the work of recent poets, but it is particularly damaging to Jarrell's since the intensity of tone and underlying plea for emotional recognition are not simply poetic devices or alternatives but recurring indications of the vague yet constant aims behind all his poetry. Stephen Spender feels, "Jarrell is very difficult to 'place' or even describe as a poet," because he "seems to complain against most of the human condition without . . . much discrimination."[2] His critique is predicated on what he sees as a lack of selectivity, of "self-control," in subject matter joined with a tedious, unchanging tone and approach. "B.," the "Opposing Self" of James Dickey's article on Jarrell, sharply dismisses his poetry on more theoretical grounds as lacking conscientious "technique" and too dependent on mere presentation of a generalized, domesticated reality.[3] Both critics quarrel as much with the intentions of Jarrell's poetry as with its aesthetics or how successfully those intentions are realized, and base their major objections on personal views of what poetry "should do." Jarrell partisans have tended to reply in kind, proclaiming how well Jarrell creates direct, moving visions of moden life free of personal prejudices and the pointless verbal gymnastics of more formal poetry.

It is my intention not to join in this general debate about the "true function" of poetry, but to define as precisely as possible that central attitude behind all of Jarrell's poems responsible for both their diversity of content and consistency of approach. One can at least gain a clearer understanding of Jarrell's real aims and accomplishments by briefly charting his development of a mature technique which he felt best expressed the basic motivations and themes behind all his work and then examining in more detail one of the finest examples of his mature verse, a dramatic monologue entitled "Seele im Raum."

Jarrell's earliest work, the poems published in "The Rage for the Lost Penny"[4] and *Blood for a Stranger* (1942), encompasses an astonishing variety of subjects, strategies, and influences. Clearly the young poet was searching among the various methods and idioms of his contemporaries for those he could best adapt to his own themes and poetic needs. The early poetry of W. H. Auden seems to have had the most dramatic effect on Jarrell's own experimentation. Early efforts like "A Little Poem" and "On the Railway Platform" adopt Auden's conversational, economical mode of address and also employ the domestic and travel imagery associated with much of Auden's best early poetry. Above all, Auden's ability to build a complex mood with a progression of concrete images, often vigorously idiomatic in nature, seems to have impressed Jarrell. He explained his special admiration for Auden's langue in a critical essay on the poet:

> They [Auden's images] gain uncommon plausibility from the terse understated matter-of-factness of their treatment, the insistence (such as that found in the speech of children, in Mother Goose, in folk or savage verse, in dreams) upon the "thingness" of the words themselves.[5]

Jarrell continued to use concrete, descriptive imagery in his dramatic poetry in order to "locate" their events and themes in scenes with their own sense of dramatic immediacy and "uncommon plausibility." His development of the dramatic monologue in the war poems of *Little Friend, Little Friend* (1945) and *Losses* (1948) and his ceaseless revision of earlier poems suggest a common impulse, an insistence on poems with their own autonomous settings and internal developments, on a total elimination of the didactic authorial voice. Jarrell's subsequent rejection of his early Audenesque models seems an outgrowth of this same basic concern, for although he first adopted Auden's brusque, declarative mode of authorial address along with his sharp, idiomatic imagery, he later abandoned it as too didactic and "omniscient" in tone and perfected a narrative approach that is more conditional, iterative, and often mildly rhetorical in its general assertions and "judgments." Auden's allegorical landscapes and his occasional tendency toward straightforward social commentary are too one-dimensional and declarative for Jarrell's purposes in his later, more investigative verse.

His rejection of the early, more assertive tone of his own poetry is clearly a factor in his personal selection of the poems to be included in the *Selected Poems* edition of 1955. Of the forty-odd poems of *Blood for a Stranger*, only ten were included, and most of those had either been revised structurally or were similar in strategy and tone to Jarrell's later poems. Perhaps the best poem from that first volume, "Children Selecting Books in a Library," is the most instructive of all in indicating the motives and effects of Jarrell's revisions. A quick comparison of the first stanzas of the original and revised versions will show what Jarrell was about:

> The little chairs and tables by a wall
> Bright with the beasts and weapons of a book
> Are properties the bent and varying heads
> Slip past unseeingly: their looks are tricked
> By our fondness and their grace into a world
> Our innocence is accustomed to find fortunate.

Our great lives find the little blanched with dew;
Their cries are those of crickets, dense with warmth.
We wept so? How well we all forget!
One taste of memory (like Fafnir's blood)
Makes all their language sensible, one's ears
Burn with the child's peculiar gift of pain.[6]

With beasts and gods, above, the wall is bright.
The child's head, bent to the book-colored shelves,
Is slow and sidelong and food-gathering,
Moving in blind grace . . . Yet from the mural, Care,
The grey-eyed one, fishing the morning mist,
Seizes the baby hero by the hair

And whispers, in the tongue of gods and children,
Words of a doom as ecumenical as dawn
But blanched, like dawn, with dew. The children's cries
Are to men the cries of crickets, dense with warmth
—But dip a finger into Fafnir, taste it,
And all their words are plain as chance and pain.[7]

The second version not only has a greater complexity and ease of rhythm and imagery but also transforms the comparatively stiff personal address of the original into a more lyrical, direct observation of characters who are involved in a process rather than serving as mere "illustrations" for a series of declarative, general remarks. The first line of the revision is more syntactically complex and manages to convey most of the raw information of the first two lines of the original. This movement toward more complex and condensed phrasing and syntax is perhaps the most consistent and characteristic stylistic development in all of Jarrell's poetry. As in these lines, the use of syntactical pauses and inverted phrases became a favorite device of Jarrell's, for they allowed syntactical rhythms that were sonorous while remaining conversational in tone. In the words of Denis Donoghue, Jarrell had a special understanding of "the relation between silence and speech, the flow of feeling between them," and could do "wonderful things with a full stop, a colon, a question mark."[8]

But even more important for our purposes is the abrupt change in the mode of address, for it is a sure technical clue to the motives behind Jarrell's mature style. The speaker in the original, who seems to control so insistently the "meanings" of his narration, withdraws to a greater distance in the revised version and refuses to generalize about the scene until it has worked itself out. The imagery likewise moves toward greater specificity and dramatic autonomy. The general category of "bent and varying heads" becomes "The child's head . . . / Moving in blind grace." The rather stuffy commentator disappears, and the "wordly wisdom" he supplied is expressed by another "character" involved in the drama, by the fantastic figure of "Care," who belongs to the scene itself and does not intrude upon it with extraneous generalizations. In short, Jarrell transforms a mere "example" into a self-realized and dramatically intact scene. The change partially relieves the author of his responsibilities as an omniscient interpreter, a stance Jarrell finds particularly uncomfortable. The worst examples of such awkward commentary and "public" imagery occur in the following lines and explain their total deletion from the revised poem:

> They are not learning answers but a method:
> To give up their own dilemmas for the great
> Maze Of The World—to turn in all their gold
> For the bank-notes of the one unwithering State.

Such major revisions throughout the poem show the key technical effects of Jarrell's later revolt against the relatively complacent moralizer who often narrates Auden's early poetry and much of Jarrell's own. The ever-increasing use of personae and dramatic scenes in the war poems of Jarrell's middle period and the adoption of the dramatic-monologue strategy almost exclusively in his most mature poetry seem a direct consequence of the attitudes and aims behind the extensive revision of "Children Selecting Books in a Library." Although Jarrell never overtly defined these aims in philosophical or critical terms, we have clear evidence of consistent and intense motives behind his revisions and the characteristic strategy he develops in his later poetry. His "speakers" become participants in concrete, dramatic situations—as wounded fighter pilots, tired housewives, or aging government employees—and Jarrell speaks *for* them if he speaks at all. Increasingly he expresses general themes *through* specific personae or the confusing, "unexplainable" circumstances which often entrap them. The ponderous "explanations" in early lines, like "Our great lives find the little blanched with dew," are strenuously avoided, are changed through a less declarative approach to specific subject matter.

Jarrell channels his general themes into intricate symbolic and syntactical patterns that express their "own" meanings through the interaction of characters and key phrases, producing less didactic but more subtle and complex expressions of emotional themes that are themselves often vague, intricate, and paradoxical. The more successful war poems, like "Eighth Air Force," where the moralizing speaker is inevitably drawn into his own judgment of soldiers who are both children and murderers at the same time, are those where the distinct, often bizarre scenes of World War II and its participants are allowed to sort out the paradoxical, absurd meanings of their own actions and machinations. The combatants, as unique representatives of human kind, are usually the real subjects of such poems and are always shown to be both victimizers and victims with equal cogency.

A wide reading of Jarrell's work begins to reveal a recurrent attitude behind the diverse events and scenes, the sense that explanation itself, as a pat, logical generalization about what human life "means," is the greatest absurdity of all. The motives behind Jarrell's own movement away from the didactic voice are best explained by the constant undercutting (and often downright parodies) of the didactic, positivist approach to experience in the later poems themselves. In his best criticism, the praise of poets like Whitman and W. C. Williams for courageously *presenting* the world of human experience with all its contradictions and absurdities intact helps us understand his own attitude. Ultimately his poetry seems designed to present specific examples of the "human condition," not in general, abstract terms, but through the direct, often consciously colloquial description of individual lives. Jarrell's final development of a personal style can best be understood as an attempt to find an approach which best *allows* such presentations. In one of his finest essays, "Some Lines from Whitman," Jarrell almost certainly speaks for his own poetics as well:

> There is in him almost everything in the world, so that one responds to him, willingly or unwillingly, almost as one does to the world, that world which seems both evil beyond any rejection and wonderful beyond any acceptance. We cannot help seeing that there is something absurd about any judgment we make of its whole—for there is no "point of view" at which we can stand to make the judgment, and the moral categories that mean most to us seem no more to apply to its whole than our spatial and temporal or casual categories seem to apply to its beginning or end.[9]

Jarrell's avoidance of absolutes or "categorical judgments" in the few comments on his own poetry and his frequent dismissal of them as useless within the poems themselves is surely related to such critical praise of the same attitudes in the work of other poets. Although I have only been able to give the most cursory attention to the development of Jarrell's mature style, it is clear even from the briefest examination that the strategies related to the dramatic monologue so widely and effectively used in Jarrell's final collections, *The Seven-League Crutches* (1951), *The Woman at the Washington Zoo* (1960), and *The Lost World* (1965), are designed to permit the most direct, concrete presentation of "things and lives" as they are in the modern world *and* thereby sponsor recognition of the human predicament. The latter can only be "judged" by the sum of its parts, and the particular characters and scenes of the final volumes compose a "gallery" of unique instances which defy logical summation.

I would now like to turn to one of the finest examples of these later poems, an interior monologue entitled "Seele im Raum," for it also expresses, perhaps more overtly than any other poem, the essential emotional motivation and quasi-mystical "beliefs" responsible for its own form. Like so many of the better late poems, it describes a persona's confused yet concrete sense of personal being and its apparent fate in a hostile culture and environment. Yet, unlike most of her "fellows," the protagonist of "Seele im Raum" manages to prevail rather than submit to "the world's one way" of defining public reality. Thus her tale becomes one of the few encouraging instances of human existence among other more despondent portrayals of personal failure like "A Girl in a Library," "The Face," and "Next Day." And in expressing those feelings and the awareness of personal being which allow her to escape the common fate, the speaker becomes especially useful to us. She becomes one of the few effective "spokesmen" for an attitude consistently fostered in Jarrell's poetry and its true "raison d'être." In short, "Seele im Raum" enunciates Jarrell's completed vision of ideal human consciousness. If there is a unifying element in all of his poetry, it is the emotional plea for this comprehensive awareness of life and the sense that it must be protected and encouraged (and especially by poetry itself) with special care in a harsh, impersonal, mechanistic age.

"Seele im Raum" begins with a typical, domestic dinner scene. Yet the setting is also "like a dream" since a place is set for a mysterious visitor who is materially invisible yet seen:

> It sat between my husband and my children.
> A place was set for it—a plate of greens.
> It had been there: I had seen it
> But not somehow—but this was like a dream—
> Not seen it so that I knew I saw it.
> It was as if I could not know I saw it.
> Because I had never once in all my life
> Not seen it. It was an eland.[10]

The halting, contorted syntax is, as I have noted, characteristic of Jarrell's later verse. It is designed to function dramatically as well as structurally and usually denotes a sense of desperation and helplessness in the speaker who attempts to explain away the absurdities of his own actions and experiences. Yet here the confusion is less desperate, for the speaker wishes to describe a familiar yet fantastic vision. She shows all the apprehension of people who fear their listeners will think them insane. Yet her "vision" is not that of a schizophrenic, for she "sees" and doesn't see a part of her own being precisely because it is so familiar to her. She characterizes it as an "eland," a part of her earliest consciousness of self, and "feels" its presence at her table without undue alarm. Her "eland" seems strange, not because it is unfamiliar, but because it is an eland.

As in "Children Selecting Books in a Library," Jarrell presents rather than defines his concept of "Seele" by making the exotic creature an active participant in the scene. The woman recalls, "Many times / when it breathed heavily (when it had tried / A long useless time to speak)" and she "touched it" and found the eland "of a different size / And order of being." And this is really the animal's function as a concrete image in the poem. It represents directly a subliminal awareness of human life that is both organic and mystical; incapable of logical articulation, it simply "breathes." In his introductory notes for the *Selected Poems* Jarrell explained that the title, "Seele im Raum," is taken from "one of Rilke's poems; 'Soul in Space' sounded so glib that I couldn't use it instead."[11] Yet it is clear that Jarrell is attempting to present with special conclusiveness his own sense of that spiritual entity in this poem, and the eland serves as its dramatic representative. A paradox, it embodies both an expansion and a reduction of human consciousness. In the context of the poem it serves as a "domesticated incarnation," mystical yet innately personal, rather than as the traditionally fearsome manifestation of a deity. Its condition invokes sympathy rather than reverence. Its exotic nature is also intentional. In the same introductory notes Jarrell suggests his reasons for choosing the animal:

> An eland is the largest sort of African antelope—the males are as big as a horse, and you often see people gazing at them, at the zoo, in uneasy wonder.

Its "wondrous" identity is important, for, like other such fabulous characters in Jarrell's poems, its physical form expresses the strange yet concrete nature of the "other self" it embodies. Jarrell's personae, like "die alte Marschallin" in "The Face" and the narrator of "A Ghost, a Real Ghost," often see in their mirrors the image of another being, comparable to the mysterious "Doppelgänger" of German Märchen, who incorporates "wraithlike" elements of human existence from which they feel estranged. For Jarrell such apparitions embody personal senses of self most evident in the child's imagination and clearly operative in dreams, myths, and imaginative literature. As such, they are no less "real" as expressions of human reality than more empirical, objective descriptions. Such "beings" appear in the poems not as mere poetic devices but as literal representatives of deeper, more irrational levels of human consciousness. Mrs. Mary Jarrell recalls that "Randall (so it seemed to me) had an affinity for what he thought of as his Other: that One he saw in ponds and photographs and mirrors."[12] So for Jarrell, children's "tales are full of sorcerers and ogres / Because their lives are." In this sense, the woman's fantasy is "childlike," but in Jarrell's view this marks her as exceptionally fortunate. She has not lost her "soul," her sense of complete and mystical being, like most of the "adults" of Jarrell's poetry.

The dramatic conflict of "Seele im Raum" does not spring from the woman's own doubts but from the necessary relationships with "the others," with her family, who make jokes about her setting a place for the beast, and "my whole city," which, "after some years . . . came / And took it from me—it was ill, they told me." The persona of "Seele im Raum," like the mother in "Second Air Force," the "Woman at the

Washington Zoo," or Jarrell himself in "Thinking of the Lost World," wrestles with the disparity between public reason and private vision, and the essential conflict responsible for the intensely sympathetic tone and air of advocacy in most of Jarrell's poetry is overtly dealt with in her internal debate. After the loss of her eland the woman's tone becomes elegiac, and in the remainder of the poem she attempts to generalize about its "meaning." In so doing she expresses precisely, not what the eland "was" (again, such generalizations are avoided in Jarrell's late poetry), but what it meant *to her*, and her ruminations assume the quality of a personal credo.

Jarrell's use of the repeated subjunctive in the following passage reinforces the conditional, uncertain tone already established in the syntax, for the woman struggles with the absurdity of her "faith":

> It is as if someone remembered saying:
> "This is an antimacassar that I grew from seed,"
> And this were true.
> > And, truly,
> One could not wish for anything more strange—
> For anything more. And yet it wasn't *interesting* . . .
> —It was worse than impossible, it was a joke.
>
> And yet when it was, I *was*—
> Even to think that I once thought
> That I could see it is to feel the sweat
> Like needles at my hair-roots, I am blind
>
> —It was not even a joke, not even a joke.

The issue remains unresolved, as such issues must in Jarrell's poetry, but the woman's remarks indicate a strength of belief and, even more important, of imagination which hold the world's rationality and derision at arm's length. Jarrell's organization of the first sentence in the second group helps show this, for the last prepositional phrase quite suddenly asserts a general attitude about the value of the "strange" beast which remains unshakable. The woman's tenacity in defending her private vision becomes the main subject of this poem and certifies her status as one of Jarrell's heroines. She defends a form of subjective mysticism, for the martyr she worships is neither "holy" in the conventional sense, nor public, but a destroyed part of her own psyche. Her faith is completely private and presumes nothing beyond itself; it is simply both an indication and a fulfillment of personal needs. The woman's imaginative memory, which allows her to *feel* the eland's presence at the slightest suggestion, saves her from the dull, lonely "reality" of less open and responsive personae in Jarrell's poems.

It would also seem at this point that she comes as near as one can to expressing Jarrell's own feelings. A prose passage describing his favorite elements of John Crowe Ransom's poetry also illuminates in remarkable detail the purposes of "Seele im Raum":

> His poems are full of an affection that cannot help itself for an innocence that cannot help itself—for the stupid travellers lost in the maze of the world, for the clever travellers lost in the maze of the world. The poems are not a public argument but personal knowledge, personal feeling; and their virtues are the "merely" private virtues.[13]

In such a context, the woman's "blind" persistence in defending her "merely private" and terribly fragile vision is both courageous and a rallying point for the "honestly defenceless." Her very admission of personal confusion is a sign of her special enlightenment. In the following passage she states her case in terms that sum up Jarrell's own fundamental attitudes as well as one could hope:

> Yet how can I believe it? Or believe that I
> Owned it, a husband, children? Is my voice the voice
> Of that skin of being—of what owns, is owned
> In honor or dishonor, that is borne and bears—
> Or of that raw thing, the being inside it
> That has neither a wife, a husband, nor a child
> But goes at last as naked from this world
> As it was born into it—
>
> And the eland comes and grazes on its grave.
>
> This is senseless?
> Shall I make sense or shall I tell the truth?
> Choose either—I cannot do both.

The key alternatives of self-definition are stated here, and the "normal," factual, social self is seen as "that skin of being," a material shell for "that raw thing, the being inside it." The former is finite, visible, and easily categorized by referring to its organic and practical activities in time, whereas the latter is unaffected by the temporal realm, is a "naked" and "raw thing," untouched by the abstract dualisms of human society and its impersonal "definitions." Inspired by its example, the woman puts a very Jarrellian ultimatum to the reader, for she distinguishes between "making sense" (in normal, rational, empirical terms) and "truth." They are judged mutually exclusive, and she, like a child or a mystic, must deal in fantastic beings and paradoxes to explain what is most important to her. Her comprehensive awareness of two opposed levels of existence keeps her, like most of Jarrell's enlightened personae, in a state of constant indecision. Yet the conclusion of "Seele im Raum" shows how well the integration of her "eland self" has helped her both judge and live with her life, and *that* is the real purpose and succor of such awareness in Jarrell's poetry. She also understands the folly of didacticism and egotism, even when defending the existence of a personal "Daemon," and that too makes her "tale" one of the most optimistic in tone among Jarrell's poems and one of the surest indications of the motives behind his own distrust of the declarative mode. She concludes, not with a logical proof, but with an enthusiastic, "childlike" cry of faith:

> I tell myself that. And yet it is not so,
> And what I say afterwards will not be so:
> To be at all is to be wrong.
> > > Being is being old
> And saying, almost comfortably, across a table
> From—
> > from what I don't know—
> > > > in a voice
> Rich with a kind of longing satisfaction:
> "To own an eland! That's what I call life!"

What sits, or sat, at her table remains beyond identification, yet her awareness of "owning" it allows her to be old "almost comfortably." One does not encounter the word "satisfaction" very often in Jarrell's poetry unless it is used ironically, but here the atmosphere and the woman's voice are "rich" with it.

It is the plea for this special awareness of personal being which lies behind most of Jarrell's poetry; his mature technique is designed to present "plausible" scenes and characters in which either its presence or, more often, its loss is shown to have specific existential consequences. The desperate tone this underlying plea promotes in many poems, along with its vague emotional outlines and Jarrell's refusal to give it conclusive theoretical or aesthetic definition, is what seems to annoy the critics who consider Jarrell's approach either too unvaried or effusively sentimental. Yet, as Douglas Dunn notes in a recent essay on Jarrell, "When poets are accused of sentimentality it is sometimes an indication that feeling in their poems has been misunderstood."[14] Such objections are based more on taste than on direct analysis of technique or the aesthetic realization of emotional yet definite intentions. Jarrell's own aims in his poetry seem remarkably constant, as we have seen in the ceaseless development of a personal style over a twenty-five-year period, and in terms of its own goals, "Seele im Raum" works extremely well. Its dramatic strategy integrates the fantastic figure of the eland and the normal, domestic setting so well in the woman's mind that they seem to bear out her final judgment and exist in a precarious but natural union. One must either judge "Seele im Raum" as the charming confession of a genuine neurotic or see it as a remarkably comprehensive explanation of the self by one who has learned to straddle its two worlds simultaneously. Jarrell characteristically refuses to step in and decide for the reader; in fact the poem's technique is designed to make such an intrusion appear artificial and unnecessary. Like so many of Jarrell's late poems, "Seele im Raum" is intended as a parable, and assessments of the speaker's "case" must themselves be subjective. Of course, by adopting a persona whose sense of the "facts" of daily life is consistently strong and who undercuts any charge of general insanity with her thoughtful, understated, self-analytical mode of address, Jarrell slants the argument in his protagonist's favor. The real intention of the poem, in both its form and content, is the direct involvement of the reader in a dilemma he may recognize as his own, and in this it succeeds admirably.

In any case, it is clear that Jarrell is often more interested in the emotional impact of his poems than in their formal artistry, and that this places him at odds with much of the practice of recent years. His increasing use of the dramatic monologue and straightforward, descriptive imagery in his last years seems a natural outgrowth of this demand for recognizable, accessible "portraits" of modern life in America. His developed style is clearly intended as a means to an end, and "Seele im Raum" suggests with special clarity the philosophical source of this shift in emphasis from "objective technique" and general assertion toward more subjective, impressionistic explorations of "private lives" and personal experiences. The concrete experience is primary; its aesthetic articulation is evaluated by its ability to *transmit* the physical and emotional outlines of a "single life" as directly and comprehensively as possible.

In developing a style capable of expressing such attitudes in the poems themselves, Jarrell drew on a wide variety of sources he felt shared his intense concern for non-rational, intuitive states of awareness. His poetry and criticism are filled with references to Freudian psychology, American Transcendentalism (of the "applied" Whitmanian school), German Märchen, and Proust's analysis of memory in *Remembrance of Things Past*, to cite only a few examples. Jarrell's extensive allusions to such diverse and wide-ranging sources, despite their single-mindedness of purpose, are a new phenomenon and suggest more about the wide-open, cross-cultural eclecticism and the explosion of "subjective" poetic conventions and systems of the last three decades than they do about the "purer," more codified theories of the Imagists or Surrealists. But because Jarrell's emotional description of ideal human awareness demands the inclusive vision of all mystical systems and feeds on paradox and unchecked observation, it is extremely difficult to define with any precision or selectivity. I have seized upon Randall Jarrell's "eland" simply because it is a distinct manifestation of this attitude with the temerity to express it literally and in precise language.

Jarrell's "eland self," as a soul or source of being, cannot be related to the Christian conception of that entity, for the Judeo-Christian soul is involved in its own linear, temporal progress toward some finite moment of redemption and is subject to all kinds of moral and existential categories and judgments. As Jarrell's speaker tells "A Girl in a Library," "The soul has no assignments . . . / it wastes its time."[15] Its functions and value for each individual must be *recognized* rather than understood; as the woman in "Seele im Raum" explains, she had "Not seen it so that I knew I saw it." These are some of the reasons I have identified Jarrell's "Soul in Space" as essentially mystical in conception; it defines enlightenment as a state of comprehensive and intuitive awareness rather than as the complex organization of logical and empirical hypotheses. In fact, the latter are impediments to a direct and unified recognition of true self. Near the end of "Seele im Raum," the speaker can only suggest the nature of her eland by defining what it "is not." In so doing she employs the process of "negative definition" found in the writings of many mystics when they describe the character of God or the soul. In like manner, Jarrell's own re-fusal to provide a theoretical definition for his aesthetic or philosophical intentions should not be judged as irresponsible or self-indulgent, but as a necessary extension of the attitudes expressed in the poems themselves. At-tempts to objectively define rather than simply present the "beliefs" behind such feelings are always self-defeating, like the speaker's attempt to define what he seeks in "A Sick Child": "If I can think of it, it isn't what I want."[16] But in "Bamberg," a short poem written the year of his death, Jarrell uncharacteristically employs simple religious imagery to suggest the depth of his belief in the unifying "powers of concentration":

> You'd be surprised how much, at
> The Last Judgment,
> The powers of concentration
> Of the blest and damned
> Are improved, so that
> Both smile exactly alike
> At remembering so well
> All they meant to remember
> To tell God.[17]

As Jarrell's "representative," the eland mocks the world's logical dichotomies (visible and invisible, material and spiritual, life and death) by adopting both alternatives simultaneously and timelessly; it "grazes on its own grave." It expresses the insistently emotional, anti-logical view of human life around which Jarrell's poetry must be unified. The varied in-terests and sources which influenced his own practice, his intense interest in Freud and the nature of dreams, his admiration for Rilke's surrealistic imagery, and his insistence on dealing with contemporary American scenes in American idioms, all relate to the subliminal nature yet concrete personal relevance of a "state of mind" his poetry is designed to en-courage. His poems are instructional without being prescriptive or under-cutting the responsibility for personal recognition of one's own condition. His tone is often desperate and painfully sharp because he feels modern culture besets his enlightened personae on all sides, insisting on a lobotomy of the consciousness and fragmented, unfocused perceptions. The world defines "real knowledge" only as the accumulation of objective, impersonal data—"divides itself into facts," according to Jarrell's positivist Mephistopheles[18]—demands that one "make sense." Yet, as the persona of "Seele im Raum" knows, such knowledge is fundamentally *useless* in helping her live her life. It is, in fact, destructive to the soul, to the emotional, imaginative sense of being that is her birthright. In a poem called "The Lost World," one of Jarrell's last works, he makes clear his own feelings about the world's wisdom with images similar to those of "Seele im Raum":

> In my
> Talk with the world, in which it tells me what I know
> And I tell it, "I know—" how strange that I
> Know nothing, and yet it tells me what I know!—
> I appreciate the animals, who stand by
> Purring. Or else they sit and pant. It's so—
> So *agreeable.*[19]

And in an essay from *Poetry and the Age* Jarrell provides an effective description of those embattled beings he wishes his poetry might encourage and protect:

> Children are playing in the vacant lots, animals are playing in the forest. Everything that the machine at the center could not attract or transform it has forced out into the suburbs, the country, the wilderness, the past: out there are the fairy tales and nursery rhymes, chances and choices, dreams and sentiments and intrinsic aesthetic goods—everything that doesn't pay and doesn't care.[20]

Again, the ultimate "utility" Jarrell strives for in his verse is akin to that of the parable or the spiritual exercise. The poems of his late period, the products of endless technical experimentation and revision, are intended as psychic "catalysts," and their direct, often highly emotional approaches to their subject matter are part of their design. We, of course, are still faced with the ongoing controversy about them, yet it seems that Jarrell's critics must at least deal with those elements of his work they find excessive as integral components of an overall method. It seems too easy to react to any consistently strong emotion in modern poetry as mere lack of artistic control, and this is certainly not the case in Jarrell's practice. Sister Bernetta Quinn, in discussing Jarrell's last book, *The Lost World*, suggests the real source of the debate over Jarrell's poetry:

> There is a great tenderness here, with a willingness to present emotion without apology, unique among poets today.[21]

Perhaps, ironically, Jarrell simply worked his design too well. We must be content, like so many of his personae, to take sides. Yet it is hoped that both Jarrell's advocates and his detractors will at least know what they are fighting about. In yet another of his critical essays Jarrell probably described the best criteria for those who would judge his own poetry:

To have the distance from the most awful and most nearly unbearable parts of the poems to the most tender, subtle, and loving parts, a distance so great; to have this whole range of being treated with so much humor and sadness and composure, with such plain truth; to see that a man can still include, connect, and make humanly understandable so *much*—this is one of the freshest and oldest of joys.[22]

Notes

1. Randall Jarrell, *Poetry and the Age* (New York, 1955), p. 90.

2. Stephen Spender, "Randall Jarrell's Complaint," *New York Review of Books*, ix, No. 9 (Nov. 23, 1967), p. 28.

3. James Dickey, "Randall Jarrell," *Randall Jarrell / 1914–1965*, ed. Robert Lowell et al. (New York, 1967), pp. 33–48.

4. *Five Young American Poets* (Norfolk, Conn., 1940), pp. 81–124.

5. Randall Jarrell, *The Third Book of Criticism* (New York, 1969), p. 155.

6. Randall Jarrell, *Blood for a Stranger* (New York, 1942), p. 15.

7. Randall Jarrell, *Selected Poems* (New York, 1955), p. 97.

8. *Randall Jarrell / 1914–1965*, p. 55.

9. *Poetry and the Age*, p. 114.

10. *Selected Poems*, p. 27.

11. *Ibid.*, p. x.

12. *Randall Jarrell / 1914–1965*, p. 279.

13. *Third Book of Criticism*, p. 313.

14. Douglas Dunn, "An Affable Misery: On Randall Jarrell," *Encounter*, xxxix, No. 4 (October, 1972), p. 43.

15. *Selected Poems*, p. 4.

16. *Ibid.*, p. 43.

17. Randall Jarrell, *The Complete Poems* (New York, 1969), p. 490.

18. *Ibid.*, p. 31.

19. *Ibid.*, p. 287.

20. *Poetry and the Age*, p. 99.

21. *Randall Jarrell / 1914–1965*, p. 147.

22. *Third Book of Criticism*, p. 302.

Unicorn to Eland: The Rilkean Spirit in the Poetry of Randall Jarrell

Charlotte H. Beck*

I

Randall Jarrell first became known as a critic whose judgments, though often caustic, always reflected the sympathy and insight which only a poet-critic can bring to the reading of another poet's work. It was Jarrell's method to judge rather than to analyze, to list those poems which he believed would survive the critical test of time, and to classify the poet in relation to his predecessors and peers. The random comments which Jarrell made concerning his predecessors provide clues to the most important influences which affected the development of his own poetic voice. Of the many poets who elicited their share of his praise, Rainer Maria Rilke had perhaps the most significant influence on the poetry of Randall Jarrell. Mary Schrader Jarrell, aware of a strong rival for her husband's affections in his adulation of German art, remarked: "I came into Randall's life after Salzburg and Rilke, about the middle of Mahler; and I got to stay through Goethe on up to Wagner,"[1] and she implied that the Rilke stage never ended; for the attitudes which the two poets shared toward art and life, their similar sensitivity to human emotion, and indeed their common conception of the very nature of reality formed permanent bonds between them. Seventeen translations which appear in Jarrell's *Complete Poems* are Rilke's tangible contribution, but more important is the Rilkean spirit which permeates Jarrell's original poems, where parallel ideas, subjects, and attitudes attest to a productive artistic affinity.

That Jarrell always considered Rilke a proper symbol of The Poet is revealed in many offhand remarks sprinkled throughout his criticism. Once, while contrasting European and American attitudes toward poetry, he remarked: "I shall never forget hearing a German say, in an objective considering tone, as if I were an illustration in a book called *Silver Poets of the Americas*: 'You know, he looks a little like Rilke.' "[2] The connective fibers are to be found, deeper than appearances, in similar poems which express interest in the human condition, especially that of women and children, whom both poets treat as victims of an often

*Reprinted from the *Southern Literary Journal*, 12 (1979), 3–17, by permission of the journal.

unfeeling world. As translator of Rilke, Jarrell became a re-creator of the Rilkean spirit. In original poems which parallel or answer those of his predecessor, Jarrell successfully transmutes the Rilkean unicorns into earthly elands, as the Rilkean influence becomes both an ideal and a creative catalyst.

Rilke's belief concerning the function of art, that it has the power to transform reality, is the subject of "The Reader," a dramatic monologue which Jarrell translated. The speaker, totally absorbed in the book he is reading, has allowed afternoon to shade into evening. As he once again becomes aware of the world around him, he finds that the two planes of reality represented by his book and his external environment have become fused:

> And now when I lift my eyes from the book
> Everything will be great, and nothing strange.
> Out there is what I live in here.
> And here and there it is all endless
> Except when I weave myself into it.
> More even, out there where my look is shaped
> To things, and the grave simplicity of masses—
> Out there the earth goes out beyond itself.
> It seems to be surrounding the whole sky:
> The first star is like the last of the houses.[3]

There is a similarity between Rilke's and Jarrell's views concerning the poet's need for distance from his creation. The poet "weaves" himself into the world of things and becomes the medium through which they are translated into poetry, rather than an emotional reactor to them. He is, however, more than a mere receiver, for there is attached to the images he has apparently recorded from his observations a weight of symbolic meaning. The illusions exists, moreover, that such association of phenomena and idea is natural and not contrived, the result of an apparently essential correlation between inner and outer reality through the medium of poetry. The illusion of complete objectivity in some of Jarrell's and many of Rilke's poems does not indicate lack of concern for feeling; rather, it becomes a means of controlling emotion. Both Rilke and Jarrell reveal in their more subjective poetry an almost overwhelming sympathy for human feeling.

Rilke himself was chiefly a lyricist, secondarily a dramatic poet. His early poetry was of a romantic, confessional sort much in tune with the popular taste of the times. As he matured, Rilke showed both a tendency to write more objectively and an increased interest in dramatic poetry. His *Das Stunden-Buch*, in that it takes the form of a dialogue between a medieval monk and his God, appears to be dramatic; but as McKay remarks, the "God" is less a separate entity than "an esthetic idea," a symbol of human despair. Thus the "dialogue" is actually an interior monologue between segments of a dual sensibility.[4]

With *Das Buch des Bilder* and *Neue Gedichte* (1900–1908), Rilke reached his peak period. This is for Rilke the period of the *dinggedichte*, the extremely objective poetry which grew out of his association with the sculptor Rodin.[5] In such poems, the poet attempted absolutely pure poetry, the creation of poems which presented things, not only inanimate objects but humans treated as objectively as things, as a sculptor produces a statue—without comments, without message.[6] In the *Duino Elegies*, which came later, Rilke allowed himself once more to consider the human situation, especially in its more tragic aspects. C. F. MacIntyre, who has translated the *Elegies*, sees them as the evidence of the poet's successful transformation of personal experience into universal expression: "The poet had developed beyond his earlier Romantic style in which he wrote of his emotions; he had created the "Thing-poems" of *Neue Gedichte*, which are almost purely objective; . . . He had learned that poetry is the result of experiences rather than of feelings."[7] Despite all the emphasis on detachment, Rilke remained what MacIntyre has described as "a man of vast sympathy for the unfortunate and the disinherited, the blind, the cripples, the beggars, the suicides in the morgues, the harlots, the old maids, the animals in captivity . . . and he understood the mysteries of childhood and the delicate nuances in the feelings of woman."[8]

It was almost certainly this element of human sympathy in Rilke, never fully concealed by the objective masks of his poems, which attracted Randall Jarrell. Making extensive use of children as subjects, both discover the child who lives on in the adult's consciousness and is not subject to change. Unlike Wordsworth, Rilke and Jarrell project their belief in man's ability to *retain* the innate divinity, the sense of oneness with the source of all Being, that comes naturally to the child. It may indeed be said of both poets that childhood is the locus from which all poetry derives. Jarrell's *The Lost World* abounds in examples of this Rilkean affinity. Common to Rilke and Jarrell is a conflict between the world of the child, which is seen as the "real" world, and the artificial world of adulthood. Their personae stand physically apart from the children they observe, while they react ambivalently to memories of their own childhoods. To Rilke, time past is full of inscrutable dilemmas that remain despite the oncoming of maturity; in short, it is useless to grow up. In his "Fourth Elegy," Rilke articulates the adult's nostalgic recollections of his childhood:

> . . . Oh, hours of childhood
> when behind the symbols was more than merely the past,
> and before us was not the future. Soon we were growing
> and often we strove to grow up sooner, half

for the sake of those who had nothing but being grown-up.
Yet we were content in our going alone
with things that last, and we stood there in the breach
between the world and the plaything, on a place
founded from the first for a pure event.[9]

Jarrell, in "Thinking of the Lost World," reacts in a similar manner to the memory of concrete things from the world of childhood:

. . . . .I seem to see
A shape in tennis shoes and khaki riding pants
Standing there empty-handed; I reach out to it
Empty-handed, my hand comes back empty,
And yet my emptiness is traded for its emptiness,
I have found that Lost World in the Lost and Found
Columns whose gray illegible advertisements
My soul has memorized world after world:
LOST—NOTHING. STRAYED FROM NOWHERE.
    NO REWARD.
I hold in my own hands, in happiness,
Nothing: the nothing for which there's no reward.
                                        (CP, 338)

In *The Woman at the Washington Zoo*, Jarrell published nine translations of Rilke's poems, which emerge as exceptionally good English poems as well as accurate renditions of the sense of their originals. Although they cover a wide range of themes and subjects—night, death, the preparation of Christ's body for burial—, three are concerned with the very human subject of childhood: "Childhood," "The Child," and "Requiem for the Death of a Boy." The last is a dramatic monologue first published in a late volume from Rilke's humanistic period, *Gedichten des Jahre*.

Rilke's use of a *dead* child as speaker is a departure from the norm in dramatic monologues but not from those of Randall Jarrell. In both poets' works, the seemingly disparate themes of childhood and death often merge. In the "Fourth Elegy," Rilke had asked, "Who makes the child's death / out of gray bread that grows hard, or leaves it there / in the round mouth, like the core of a fine apple? . . . to accept death, even before life, so gently, / the whole of death, and not to be angry, is past description."[10] The source of Rilke's fascination with the subject of *kindertod* is, then, the unique passing of the self from one world, not yet understood, to another which can hardly be more enigmatic; it is to leave life without any sense of loss. To the child in Jarrell's translation of the "Requiem," death is simply another new experience, a new set of questions to be answered:

Why did I print upon myself the names
Of Elephant and Dog and Cow
So far off now, already so long ago,

> And Zebra, too . . . what for, what for?
> What holds me now
> Climbs like a water line
> Up past all that. What help was it to know
> I was, if I could never press
> Through what's soft, what's hard, and come at last
> Behind them, to the face that understands?
>
> (*CP*, 247)

More real to the child than to the adults who talked and laughed, but were never "inside the talking or laughing," was the reliable world of things:

> The sugar bowl, a glass of milk
> Would never waver the way you would waver.

For Rilke death becomes a unique perspective, a way of viewing life in order to criticize it. Such a viewpoint on reality must have captured the imagination of Randall Jarrell, whose renditions of the voices of children who are isolated by sickness or death from contact with the world of common existence are among his best dramatic poems. The speaker in "Requiem" remarks that "Surely there're some other children / Who've died, to come play with me—They're always dying; / Lie there in bed, like me, and never do get well." In his original poem, "A Sick Child," another little boy has an imaginary conversation with a postman who is bringing a letter which invites him to be president of a republic; and he conjures up a "ship from some near star" to land in his back yard. Yet he becomes dissatisfied with his imaginings, being dimly aware of the other reality beyond this world of appearances:

> And yet somewhere there must be
> Something that's different from everything.
> All that I've never thought of—think of me!
>
> (*CP*, 53)

The boy desires that the other dimension of reality establish contact with him.

In another of Jarrell's child poems, "The Prince," the royal child feels the presence of his father's ghost trying to contact him in the dark of his room at night. He has learned quickly the adult conception of death from those who gave him a rabbit on the day his father died. He asks, with cynically mature logic, "What will they pay me, when I die, to die?" And in "90 North," Jarrell employs a double perspective, somewhat similar in basic concept to that which Rilke makes use of in "The Child." In Rilke's poem, which Jarrell translated, the distance, the impossibility of communication which separates the child's vision of reality from that of the adult, is presented descriptively with typical Rilkean objectivity. The poet stands apart and looks, Janus-like, at both worlds:

> Without meaning to, they watch him play
> A long time; once or twice his profile
> Turns and becomes a live, full face—
> Clear and entire as a completed
>
> Hour that is raised to strike its end.
> But the others do not count the strokes.
> Exhausted with misery, enduring their lives,
> They do not even see that he endures . . .
>
> (CP, 245)

In Jarrell's "90 North," the double perspective is managed dramatically, as the speaker seems at first to be a child just awakened from a vivid dream:

> At home, in my flannel gown, like a bear to its floe,
> I clambered to bed; up the globe's impossible sides
> I sailed all night—till at last, with my black beard,
> My furs and my dogs, I stood at the northern pole.
> . . . .
> . . . . .I stand here,
> The dogs bark, my beard is black, and I stare
> At the North Pole . . .
>   And now what? Why, go back.
>
> (CP, 113)

As the perspective shifts to that of the adult who remembers his childish dream, to "go back" has a double significance; and the "night's voyage" becomes the symbol for the journey from childhood to maturity, which brings the speaker to a sense of knowledge without wisdom:

> I reached my North and it had meaning
> Here at the actual pole of my existence
> Where all that I have done is meaningless,
> Where I die or live by accident alone—
>
> Where, living or dying, I am still alone . . .

For Rilke, the beginning of knowledge of earthly existence comes after childhood when one realizes that death is inevitable and that pain and sorrow are man's lot. Jarrell's speaker becomes mature when he realizes the meaninglessness of man's attempts to wring knowledge from experience: "Pain comes from the darkness / And we call it wisdom. It is pain." Jarrell's children, like Rilke's, are privy to a sort of wisdom which transcends corporeal existence. Those who die in childhood leave the world without losing this wisdom. But with an awareness of death comes the end of one kind of wisdom and the beginning of another: that life is a process of physical attrition, a preparation through suffering for the passage into the world of being.

II

In Rilke's poems about two women the theme of life's transience, of existence dominated by the harsh reality of growing older, becomes another link with the poems of Randall Jarrell. Two of his Rilkean translations, "Faded" and "The Widow's Song," are evidence of his appreciation of this subject, one which he was to treat in a number of original poems. "Faded" is dramatic in the sense that it describes the actions and attitude of a human subject in the present tense; its speaker is an omniscient observer of a woman at her dressing table:

> She carries her handkerchief, her gloves
> As lightly as if she had died.
> The odor of her dressing table
> Smothers the scent she loves—
>
> The scent she knew herself by, once.
> But nowadays she never asks
> Who she is (: a distant relation)
> And goes worriedly about her tasks,
>
> Fretting over the poor anxious room
> She must care for and set in order
> —Because, the same young girl
> May be, after all, still living there.
>   (*CP*, 480)

"The Widow's Song," Jarrell's rendition of Rilke's "Das Lied der Witwe," is a dramatic monologue spoken by a similar, perhaps older woman also reflecting on the passage of time: "In the beginning, life was good to me. / It humored me, it encouraged me. / It does that to all the young—." This feminine persona sees herself as the victim of "Fate," coming like an extortioner to take away, piece by piece, the physical being, the only means of self-identity:

> Then what was mine—my own, mine?
> Wasn't even my misery
> Only lent me by fate?
> Fate wants back the torture and the screaming,
> And it buys the wreck second-hand.
>
> Fate was there and got for a song
> Every expression of my face,
> Even the way I walked . . .
>   (*CP*, 483)

Jarrell's own poems on this theme, such as "The Face" and "Next Day," similarly emphasize the horror with which the woman, particularly the woman to whom youth and beauty are life, contemplates the deterioration that comes with age. The speaker of "The Face," like the subject of "Faded," no longer identifies with the image in her mirror:

> Not good any more, not beautiful—
> Not even young.
> This isn't mine.
> Where is the old one, the old ones?
> Those were mine.
>
> (*CP*, 23)

The speaker of "Next Day" looks into her rear-view mirror and is afraid of her face: ". . . the eyes I hate, / The smile I hate. Its plain, lined look / Of gray discovery / Repeats to me: 'You're old.' . . ." For both Rilke and Jarrell, inner transcendence of physical deterioration provides the only element of hope for man in his bodily prison. The flesh must be recognized to be an unreal state against which the unchanging soul wages a frustrating battle throughout life.

The theme of the imprisoned spirit recurs in various guises in the poems of Rilke and Jarrell. The striking similarity which exists both in theme and imagery in Rilke's "The Panther" and Jarrell's "The Woman at the Washington Zoo" suggests that Jarrell might have had Rilke's poem in mind. The poems are quite different in kind, "The Panther" being a typical *dinggedicht*, while "The Woman . . ." is one of Jarrell's most emotionally expressive dramatic monologues. Rilke's poem is a study of the condition of a magnificent animal in captivity. Through the poet-speaker's sensitive powers of perception, the reader experiences both the visual image of the animal in his cage and a sense of the tension and futility which the wild spirit within the panther is suffering in a world of endless bars:

> His sight from ever gazing through the bars
> has grown so blunt that it sees nothing more.
> It seems to him that thousands of bars are
> before him, and behind them nothing merely
>
> The easy motion of his supple stride;
> which turns about the very smallest circle,
> is like a dance of strength about a center
> in which a mighty will stands stupefied.[11]

In Jarrell's "The Woman at the Washington Zoo," the sense of empathy which Rilke forces his reader to feel with the caged animal is transformed into a felt and articulated identification between the speaker of the monologue, a woman who often visits the zoo, and the animals which she sees in their cages. In their situation she sees the mirror image of her own trapped existence:

> .... this serviceable
> Body that no sunlight dyes, no hand suffuses
> But, dome-shadowed, withering among columns,
> Wavy beneath fountains—small, far-off, shining
> In the eyes of animals, these beings trapped
> As I am trapped but not, themselves, the trap.
> Aging, but without knowledge of their age,
> Kept safe here, knowing not of death, for death—
> Oh, bars, of my own body, open, open!
>
> (*CP*, 215)

The woman's body dressed in its serviceable blue uniform is a cage from which there is no escape, unless the spirit can break out of the body's confining bars, unless the vulture can take off its red helmet and black wings, step to her "as man," and change her to a new order of being. Jarrell takes from Rilke this attitude toward the isolation of the individual, his feeling of captivity in the world of appearances. Rilke's caged panther, a powerful symbol of isolation and enslavement, is an appropriate correlative to the woman trapped in the prison of her own body. Jarrell has called her "a distinct relative of women written about before" in such poems as "Cinderella," "The End of the Rainbow," and "Seele im Raum," all representative of the modern in his condition of isolation and captivity.[12]

Jarrell's poem which illustrates most clearly the Rilkean spirit *is* "Seele im Raum." The poem derives from two of Rilke's poems, one actually entitled "Seele im Raum" and one an adaptation of the fourth in the second series of *Sonnets to Orpheus*, which Jarrell calls "The Unicorn."

In his notes to the *Selected Poems*, Jarrell confirms his use of Rilke's title, remarking that to have translated the title as "Soul in Space" might have "sounded too glib." He goes on to explain that the eland, which replaces the unicorn of the sonnet, is "the largest sort of African antelope—the males are as big as a horse, and you often see people gazing at them, at the zoo, in uneasy wonder."[13] The eland in the poem is imaginary, the embodiment in the speaker's mind of her "soul in space." She has begun to see the eland sitting across the dinner table, eating from its own plate, and somehow satisfying for her a deep inner need. It is "of a different size / And order of being, like the live hard side / Of a horse's neck." Its Rilkean ancestor is the less earthy unicorn of the sonnet:

> This is the animal that never existed
> None of them ever knew one; but just the same
> They loved the way it moved, the way it stood
> Looking at them, in pure tranquility.
>
> Of course there wasn't any. But because they loved it
> One became an animal. They always left a space.

And in the space they hollowed for it, lightly
It would lift its head, and hardly need

To exist. They nourished it, not with grain
But only, always, with the possibility
It might be. And this gave so much strength to it

That out of its forehead grew a horn. One horn.
Up to a virgin, silverly, it came
And there within her, there within her glass, it was.

                                                    (CP, 482)

The latter poem has quite obviously furnished Jarrell with most of the imagery of "Seele im Raum." The imaginary animal, which for ages func-
tioned as symbol of that which man needs to believe in, has become for
the trapped housewife an eland, fulfilling that need in her. The shift from
unicorn to eland is a significant one, as Suzanne Ferguson has pointed
out: "In Jarrell's poem the eland seems almost to invert the significance of
Rilke's unicorn, even as the ungainly figure of the animal contrasts with
the idealized form of the mythic beast. Perhaps to the woman the eland
represents *doubt* 'in [what Rilke calls] the worth . . . of that which our
spirit has . . . created.' "[14] Truly the woman has come to doubt her own
worth, and her creation of the eland, less graceful but more identifiable—its "great melting tearless eyes / Fringed with a few coarse wire-like
lashes"—gives her something of her own, something to reach out to when
others reject her. Trying to humor her, her husband and children have
first pretended to see the creature:

An eland! *That* is why the children
Would ask my husband, for a joke, at Christmas:
"Father, is it Donner?" He would say, "No, Blitzen."

                                                    (CP, 37)

Lately, in order to "cure" her, they have tried to convince her that the
eland is dead, not realizing that in its death occurs the death of her sense
of being. When it lived, she also felt alive; and to touch her eland was to
reach out to another dimension of reality:

. . . . Many times
When it breathed heavily (when it had tried
A long useless time to speak) and reached to me
So that I touched it—of a different size
And order of being . . .

                                                    (CP, 37)

In Rilke's monologue, the speaker *is* the soul-in-space, separated
from the corporeal form which has recently housed it and speaking about
its past life with a weak and impermanent other self:

> True, I endured through the timid body
> Nights: I befriended it,
> finite earthen stuff, with infinity
> sobbingly
> its simple heart overflowed when I left.[15]

Jarrell takes from Rilke's poem the concepts of duality and of the inferiority of the body to the soul. In Jarrell's poem, the body, rather than the soul, is the persona. The speaker herself realizes that the eland is only a symbol of her *elend*, her wretchedness. She sees also that reality resides apart from the physical being who plays the role of wife and mother:

> Yet how can I believe it? Or believe that I
> Owned it, a husband, children? Is my voice the voice
> Of that skin of being—of what owns, is owned
> In honor or dishonor, that is borne and bears—
> Or of that raw thing, the being inside it
> That has neither a wife, a husband, nor a child
> But goes at last as naked from this world
> As it was born into it . . .
>
> <div align="right">(<i>CP</i>, 39)</div>

Rilke's "Seele" is that naked being, and because of its formlessness, it faces, like the eland, the problem of incredulity. It asks, "But now, who'd be impressed if I said . . . I am the soul?" Both poets see the tragic implications of man's duality in the "real" world of sane men who, in the words of Jarrell's speaker, choose to "make sense" rather than to "tell the truth."

The transformation of unicorn to eland thus epitomizes the way in which the Rilkean spirit operates in the poetry of Randall Jarrell. Jarrell embraces the Rilkean metaphysic and brings it into the world of the physical, giving sensuous expression to Rilke's presentations of the ideal, statuesque, or nonhuman subject. Jarrell has taken from Rilke a shared concern with the dilemma of the child and the woman, enriching these by addition of analogous references to Rilke's nonhuman world of panthers, unicorns, and disembodied voices, through which he objectified human emotions. Jarrell learned also from Rilke how to balance sentiment with objectivity, although the two poets approached that synthesis from opposite poles: Rilke's excessive coldness and Jarrell's sentimental tendency. The result is a most successful proof of the invaluable appropriation and subsequent transcendence of influence.

Notes

1. Mrs. Randall Jarrell, "The Group of Two," in *Randall Jarrell, 1914–1965*, Robert Lowell, Peter Taylor, and Robert Penn Warren, eds. (New York: Farrar, Straus, and Giroux, 1967), p. 274.

2. Randall Jarrell, "The Obscurity of the Poet," in *Poetry and the Age* (New York: Vintage Books, 1953), p. 6.

3. Randall Jarrell, *The Complete Poems* (New York: Farrar, Straus, and Giroux, 1969), p. 484. All subsequent quotations from Jarrell's poems will be indicated by *CP* and page number following the quotations.

4. G. W. McKay, "Introduction" to *Rainer Maria Rilke: Selected Poems* (New York: Oxford Univ. Press, 1965), pp. 18–19.

5. H. W. Belmore, *Rilke's Craftsmanship* (London: Oxford Press, 1954), p. 193.

6. McKay, *Selected Poems*, p. 21.

7. C. F. MacIntyre, "Introduction" to *Rilke: Duino Elegies* (Berkeley and Los Angeles: University of California Press, 1961), p. v.

8. C. F. MacIntyre, "Introduction" to *Rilke: Selected Poems* (Berkeley and Los Angeles: Univ. of California Press, 1962), pp. 5–6.

9. MacIntyre, *Duino Elegies*, p. 33.

10. *Ibid*.

11. McKay, *Selected Poems*, p. 65.

12. Randall Jarrell, "The Woman at the Washington Zoo," in *A Sad Heart at the Supermarket* (New York: Atheneum Press, 1962), p. 162.

13. Randall Jarrell, *Complete Poems*, p. 5.

14. Suzanne Ferguson, *The Poetry of Randall Jarrell* (Baton Rouge: Louisiana State Univ. Press, 1971), p. 152.

15. J. B. Leishman, trans., *Rainer Maria Rilke: Later Poems* (London: The Hogarth Press, 1938), p. 94.

Randall Jarrell: Landscapes
of Life and *Life*

Sister M. Bernetta Quinn*

Landscapes exist in the mind long after they stop being present to the eye. In both modes, they are partly created out of emotions aroused by what has happened in certain places. Through landscapes as laminated as those of Vuillard, Randall Jarrell tells the story of an individual life (his own or another's) and in addition relates the more comprehensive tale of *life* itself.

His days at Tarbox School, Nashville, Tennessee, brought him little happiness, if one can judge from the cumulative negative emotions built up by poems about his early youth. Yet with an inverted primitivism he persists in wandering back to the country of his childhood. His most vivid grade-school flashback has as its title "The Elementary Scene," arrived at after "The Daughters of Memory" and "The Child's Dream," were discarded as titles (as shown by worksheets at the University of North Carolina, Greensboro). By stressing the landscape connotation of *scene* he is able to communicate pictorially the pain he endured as a boy, a pain common enough among sensitive children. In "The Elementary Scene" symbol-equivalencies for *sun* weld the links in a chain of "interior landscapes," as the protagonist goes through his routine of schooldays.

> The white sun like a tin plate
> Over the wooden turning of the weeds;
> The street jerking—a wet swing—
> To end by the wall the children sang.

A tin plate has the unpleasant association with prison—the familiar child's attitude towards school but here representing something much deeper which has persisted into adulthood. "The Elementary Scene" is world stripped of divinity. The attribution of *wooden* to the moving weeds carries a sensation of numbness, as in "He looked at her woodenly." The thin, straggling, yellow-rotten grass by the girls' door and "the gaunt field with its one tied cow" (the animal symbolic of the schoolboy) consti-

*Reprinted from *Shenandoah: The Washington and Lee University Review*, 20, No. 2 (1969), 49–78, with permission of the editor. Copyright © 1969 by Washington and Lee University.

tute a situation expressed thus: "The dead land waking sadly to my life—"
Imagery of an earlier version heightened the distastefulness:

> And the gaunt field with its one tied cow
> like a sodden paper in the death
> that wells like evening over everything.
>
> (manuscript at U. of N.C.G.)

With hardly the exhilaration of Stevenson's little song in *A Child's Garden of Verses*, the boy, playing at recess on the wet swing of "The Elementary Scene," jerks the street into a distortion broken again and again by Humpty-Dumpty's wall.

The poet bends over the alienated child he then was as its phantom lies tossing toward sleep in a darkness conceived of as the absence of a star:

> Till, leaning a lifetime to the comforter
>   [the quilt on his bed]
> I float above the small limbs like their dream:
>
> I, I, the future that mends everything.

When he was a child he had expected miracles of the future, not realizing that *he* was and would always be that future. The free manipulation of tenses corresponds to a sentence on the dust jacket of a science-fiction novel on Jarrell's bookshelves at the time of his death, *Timeliner* by Charles Maine Erie: "Here is a provocative story of tomorrow and of one man forced to fight through future eras to return to his own world and his own identity."

Unquestionably, the author of this lyric, "The Elementary Scene," anticipates throughout it the neo-Romantic, subjective, plunging image of his own later poetry. More significantly, he shows himself here as elsewhere to be the single tie between the formalistic witty ironies of Auden, Tate, Ransom, Moore, and others of the Older Generation, and the intuitive, almost surrealistic landscapes of James Wright, Robert Bly, Theodore Roethke, Denise Levertov. Either Bly or Wright might have written "the bare night of the fields" and "the wind jumps like a dog against her legs" of Jarrell's "A Ghost, A Real Ghost." Preceding contemporary experiment in this vein is "The cow wandering in the bare field," a poem greatly admired by Robert Penn Warren and published at twenty by Jarrell in *The American Review*. In giving a body to loneliness, dream (waking or sleeping) forms the common denominator with recent poets: the freedom of the unconscious. A lesser bond is Jarrell's way of heightening melody not by a pre-determined pattern but by letting intuitive alliteration hold the poem together, with occasional rhyme-echoes or assonance: *swing* and *sang; Stir* and *curl; switches* and *witches* ("The Elementary Scene").

Experience in the first person, seen as a landscape painter might see it, also comprises the data for "A Country Life," "The Orient Express," "Field and Forest," "A Game at Salzburg." Though they range in setting as far as Austria these four verse-reveries are like a series of Bergman throwbacks worked into an American context. They are all richly autobiographical. The poet's Kenyon College roommate and longtime friend, Robert Lowell, wrote about him thus in the commemorative issue of Greensboro's University of North Carolina *Alumni News*: "But what Jarrell's inner life really was in all its wonder, variety, and subtlety is best told in his poetry."

Very different from "Binsey Poplars" with its "sweet especial rural scene," the farmland of "A Country Life" is desolate without being hopeless. A personalized reaction of what living "in the country" is like, the poem is cast in a formal pattern which leans backwards toward the Fugitive group once gathered at Vanderbilt. The view contemplated by the speaker arouses a feeling in him which deepens from dissatisfaction to grim repulsion, as indicated by the diction (*Hunched, scarecrow, sideways, heat, lagging, parched*). Monotony is underscored by the title, which implies that all the inhabitants of the region lead the *same* life. As an opening the lyric uses a fine illusion based on a metaphor unconsciously present when announcers report the weather:

> A bird that I don't know,
> Hunched on his light-pole like a scarecrow,
> Looks sideways out into the wheat
> The wind waves under the waves of heat.

Though the most noticeable ripples are those of the grain, the air itself, half-visible, rolls over the field in heatwaves. No mocking bird is singing here in a lacy deodar tree as at home; rather a nameless bird huddles on the dead trunk of an electric-light pole.

Then Jarrell adds to this bleak landscape a blowing locust tree, sketched in with colors which might well have been taken from the labels on tubes of oil-paints (*leaf-green, shade violet*), a natural choice, since he had always wanted to be a painter. In his Greensboro home, this dream lingers on in a portrait he did of himself shaving and in a picture, executed in the A. E. Russell manner, of a woman's dark head floating in pastel clouds—souvenir of a painfully broken-off early romance. The locust in "A Country Life" is an emblem comparable to the psalm of fertility in the Old Testament:

> The field is yellow as egg-bread dough
> Except where (just as though they'd let
> It live for looks) a locust billows
> In leaf green and shade violet,
> A standing mercy.

The tree has an equal value though not the same tenor as the willow mourning in "Lady Bates."

There is no one to interrogate about the bird's name, though in the poet's heart he recognizes it as the scarecrow death; or about its human neighbors:

> Or why, for once, the lagging heron
> Flaps from the little creek's parched cresses
> Across the harsh-grassed, gullied meadow
> To the black, rowed evergreens below.

Landscape here is a diminished thing—an awkward heron, a rivulet threading its way through an overgrown pasture pitted with holes, the "prospect" brought to a halt by a row of black pines. Around Nashville, as around Greensboro, the soil is burnt-orange, marvelous for growing if kept irrigated but as sterile as brick if not. When the bird calls "*Red* clay, *red* clay" (italics mine), its sound might as easily be understood as "Directly, directly." Directly death will lower the "red, clay face" (how much significance the comma gives!) of native son after native son into "the naked clay."

This landscape has been rendered in conversational words, as close to talk as an excellently counterfeited emerald is to the genuine article. Since the "I" is alone, the poem is obviously an "interior monologue," or perhaps better, a meditation. As it fades away, Jarrell introduces stars as signs of affirmation, in this case reinforced by a church steeple:

> From the grove under the spire
> Stars shine, and a wandering light
> Is kindled for the mourner, man.

Milton too in "Lycidas" grieves for himself and for all humanity, consoled, however, in his lament by music, not light: the singing from afar of angelic societies.

Stars are customarily symbols of hope in Jarrell. The Rilke translations "The Breath of Night," "Death," "Lament" and "Evening" all draw on astral imagery to save these lyrics from absolute melancholy: the fact that he liked them enough to turn them into English makes each a window into his own landscape-responses. "Second Air Force" changes planes and beacon lights at a base into stars that answer each other. "Nestus Gurley" plays on the word *Star* across a newspaper, connecting it by invisible lines to Orion, a constellation beloved by Jarrell, and to the Moravian many-pointed star, an ordinary part of his Greensboro environs with its Moravian congregation. Most touching of all stellar allusions is that in "The Meteorite":

> Star, that looked so long among the stones
> And picked from them, half iron and half dirt,
> One; and bent and put it to her lips

> And breathed upon it till at last it burned
> Uncertainly, among the stars its sisters—
> Breathe on me still, star, sister.

Dead matter kindled into fire becomes here creative power.

When even the stars, those presences of faith, vanish, the world becomes a giant cemetery. Later the poet adds: "The stars go down into the West; a ghostly air / Troubles the dead cities on the earth" ("An English Garden in Austria").

Perhaps in Jarrell's childhood the dark was a forest, a dread projected now into adult terms in "Field and Forest," identifiable with the mysterious, repeated in fantasy by the landscape below his flight, as it stood before men's axes had cleared out blocks for cultivation. Even now, forests are to be feared since they shelter the fox that steals out at night to eat chickens, and the crop-destroying deer. Penetrating in daydream the farmer's consciousness, the man in the plane speculates, in a voice very much like Frost's, on how profitable it would be to turn the entire forest to farm, if marsh and rock would permit.

"Field and Forest" opens: "When you look down from the airplane you see lines, / Roads, ruts, braided into a net or web—" Already the landscape serves as transference for a trapped sensation the spectator is experiencing. Topographical features and language are identified: when Heaven asks the farmer "What's your field?" his silent answer to the personified sky is a pasture. As in Constable, his herd of cows is a picture worth a thousand words—the animals themselves the best definition possible of dairy-farming, even though his response to the question does not especially matter because his trade is as insignificant as "a boy's toy cow." Through the echo device Jarrell noted in Williams when he brilliantly reviewed the first part of *Paterson*, he imitates in the lines "the terrible monotony of the fields."

The final landscape in this lyric is animated, like Charles Burchfield's woodland canvases, with humanized trees. Stirred by a death-wish, the boy that the plane-traveler once was stands looking at the cave sheltering a sleeping fox, the fields all around him dreaming; without farmers and farms they have turned to forest again, just as the boy and fox exchange roles, until "the trees can't tell the two of them apart." Since the field has become woods (for which these trees stand as synechdoche) the poem ends by "assuming" the voyager into the primeval spell of darkness.

To achieve dramatic distance Jarrell can shift to impersonality in landscaping the country of the soul. "Leave" brings a painter's eye to the desert of southern Arizona, where as the author's notes to the lyric say, "isolated mountain ranges rise nine or ten thousand feet, like islands from a sea of sand." This equation of desert and ocean justifies the reader in attributing to the mountain on which the pilot is spending his furlough all that an island symbolizes in Yeats and Auden. There is here, as elsewhere in Jarrell, an explicit reference to Chinese landscape. With economy of choice Jarrell summons from his air force memories the firs girded with waist-high brown ferns, the huge aspens, pine trees hammered at by upside-down woodpeckers, a stalky meadow: "But the plants evolve into a rock, the precipice / Habitual, in Chinese ink, to such a scene." Habitual, too, is the cascade tumbling from rock to rock. As he stares down the cliff's side, the man on leave inserts into the view the usual Confucian sage:

> Persisting in a cleft, one streaming fir
> Must shelter at its root a fat philosopher
> Reducing to his silence this grey upper world.

The key word is *grey*, with its invariable depressing or at least negative effect. Jarrell preferred all other colors to this drab neutrality, in "Leave" symbolizing the "non-existence" of war routine from which this appraiser of landscape has come and to which he must shortly return, even though the *grey* applies here to the world of his reprieve: the furlough cannot escape being blighted by its brevity. Within sight of bombers and fighters the soldier cannot achieve the Oriental serenity evoked by the seven peaks rising over the dim fields of the air base. Japanese landscape art dominates the mother-son lyric "The Rising Sun," also out of the war years, a poem Jarrell wrote after seeing a documentary on Japan shown while he was flight instructor in WW II. This second "canvas" depicts black pines and a cloud-girdled mountain painted against a background of starlight. The soldier whose experience is tenuously captured here dreams that his mother is with him, her head "a five-colored cloud" bobbing over his bed. Reality, in war, is always somewhere else.

"The End of the Rainbow" is unique in that it is an extended verse-biography of a landscape painter. Set on a California beach similar to Laguna, where Jarrell spent peaceful vacations, listening to the sun-warmed surf, it begins:

> Far from the clams and fogs and bogs
> —The cranberry bogs—of Ipswich,
> A sampler cast upon a savage shore,
> There dwells in a turquoise, unfrequented store
> A painter; a painter of land- and seascapes

This turquoise store is in southern California, not northern; the location is as symbolic as that of northern and southern Italy. Against the Pacific's beauty rises, in the painter's mind, the rocky coastline of Massachusetts, a Puritan severity clinging to it. At the very outset, Jarrell makes a place into an art-form: the Ipswich cranberry bogs become "A sampler cast upon a savage shore."

The heroine works away at her easel, light streaming unlovingly over the routine gesture of her "spare, paint-spotted and age-spotted hands" as they finish a water-scene:

> Beyond the mahlstick a last wave
> Breaks in Cobalt, Vert Emeraude, and Prussian Blue
> Upon a Permanent White shore.

Capitalizing these colors is a means of reducing them to bright wet substances squeezed out of tubes onto a palette so that one sees a mechanical response remote from the improvisations of a man like Wallace Stevens regarding in pensive vein the same blue and green sea breaking upon white sand. Like a dull ache, the hopelessness of the woman pulses through the last line ("Upon a Permanent White shore"). In one ambivalent sentence Jarrell then compresses all her years to a single brushing of her hair, "finer and redder once / Than the finest of red sable brushes" but now "brushed / Till it is silver." Like Rip Van Winkle, she has aged in an instant, as she sees in that electrifying surprise no stranger to aging hearts.

The Californian littoral landscape of "The End of the Rainbow" exists on multiple levels. The sea belongs to a marine painting (a page of an interminable "book") and is also the actual ocean. Both have betrayed the artist, leaving the traces of their treachery on her false-blue hair: "And blue / Are all the lights the seascapes cast upon it, blue / The lights the false sea casts upon it." Only the dog, Su-Su, is naturally black. In the East, the woman's former lover lives in a great-windowed (glass) house on a New England strand, "the owner / Of the marsh-o'erlooking, silver-grey, unpainted salt-box." Jarrell converts him into the Frog-Prince, inhabiting an environment of cattails and darting tadpoles: the rushes "rustle again / In flaws or eddies of the wet wind." Metamorphosis mingles water images with the Marsh-King's appearance. In a preliminary stage of composition the Frog-Prince was pictured as "Overlooking a landscape like the ghost of Loss." (U. of N.C.G. ms.) When the woman sends him an occasional letter, she feels as if the mailbox marked THE STATES is a pool in which her one-time suitor lives.

The view next presented externalizes the self this landscape-painter has become:

> She turns away
> Into the irrigated land
> With its blond hills like breasts of hay,
> Its tall tan herds of eucalyptus grazing
> Above its lawns of ice-plant, of geranium,
> In meadows of eternal asphodel.

The eucalyptus trees, source of that Vicks Vapor Rub whose factories are prominent both in Jarrell's Californian and North Carolina landscapes, eat away like cattle at the hills, here represented as blonde women. The artificially watered slopes constitute an Elysium no more satisfying than that of Achilles, in *The Odyssey*. It is as if her life were already over and she was on the other side of eternity:

> The dark ghosts throng by
> Shaking their locks at her—their fair, false locks—
> Stretching out past her their bare hands, burnt hands.

Reading this, one cannot miss the repetition of how her own hands and hair were earlier described. To emphasize the resemblance, the poem elaborates on her deep tan:

> And she—her face is masked, her hands are gloved
> With a mask and gloves of bright brown leather:
> The hands of a lady left out in the weather
> Of resorts; the face of a fine girl left out in the years.

Where one expects weather, Jarrell in the manner of Auden or Dylan Thomas substitutes years; even more like Auden is the preceding combination "the weather/ Of resorts."

Polarized throughout "The End of the Rainbow" are California and Massachusetts, the first with its seals barking on the rocks and the second with frogs croaking by night on their marshy islands. Each Western detail is balanced with an Eastern one. After a battery of remembered proverbs (residue of her schooldays), the woman lapses into a mournful recollection of Arnold's "The Forsaken Merman," a variation of the plot of Jarrell's children's book *The Animal Family*. The sterility of her fate is not unusual in this Californian artists' colony of empty lives:

> Little Women, Little Men,
> Upon what shores, pink-sanded, besides what cerulean
> Seas have you trudged over, nodded over, napped away
> Your medium-sized lives!

How right Thoreau was when he declared: "The mass of men lead lives of quiet desperation."

When the woman retreats to her childhood, it too looms up in terms of landscape. Her bedroom as imagined is the ocean, her rag rug moving in a crescendo from an island, to the Pole, to the Northwest Passage, to the Hesperides. The candle by which she reads *The Swiss Family Robinson* creates a "warm, flickering / Hemisphere." Now, that light is "gone, gone forever / Out into darkness." She has grown old enough to be invisible, like the shopping housewife in the first lyric of *The Lost World*.

After lunch the woman goes back to her studio:

> Opening the belled door,
> She turns once more to her new-framed, new-glassed
> Landscape of a tree beside the sea.
> It is light-struck.
>
> If you look at a picture the wrong way
> You see yourself instead.

This version achieves a conciseness and poetic tension beyond the U. of N. C. G.'s draft, even though the latter is shorter:

> If a landscape's glassed
> And you look from the wrong direction, you cannot see
> The landscape, but only yourself.

How many people walk through art galleries talking about themselves rather than the masterpieces, looking at the landscapes "the wrong way"? Every art form is in a sense a mirror. Jarrell never came near a looking-glass without examining his face in it, increasingly concerned with the approach of death his reflection revealed. But a mirror, whatever its secrets or prophecies, is only the first step. The landscape under glass must be looked at from the right direction, in a *light* which like *dark* is symbolic.

Besides her own countenance, the woman-painter sees in the light-struck landscape, once she moves a little, her spiritual destiny as a lonely tree planted next to the waves. The metaphor recalls Jarrell's rendition of Masha's song in *The Three Sisters*: "By the sea-strand a green oak stands," and the very next words, appropriate because "The End of the Rainbow" is so heavily weighted with financial images: "a chain of gold upon it." Played first professionally by New York's Actors Studio Theatre with Kim Stanley as Masha, Randall Jarrell's *The Three Sisters* is destined to be one of the great translations of the century, partly because he felt Chekhov to be the most intimate friend of his own spirit. Careful study of how he treated this play throws into a different focus many of his original lyrics and the method behind their patterning.

A major preoccupation of his last years was his struggle to turn Goethe's *Faust* into English, a project fortunately completed at the time of his death in 1965, except for a few songs. Goethe was for him a literary idol, together with Chekhov, Yeats, Rilke, Hardy, Kipling, Proust. The following lines in "The End of the Rainbow" seem to be Jarrell's rather ironic meditation rather than the thought of his protagonist:

> A quarter of an hour and we tire
> Of any landscape, said Goethe; eighty years
> And he had not tired of Goethe. The landscape had,
> And disposed of Goethe in the usual way.

Earth, he implies, had received her honored guest, only to quickly make havoc of his physique. Goethe's apothegm refers to an unpeopled landscape or to one cut off from any empathetic relationship with the beholder. Jarrell's are no more unpeopled than Breughel's and almost as capable of holding interest indefinitely. The woman-artist's landscapes are the type which would have bored Goethe. One discarded draft continues the passage about the German writer's dissolution into earth with a description of her work:

> Here the landscapes
> Are uninhabited through Art. The seascapes
> Seal-less through Art.
>
> (U. of N.C.G.)

As in "The Märchen," seals are equated with men; a pun on the German noun for soul (*seele*) may also be intended. Later in transforming the passage into "The unpeopled landscapes / Run down to the seal-less, the merman-less seas," Jarrell entirely drops the agency "through Art."

Of all late medieval or early Renaissance landscapes, those of manuscript-illuminators are perhaps the most fruitful for a study of symbolism. From museum to museum in Europe, the Jarrells contemplated with delight pages from the Duke of Burgundy's *Book of Hours*. The initial letter in the specimen from this work which hangs over the woman's bed begins a poignant half-truth: HE WHO HAS HIMSELF FOR FRIEND IS BEST BEFRIENDED:

> One sees, through the bars of the first *H*, a landscape
> Manned with men, womened with women, dogged with a
>   dog,
> And influenced—Content says—by the influence
> Of *The Very Rich Hours of the Duke of Burgundy*.

Content is a first name like Prudence or Hope, borrowed from Mary von Schrader Jarrell's Massachusetts family, a member of which ("Cousin Bertha") moved out to California and at her death left Mrs. Jarrell the beach house incorporated into this poem, as are other real details, such as the dog Su-Su.

A shift occurs from *Hours* in upper case, here a brilliant wealthy image, to *hours* as suffered through by an insomniac ("the very long hours"). Though the landscape-painter is only half-sleeping under the whisperings of wind and waves, she dreams of a man out of her past, someone smelling of peppermint after-shave lotion and standing in the water holding out to her with enormous hands a corsage of watercress shining with drops that contain cupids, water babies, little women, little men. She is young again, her silver hair gone back to red and as long as a fairy princess's—long enough to float out to him as she calls out the word *Father*, half in address and half as a threat to summon her parent. He melts away into Su-Su, in Su-Su's dark little grave, described in landscape-terms: "The Prince is dead. . . . The willows waver / Above the cresses of his tomb." Steeped in the writings of Sigmund Freud, Randall Jarrell saw in dream-phenomena that author's interpretations.

On the non-Freudian level, Jarrell in "The End of the Rainbow" is pursuing a stratified attack in the Vuillard manner on the development of his key-idea, holding together in a fabric of fact and fantasy the poetic psychography. The ballet of Death and Life next introduced revives the ghost-ship episode from Coleridge's "The Ancient Mariner":

> Beside her, Death
> Or else Life—spare, white, permanent—
> Works out their *pas de deux*: here's Death
> Arranging a still-life for his own Content.

As intimated above, Death and Life are all but indistinguishable in her barren existence: here, the fusion is emphasized by the singular verb *works* with the plural "their *pas de deux.*" Permanent White has become "white, permanent," the blankness persisting. The heroine belongs to Death (she is "his own Content") and at this point in the poem he acts for her, arranging a still-life; digging for gold at the end of the rainbow but striking only water and oil; washing out her brushes in the Hopi jar and handing them to her. When she dies, he will submit to the trustees of her estate "a varied / Portfolio": paintings and stock-certificates.

A microcosm of the title-image, and the most beautiful line in the work, slips in quietly as an iridescent screen between the artist and her mirror ("—The little home-made rainbow, there in tears—"). She pathetically begs her reflection for reassurance, as does the Queen in *Snow-White*:

> She says: "Look at my life. Should I go on with it?
> It seems to you I have . . . a real gift?
> I shouldn't like to keep on if I only. . . .
> It seems to you my life is a success?"

Death answers, *Yes. Well, yes.*

Then she surveys the collection of unsold landscapes in her little shop:

> She looks around her:
> Many waves are breaking on many shores,
> The wind turns over, absently,
> The leaves of a hundred thousand trees.

The meaninglessness of her past comes through in the figure of the wind as a distracted reader leafing among the pages of a dry book. This woman has put all her eggs in one basket. Now, as the poem arrives at its goal, paralleling the progress of her life, she sees the world she has fashioned for herself as an artifact similar to the "sampler cast upon a savage shore," though now it takes the form of a patchwork quilt, such as Jarrell, both as child and adult, slept under:

> How many colors, squeezed from how many tubes
> In patient iteration, have made up the world
> She draws closer, like a patchwork quilt,
> To warm her, all the warm, long summer day!

Landscapes and comforters have often been compared: "The blocked-out Tree / Of the boy's Life in gray / On the tangled quilt. . . ." (A Quilt-Pattern"). Symbolic of her low spirits and at the same time punning on the neutral appearance of the arid region, the pictures lose their primary hues:

> The local colors fade:
> She hangs here on the verge of seeing
> In black and white,
> And turns with an accustomed gesture
> To the easel, saying:
> "Without my paintings I would be—why, whatever
>   *would* I be?"

The pun on *local* is typical of Jarrell's compassionate wit.

In posing this question in the words of a character talking to herself, Jarrell, as so frequently, wrestles with the problem of identity. Earlier in the lyric-narrative, "She has looked into the mirror of the marsh / Flawed with the flight of dragonflies, the life of rushes, / And seen—what she had looked for—her own face." Her canvases make an even more obscure glass than the Massachusetts marsh. The weird effect of finding the unexpected in a mirror is elsewhere exploited from the point of view of a character literally rather than spiritually dead:

> The first night I looked into the mirror
> And saw the room empty, I could not believe
> That it was possible to keep existing
> In such pain: I have existed.
>
> ("A Ghost, a Real Ghost")

One sheet of Jarrell's "The End of the Rainbow" manuscripts achieves an equally startling impact by exchanging art for mirrored life:

> She turns once more to her new-framed, new-glassed
> Landscape of a tree beside the sea.
> She looks: no tree, no sea: it is light-struck.
>
> (U. of N.C.G.)

She feels as if both she (the tree) and her world (the sea) have been annihilated by a thunderbolt, a reaction that the ellipsis of the final version causes, perhaps, to go unnoticed.

No landscape element except the star is more of an integral symbol in Jarrell than water-mirrors. In "The Skaters" the ice, as well as its mutation into a face, is "the fast and flattering glass." In "A Rhapsody on Irish Themes" Orion's points of light float in the Irish Sea. All of these "removes from reality" press home the fact that the natural world is changed by imagination.

Southern California, in "The End of the Rainbow," is the realm of the actual; Ipswich, for the painter at least, that of fantasy (dream, memory, reverie). Ipswich is the Promised Land turned sour, the wrong end of the rainbow. All the traditional symbolism of this colored arch spanning the skies, all its physical loveliness as captured by Turner and

Cole, Heade and Bierstadt, collapse before the ironic gaze of the poet who writes in "A Girl in the Library" that "the ways in which we miss our lives are life."

Life viewed collectively forms the subject for two of Randall Jarrell's finest achievements: "The Märchen" and "Deutsch Durch Freud." The first presents the *märchen* themselves as Life in a child's eyes. It develops the idea of enclave so pervasive in this poet, here as the "inland island." The forest is an evertossing sea, primeval and murmuring, like the forest in "Evangeline." As the pioneers chopped down its trees, they created art-forms for habitation, whereon the sunlight fell to them as to their wish, an echo of that story Jarrell praises in superlatives: "*The Fisherman and His Wife* was collected by the Brothers Grimm, and to me it's the best fairy tale ears ever heard or tongue ever told" (*The Rabbit Catcher and other Fairy Tales of Ludwig Bechstein*, p. 6). Called out of fiction by the reading child, these gold-lit retreats from the harsh world stand forth against the dark of Necessity, that "unbroken wood" of his daily unexistence.

In "The Märchen" the sun is ultimately a pejorative symbol. At first, while the islands are being carved out by axes, it promises happiness, a hope coursing through the start of this passage but checked with its changing refrain:

> The sunlight fell to them, according to our wish,
> And we believed, till nightfall, in that wish;
> And we believed, till nightfall, in our lives.

The shifting pronouns make clear that "the lost world" is viewed with a subjectivity which increases as, at noon, the gold sun becomes nothing but a "homely, mercenary, magnified" circle drawn with India ink on a green background. By evening, the sun is the "foolish gold" guiding soldiers onward who wander on crutches through leagues of shadows, an image suggesting the title of one of Jarrell's collections of poems. A Bosch or a Breughel might well have depicted the total disillusion of

> the plots
> Where life, horned sooty lantern patched with eyes,
> Hides more than it illumines, dreams the hordes
> Of imps and angels, all of its own hue.

From rain-clouds, lightning sent by an avenging Father flashes out. Life has shrunk from the landscape of fairy tale, no longer believed in, to a troubled sleep frustrated by the need to change which the *märchen* urge without divulging their secret of how to do so.

"The Carnegie Library, Juvenile Division," much altered from its first published version ("Children Selecting Books in a Library" in *Blood for a Stranger*) also centers throughout on the folktale as metaphor for life. It begins with the child-patron looking out at the "hills and stone and steeples of the town / Grey in the pure red of the dying sun," the landscape set in antithesis to the safe cavern of the library. Jarrell uses again the identification of Life with the *märchen*, together with a repetition of island-imagery, accented here by his turning the noun *isle* into a verb:

> . . . the beasts loom in the green
> Firred darkness of the märchen: country the child thought life
> And wished for and crept to out of his own life—
> Must you still isle such, raiders from a world
> That you so long ago lost heart to represent?

Unexpectedly, darkness is longed for, its fearsome connotations cancelled out by the excitement of this special realm of green shadows prowled by magic animals. The entrance to Life, where waves are roofs; seals, men; and twilight hues are rhymes, is "the hole / That widens from the middle of a field / To that one country where the poor see gold," a gold easily tainted by avarice, as the fisherman and his insatiable wife discover.

Jarrell concludes "The Märchen" with a microcosm-macrocosm analogy. To buy Life on the *märchen's* terms, non-existence must be laid on the library-counter:

> How many here will purchase with a world
> These worlds still smoldering for the perpetual
> Children who haunt this fire-sale of the centuries.

Some people never grow up, childhood being for them a "perpetual" state. With his racing cars and science fiction magazines, his love of fairy tales and of assigning to birds and animals humanity in conversation, fiction, and verse, Randall Jarrell was a child to the end.

The *märchen* as enclave is replaced in "A Girl in a Library" by a room full of books treated as landscapes that their authors have dreamed through the ages:

> Here in this enclave there are centuries
> For you to waste: the short and narrow stream
> Of Life meanders into a thousand valleys
> Of all that was, or might have been, or is to be.

The New Testament's straight and narrow path becomes a short and narrow stream through which the united waters of Life rather than an individual life leisurely flow. Over the panorama a rosy nimbus gathers about the visionary:

> Those sunrise-colored clouds
> Around man's head—that inconceivable enchantment
> From which, at sunset, we come back to life
> To find our graves dug, families dead, selves dying:

Asleep but not dreaming, a Wooden not a Golden Mean, the student of the title stands for the New World of pragmatism; the enclave of books, for the Old World of more humane values—a childhood of the race which, paradoxically, is its maturity.

As early as 1950 Jarrell seized upon the German language as an equivalent not only for his interior landscape but for Life itself. "Deutsch Durch Freud" opens: "I believe my favorite country's German," a line which if taken in all its implications demands logically that everything he says about German apply also to a country. The result is his version of another American writer's landscape symbol for Life: Thomas Wolfe's in "Only the Dead Know Brooklyn." Underlying both is the frightening insight that none but the dead can completely master Life: "The thought of *knowing* German terrifies me." Jarrell never learned to speak German nor to read it easily, despite his translations of Rilke, Mörike, Goethe, and others. This poem is his *apologia*:

> —But surely, this way, no one could learn German?
> And yet . . .
>   It's difficult; is it impossible?
> I'm hopeful that it is, but I can't say
> For certain: I don't know enough German.

Jarrell has no wish to be another Dr. Heidegger. "Sailing to Byzantium" and "Ode on a Grecian Urn" disguise the same preference for imperfection, which is in reality a preference for life over lifelessness: "If God gave me the choice—but I stole this from Lessing— / Of German and learning German, I'd say: Keep your German!" The theft from Lessing comes from "If God said to me, 'I have the search for Truth in my left hand and the Truth in my right, choose,' I would fall into his left hand and say the Truth is for You alone." (Mary Jarrell's note in her copy of *The Woman at the Washington Zoo*, p. 59).

The Chinese define landscape as a space to walk about in: to be pleasurable it must be capable of discoveries:

> Ah, German!
> Till the day I die I'll be in love with German
> —If only I don't learn German. . . .

When a country is thoroughly explored, it is exhausted. Ignorance of vocabulary keeps one safe from death, since a person can't die until he knows the right inflection of *sterben*:

> I can hear my broken
> Voice murmuring to *der Arzt: "Ich—sterber?"*
> He answers sympathetically: *"Nein—sterbe."*

The final words of Chekhov, whom Jarrell considered his *doppelgänger*, were *"Ich sterbe."*

In the second line of "Deutsch Durch Freud," the expansion of German as a country takes the form of "I wander in a calm folk-colored daze," the speaker following the same road that Kant reels down "*im Morgenrot / Humming Mir ist so bang, so bang, mein Schatz—*" Kant fits in well as a citizen of Jarrell's chosen country. The poet, who in his last two years read straight through William James, was consistently interested in idealism and gave some of his best thought to the connection between word and thing which integrates this poem. When he is in his land of German, he does not doubt reality; the Word falls on his head like a blessed rain, inspiring him with a faith unknown to "hard-eyed industry" and to "the school's dark Learning." In German viewed as landscape a wonderfully beautiful linden tree stands in the moonlight. Luckily *business, teaspoon, soap, sidewalk, suitcase* and other trivialities are outlawed here ("*Schweig stille, meine Seele!* Such things are not for thee") but not *world, moon, heart, grief, time, eternity.* Because he knows the names of the latter in German, they belong, without bitterness, to his preferred country, Life, across the limits of which, he says cleverly, the Norns can't pursue him because he doesn't know the German word for scissors. It is dangerous to learn too much; not only does one lose the secret joys of childhood belief in metamorphosis but the assignments become all but prohibitive: "It is by Trust, and Love, and reading Rilke / Without *ein Wörterbuch*, that man learns German." Though merely the neutral pronoun in German, *man* serves admirably to enlarge the scope of the lyric.

In "Second Air Force," Randall Jarrell concentrates on a depressing landscape correlative to a scene in the life of a mother come to visit her pilot-son. What he says about William Carlos Williams in *Poetry and the Age*—that colors and surfaces in landscape matter only in so far as they reveal its analogical, anthropomorphized life (p. 214)—seems particularly apropos here. Reading the lyric, one thinks, perhaps, of Chekhov, who for years wore a seal ring engraved "To the lonely man the world is a desert." Written in 1944, during World War II, it adopts experimental-film technique in presenting the air-base hangars as swaying hills looming above the summer-dried plain. The woman's spirit matches the desert inferno which lies before her:

> She sees a world: sand roads, tar-paper barracks,
> The bubbling asphalt of the runways, sage,
> The dunes rising to the interminable ranges,
> The dim flights moving over clouds like clouds.

The planes, "green made beasts," at night turn to stars, huge globes of fire drifting in from Mars. By the use of the participle as applied to the returning aircraft ("great lights floating"), Jarrell initiates the metaphor of air as ocean, continuing it in poetry almost as beautiful as the corresponding lines in Robert Penn Warren's "Bearded Oaks." The base might be Atlantis:

the woman and her son
Stand in the forest of the shadows, and the light
Washes them like water. In the long-sunken city
Of evening, the sunlight stills like sleep
The faint wonder of the drowned; in the evening,
In the last dreaming light, so fresh, so old,
The soldiers pass like beasts, unquestioning.

The sky's "steady winter" is hostile. When Jarrell writes that the twilight takes *everything*, one senses that the woman recognizes how truly it symbolically does.

If Randall Jarrell can paint the landscapes of Hell, he can also paint Paradise. Like all human beings, he longs for a Never-Never Land. "A Rhapsody on Irish Themes" is a lilting song which celebrates Ireland as the lotus-eaters' retreat, or, again, as "the Western Isles." The enclave of "The Märchen" and other poems returns: Erin is one more refuge from the matter-of-fact, the quotidian ("You Eden of Paleolithic survivals, / You enclave of Brünn and of Borreby man"). The Irish landscape as seen from a ship as angle of observation is green under a blue sky, with a blood-red patch cut out on a treeless hillside. Jarrell's great-grandmother becomes Cathleen ni Houlihan, "A sleep-walker fallen from the edge of Europe, / A goosegirl great among publicans and censors"—appositives echoing the substitutions of "Fern Hill," which also praises heaven from which its laureate (Dylan Thomas) is banned. No other Jarrell lyric has the lightheartedness of this, capturing as it does the very idiom of Ireland's musical tongue.

Next to "The End of the Rainbow" the most extensive treatment of poetic as connected to painted landscape in Jarrell is "The Old and the New Masters." It gives an answer to the question Breughel posed in *Landscape with the Fall of Icarus*: the problem of evil in the universe. In depicting the myth of the Cretan carpenter and his son, the Flemish artist shows a shepherd looking up into into the empty sky and a farmer staring down at the soil; the only eyes gazing at the drowning boy are those of a single sheep. Although one person in the vessel sailing past is in direct line of vision this man indicates by his static position a complete indifference to the plight of the fallen Icarus. Albert Skira in *Bruegel* affirms what landscape means to the merits of such a pictorial commentary:

> For Bruegel was essentially an open-air man, a lover of the windswept countryside of his native land, as well as a landscape painter born, and we feel this in all his work even when landscape is not the leading theme. (Skira, 1959, p. 38)

The name of the canvas hints that landscape is hardly a subordinate concern in the tale of Icarus.

Using the same opening words as Auden's in "Musée des Beaux Arts" ("About suffering they were never wrong, / the Old Masters") Jarrell goes on to change a satiric over-simplification to a truth: "About suffering they disagree—the Old Masters." The first painting he analyzes is Georges de la Tour's *St. Sebastian Mourned by St. Irene*, about which he has much to say in his *Art News* essay "The Age of the Chimpanzee" (Summer 1957, pp. 34–36) and which elevates suffering to perhaps the only universal. After describing this scene of mourning painted by a mourner, he moves backwards to the fifteenth century and to van der Goes.

In the 1470's Hugo van der Goes' *Adoration of the Shepherds* had interpreted the Christmas *tableau* as one in which everything, like the needle of a compass, points toward "the naked / Shining baby" born to bear the world's pain. On a trip to Florence, Jarrell found a good copy of this Uffizi altar-triptych which, displayed thereafter on a metal stand in his Greensboro home, provided increasingly illuminating detail under his magnifying glass, always as ready to hand as the binoculars he used in scrutinizing the landscapes adjacent to the house. Even though Jarrell re-titled the work *The Nativity* in order to focus the theme around which he built his poem, he must have been affected in every such period of contemplation by the wonderfully diversified expressions of the herdsmen adoring Jesus. Jarrell omits sense-particulars in favor of relevance to the organizing idea:

> Even the offerings, a sheaf of wheat,
> A jar and a glass of flowers, are absolutely still
> In natural concentration, as they take their part
> In the salvation of the natural world.

Just as all orders and sizes of creation are included in the van der Goes (angels, simple folk, nobility, saints, animals, plants, rocks), so are the various genres: still-life, portrait, landscape. Van der Goes blends levels of existence: the monster on which one of the women-saints stands could not possibly be there, as Randall Jarrell remarks in "The Age of the Chimpanzee" (p. 35), any more than could the Little People; these two orders exist in their own right, however, even if not visible to the naked eye as are the ox and ass.

As in medieval art, a prefigured Cubist treatment of time brings together events in defiance of chronology. Three of these "anecdotes" (the approach to Bethlehem of the Holy Couple, the announcement to the shepherds by angelic song of Christ's birth, and the coming of the Magi) involve symbolic landscape. All action is directed toward the miraculously conceived Infant newly issued from His mother's womb:

> The time of the world concentrates
> On this one instant: far off in the rocks
> You can see Mary and Joseph and their donkey
> Coming to Bethlehem;

Immediately above the patron-saint of the donor's two sons, Joseph is helping his spouse, who has the look of the Mater Dolorosa, as they move down the path while the donkey walks behind them. Irregular, harsh-appearing, Giotto-esque cliffs dramatize the difficulty of the journey, as does one tree bare of sheltering leaves. Only the light-apricot sky over the pair suggests a happy end to the pilgrimage. Jarrell describes the second landscape thus:

> on the grassy hillside
> Where their flocks are grazing, the shepherd's gesticulate
> In wonder at the star.

Deliberately made tiny to denote recession into the past, these sheeptenders, placed amidst their flocks in an olive-green area, are in communication with a diminutive white angel, the only angel not gazing at the Child: its role is one of communication rather than worship. Van der Goes departs from the Gospel narrative by setting the shepherds' vision in daylight, since the central panel, contrary to pictorial tradition, shows the Nativity by day rather than at night. Close in space to the climactic Babe is the cortege of Wise Men:

> the Magi out in the hills
> With their camels—they ask directions, and have pointed out
> By a man kneeling, the true way;

Curves on the earth's surface rather than jagged peaks bespeak imminent joy, as do trees housing Breughelian birds. The aristocrats who commissioned the five-hundred-year-old painting are as lasting as it is: they kneel in the future, like the advent of the Magi brought back to the "eternal instant" in the same manner the journey was brought up to Bethlehem, together with the message of the angels:

> and so many hundreds
> Of years in the future, the donor, his wife,
> And their children are kneeling, looking; everything
> That was or will be in the world is fixed
> On its small, helpless, human center.

As a summary of "The Old and the New Masters," one might allude to what Jarrell himself specifies as a connection between the de la Tour and the van der Goes in "The Age of the Chimpanzee" (p. 34). He regards the hands in both pictures as metaphors relating the represented world to its subject "out there" and also to the world inhabited by the viewer of these masterworks. Modern abstraction, he feels, has no "meaning" beyond what it is: the joined fingers are parallel cylinders only. By simplification, artists have lost the most valid reasons for painting. Intelligently eclectic though his tastes in art were, he disliked Abstract-Expressionism on grounds which he explains in his *Art News* feature:

> Earlier painting is a kind of metaphor: the world of the painting itself, of
> the oil-and-canvas objects and their oil-and-canvas relations, is one that

> stands for—that has come into being because of—the world of flesh-and-blood objects and their flesh-and-blood relations, the 'very world, which is the world / Of all of us,—the place where, in the end, / We find our happiness or not at all.' (*Ibid.*)

Three worlds exist here: the pictures, Nature, and our relation to both. Jarrell rejects the idea that the universe can be wrung into what lies at the end of a paint brush, even while he sees artists accepting this qualitative change which has finally grown out of the quantitative changes of the century.

"The Old and the New Masters" concludes:

> The earth is a planet among galaxies.
> Later Christ disappears, the dogs disappear, in abstract
> Understanding, without adoration, the last master puts
> Colors on canvas, a picture of the universe
> In which a bright spot somewhere in the corner
> Is the small radioactive planet men called Earth.

The Passion, relegated after the Renaissance to a minor portion of the composition, as in Breughel's *Way of the Cross*, has been replaced by a luminous dot which the men who used to inhabit it called Earth. Here, that extrapolation underlying the S-F tales by Heinemann, Bradbury, and others that Jarrell enjoyed furnishes the subject for the painter. Technological powers of destruction have led to a new landscape: the whole universe as recorded by the last artist before total demolition.

"The Age of the Chimpanzee" mitigates this cry of despair: "Man and the world are all that they ever were—their attractions are, in the end, irresistible: the painter will not hold out against them long" (p. 36). Jarrell is joined in this optimism by Sir Kenneth Clark, whom he strongly recommends. Clark examines in *Landscape into Art* a recurrent dread of the dissolution of creation, calling this fear Chiliasm. He traces its history up to the present era: "And in the last few years nature has not only seemed too large and too small for imagination: it has also seemed lacking in unity" (p. 141). Yet for all that, the critic believes that new forms will be found to express the human spirit, perhaps in an expressionism of the future inventive as the work of other Chiliastic artists such as Grünewald.

Jarrell holds no brief for Old Masters exclusively. He admired Oskar Kokoschka, for example, who painted into shapes the subjectivity struggling to emerge from the terrain of spirit, shapes that often came forth as enchanted, non-realistic landscapes like Franz Marc's *Water-Mill* in the Chicago Art Institute. For years an excellent, very large reproduction of Kokoschka's *City of Lyons* hung over the sideboard in his Greensboro home, taken from the original he must often have seen at the Phillips Gallery during his stay in Washington, D.C. In writing for an art-club meeting, Mary Jarrell communicates some of her husband's enthusiasm for Kokoschka, of whom she says: "He became the unrivaled landscape painter of his age, and the landscapes, too, are portraits; portraits of great historic cities in all their individuality."

The nearest analogue in Jarrell to Kokoschka's landscape-portraits of cities is "Thinking of the Lost World," wherein he returns as if in a time-machine out of one of his science-fiction novels, to the land of his child-hood. Though the setting resembles Greensboro, an ambiguity allows the reader to choose between the freedom of reverie and the possibility that he actually is again in California with his wife Mary, who before they met lived near him in Los Angeles:

> Come back to that calm country
> Through which the stream of my life first meandered,
> My wife, our cat, and I sit here and see
> Squirrels quarreling in the feeder, a mockingbird
> Copying our chipmunk, as our end copies
> Its beginning.

When he continues "Back in Los Angeles, we missed / Los Angeles" he symbolizes that bright joy lacking to them then because of their separateness by shifting from the thoughtlessly used name of the city to the Spanish word for angels. A trip today to Los Angeles and the adjoining Hollywood, with its Sunset Boulevard alluded to in this poem, shows that the "calm country" has suffered a fate like the one Natasha prophesies in her speech from the last act of *The Three Sisters*: "First of all, I'm going to have them chop down all those fir trees along the walk—then that maple . . . and I'll have them plant darling little flowers everywhere" is her tri-umphant response to the Baron's earlier burst of lyricism: "It's as if I were seeing for the first time in my life these firs and maples and birches, and they are all looking at me curiously and waiting. What beautiful trees, and how beautiful life ought to be under them" (Jarrell translation). The firs, maples, and cherry trees of Chekhov have all gone, like the Binsey poplars; so have the orange groves of Los Angeles:

> The sunshine of the Land
> Of Sunshine is a grey mist now, the atmosphere
> Of some factory planet: when you stand and look
> You see a block or two, and your eyes water.
> The orange-groves are all cut down . . .

The intensification gained in going from *sunshine* to *Sunshine* duplicates that in landscapes of *life* and *Life*.

In 1960 Mary and Randall Jarrell moved into the Garden Lakes development on the outskirts of Greensboro, North Carolina, near Guilford College. Theirs was the second of the houses breaking the "wilderness" which *The Bat-Poet* drew on for landscape-symbolism. Among the lyrics punctuating the prose of this book is "The Mockingbird," also included in *The Lost World*: its imagery of sunset, rising moon, willow, sparrows, thrushes, thrashers, jays, chickadees makes up the whole world this bird drives away with his pantomime in sound, his imitative music which may possibly *be* that world. Over and over, Jarrell in his verse concerns himself with the problem of art versus life/Life.

Each window in the home he liked to call his "House in the Woods" framed a landscape. From spring throughout summer, any of these points of observation rejoiced his heart with vistas of periwinkles, honeysuckle, azaleas, violets, roses, and in June the marvelous blossoms of the rhododendrons. From the east, Jarrell could see the long-needled pine, visited by birds in which he always took an extraordinary interest, both through binoculars and books. The west view from his bedroom showed a comma-shaped stone bench next to a tree stump and a stone rabbit, the latter symbolic of that desire to "hold the moment," a goal the unattainability of which was Faust's salvation. From the front bedroom window, facing south, he could watch the boy Nestus Gurley coming up to deliver his newspaper "While the soft, side-lit, gold-leafed day / Lingers to see the stars"—the reference gold-leafed transferable from the day to the trees beyond the L-shaped porch. In the yard flourished Scotch pine; tulip tree with its pink blossoms appearing before the leaves; sweet gum; wild judas; red gum; holly; black gum with its star-shaped flowers; dogwood; oak; deodar ("gift of God"); Southern cedar; mimosa; japonica. With all their "staggered" floral life, these kept these window-framed pictures, or the closer views from porch seat or hammock, just so many variegated joys capable, as in Jarrell's beloved Wordsworth, of elevating the soul.

Inside the house, the Kokoschka portrait of Lyons was but one testimonial among many to Jarrell's deep involvement with painting, including landscape. While he was not fond of the early English landscapists, he loved Cézanne, an example of whose work (a town in southern France) hung above his bed. His friends brought him presents according to his art-tastes: Peter Taylor, for instance, gave him a copy of a Hieronymus Bosch in the Prado collection—a peopled landscape featuring a lake alive with weird, half-formed figures. In the living room he had placed a detail from the Constantine series of Piero della Francesca, a genius at one time something of a passion with Jarrell, though later supplanted by Carpaccio among Quattrocento masters. In his office in the English department of the University he kept a reproduction of Breughel's *The Hunt*, with a smaller one at home; on winter evenings, from his western windows on the little road that is South Lake Drive, he could see its landscape images duplicated. When Robert Lowell returned from a trip to Italy he presented his friend with Uccello's *Battle of San Romano* (Uffizi), predecessor of a larger copy Jarrell himself later purchased in Florence. The arcs of this fifteenth-century painting are as if drawn with a compass, effecting a design as eloquent as the chain of hands in van der Goes. Rectilinear patterns also appear, the "pied" fields of the farthest distance in the Uccello foreshadowing Hopkins. In casual yet significant background action, a hound pursues a hare, while another hare streaks off in the opposite direction. Such "echoes" of the battle of San Romano correspond to digressions in a poem, a method of composition Jarrell employed constantly as he "worked" his conversational idiom into involutions of his theme through interrupted sentences and parenthetical remarks.

The complication of Uccello, then, relates meaningfully to Randall Jarrell's practice of turning a fascinating idea into an artifact through layer after layer of connotation. Towards the end of his career he consciously settled upon Vuillard for a model in this type of construction. As early as 1956 he gives evidence of a warm interest in the French painter as he reviews Adrienne Rich's *The Diamond Cutters*, praising her on the whole but defending Vuillard against her interpretation:

> Nor does her 'Pictures by Vuillard' contain any intimation of the frozen pictures, exact, photographic, almost academic, that testified during his later years to the boredom and passiveness that had always waited unpainted over at the side of those Victorian rose-windows, small bourgeois paradises, that he half-witnessed, half-created. (*The Yale Review*, XLVI, p. 101).

Far less popular than his contemporaries the Impressionists, Vuillard perfected a style which tallies point by point with Jarrell's way of increasing the complexity of his art, as his personal copy of Claude Roger-Marx's *Vuillard His Life and Work* reveals. The chapter entitled "Visual Memory and Organization of the Picture" discloses what passive observation of Vuillard's rather muted canvases can miss.

Vuillard, like Turner, painted from memory. Jarrell followed them here. One seldom gets the sensation that he is directly confronting the subject of a lyric, as Yeats confronts Coole Park or Williams the Passaic. From childhood on, his unconscious gathered for him symbolic places and objects which combine after years of meditation and months (or even years) of choice among multiple images until such poems result as "The Night before the Night before Christmas" or "Hohensalzburg." What Roger-Marx says of Vuillard applies equally to Jarrell:

> Vuillard was privileged to possess in the supreme degree the gift of preserving the precious sediment deposited by things—an imponderable substance which is a forecast of the picture itself. (p. 173)

And in another place: "Whether it was the matter of an interior, a landscape, a figure, the essential was registered and reconstituted within himself" (p. 182). He made paintings out of ordinary things which acquire an interior reality as they live on and on in his memory, needing no startling novelty when they rise up into the consciousness but rather a kind of patterning which gives them inexhaustible depth.

Roger-Marx sums up Vuillard's greatest merit thus: "The layout demonstrates the sway of a skillful system of verticals, horizontals, and obliques" (p. 175). In all his longer poems Jarrell shows this same almost geometrical preoccupation, which he discusses in "The Age of the Chimpanzee" and demonstrates in "The Old and the New Masters" and "The End of the Rainbow." Because he can endlessly vary a design he is never afraid to repeat a subject.

Another characteristic wherein Jarrell not only resembles but surpasses Vuillard is his obsession with mirrors: "He [Vuillard] liked to mingle actual objects with their reflections and made great play with the mirror which favours all sorts of mystifications, exchanges, interference, and penetration" (p.184). The whole of Life to Jarrell took on more and more the contradictions of secret presences such as imagination can conceive of as lurking behind painted landscapes or a mirror's glinting surface.

Mary Jarrell, his faithful reader, in bringing to publishable form the notes he left for an introduction to his translation of *The Three Sisters*, illustrates by innumerable single-line quotations from the play, guided by her husband's markings or by the cataloguing device habitual to him, how Chekhov's drama weaves a texture of symbols and *leit-motifs* so carefully as to permit none to dominate, achieving a symmetrical arrangement led into by one "spot-surface" after another. This she compares, ordering Jarrell's insights, to the randomness and personalness of real life as Vuillard transcribed it in paint:

> A visual counterpart of this very method [Chekhov's, that writer whom above all others Jarrell thought of as being nearest to his own nature] uncannily exists in the work of the painter Vuillard. In certain of his indoor and outdoor scenes of French domestic life, the foundation areas on the canvas are made less emphatic by the swarms of particles that mottle the walls with rose-printed paper, the rugs with swirls, the lawns with pools of sun and shade. From such variation and variegation comes his cohesion. (Introduction to Jarrell's translation of *The Three Sisters*).

The "spot-surface" attack she refers to in Vuillard finds documentation in his *Girl at Table*, a reproduction of which hangs in their Greensboro living room. The first "spot" the viewer sees is the open door. Why is it open? Already the basic idea starts to become intricate.

This unity evolving from variety takes infinite pains. In Jarrell's "The End of the Rainbow," by presenting a rather dull ground as opening landscape (the cranberry bogs of Ipswich) the poet is able to set forth with greater flamboyance the metamorphic Marsh-King:

> with a seal's angelic
> More-than-human less-than-human eyes, a strange
> Animal, some wizard ruling other realms.

Thus he himself follows his counsel in editor Ciardi's *Mid-Century American Poets*: "If the poem has a quiet or neutral ground, a delicate or complicated figure can stand out against it: if the ground is exaggerated and violent enough, no figure will" (pp. 182–183).

In discouraged moods, Jarrell might perhaps have sensed psychological kinship to Vuillard whose pictures he called in the Adrienne Rich review "miracles free to us, but that the painter paid for—paid for with part of himself; and when that part was gone the poetry of objects, by the light of common day, became their prose." Yet the last poem in his last book, "Thinking of the Lost World," contradicts by its achievement any fear of diminishing creative power which he may have entertained. Unlike Vuillard's, Jarrell's talents could be labeled "Ceiling unlimited."

Poets, Jarrell says in the *Partisan Review*, are first of all hypotheses, then facts, and at last values. Until mid-century his own greatness was a hypothesis. Gradually it has climbed to the stature of fact, so gradually that the ascent, though real, has been invisible to some. When a poet is in the first stages of his career, he is like a new window. "But in a quarter of a century even the chairs see through that window not a landscape but the Beautiful" (XII, p. 120).

In *The Bat-Poet*, the title-character says to himself: "The trouble isn't making poems, the trouble's finding somebody that will listen to them" (p. 15). Across the world that Jarrell left behind in 1965, the goodly company of listeners to his poetry grows daily. Gratefully, such persons learn from his life and lives about life.

[From "The Man Who Painted Bulls"]

Mary Kinzie*

.   .   .   .   .   .

Jarrell was, I believe, one of those narcissistic poets to whom, as to Wordsworth and Arnold in their periods, we owe one of the most important of the modern age's definitions of the self. For Jarrell, the self is what comes into being without our help, without our notice, and without our having been, at any point, able to alter what we have become:

> That is what happens to everyone.
> At first you get bigger, you know more,
> Then something goes wrong.
> You are, and you say: I am—
> And you were . . . I've been too long.

This is a paradoxical attitude for a good Freudian to hold, although commensurate with Freud's thought as I will try to show later, and equally paradoxical for a poet as characteristically attuned to children and to his own childhood as Jarrell was. With respect to childhood, in fact, Jarrell had the uncanny ability to think himself back to states of mind, attitudes of hope, dread, and tremulous expectancy that the combative passages of adolescence arrange to hide from most of us:

> We wept so? How well we all forget!
> One taste of memory (like Fafnir's blood)
> Makes all their language sensible, one's ears
> Burn with the child's peculiar gift for pain.[1]

This ability to *think back* was so highly defined—Jarrell's self as a child is so neutral to and hence indifferently compatible with his later self—that he was able to extend the principle to the minds of others. He was able to relinquish himself to those monologists who are aging, misplaced, bewildered, dying; to become those speakers caught in the dark wood of a fairy tale or dream; to mime those voices audible among the dead.

Neither Wordsworth nor Arnold was especially good at this kind of

*Abridged and slightly revised from the version printed in the *Southern Review*, NS 16 (1980), 829–52. By permission of the author.

transfer of allegiance from their own to the lives and minds of others. The scholar-gypsy and Empedocles were counters for Arnold's ego and desire, just as the leech-gatherer and the old Cumberland beggar, half-erased transparencies that they were, were agreeable places for Wordsworth to project himself upon the landscape. It is part of Jarrell's great difference from them, and part of his suitability to his period, that his concept of self does not allow for projection; the self is not continuous. Jarrell cannot rehearse the *changes of state* from infant to child, child to adolescent, adolescent to adult. He can only record the sense of confusion *within a state* that has no clue as to how to get itself changed. This is the source of the trapped, bewildered pathos on the part of the child questioning the adult world, the sense of loss of the mature being looking back on the child, and of the dead looking back on the living. Often, Jarrell will insist that the two are one, the man the child, the living the dead.

Among so many pairs of opposites in the poems—men vs. children, living vs. dead, bad vs. good, the masses vs. the human soul—there is one recurring mediating state: the dream. It is this uncertain threshold to which Jarrell the poet tried to hold himself, sometimes unsteadily or too vaguely, sometimes tipping over into rivers of mythic blood (*Orestes at Tauris*, "Che Faro Senza Euridice," "The Märchen"), sometimes falling into Freudian bathos ("A Little Poem") or its Audenesque variant ("The Iceberg," "Love, in Its Separate Being . . ."), and sometimes dwelling too obsessively on detail ("The End of the Rainbow," the longer of the two poems entitled "Hope"). But even in poems I would call failed or strained, the main business is dream-work, which translates the experience of the childhood self into the language of the adult. Not that the poetry is literally the product, as some poetry can appear to be, of dreams the author may actually have had; Jarrell's program is a deliberate dreaming-back, a relatively conscious act. It is further significant that the realm of early years to which his poetic dreams recur is principally the period of latency, not the earlier precognitive period. It is as if the two great periods of libidinal and aggressive energy, infancy and adolescence, had been erased by their very violence, and what remained were the states among which Jarrell holds his dialogue, childhood and maturity, two periods of achieved quiescence that do not know their real histories or their real names:

> Today, the child lies wet and warm
> In his big mother; tomorrow, too, is dumb,
> The dry skull of the cold tomb. "Between?"
> Between I suffered.
>
> ("The Difficult Resolution")

Some of the characteristic exclamations and insistent questions in Jarrell's poems echo this unconsciousness, as if each version, child and adult, of the self-in-arrest were asking about its dark, forgotten, torrential years, suspecting that there is a link, a point of passage between them, but unable to prove anything. The terminal convalescent in "The Long Vacation" in *Blood for a Stranger* (called "A Utopian Journey" in *Collected Poems*) asks of his experience, "*But what was it? What am I?*" In the dream of "The Night before the Night before Christmas" the girl's little brother learns that he is dying. He replies, "I didn't know," indicating a touching acceptance, while the girl whose dream it is cries out her unaccepting "I don't know, I don't know, I don't know!" The sick child in bed in "A Quilt-Pattern" discovers, or nearly discovers, strange truths in his feverish hallucinations; he almost knows that the true witch is the gingerbread house:

> the house of bread
> Calls to him in its slow singing voice:
> "Feed, feed! Are you fat now?
> Hold out your finger."
> The boy holds out the bone of the finger.
> It moves, but the house says, "No, you don't know.
> Eat a little longer."
> The taste of the house
> Is the taste of his—
> "I don't know,"
> Thinks the boy, "No, I don't know!"

In Jarrell, one might say, the self defines itself by its desire to be unlike the eternal rule, the law of the masses, the voice that says, You too will die and be unimportant, or, Your very unimportance is the equivalent of your death. But still the self hopes to escape the law of large numbers, the force of history's evidence, by being—itself. Some early poems of Jarrell's close on the irrevocable fact of this bleak knowledge:

> I see at last that all the knowledge
>
> I wrung from the darkness—that the darkness flung me—
> Is worthless as ignorance: nothing comes from nothing,
> The darkness from the darkness. Pain comes from the
>   darkness
> And we call it wisdom. It is pain.

("90 North")

But increasingly throughout his poetic career Jarrell inserts a strange keynote following the characters' recognition that pain outstrips knowledge, and this keynote is the tenacious belief in *something*, something else, something more, something one hasn't thought of yet that must nevertheless be there, something that will make a more human sense out of this human discomfort. Often these assertions of the necessary existence of the saving residue are called, simply, "something":

> *Say again*
> Say the voices, *say again*
> *That life is—what it is not;*
> *That, somewhere, there is—something, something;*
> *That we are waiting; that we are waiting.*

What I find chilling about those lines is the fact that they are spoken by people who have died. As the dead implore in "The Survivor among Graves," so Jarrell's characters persistently ask that life be—*what it is not.* But when his people try the statement out, and turn "Life is life" into "Life is not life," "it sounds the same." The simple contrary, the insertion of the negative into the most desperate confession, makes very little difference:

> In the great world everything is just the same
> Or just the opposite, we found (we never went).
>
> ("The Märchen")

This perverse, affronted, ambiguous mood, in which to say *Life is life* amounts to the same thing as saying *It isn't*, is part of Jarrell's flat style, the undercurrent of nihilism that runs through the verse. In the original version of "The Memoirs of Glückel of Hameln" in *Blood for a Stranger*, Jarrell addresses the memoirist with the dismissive conclusion that about her

> there is none to care.
> Glückel, Glückel, you tell indifferently
> To ears indifferent with Necessity
> The torments and obsessions of our life:
> Your pain seems only the useless echo
> Of all the evil we already know.

In a poem he did not publish, Jarrell makes the same sort of heavily careless statement: "Life is—why, life: / It is what all our evils have in common." Such statements are part of Jarrell's melancholy determinism, especially evident in the first three volumes, according to which nothing the individual does will make a difference to the States who are conducting the war with *his* life. "The Wide Prospect" in *Little Friend, Little Friend* is an apt example of the Jarrell allegory of Trade fed by the bodies of living men. In the same volume, guns practice against the thin body of a soldier "pinned against the light." A tormented life is nothing more than the fly caught in "the lying amber of the histories." "The Difficult Resolution" exhorts us to realize that we have no way to exercise the will except in realizing that we cannot exercise it. The warrior dressed in an ancient name to fight a modern war in "Siegfried" chants over and over to himself that "It happens as it does because it does." The great thinkers of the dawn of the scientific age, Bruno, Galileo, and Newton, have at last taught us how "to understand but not to change." The world tells the dead child that it "will not be missed." What is left to us in this dreary program is but the "bare dilemma of the beast—to go on being."

. . . .

I would like to suggest very briefly the early poems one would look to in order to trace this experience of the separation of the young self from the solid, comforting world and of the self's first insight into its imprisonment in being. In *Blood for a Stranger* (1942) Jarrell treats the coming of the self to the self as a polarity between love for the world and a sense of betrayal by it. "A Little Poem" and "Love, in Its Separate Being . . ." give us two variants on the theme of betrayal; in the former, a child has been usurped by the arrival of an interloper, another child, to whom he speaks while the other is still in the womb; in the second poem the child is betrayed by the forces of history. In a third poem, "Fear," Jarrell articulates this abused estrangement of the child by suggesting that the little girl here is caught and compromised by being a cipher in the dreams of the adult world, and in a grim forecast of the willful retreat of the chairs and tables of the world in "The Orient Express," the child is encouraged by the statues, those substitute adults, to "be like us, absolute."

"The Iceberg" and "90 North" are children's adventure dreams of Arctic exploration and deep-sea diving in which the outcome of the exuberant voyages is a fierce despair. The iceberg is a symbol of Necessity in a poem where even air and water are malevolent. In "90 North," when the child decides (as the strange arbitrary power-shifts of dreams permit him to do) to leave the North Pole and go home,

> Turn as I please, my step is to the south.
> The world—my world spins on this final point
> Of cold and wretchedness: all lines, all winds
> End in this whirlpool I at last discover.
>
> And it is meaningless.

Although this voyage to the north had meaning for him as a child, now the speaker sees that (as we quoted earlier) the knowledge he thought he had gained was worthless, and that the pain he wrung from the darkness and called wisdom was really only pain.

On the other side of the picture we find ambiguous, painful dream poems in which love for the world and the state of being loved by it—the self's adventuresomeness rewarded—are emotions that the dream keeps curiously blocked or inflexible. In "The Lost Love" a dead woman (the mother as lover) returns to caress the dreaming child; when the child responds, something fearful is suggested: "When I touched you / My hand was cold." "The Skaters" is the early apotheosis of the adventure poem and of the category of poems like "Fear," which are broodings on hidden losses when the self and the world dream together. But "The Skaters," like "The Lost Love," is also a poem of yearning that nearly becomes passion, a passion repressed by the eeriness of the rhythms of the dream; "How long we pled our love! / How thorough our embrace!" is followed by the two lovers' rout into

> The abyss where my deaf limbs forget
> The cold mouth's dumb assent;
> The skaters like swallows flicker
> Around us in the long descent.

The original love of the child and the mother finds its place here, in the pleading and thorough embraces of stanza six, just as the mother returns to the child in "The Lost Love"—and in many later poems ("2nd Air Force," where the mother, perhaps to his infinite aggravation, visits her son in basic training; "Mother, Said the Child," the first of the many *Kindertotenlieder* Jarrell was to write, among them "Come to the Stone . . . ," "Protocols," and "The State," in the same volume of which we are now speaking, *Little Friend, Little Friend*, 1945).

Many intonations are given to the central theme of the child's family struggle, which is also the struggle to import the flexibility and childish sense of adventure into the world of action without being haunted by sexuality. The escape to dream in "The Skaters" is linked to the poems in which the child escapes yet further from his life and makes his family pay yet more dearly for his loss. The schoolboy's fantasy of his own disappearance in "A Story" in *Blood for a Stranger* (1942) is written in the same ingenuous, sorrowing mood as the later laments of those who are actually dead in *Little Friend, Little Friend* and in *Losses* (1948), "Lady Bates," "Jews at Haifa," and "In the Camp There Was One Alive." When these songs of the dead children in *Losses* are compared to the living child's bereavement at the loss of his father after his parents' divorce in "A Child of Courts" in the same volume (called "The Prince" in *Collected Poems*), it is clear what equivalences have been enforced between the living and the dead. The child construes loss not as the absence of the good but as the presence of the good turned into the bad, into the dead. The child lies in an agony of fear, shrinking up like his pet rabbit, when he hears the father's hand like a rabbit's paws scraping at the dirt. Then, in a majestic act of courage and forgiveness, the boy "inch[es] my cold hand out to his cold hand." In the third stanza, after nothing has grasped his heroically offered hand, the boy throws his "furs" off, then hears a sentry calling.

> I start to weep because—because there are no ghosts;
> A man dies like a rabbit, for a use.
> What will they pay me, when I die, to die?

The transfer in the child's reason from the retreat of the parent to his own retreat in death is made here by the sudden additional knowledge, or recollection, that the child is grown, asleep in a barracks in wartime, that they have all long since really died, father, rabbit, many military cronies, many millions of Europeans, and that the smaller deaths were to be followed by the greater ones. Across the chasm of guilt abruptly opened as the child turns—before his eyes as well as ours—into a grown man, the speaker has no opportunity to enact the desired retribution: to make *them* pay for their "deaths" by dying himself. When he does die, it will be for a small use, as a rabbit dies for a use, as a soldier dies in his numbers.

. . . .

I began by claiming that Jarrell's influence on modern poetry derives from his definition of the self as something that got to be the way it is without the human's conscious ability to control what he would become, or even to record the process of change. The dream seemed to me to be the mediating state in which Jarrell's children discover or combat the discovery of what they are becoming, and where his grown-ups become children by forgetting the same knowledge, or courting an earlier, less lethal form of it. (Jarrell is a poet who proceeds in shadow language, as if to say the truth in a dream released him from the guilt of revealing it.) The characteristic pleas, *Let me be what I was, Let nothing matter, Change me, change me!* resemble the characteristic questions, *But what was it, what am I?* and the brilliant exclamations, *I don't know, I don't know!* as well as the repeated assertion of belief in *Something, something*, because they all rehearse, after their fashions, the principles of avoidance and incredulity in the developing life. Thus the urgency on the part of things to turn into things, and on the part of men to turn into things or to share with things the bare property described in the statements *These are*, or *I am*, are solutions with a double edge. On the one hand, to feel that one *is* makes one the center of a reverently circumscribed world; but on the other hand, one shares that simple, dull, and unqualified being with everything that lies beyond, sometimes only a short distance away, just as unknown, but also unwanted.

. . . .

The pull of the fairy tale is particularly strong in *The Seven-League Crutches*, doubtless Jarrell's best book. The parable of the two children who are turned into birds in "The Black Swan" presents the love of a girl for her sister, who has been turned into a black swan, as a willingness to follow the changed one into death. Both Sister Bernetta Quinn and Suzanne Ferguson have traced the fairy tale sources in many of the poems. And yet no one, in talking about Jarrell's use of Grimm, has indicated the persistent divergence of the poet from the spirit of these tales. Jarrell has imposed something closer to Hans Christian Andersen's conception of final metamorphosis, immutable change, upon the essentially restorable world of the Brothers Grimm. The maimings in the *Märchen* are fierce, bloody, and gratuitous, but in the end, really, no harm will come. The severed head is restored to the body, the hands that were cut off are put back, the bear turns back into the prince, the blind see, the foul are cleansed. But though there is less bloodshed in the Andersen stories about the little mermaid, the red shoes, the snow queen, and little Inger, the girl who stepped on bread in order not to dirty her fine new clothes, the maimings and changes of state, when they do come, horrify the more because they are more endless, more final. Consider the many long years during which little Inger must stand like a caryatid in the peristyle of hell until her heart is softened by her mother's tears. At last Inger is allowed to become a sparrow who gathers crumbs for the other birds to expiate her wastefulness. But she is never turned back into a girl, whereas the seven swans or seven ravens into which a witch has transformed the princess' seven brothers in several Grimm tales are allowed to return to human shape after seven years of their sister's silence, and finally they are all human again, and they can all speak, and they have not grown in the meantime very much older. In Jarrell's "Black Swan" the little sister wants to expiate some sin—perhaps that she has a "bad sister," as the child in "A Quilt-Pattern" has a "Good Me" and a "Bad Me"—but the form of expiation is union with her sister, so that love and longing are indistinguishable from remorse and complicity. The poem tells us (and the little sister knows this too) that the transformations into swans are only happening in a dream,

> But the swan my sister called, "Sleep at last, little sister,"
> And stroked all night, with a black wing, my wings.

In other words, the poem tells us that its experience is not real, but in a way it then retracts: we get no comfort from the proviso that it's only a dream. The little girl whose sister was turned into a swan, who yearned toward her in the center of the lake where she, too, was transformed into one, keeps on being a swan stroked by the black wings of the other. Although it is true, as Jarrell writes at the end of "The Märchen," that the tales are allegories of the human heart, and that the exercise of power in forming and delivering the wishes one is allowed to make is a version of the desire *to change, to change!*, the spirit of this and other poems of Jarrell's tell us that the change we wish for is never the one that visits us.

More and more in the later poems in *The Woman at the Washington Zoo* (1960) and *The Lost World* (1965), the world of the great fantasies, in which tales like "Hansel and Gretel" had figured, contracts. Consider the use of the tale in "A Quilt-Pattern":

> Here a thousand stones
> Of the trail home shine from their strings
> Like just-brushed, just-lost teeth.
> All the birds of the forest
> Sit brooding, stuffed with crumbs.
> But at home, far, far away
> The white moon shines from the stones of the chimney,
> His white cat eats up his white pigeon.

and in "The Elementary Scene" from *The Woman at the Washington Zoo*:

> Looking back in my mind I can see
> The white sun like a tin plate
> Over the wooden turning of the weeds;
> The street jerking—a wet swing—
> To end by the wall the children sang.

It is interesting that "The Elementary Scene" rejects the child's point of view to speak from the adult's: "I float above the small limbs like their dream: / I, I, the future that mends everything." Another poem from *The Woman at the Washington Zoo*, "A Ghost, a Real Ghost," in which the present time is just as dreary, dead, and removed, contains an equally harrowing formulation of the principle we have already found at work in so many of the poems: "The child is hopeful and unhappy in a world / Whose future is his recourse." But there is no future in this poem, only mourning:

> The first night I looked into the mirror
> And saw the room empty, I could not believe
>
> That it was possible to keep existing
> In such pain: I have existed.
> . . . .
> Am I dead? A ghost, a real ghost
> Has no need to die: what is he except
> A being without access to the universe
> That he has not yet managed to forget?

It is as if the girl in "The Night before . . . Christmas" were speaking from the other side of maturity; as if the sister turned into a swan were addressing the world she loved from the vantage of her paralyzed, disenfranchised doom.

. . . .

Randall Jarrell was very much a poet of the homely horrors, for at the back of every transcendent impulse he saw the doom of common disappointment crouching in its lean and idle way behind the bolster. In his brilliant essay on Jarrell's ideology, as much a tour de force as Jarrell's essays on the stages in Auden's, Jerome Mazzaro (*Salmagundi*, Fall 1971) suggests that Jarrell was done in by happiness, and that to have been comforted and forgiven was equivalent to having been bereft of every defense against his own accepting world: "The mechanisms by which one's self has been defined, once withered away by forgiveness, leave one nothing by which to define self—a fear implicit in any real skepticism and here expressed 'in happiness.' " Jarrell's imagination followed Freud, dwelling not on illness but rather on what Freud supposed to be our common condition, human suffering and yearning. Randall Jarrell wrote about life as a matter of helplessness: the child cannot elude its fate, the pressure of consciousness; the adult cannot yet manage to forget the loved earth. The self in Jarrell participates in a perennial abdication of power, until it can only hover, weakened and disembodied, over the loved object. More critical attention might be devoted to Jarrell's image of the self that "float[s] above the small limbs like their dream" and to his deep impression on the poetic world of the mid-century above which he hovered, condemning, accepting, helpless, unable to leave:

> We learned from you so much about so many things
> But never what we were; and yet you made us that.
>
> We found in you the knowledge for a life
> But not the will to use it in our lives
> That were always, somehow, so different from the books'.
> We learned from you to understand, but not to change.
> ("The Carnegie Library, Juvenile Division,"
> *Little Friend, Little Friend*, 1945)

Note

1. "Children Selecting Books in a Library," *Blood for a Stranger* (New York, 1942). Because of quotations like this one, whose revised form in *Selected Poems* strikes me as somehow bland and "off," I have decided to quote from the original volumes. The others are *Little Friend, Little Friend* (New York, 1945), *Losses* (New York, 1948), and *The Seven-League Crutches* (New York, 1951). Quotations from the subsequent volumes, *The Woman at the Washington Zoo* (1960), *The Lost World* (1965), and the posthumous *New Poems* are taken from *Complete Poems* (New York, 1969). There is a great need for a new text of Jarrell's poems placed in chronological order with revisions printed en face. Jarrell's own order for poems from the first four volumes is confusingly achronological, though his arrangement highlights some issues.

Jarrell's "The Death of the Ball Turret Gunner"

Leven M. Dawson*

The theme of Randall Jarrell's "The Death of the Ball Turret Gunner" is that institutionalized violence, or war, creates moral paradox, a condition in which acts repugnant to human nature become appropriate. The "they" of the last line of the poem are not insensitive nor are they intended by the author to be unsympathetic; their "unnatural" action, given their abnormal situation, is the only appropriate one. "The Death of the Ball Turret Gunner" works generally through paradox, for consistently in it reversals of conventional conditions or attitudes become correct as a result of the overall unnatural or paradoxical condition created by war.

The basic figurative pattern of the poem is a paradoxical one of death being represented in terms of birth. The "belly" of the "State"—which is the name of the B–17 or B–24, but also represents the persona's "state" (condition or country)—has replaced the secure womb of the "mother's sleep" (the full sleep of complete battle fatigue dreaming of home or the general security of peacetime existence), and the Gunner undergoes the birth trauma: he *falls* "from [his] mother's sleep" (the womb) and is *awakened* to the "nightmare" unnaturalness of institutionalized "life." (This birth may be seen as the rebirth or initiation into a mature vision of reality and evil.) But the birth of the Ball Turret Gunner is reversed in purpose, for "Six miles from earth" he is "loosed from its dream of *life*"; the birth in his "state" is death.

The paradoxical structure as well as the imagery of "The Death of the Ball Turret Gunner" originates in Shelley's elegy for John Keats, "Adonais," stanza XXXIX:

> Peace, peace! he is not dead, he doth not sleep—
> He hath awakened from the dream of life—
> 'Tis we, who lost in stormy visions, keep
> With phantoms an unprofitable strife. . . .

The Ball Turret Gunner also awakens from the "dream of life." As, paradoxically for Shelley, the death of Keats was birth, birth in the Gunner's new "state" is death; in his condition life is an unnatural, insecure

*Reprinted from *Explicator*, 31 (1972), item 29, by permission of the journal.

"dream" from which one awakens to "stormy visions" of "strife" with "phantoms" ("black flak and the nightmare fighters") and then dies. Ascension into the heavens is to find death, not apotheosis; and the "*Six miles from earth*," the ascent of the Gunner where he finds death, must suggest the reverse direction, the conventional six feet under earth of burial. Water, which is conventionally associated with rebirth and the womb, in the Gunner's condition is either cold or is used to eject, rather than secure, the individual in his protective container. The umbilical "hose" is reversed in function also, being used indifferently to eject the dead body of the gunner.

The most effective phrase in economically expressing the unnatural condition of war is the image of the Gunner's "wet fur" *freezing* while he "hunched" in the "belly" of the "State." This "fur," of course, is merely the pile of his flight jacket soaked in the early morning mist of takeoff, freezing in the temperature change of high altitude (suggesting the constant fatigue and general discomfort of the Gunner's occupation); but it must also turn the reader's mind to the fact that man in his natural state does not have fur, is not naturally equipped for the environment in which the Gunner finds himself, and to the fact that the human fetus does, however, go through an "unnatural" regressive "state" in which it is completely covered in down or "wet fur."

Everything in war, the state of institutionalized violence, is reversed: up is down, one ascends to die, life is merely a *dream* of earth, *awakening* or realization is "nightmare," for truth is horrible, birth becomes death, and death is the only reality and release. But more importantly man becomes part of the paradox, because he enters into abnormal states where he must dress unnaturally and regressively and where insensitivity becomes a sustaining virtue. Without "Peace" he is truly "*lost* in stormy visions" and "keeps / With phantoms an *unprofitable* strife." In the moral paradox of war, where everything is reversed, moral intention and virtue have no meaning and the release of death is a blessed event, or at least, indifferent, even to the living. Jarrell writes "The Death of the Ball Turret Gunner" in the first person because so inherent is the paradox of institutionalized violence that it is only after this release that one can even see the pervasive reversal; Jarrell is saying that this vision is the only apotheosis available to those trapped in the belly of the state engaged in dehumanizing violence.

Jarrell's "The Death of the Ball Turret Gunner"

David K. Cornelius*

In reading Leven M. Dawson's note on Jarrell's "The Death of the Ball Turret Gunner" (*The Explicator*, 31, Item 29), I began to wonder whether the consistency of Jarrell's imagery has yet been fully noted—particularly in its relationship to the structure of a World War II B–17. Dawson cites the "womb" imagery of the poem, and even remarks that "the umbilical 'hose' is reversed in function also, being used indifferently to eject the dead body of the gunner." This may be twisting the metaphor. (Incidentally, tales—and predictions—of disintegrated gunners being flushed out of turrets with hoses were a commonplace during the war—a gallows-humor cliché.) In any case, the ball turret, protruding from the plane's belly, is rich in metaphoric suggestions. The turret was small. Inside, the gunner sat in a fetus-like posture, with his knees drawn up nearly to his chin. Like the child in the womb, he was part of the larger organic life of the plane, yet, once his hatch was closed, isolated from it. His umbilical cord was his oxygen hose, plugged into the main oxygen line of the plane, as the child is attached to the life-support system of the mother. The ground crew's hose is probably simply the instrument that completes the abortion.

*Reprinted from *Explicator*, 35 (1977), 3, by permission of the journal.

The Woman at the Zoo's Fearful Symmetry

Michel Benamou*

I begin with a sense of danger. Explicating poetry is usually a pretty safe game. Most poets either are dead or do not care; Valéry once said that his poems had the meaning the reader gave them. But Randall Jarrell is very much alive; he is an intelligent critic; and he hates obscurity in his own poems. When he published a selection of them in 1955, he took the trouble to add prose crutches, *realia*, bits of information not only for the American reader, who might know what a *blind date* is, and what *he stood you up* means, but also for the foreigner who might not. "Prose helps," he remarked. "It helps just by being prose." Of course, to Valéry at least, such a practice would seem nothing short of sacrilegious. But clearly Jarrell belongs to an altogether different tradition. He is thoroughly American, although he claims that his "favorite country's German" (not Germany). He resented Wallace Stevens' "old-fashioned Europe," as he called it in an important essay of *Poetry and the Age*. Being a foreigner, I perceive that both Jarrell and Stevens are most American when they speak about Europe. And when it comes to Americana, I do need the prose crutches. Hence the sense of danger. A prose gloss may one day accompany "The Woman at the Washington Zoo." Whether the "dome-shadowed" office in which that lady works is or is not in the Library of Congress, and the Deputy Chief Assistant a staff member of that Institution where Jarrell was Poetry Consultant, will be known sooner or later. It will have devastating effects on my analysis, unless I confine myself to the poem as a work of art, taking it at its face-value, and inferring from its structure whatever can be inferred about Jarrell as a writer.

"The Woman at the Washington Zoo" is rightly the title poem. Its title is the best in the book: humorous and disquieting. Article and preposition—*a* woman would be tame—establish the central theme: she is both visitor and inmate. The local color, the surface of things in Washington appear with the impressionistic first lines:

The saris go by me from the embassies.

*Reprinted from *Analects*, 1, No. 2 (1961), 2–4, by permission of the author's estate.

> Cloth from the moon. Cloth from another planet.
> They look back at the leopard like the leopard.

Apart from their foreignness, the anonymous, almost faceless, saris have a disturbing quality: their weird resemblance to the leopard. This, I think, is the central theme of the poem, and not the trite self-pity of the aging secretary. Superficially, this is a poem about a female Prufrock. In contrast to the bright saris and the leopard, she sees herself dressed in the standard color of the American career woman, Navy blue:

> this dull null
> Navy I wear to work, and wear from work, and so
> To my bed, so to my grave, with no
> Complaints, no comments . . .

But though she complains rather sentimentally, she also sees herself "small, far-off, shining / In the eyes of animals," an act of Rilkean perception which enhances the theme of animality. Her image in the pupils of the inmates of the Zoo reminds one of the Jardin des Plantes poems, especially "the Panther":

> Nur manchmal schiebt der Vorhang der Pupille
> sich lautlos auf——. Dann geht ein Bild hinein. . . .

Jarrell's beautiful translations of Rilke bespeak this affinity. But what interests him here is not the beasts themselves so much as what they mean to the woman. His imagination musters all the predatory animals of the zoo: even the sparrows and the pigeons prey upon each other's food. To follow Northrop Frye's convenient archetypal category, Randall Jarrell's imagination is of the demonic kind: the animal world is portrayed in terms of buzzards, vultures, rats, foxes and wolves. The frightening thing that was sensed in the title could now happen: the vulture could take off his red helmet and step to her, the she-wolf in a Navy print, as man. Or she might be turned back into "what she was." Then the "saris" who look back at the leopard would notice her, whereas now "The world goes by my cage and never sees me." This cage is not the animals' trap, but her own body—a pretty hackneyed metaphor, were it not for the extraordinary theme of woman-into-beast and beast-into-man palingenesis which the cage image supports. This poem makes us grope for a dark truth about human nature: our punishment is metamorphosis from the animals we were into the beings we are. Do not most of Ovid's changelings seem more truly themselves *after* their mutation?

The style of this poem reflects its thematic tension between the Prufrock motif and the animal motif. Its structure is consistently binary, with repetition its main device. But one should perhaps distinguish between the style of the poem and the style of the poet. For instance:

> In the eyes of the animals, these beings trapped
> As I am trapped but not, themselves, the trap,
> Aging, but without knowledge of their age,
> Kept safe here, knowing not of death, for death—

belongs to the style of the poem. The paired words, *trapped, aging, death*, are set either at maximum or minimum distance from each other through admirable control of both sense and prosody, with the effect of heightening the contrast while keeping the thematic parallelism between woman and beasts. The same thing occurs with "leopard like leopard." Repetition functions as the very structure of the poem, placing words in the fearful symmetry of the woman-beast analogy. Other repetitions such as

> Oh, bars of my own body, open, open!

are saved from the emphasis of sentimentality by the close relationship of the words within the image, in the same way as Rimbaud's line

> O, que ma quille éclate! O, que j'aille à la mer!

is not sentimental. But when I said that the style of the poem and the style of the poet are not one, I meant that some repetitions are justified in terms of a manner, which is Randall Jarrell's very own, rather than in terms of the structure of the poem. Possibly this has already been noticed and discussed elsewhere, but I am unaware of it, and shall offer the following discussion for what it is worth, very tentatively. I shall first quote again from "The Woman":

> Cloth from the moon. Cloth from another planet.

In contrast with the other repetitions already examined, it can be seen at once that this one fulfills no role in the poem. Its stylistic value may, however, be quite considerable, as will appear from an appraisal of similar features elsewhere in the same volume.

First, how frequent or characteristic is the device? A quick tally shows that it appears at least once in half the original—not translated—poems in *The Woman at the Washington Zoo*. Here are a few examples:

> Far from the clams and fogs and bogs
> —the cranberry bogs—of Ipswich
> > ("The End of the Rainbow")

> But in some the lights still burn. The lights of
> others' houses.
> > ("Windows")

> He is naked, Shod and naked. Hatted and naked.
> > ("The Bronze David of Donatello")

> In the darkness that is not lit by anything,
> In the grave that is not lit by anything
> Except our hope: the hope
> That is not proofed against anything . . .
>
> ("Nestus Gurley")

The last example exemplifies the musicality of the device as used by Eliot in *Four Quartets* for instance, a repetitive effect native to English poetry and impossible, as Péguy proved it to be, in French verse. Something besides auditory imagination, however, is evinced by these repetitions: something about Jarrell's perception of the world, and about his use of language. I am referring to the many appositive explanations, the way in which a word is repeated in apposition and its meaning specified. The bogs are *cranberry* bogs, the lights are *others'*, the moon is *another* planet. Now, this device is not euphonic. Neither is it mere word-play of the serious kind indulged in by Gertrude Stein (although Randall Jarrell out-steined Stein in *Pictures from an Institution*, a novel whose heroine was precisely named Gertrude). It is a device closer to vision than to language, akin to the poet's prose notices preceding his *Selected Poems*, pointing out for example that the hose in "The Death of the Ball Turret Gunner" was a *steam* hose. The first perception, the first expression, do not satisfy Jarrell's need for precision. His approach is iterative, analytic, piecemeal. On the one hand, one has the life-like effect of a deliberately unartificial search; the impression that life and poetry coincide. On the other hand, the search may make us wish that he had found *before* he started writing. Both effects merge in this excerpt from the best poem in the book, "The Bronze David of Donatello":

> To so much strength, those overborne by it
> Seemed girls, and death came to it like a girl,
> Came to it, through the soft air, like a bird—
> So that the boy is like a girl, is like a bird
> Standing on something it has pecked to death.

One might wish that the beautiful bronze of the last two lines—an image of loveliness and predatory obsession—had been arrived at without successive plaster shapes from which it was finally cast. Jarrell's favorite repetitive pattern has prevailed: girl, bird, girl and bird. The words which make up the image are brought together from two separate lines into a third, while we watch. The aesthetic surprise is deliberately renounced, for Jarrell depends more on repetition than on metaphor, or rather, he finds his metaphors through repetition. But in this particular poem, the iterativeness of the style is appropriate to the slow motion of the gazer as he goes round the statue, making the most of every detail.

Randall Jarrell as a writer proclaims his distrust of fabricated beauty. If one had to be either on the side of art or on the side of life, he would choose life. His vision, sympathetic though uncompromising, even cruel in its obsession with the animal-and-dream-worlds, is one of the most original today. In the better poems of *The Woman at the Washington Zoo*, his style is appropriate to his material. His chief mannerism, the use of repetition—musical, appositive and metaphoric—indicates that to him language is a means not merely to convey but to discover. His style lies closer to life's slow patterns of metamorphosis than to the golden effigies of Byzantium.

The Criticism

The Poet as Humanitarian: Randall Jarrell's Literary Criticism as Self-Revelation

Janet Sharistanian*

Reluctantly providing "Answers to Questions" posed by John Ciardi in his 1950 anthology of *Mid-Century American Poets*, Randall Jarrell irately asserted that "To write . . . about one's own poetry is extremely unpleasant and unnatural."[1] He was willing to say something about his audience or about the oral quality, subjects, imagery, and meter of his poems, but regarded a request to make a statement "about the ethical-philosophical relation of the poet to his writing" perfectly superfluous, since "My poems show what this relation actually is for me; what I say it should be matters less." In fact, despite the considerable amounts of criticism which Jarrell published—three collections, and approximately fifty additional essays and reviews—and in contrast to the close attention which he turned to the work of other writers, he rarely wrote about his own poetry. His one detailed piece of self-analysis is his extremely useful account of "The Woman at the Washington Zoo," which is printed in Brooks and Warren's *Understanding Poetry*.[2] And one can hardly fault him for otherwise refusing to be a self-critic, since his analyses of other writers implicitly attest to his understanding of the distinction between stated and achieved intention. At the same time, however, a reading of his literary criticism shows that in discussing and, especially, in evaluating the work of other writers, Jarrell was expressing his own ideas about the nature and uses of poetry. For Jarrell, whose criticism is committed and opinionated rather than coolly detached, writing about other writers was an informal and implicit way of working out a poetics of his own, and one in which "the ethical-philosophical relation of the poet to his writing" was of supreme importance.

In criticism early and late—whether he writes about favorites like Whitman, Frost, Yeats, Williams, and Ransom, discusses poets such as Auden and Stevens about whom his opinions shifted drastically, or deals with a writer like MacLeish for whom he harbored disdain—Jarrell sounds over and over a note very important to his own work: one of the modern poet's most important subjects should be real, that is, *ordinary* men and women, and their "everyday affairs of life and death."[3] Robert

*Reprinted from the *South Carolina Review*, 10 (1977), 32–42, by permission of the journal.

Frost, whose acceptance as a serious poet was largely precipitated by Jarrell's 1947 and 1952 essays on him, was for Jarrell [with Stevens and Eliot] "the greatest of the American poets of this century"[4] precisely because of his fidelity to such affairs. Delivering a lecture on "Fifty Years of American Poetry" at the National Poetry Festival in Washington, D.C., in October, 1962, and speaking in terms which echo the earlier Frost essays, Jarrell declared that

> Frost's virtues are extraordinary. No other living poet has written so well about the actions of ordinary men; his wonderful dramatic monologues or dramatic scenes come out of a knowledge that few poets have had, and they are written in a verse that uses, sometimes with absolute mastery, the rhythms of actual speech. It is hard to overestimate the effect of this exact, spaced-out, prosaic movement, whose objects have the tremendous strength . . . of things merely put down and left to speak for themselves. . . . Frost's seriousness and honesty; the bare sorrow with which, sometimes, things are accepted as they are, neither exaggerated nor explained away; the many, many poems in which there are real people with their real speech and real thoughts and real emotions—all this, in conjunction with so much subtlety and exactness, makes the reader feel that he is not in a book but a world, and a world that has in common with his own some of the things that are most important in both.[5]

It is no surprise to hear Jarrell praise Frost for dramatizing the "actions of ordinary men," "the rhythm of actual speech," and the acceptance in "bare sorrow" of "things . . . as they are" in poetry that is more like "a world" than "a book," for these are as central to Frost's poetry as they are to Jarrell's. What is perhaps more pertinent is that in writing about poets quite unlike Frost, Jarrell tends to praise or condemn on the basis of similar preoccupations. He is particularly concerned with stressing a poet's allegiance to commonplace existence and his recognition of the very limited power which men and women have over their lives. Thus Jarrell praises John Crowe Ransom's poetry for being "not 'modernist' poetry at all,"[6] and finds it "remarkable how much narrative, dramatic, non-lyric, not-highbrow [sic] interest the best poems have."[7] In the poems of William Carlos Williams, as in Ransom's, Jarrell looks for "generosity and sympathy, . . . moral and human attractiveness."[8]

These terms, with others like "tenderness," "pity," and "affection," appear frequently in reviews and essays in which Jarrell is enthusiastic about his subject (he is never merely indifferent). They have very little to do with a concept of the poet as rebel, seer, or creator of artifacts, but much to do with a definition of the poet as humanitarian and representative spokesman of his age. Jarrell titled one essay "The Development of Yeats's Sense of Reality," and in it concentrated on this aspect of Yeats's work almost to the exclusion of his symbolism, belief in the occult, concept of the mask, or visionary creation of his Sacred Book of the Arts. For Jarrell, Yeats's greatness lies in the fact that he discovered a philosophical and historical system by which history itself, the universe itself, *made* the present change into the past. Now, instead of rejecting or escaping from the modern world, the process of history; instead of accepting it under compulsion, full of doubt and hatred; he could fully accept it, urge it violently on. History, politics, the modern world became enormously meaningful for Yeats, became materials that he could accept and use as finally important. And it was in this way that Yeats escaped from the greatest weakness of modernist poetry, the modern poet's highly specialized relationship to contemporary life: his rejection of the present, his inability to write about the life of his own times (which is, in the end, his only material) as anything but a special case, an aberration, a degeneration.[9]

The praise, while accurate, is couched in terms which many readers of Yeats would find startling. They would argue that Yeats's creation, in *A Vision*, of a cosmology which allowed him to "accept and use" modern history, not as "an aberration" but as part of an inevitable pattern of universal cyclical change, is the *result* of his "highly specialized relationship to contemporary life."

What "the modern world" in general means to Jarrell is clear from other essays. Implicitly comparing himself with Theodore Roethke in the 1962 National Poetry Festival address, Jarrell says that Roethke's reader "is struck by what the world of his poems is full of or entirely lacking in; plants and animals, soil and weather, sex, ontogeny, and the unconscious swarm over the reader, but he looks in vain for hydrogen bombs, world wars, Christianity, money, ordinary social observations, his everyday moral doubts."[10] Later in the talk Jarrell generalizes again in similar terms. Most poets, even good ones, he says, "no longer have the heart to write about what is most terrible in the world of the present: the bombs waiting beside the rockets, the hundreds of millions staring into the temporary shelter of their television sets, the decline of the West that seems less a decline than the fall preceding an explosion."[11] For Jarrell what is "most terrible" is what is most important, and what is most important is the large-scale social and historical circumstances which affect us all, rather than the joys and obsessions which may engage us only as private individuals. In effect, Jarrell is asking Roethke to write different poetry, poetry about Jarrell's own favorite subjects: war and a peace that is unfulfilling; soldiers and typically American, middle-class, middle-aged men and women.

Jarrell's reactions to Wallace Stevens are also instructive. In his 1951 essay "Reflections on Wallace Stevens," a quite hostile and witty overview of the poetry between *Harmonium* (1923) and *The Rock* (1954), he decried Stevens' tendency to be "philosophical, abstract, rational. . . ."[12] "Poetry is a bad medium for philosophy," Jarrell says, and goes on:

> When the first thing that Stevens can find to say of the Supreme Fiction is that "it must be *abstract*," the reader protests, "Why, even Hegel called it

a *concrete* universal"; . . . Stevens had the weakness . . . of thinking of particulars as primarily illustrations of general truths, or else as aesthetic, abstracted objects, simply there to be contemplated; he often treats things or lives so that they seem no more than generalizations of an unprecedentedly low order. . . .

As a poet Stevens has every gift but the dramatic. It is the lack of immediate contact with lives that hurts his poetry more than anything else, that has made it easier and easier for him to abstract, to philosophize, to treat the living dog that wags its tail and bites you as the . . . "cyclindrical arrangement of brown and white" of the aesthetician analyzing that great painting, the world.[13]

Jarrell's vehemence and verbosity are revealing. For him it is important that the poet dramatize modern history as it is lived on a daily basis by quite commonplace people; "The World Is Everything that Is the Case," he called one section of his *Selected Poems* (1955). Consequently he suspects generalizations, aesthetic or otherwise, because they imply considerable distance between poet and subject, while a sympathetic and "immediate contact with lives" should reveal itself in details, particulars, the opposite of the abstract. For Jarrell, an abstract generalization is tantamount to ignorant and elitist condescension.

None of this means that Jarrell's concern for the ordinary automatically includes praise for it. In the first place, Jarrell saw human life as essentially unheroic and limited: a matter of powerlessness, solitude, and a constant need for change, for escape from the destructiveness and meagerness of one's existence. This need for change is never satisfied in actual life (except perhaps ironically, as when the life-long cry for transcendence is finally answered by the decline into old age), but is answered only temporarily, in dreams, memories, myths, and in the contemplation or creation of works of art. In the second place, despite his interest in and sympathy for them, Jarrell recognized with wry understanding that the people he wrote about in his poems, though in the main products of universal education, are not people who read his or anybody else's poetry, or if they do, read it for the wrong reasons. He knows that they are rarely touched by genuine art of any kind, but instead rely upon the distractions of *kitsch*, middlebrow entertainment, and a massive consumerism which even they often recognize as meaningless and insufficient.[14]

For Jarrell, unlike many other writers, this constitutes a genuine problem. His subject and his audience should be one, yet they are not. Jarrell puts the problem in poetic terms in "A Conversation with the Devil." It takes "uncommon" readers, the speaker knows, to recognize that the poet's best function is "To see things as they are, to make them what they might be." The "artful, common, unindulgent others" are readers who want to be able to say of a work of literature, *"Not like a book at all. . . . Beats life."*[15] Such readers demand that the poet dramatize or narrate a complacent and flattering acceptance of people and events. They correspond to what Jarrell defines as the audience for "Instant Literature," which—"whether . . . a soap opera, a Broadway play, or a historical, sexual best seller—tells us always that life is not only what we wish it, but also what we think it."[16] Comparing Jarrell's essays with his poem, one sees a paradox emerging. Intelligent readers, the only ones worth writing for, are "uncommon" and "few." The more numerous, "common . . . others" see no line between literature and life; or, rather, the less line they see, the better they like the literature. Yet in his criticism of other poets, Jarrell uses as a standard of judgment fidelity to precisely the same commonplace multitudes whom he criticizes in this poem. And in praising Frost for making the reader "feel that he is not in a book but a world, and a world that has in common with his own some of the things that are most important in both," Jarrell himself skirts dangerously close to saying of Frost's work that it is "*Not like a book at all. . . . Beats life.*"

How clearly Jarrell recognized this paradox is not clear. What is clear is that he expressed over and over again, in verse and prose, his unqualified dismay at the diminution of the reading public in modern America, and the consequent disappearance of the poet. His sense of the poet's invisibility is stressed in some of his best-known essays, such as "The Obscurity of the Poet" and "The Age of Criticism" in *Poetry and the Age* (1953); or "The Intellectual in America," "The Taste of the Age," "A Sad Heart at the Supermarket," and "Poets, Critics, and Readers," in *A Sad Heart at the Supermarket* (1962). Reflecting on the tale of the philosopher Diogenes being visited by Alexander the Great (the latter asked if there was anything he could do for Diogenes: " 'Yes,' said the philosopher, 'you can get out of my light' "), Jarrell comments: "when our age, our country, listens to the story of how Alexander stood in Diogenes' light, it asks perplexedly: 'What was he doing *there*?' Why should a statesman, a general, make a sort of pilgrimage to a poverty-stricken philosopher, an intellectual of the most eccentric kind? We wouldn't. Most of us distrust intellectuals as such: We feel that they must be abnormal, or else they wouldn't be intellectuals."[17] In a less humorous vein, he sums up his position in "A Sad Heart at the Supermarket": "Mass culture either corrupts or isolates the writer. . . . True works of art are more and more produced away from or in opposition to society. And yet the artist needs society as much as society needs him: as our cultural enclaves get smaller and drier, more hysterical or academic, one mourns for the artists inside and the public outside."[18]

While Jarrell's preoccupations in his criticism can in part be traced straight to what he defines as the reality of "our age, our country," some of them are more dependent on his preception of human existence as a whole. That he saw human life primarily in terms of limitation rather than potentiality (which he called "the greatest single subject of the romantics")[19] is demonstrated again and again in his prose. "Recognition of the essential limitations of man, without denial or protest or rhetoric or palliation"[20] is one of the characteristics which he praised in Frost. "Without denial or protest" but with sympathy and understanding, one assumes. Thus in his satiric academic fable, *Pictures from an Institution* (1954), one of the charges which the poet/teacher/narrator levels against Gertrude Johnson (Mary McCarthy?), the devastating lady novelist, is that "she was far more of a moralist than Spinoza. Did he not say that he had *'labored carefully not to mock, lament, and execrate, but to understand'*? Gertrude had labored carefully to mock, lament, and execrate—to condemn utterly; and to do so it had also been necessary for her to understand, for her to have at the tips of her fingernails the Facts."[21] For Jarrell, the primary Fact is that "Reality is what we want it to be or what we do not want it to be, but it is not our wanting or our not wanting that makes it so";[22] but this was not one of the Facts that Gertrude Johnson understood. The definition of reality appears in a review of Malraux's *The Voices of Silence* (1953), in which Jarrell objects on philosophic grounds to Malraux's tendency to arrive triumphantly at an explanation for every artistic phenomenon he writes about. Jarrell writes, "if someone has a good enough eye for an explanation he finally sees nothing inexplicable, and can begin every sentence with that phrase dearest to all who professionally understand: *It is no accident that*. . . . We should love explanations well, but the truth better; and often the truth is that there *is* no explanation, that so far as we know it is an accident that. . . ."[23]

Jarrell's belief that man is basically a limited creature who cannot understand his world because he cannot control it (rather than the possibly more hopeful reverse) is one reason for his strongly worded denunciations of Archibald MacLeish and Yvor Winters. In reviewing MacLeish's radio play, *The Fall of the City*, Jarrell castigates the author for being "an extraordinary case of arrested development. . . ." He is "a survivor from an almost extinct past," says Jarrell: "there is something consciously neo-primitive about his eager adoption of the optimistic voluntarism of frontier days, when . . . plenty of people thought that you can if you think you can; that the world is what we make it; that there's no limit." The result, Jarrell believes, is not only philosophic superficiality but artistic inferiority, since, he states, a "tragic view of life" is "the point of view of any great dramatist—who is, necessarily, a specialist on limits; who knows that the world is, at a given moment, what we find it; who understands well enough to accept, with composure even, the inescapable conditions of existence. MacLeish passionately dislikes any determinism, even an optimistic one; his response to any inescapable condition is to look strong and deny that it exists."[24] Consequently, Jarrell sees MacLeish's play as an easy, cheap avoidance of "Fate or Necessity."[25]

Similar language marks his almost parodic view of Winters'
Maule's Curse (1938), which he bluntly calls "simple-minded" because for
Winters

> there are few questions unanswered, and none unanswerable. If ours is
> not the most rational of all possible worlds (for even Mr. Winters some-
> times entertains the doubt), that does not excuse any confusion about it on
> our part; we *have* absolutely valid standards, both adequate and relevant,
> by which the universe can be understood and evaluated; if we are unfor-
> tunate or foolish enough to disregard these, we must take the conse-
> quences—which are disastrous. He writes as if the last three hundred
> years had occurred, but not to him. . . .[26]

Both writers, then, though in different ways, commit what is for Jarrell
the cardinal sin of reducing complexity to simplicity, of exchanging the
open-ended, uncontrollable, and pessimistic thing that is the world for a
simple, satisfying, but faithless substitute in which life is "what we think
it."[27] Defending Whitman's refusal to be consistent, in "Some Lines from
Whitman" from *Poetry and the Age*, Jarrell summarizes: "When you
organize one of the contradictory elements out of your work of art, you
are getting rid not just of it, but of the contradiction of which it was a
part; and it is the contradictions in works of art which make them able to
represent to us—as logical and methodical generalizations cannot—our
worlds and our selves, which are also full of contradictions."[28] A similar
inconsistency is another admirable quality which Jarrell finds in Ransom's
poetry, along with its sympathy and tenderness. He explains with an
anecdote:

> Once I took a little girl to a Tarzan movie; and as each new actor, each
> new cannibal, each new leopard and monkey and crocodile came on the
> scene, she would whisper to me desperately: "Is that a *good* one? Is that a
> *bad* one?" This great root-notion, this imperative at the bottom of our be-
> ings, is ill satisfied by Ransom's poems, anomalous things that keep whis-
> pering to us, "Both"—that keep whispering to us, "Neither."[29]

The distaste for moral absolutism which is evident in Jarrell's judgments on Winters and MacLeish is expressed even more passionately in his
review of Alex Comfort's book of war poems, *The Song of Lazarus* (1945).
Here, Jarrell is abrupt and irate. He grants Comfort "both courage and
individual judgment" in becoming a conscientious objector, but asserts
that because Comfort served out his term as an interne in a London hospital, instead of as "a laborer in some concentration camp in the
country,"[30] he was insulated from the truth of war. As in so much of the
criticism I have been quoting, Jarrell takes the side of the average, anonymous millions against what he sees as Comfort's supercilious and wrong-
headed condescension:

> . . . he is the isolated, pacifist, individualistic anarchist who tells the truth
> about things to the deceived homogeneous mass that is everybody

else. . . . Mr. Comfort believes in conscientious disobedience: if no one obeys the government there will be no war. . . . The poet's irritation at the stupidity of the corpses weakens his pastoral and generalized grief for them; besides, these are the wholesale deaths that happen to other people. . . . And he never wonders: how does it feel to be a dupe? . . .

Between Mr. Comfort and the soldiers there is a final barrier: he is right and they are wrong; and he cannot share the . . . unwilling identity in which all their differences are buried. . . . It is hard for him to feel for one of them an unmixed sorrow, since he can't help thinking, "He'd have been all right if he'd only had sense enough to disobey." But he means, *if they'd only all had sense enough to disobey*; though he seems to think he is making plausible political proposals, he is actually making impossible moral demands."[31]

The misgivings about free will and easy ethical judgments which are evident in these reactions against Comfort's poems are clearly related to Jarrell's disappointment in and distrust of Christian belief. Indeed, if one were to characterize Jarrell in religious terms on the basis of either his critical prose or his poems (e.g., "The Night before the Night before Christmas," "In the Ward: The Sacred Wood," "Burning the Letters," "A Camp in the Prussian Forest"), it would have to be as what the Middle Ages would have termed a Manichean. For Jarrell the modern, however, the duality of good and evil is not based on the conflict between spirit and the material world, but on the gulf between transcendence and inevitability. Writing on R. P. Blackmur's *The Good European* in 1948, Jarrell defined the subject of Blackmur's poems as "evil: evil as such, a real and final evil; so they are not Christian poems at all." Real evil, he goes on, "surely is what is arbitrarily *so* in the universe, all that is undeserved and irremediable," and the definition corresponds precisely with Jarrell's own description of Fate or Necessity as synonyms for reality. As Jarrell recognizes, Christian belief is based upon a monistic universe, and an insistence on the free will of the individual. Still discussing Blackmur's poems, he says, "so long as *we* are to blame for evil, so long as God is free from it—free to save us from that evil which we are and have deserved to be—real evil, final evil, does not exist."[32] But real evil, defined in these terms, *does* exist in Jarrell's world, where "free will" is only a specter. Thus, in a lengthy and extremely capable analysis of "Changes of Attitude and Rhetoric in Auden's Poetry," Jarrell is able to get at the cause of some of the pious profundities in Auden's Christian poetry:

Remembering some of the incredible conclusions to the later poems—*Life must live*, Auden's wish to *lift an affirming flame*—the reader may object that this sort of thing is sentimental idealism. But sentimental idealism is a necessity for someone who, even after rejecting a system as evil, finally accepts it—even with all the moral reservations and exhortations possible. The sentimentality and idealism, the vague abstraction of such prayers and exhortations, is a *sine qua non*: we can fool ourselves into praying for some vague general change of heart that is going to produce, automatically, all the specific changes that even we could never be foolish enough to pray for. When Auden prays for anything specific at all; when he prays against the organization of the world that makes impossible the moral and spiritual changes he prays for, it will be possible to take the prayer as something more than conscience- and face-saving sublimation. . . .[33]

Jarrell recognizes a similar problem in a very different writer, Kipling, and relates it to the role of Kipling's parents in the misery of his young life. "If Father and Mother were not to blame for anything," Jarrell says in his 1961 introduction to an anthology of Kipling's stories, "yet what did happen to you could happen to you—if God is good, and yet the concentration camps exist—then there has to be *someone* to blame, and to punish too, some real, personal source of the world's evil. But in this world, often, there is nothing to praise but no one to blame, and Kipling can bear to admit this in only a few of his stories."[34] In the poetry of Jarrell the humanitarian, on the contrary, the fact that often "there is nothing to praise but no one to blame" is admitted to again and again. The questions of where, how, and with what degree of success, can only be answered by a reading of *The Complete Poems*; but Jarrell's "amusing, high-spirited, accurate, original, and humane"[35] critical prose offers some important clues to his vision and values.

Notes

1. *Mid-Century American Poets* (New York: Twayne, 1950), p. 184.

2. Cleanth Brooks and Robert Penn Warren, eds., *Understanding Poetry*, 3rd ed. (New York: Holt, Rinehart and Winston, 1960), pp. 531–38.

3. From Jarrell's review of Eleanor Ross Taylor's *Wilderness of Ladies*, in his *A Sad Heart at the Supermarket* (New York: Atheneum, 1962), p. 210.

4. "Fifty Years of American Poetry," in *The Third Book of Criticism* (New York: Farrar, Straus & Giroux, 1969), p. 300.

5. *Ibid.*

6. *Poetry and the Age* (New York: Vintage, 1955), p. 92.

7. *Ibid.*, p. 93.

8. *Ibid.*, p. 226.

9. *Southern Review*, 7 (Winter 1942), 665.

10. *The Third Book*, p. 326.

11. *Ibid.*, p. 333.

12. *Poetry and the Age*, p. 129.

13. *Ibid.*, pp. 128–29.

14. Jarrell parodies universal education in the dialogue called "The Schools of Yesteryear" from *A Sad Heart at the Supermarket*, pp. 43–63. See also "A Girl in a Library," "The Night before the Night before Christmas," "Next Day," "In Montecito," "Three Bills," and the second of two poems called "Hope" in *The Complete Poems* (New York: Farrar, Straus and Giroux, 1969).

15. *The Complete Poems*, pp. 29–33.

16. *A Sad Heart*, p. 26.

17. *Ibid.*, pp 3–4.

18. *Ibid.*, p. 84.

19. *Poetry and the Age*, p. 88.

20. *Ibid.*, p. 39.

21. (New York: Alfred A. Knopf, 1954), pp. 132–33.

22. *A Sad Heart*, p. 191.

23. *Ibid.*, p. 180.

24. *Sewanee Review*, 51 (April–June 1943), 276.

25. *Ibid.*, p. 277.

26. "The Morality of Mr. Winters," *Kenyon Review*, (Spring 1939), 213.

27. *A Sad Heart*, p. 26.

28. *Poetry and the Age*, p. 116.

29. *Ibid.*, pp. 91–92.

30. *Ibid.*, p. 141.

31. *Ibid.*, pp. 141–42.

32. *Ibid.*, p. 152.

33. *The Third Book*, p. 124.

34. *A Sad Heart*, pp. 134–35.

35. R. W. Flint, "On Randall Jarrell," in Robert Lowell, Peter Taylor, and Robert Warren, eds., *Randall Jarrell 1914–1965* (New York: Farrar, Straus and Giroux, 1967), p. 77.

Principle and Practice in the Criticism of Randall Jarrell

Keith Monroe*

For twenty years, from the outbreak of World War II through the late 1950s, Randall Jarrell was the archangel of American poetry criticism. He began by guarding the gates to the realm of poetry against interlopers with ferocious purity; he ended by interceding on behalf of excellences previously undetected. From the late 1940s on he turned his talents for invective and polemic away from individual poets and toward the defense of poetry itself against larger enemies. Fifteen years after his death almost all his criticism remains in print, and he is regarded by many as without peer as a practical critic of poetry.

This accomplishment is made the more interesting by the fact that with few exceptions his criticism took the form of brief book reviews or stylish personal essays—forms of criticism more characteristic of the nineteenth than of the twentieth century. The deceptive ease with which he was able to make a memorable essay out of the most mundane occasion was founded on two factors. Jarrell, though generally disdaining theory in favor of practical attention to a given poetic object, had a clear, ample, consistent view of the nature of poetry which can be extracted from his criticism as a whole. And Jarrell possessed a rare rhetorical mastery. These two qualities lend importance to even the slightest of his nearly one hundred critical essays and reviews. These two qualities *and* a subject worthy of attention produced a number of critical landmarks—his famous essays on Frost, Whitman, Graves, Williams, Stevens, and Lowell—and his finest polemics—"The Age of Criticism," "The Taste of the Age," and "A Sad Heart at the Supermarket." In the following pages I will attempt to isolate Jarrell's view of the nature of the poet and poetry and to describe the rhetorical means he employed to express judgments based upon it.

The kernel of Jarrell's view of the nature of poetry may be found in a remark in praise of Auden's early poems. Jarrell said they were produced by Auden's whole being, "as much unconscious as conscious." He went on to contend that, though the "rational intelligence guides and selects, it

*This essay was written especially for this book and appears by permission of the author.

does not produce and impose; we make our poetry, but we make it what we can, not what we wish." Thus, for Jarrell, trained as an undergraduate in psychology, the true source of poetry is in the unconscious, and this source can be "dried up, by too rigorous supervision."[1] One of Jarrell's most used words of praise about poems is "magical," and he very politely defines it as having to do with "levels which we are not accustomed to verbalize or scrutinize."[2] Poetry which is "magical" speaks to those levels in the reader and emerges from them in the writer.

Because the unconscious is the source of poetry, and because the poet is liable to dam that source by too much application of rationality or ego, he is more helpless victim of the capricious unconscious than controlling intelligence. He is "a sort of accident-prone worker to whom poems happen," which leads Jarrell to conclude: "A good poet is someone who manages, in a lifetime of standing out in thunderstorms, to be struck by lightning five or six times; a dozen or two dozen times and he is great."[3] His belief in the unconscious and largely uncontrollable fountainhead of poetry leads Jarrell to endorse Blake's "There is no competition between true poets." For how can the unconscious be expected to compete?

Still, this conclusion does not mean that there are no distinctions to be made among poets. They may all be at the mercy of the muse, but all are not treated equally by her. Some poets are simply struck by lightning more often than others, are more fully open to the unconscious. And, though this is the *sine qua non* for writing good poetry, it is not all that is required of a poet. A very delicate balance is required. Too much unconscious and too little rational control is bad, but so is too much rational control because it can censor the unconscious offerings. Before examining some of Jarrell's remarks on this balance, it should be pointed out that all of it applies only to true poets. There is also a sort of pseudo-poetry in which "people's hard lives and hopeless ambitions have expressed themselves more directly and heartbreakingly than they have ever been expressed in any work of art: it is as if the writers had sent their ripped-out arms and legs, with 'This is a poem' scrawled on them in lipstick." Such poetry lacks both technique *and* the unconscious, which speaks indirectly. It is simply a conscious scream or moan or sign. Such poets "have never made anything, they have suffered their poetry as helplessly as they have anything else."[4] This is Eliot's idea of the objective correlative, restated. If you want the reader to feel the same sickness you do, you cannot simply say: "I feel sick." As Jarrell says more than once, "true art is indirect," "art lies to tell the truth."

But even among true poets the luck of being in touch with the unconscious is parceled out unevenly, and this inequity makes hierarchical judgments possible. Most good poets are "partial poets"; only the greatest have so much contact with the unconscious that it provides them with a complete vision. Wordsworth, Rilke, and Yeats are examples, and when you compare them with a partial poet, however brilliant, "you are comparing a rearrangement of the room with a subsidence of continents."⁵ And that distinction is primarily based on one's lucky relations with the muse.

The worst thing one can do is become too conscious. Philosophy is dangerous for a poem: poetry "specializes in muddles." It is the poets' "subordination to the poems they write that makes them admirable." The poet should write "his poem for its own sake," not for his sake or the audience's sake. He should use consciousness to acquire "The chameleon's shameless interest in everything but itself," for otherwise the ego gets in the way and kills the poem. Many of Jarrell's individual judgments are based on this principle. In Jarrell's view, Auden, for example, lost touch with the unconscious source of poetry, becoming "the most professional poet in the world." But that "is not necessarily to be the best: Minerva says, 'But *you* don't need *me*!' "⁶

This, then, is Jarrell's view of a true poet—someone lucky enough to be open to the unconscious, who has acquired sufficient technical skill to complete the gifts the muse provides, but who is not so conscious of himself and his technique as to close the channel to the unconscious. Most are partial poets. All write much poetry that is less than completely successful—a few successes redeem all the rest. Each poet has his own difficulty in maintaining this balance: Williams tends to refine too little; Stevens tends to philosophize too much; Pound's interest in himself obtrudes.

If we now have a sense of what a poet is for Jarrell, we must still ask what a poem is. In addition to magical, the words Jarrell uses most often to approve poems are "real," "truthful," and "imaginative." As we have seen, the kind of imagination he praises is not involved with the ego, but with its effacement. Imagination is the vehicle by which the poet escapes the self, submerges himself in other lives. This immersion allows the poet to treat reality, Jarrell's key word in defining poetry. As both poet and psychologist, Jarrell insists that the unconscious, subjective world of feeling and emotion, dream and wish and contradiction, is the medium through which poets (but not just poets) apprehend the logical, quantifiable, rational side of life we are accustomed to call reality. It is the poet's business, by this method, to plunge "into the very blood of the world," and create a real object which "is simply there, in indifferent unchanging actuality."⁷ The poet halts the flux of existence for a moment, captures the bug of life in amber, but an amber capable of letting it out again alive: he has an "immemorial power to make the things of this world seen and felt and living in words."⁸ And since literature encompasses life, it also embodies a sort of truth, "our truth, truth as we know it; one can almost define literature as the union of a wish and a truth, or as a wish modified by truth."⁹

Poetry thus combines what is real and how we feel about what is real to create "animals no one has succeeded in naming, young things nothing has succeeded in aging." "How can anybody write about unreality?" Jarrell asks. Since the raw materials of poems are so essentially human, the interplay of consciousness and the unconscious with the material world, it follows that "human life without some form of poetry is not human life but animal existence."[10] It also follows that, since poetry is the product of the individual mind, the potential forms of poetry are infinite. It is a "delusion that a single poem can serve as a model for the poet's poems or for Poetry. . . ."[11] One measure of a poet is, therefore, in his diversity—in how much of reality he can encompass. Graves is praised because his poems are "different either from one another or from the poems of any other poet. His poems have to an extraordinary degree the feeling of one man's world, one man's life."[12]

This is a recurrent refrain. If poems are what the unconscious makes of the world, refined by conscious technique, then a poet's success is measured by the size and individuality of that imaginatively reconstructed world. Thus, Ransom's poems give us "parts of one world." Reading Frost we are "not in a book but in a world." There is in Whitman "almost everything in the world." Lowell provides us not with "themes or generalizations but a world."[13]

This last remark brings us to the point where the three elements Jarrell has defined intersect. First, there is the world itself, and poets are praised for knowing as much of it as possible and damned for being the " 'alienated artist' cut off from everybody who isn't, yum-yum, another alienated artist."[14] The first thing a poet should do is imagine, observe, be "faithful to reality," obsessed by "lives, actions, subject-matter," "shaken out of himself, to have his subject individualize his poem."[15] The second link in the chain that produces art enters here. A great poet must be a great observer, but next he must be an individual personality whose mind is open to all he observes. From the interaction of observed world and observing mind, poetry is produced, and the third element, technique, enters. The process can fail at any point. If the poet knows too little of the world his poems will be slight. If the poet does not bring his data back alive, he has failed. Yet he must not give us a poem with only "as much reality as the brick one stumbles over on the sidewalk," because then too little has been done to the raw materials.[16] His technique or consciousness must organize, subordinate the part to the whole. Poems must be concrete, singular, compressed, concentrated life. They must be exact and concise. Blake's "minute particulars" matter—not only the minute particulars of the world but of technique.

Yet Jarrell thought conscious technique dangerous. He often quoted Ruskin's remark that perfection ought not to be expected of a work of art; praised a Whitman passage that had faults that did not matter; and said that logic was not crucial, that "the contradictions in works of art . . . make them able to represent us. . . . [since] our world and our selves . . . are also full of contradictions."[17] He believed a style could become habit-forming and remove the reality from the poem, or limit the amount of reality that could be encompassed. Tennyson was restricted by his tight forms, Whitman liberated by his freer ones.

Considering all the ways in which a poet may fail according to this scheme, it is no surprise that Jarrell considered a successful poem a miraculous creation, a great poet the rarest of beings. His view that all of reality—objective and subjective—was the province of the poet, that form might grow organically out of the material, meant that he was able to appreciate a great range of poetry—Williams and Whitman, Stevens and Yeats, Frost and Moore, Graves and Pound. These attitudes allowed him to read a poem as if he were "entering a foreign country whose laws and language and life [were] a kind of translation" of his own.[18] He could do so because he believed the function of art was to show us excellence "unlike our own" which would extend and complete us.

This view of the nature of poetry lies behind Jarrell's criticism of it, is the essential engine which drives the criticism. But it also dictated the style and method Jarrell evolved. As a poet-critic, he belongs to a critical tradition that, at least as far back as the Renaissance and increasingly since Wordsworth, has taken as its starting point the human necessity, worth, and centrality of poetry. All of Jarrell's criticism is, in effect, a defense of poetry as an essential human activity. Jarrell defended poetry against incompetent poets and against its critics. He protested against any specialization of literature into an airtight compartment, contending rather that, since poetry springs from universal human sources and is a part of life, it should be as widely disseminated as possible, should live in the world.

These attitudes led him to adopt a style of criticism that ran counter to most of that of his time. Instead of an increasingly druidical criticism intended for an audience of other initiates, Jarrell attempted to make his criticism accessible to as wide an audience as possible, by writing whenever possible for organs likely to penetrate beyond the scholarly and academic realms—the *Nation*, the *New Republic*, the *New York Times Book Review*, *Partisan Review*—and by eschewing the scholarly article in favor of the modest review. He often made public lectures the starting point of his criticism, and he developed a richly personal style in opposition to the sort of criticism he scorned, which "might just as well have been written by a syndicate of encyclopedias for an audience of International Business Machines . . . an astonishingly graceless, joyless, humorless, long-winded, niggling, blinkered, methodical, self-important, cliché-ridden, prestige-obsessed, almost autonomous criticism."[19]

The first problem he faced in carrying out this program grew out of the fact that the sorts of reviews he chose to write are often limited to a thousand or at most two thousand words. Often more than one book is to be discussed. How does one give the reader a real feeling for a poet's quality, if the poet is an unknown one, in under a thousand words?

Quotation is the most obvious method, of course, but if space is being allocated not in words but in columns or column inches, this can be self-defeating. A relatively few lines of poetry can take up the better part of a magazine column, a disproportionate amount of space for what is conveyed.

In order to solve this problem Jarrell adopted some devices that he used consistently. He would describe poets as belonging to the school of Winters or Wilbur, or as romantic or Victorian mastodons left over from an earlier time. This was classification by type for those poets who deserved it. He also classified poets in terms of value. He said, for example, that it might make sense to say Frost was not in Rilke's class, but that it did "*not* make much sense if you substitute for Rilke's name that of Eliot or Moore or Stevens or Auden, that of any living poet."[20] Likewise, "Can Whitman really be a sort of Thomas Wolfe or Carl Sandburg or Robinson Jeffers or Henry Miller—or a sort of Balzac of poetry, whose every part is crude but whose whole is somehow great?"[21] Such classifications are not only normative, not only establish a hierarchy, a peerdom, but also help give a shorthand feeling for a writer's qualities.

As classification shades into comparison, Jarrell acquires another method for briefly giving a feeling for a writer's own tone. When he began writing criticism he was fond of comparisons drawn from the sciences. This was undoubtedly a result of his scientific education, but he may well have learned from Eliot's famous equating of the poetic process with the chemistry of platinum that such comparisons conferred on mere opinion a solidity and weight they might otherwise lack, making mere judgments look like scientific proofs. Thus *Paterson* (Book I) is "a geological event"; Frost's poems are "geometrical"; Marianne Moore's have "the lacy, mathematical extravagance of snowflakes"; romanticism evolving into modernism is "a vector"; and so on.

In the fifties, Jarrell began to use fewer such comparisons, and more from the worlds of art and music, apparently hoping that an audience ignorant of poetry might still have some cultural reference points he could play on. As in the case of the scientific allusions, these came readily to his mind. So, Aiken poems are like Delius or Liszt finger exercises; Bishop's are compared to Mahler songs, Vuillard and Vermeer paintings; Marianne Moore resembles Mozart "choosing unpromising themes for the fun of it"; MacLeish's best lyrics are like Georgia O'Keeffe paintings; and so on.

One final shorthand device Jarrell used in reviews where space was at a premium was the coining of mottos meant to sum up a poet's stance in a phrase. They were often, though not always, a trifle snide. Kenneth Patchen's motto is "Too Much!" Jeffers's is "More! more!" Lowell's is "Make it grotesque." Williams's is "In the suburbs, there one feels free." And the early Pound's is "Write like speech—and *read French poetry!*" All of these devices often make for a fairly dense thousand-word review, but they do not constitute overkill; rather they represent Jarrell's attempt to give the reader numerous clues to a writer's special qualities. If he does not profit from one device, he may from the next. And they add up to a formidable erudition and authority, however lightly carried, which is bound to exercise a persuasive force on the reader.

Lest the erudition alienate readers, Jarrell counterpoised against it an elaborately built-up persona. By employing a whole range of rhetorical devices not usually found in literary criticism, Jarrell attempted to create a personal criticism with all the human qualities he stressed in the poetry he discussed, criticism as conversation among friends. Jarrell's mature criticism is certainly noteworthy for this quality, but a look at his critical work in chronological order reveals that the style he finally achieved was the result of painstaking refinement. Several elements went into this mature style and contribute to its success in removing barriers between author and audience so as to better convey to the reader an accurate sense of the work being discussed in an atmosphere of attentive, often festive, appreciation.

For example, the range of diction is far greater than usually encountered in such writing. Though the sentences are supple and well-crafted, the diction rises to oratorical and poetical flourishes and dips into colloquialism. When Jarrell says that if in making an anthology "you leave out Spenser you mean business," when he speaks of "Breakfast-Club-Calisthenics, Radio-Kitchen heartiness" in explicating a poem, he is miles from the standard reviewer's tone of voice and diction.[22] Lowell has remarked on an aspect of this in pointing to a passage in "To the Laodiceans" when Jarrell breaks into a recommendation of some long poems to say he feels "frustrated at not being able to quote and go over them, as I so often have done with friends and classes."[23] Lowell remarks that "few critics could so gracefully descend from the grand manner or be so offhand about their dignity."[24] Furthermore, Jarrell knew perfectly what he was about, as is suggested by his remark that in Whitman's similar "changes of tone" was contained "the essence of wit."[25]

If Jarrell's persona is manifest in his diction, it is also apparent in the range of emotion he allows himself to show. He refused to maintain a safe, tepid tone. His criticism is full of exclamations, generally enthusiastic, and imperatives, rhetorical questions, italics, capitals, and hyperbolic series designed to close the distance between himself and his audience.

Another element common to all of Jarrell's criticism is a reliance on humor. Often the humor arises simply from a well-turned phrase, but there were several formulas to which Jarrell was addicted. One was the interpolation of little stories, or parables. In discussing Frost's "Design," Jarrell breaks off to describe a witless coed's misinterpretation of the poem. In discussing Marya Zaturenska's pastorals, Jarrell begins by imagining her

> perplexed with this sick disease of modern life standing in the subway reading *Finnegans Wake* . . . it is like a nightmare. A schoolgirl begins to recite her homework, "Corinna's Going A-Maying." Word by word, stanza by stanza, the repose and order of the pastoral settle over Miss Zaturenska's troubled mind, over Miss Zaturenska's feverish spirit, like a wet blanket. Joyce, Einstein, Engels fade away, are quite forgot; the subway is a mass of Ivy.[26]

These little tales can be condensed into a metaphor, as when Jarrell describes Aiken as "a kind of Midas: everything that he touches turns to verse." Often, however, they leave such relatively simple dramatic comparisons behind and grow into quite elaborate allegories. This is particularly common in the polemics. "The Intellectual in America," is half given over to an updated retelling of the story of Diogenes and Alexander. "The Age of Criticism" contains an allegory about various types of readers. There are little dramatic scenes involving Queen Victoria and Matthew Arnold.

Comic comparisons are also common in Jarrell's work. Frost sometimes makes "a point like the end of a baseball bat." Arnold's touchstones "remind one of the charm bracelets little girls wear." Expecting Tate and Warren to be influenced by Ransom "is like expecting two nightmares to be influenced by a daydream." These humorous metaphors often turn into parables. The two devices overlap, as in this passage which begins with a kind of pun on the title of Hyman's *The Armed Vision*.

> Critics are so much better armed than they used to be in the old days: they've got tanks and flamethrowers now. . . . Can't you imagine an age in which critics are like paleontologists, an age in which the last bone that the youngest critic had wired together is already hundreds of years old?[27]

Another source of humor is in two related devices, the submerged or unattributed quotation and the altered cliché. At one point Jarrell says, "I have only begun to quote." He says the moral of "Provide, Provide" is that you should "settle yourself for life in the second-best bed around which the heirs gather, the very best second-best bed." In discussing literary quarterlies, Jarrell says there are a few poems and stories, "the rest is criticism." And in some of the polemics, Jarrell took this technique a step further and wrote clichés with appendixes. "If you have been put in your place long enough, you begin to act like the place." Or, "Big Fleas have little fleas to bite 'em, especially when the little ones know that they are going to get applauded by the dog."[28]

Many of these examples also employ direct address to the reader. Jarrell is always talking to him, addressing him as "you," introducing him into the essay with invented dialogue.

One final device is the most noticeable of all in Jarrell's repertoire: the use of quotation. Several writers—Shapiro puts it best—have remarked that he wrote "a style of inlay in which quotation is so exquisitely handled that everything Jarrell quotes sounds as if he wrote it."[29] This is true, and I think there are several reasons for it. First, amid so much invented dialogue, direct address, and wit, his quotations seem perfectly at home. His style was already so dramatic that a wise saying or two did not stand out. Also, in most cases, he really did possess the quotations he used. They were not hunted up for the occasion, but sprang to his lips unbidden and so sound that way.

Jarrell's motive in employing all these devices was to make poetry matter, to dramatize the issue by turning each book review into an occasion to force the reader to participate as the reviewer's ally for or against the work under discussion. And this impulse grew out of Jarrell's central concern that poetry is a crucial human activity to which attention must be paid. This may be the ultimate value and significance of Jarrell's criticism. His defense of Williams, his early championing of Lowell, his discovery of new merits in Frost and Whitman, his withering attacks on inflated reputations may now be simply footnotes to literary history, but the style and attitude he brought to criticism are timeless. Jarrell believed he knew what poetry was, believed in its importance, and developed a criticism meant to persuade others to share his views. That his book reviews, a most ephemeral species of writing, still command attention nearly twenty years after the last of them was written, suggests he was successful. And this fact also suggests that his example is one worth heeding. His criticism reflects the attitude not so much of a critic or even a poet but of an ideal reader confronting each new work with humility, attention, and openness to experience. Jarrell once contended that the true reader must become as a little child again, and by his example he helped a generation learn how to achieve that goal, how to read poems and write about them as they deserved.

Notes

1. Randall Jarrell, *The Third Book of Criticism* (New York: Farrar, Straus and Giroux, 1969), pp. 148–49.

2. *Third Book*, p. 155.

3. Randall Jarrell, *Poetry and the Age* (New York: Noonday, 1972), p. 113.

4. *Poetry and the Age*, p. 178.

5. *Third Book*, p. 94.

6. Randall Jarrell, *Kipling, Auden and Co.* (New York: Farrar, Straus and Giroux, 1980), p. 230.

7. *Third Book*, p. 142, and *Poetry and the Age*, p. 186.

8. *Poetry and the Age*, p. 186.

9. Randall Jarrell, *A Sad Heart at the Supermarket* (New York: Antheneum, 1967), p. 26.

10. *Poetry and the Age*, p. 23.

11. *Third Book*, pp. 145–46.

12. *Third Book*, p. 193.

13. *Poetry and the Age*, pp. 96, 126, 217.

14. *Poetry and the Age*, p. 31.

15. *Poetry and the Age*, p. 141.

16. *Poetry and the Age*, p. 244.

17. *Poetry and the Age*, p. 128.

18. *Poetry and the Age*, p.12.

19. *Poetry and the Age*, p. 73.

20. *Poetry and the Age*, p. 38.

21. *Poetry and the Age*, pp. 113–14.

22. *Poetry and the Age*, pp. 171, 47.

23. *Poetry and the Age*, p. 63.

24. Robert Lowell, "Randall Jarrell," in *Randall Jarrell: 1914–1965*, ed. Robert Lowell, Peter Taylor, and Robert Penn Warren (New York: Farrar, Straus and Giroux, 1967), p. 106.

25. *Poetry and the Age*, p. 116.

26. *Kipling, Auden and Co.*, p. 68.

27. *Poetry and the Age*, p. 93.

28. *Sad Heart*, pp. 10–11.

29. Karl Shapiro, "The Death of Randall Jarrell," in *Randall Jarrell: 1914–1965*, p. 196.

The Fiction

Randall Jarrell, Novelist: A Reconsideration

Sylvia Angus*

In an issue of the *New York Review of Books* several months ago, the poet Robert Lowell has a long and affectionate essay on his friend, the late Randall Jarrell. It traces Jarrell's life, discusses his personality, and treats in considerable detail the excellence of his poetry. Two sentences only are devoted to Jarrell's one novel: "His novel, *Pictures from an Institution*, whatever its fictional oddities, is a unique and serious joke-book. How often I've met people who keep it by their beds or somewhere handy, and read random pages aloud to lighten their hearts." One is left with the uncomfortable sense that Lowell wished he did not have to comment at all on his friend's one fictional excursion. "Joke-book." This is a destructive epithet, the more astonishing because it stands alone in a sea of praise and poetic perceptiveness.

Lowell's attitude is additional evidence of the remarkable degree to which Jarrell's novel has been undervalued and misunderstood by the reviewers. It has been seen almost exclusively as a tour de force of wit—and it *is* probably the most consistently and devastatingly witty book of our generation. Nearly every line in it is instinct with light and sparkle, an overflowing of intelligence which makes one grope back toward *Tristram Shandy* in an effort to find suitable comparisons. No one, however, seems to have noticed that the book is a multilevel creation of enormous subtlety and depth, musical in structure and moving simultaneously on psychological and on allegorical levels.

I

Pictures from an Institution: A Comedy, originally published in 1954, is about the institution called Benton College, an ivy-covered Eden so dedicated to liberal thinking and social adjustment that its students are often moved to cry out to their advisors: "Whip me, whip me, Mother, just don't be Reasonable!" In this modern, green, semi-intellectual paradise, Jarrell has gathered together a galaxy of characters which is at once a humorous cross section of college "types," a sensitively understood

*Reprinted from the *Southern Review*, NS 2 (1966), 689–96, by permission of the author.

266

group of individuals, a collection of interlocking, contrapuntal motifs, and a group of allegorical archetypes quite clearly representing the mythic vision of heaven and hell. It is a remarkable achievement, perhaps most unusual in that it is illuminated throughout with a coruscating wit which has blinded reviewers to all else. Perhaps only James Joyce in our century has had the brilliance and audacity to use the tool of wit in treating so fundamentally large and somber a subject as the condition of man in our time. The lines in Jarrell's book, as in *Ulysses*, are jewels, but they could never make up a joke book because the essence of their wit is that they are indissolubly wedded to the characters they formulate.

Full in the foreground of Benton, that "other Eden," stands Gertrude Johnson, lady novelist, whose cynical intelligence and hatred of life—and fundamentally of herself—are expressed in verbal attacks which flay everyone alive. Her first comment on Benton, where she has come to teach creative writing, is typical of her: "When I first got here I said to myself 'How well the animals get on together!' but then I saw they were vegetables." Her smile, Jarrell says, was "like a skull, like a stone marten scarf, like catatonia, like the smiles of the damned at Bamberg . . . . torn animals were removed at sunset from that smile."

Gertrude's smile is a clue. She is, indeed, one of the damned, if not the devil himself. Like most of the great devils in literature she is cursed with intellectual pride; she cannot admit a superior, or even an equal. Satanic, too, is her incapacity to feel. Gertrude's novels are brilliant, erudite, factual. They lack only humanity, the gift of love. The novel is full of details which illustrate Gertrude's allegorical nature. She is, for instance, tone deaf; there is no harmony in her soul. She has, for another pointer, a constant dull pain in her chest—like the absence of some necessary thing, a heart perhaps. All the great satanic figures in literature also have some such flaw or "absence."

But it is too simple to write Gertrude off as a symbol of the devil. She is a hag-ridden human being whose intelligence is her only defense against the howling emptiness within her. There are many clever, psychically flawed people like her. One can recognize Gertrude without the mythic level if one wishes. Jarrell says of her: "The world was the arsenal Gertrude used against the world. She felt about anything: if it's not a weapon, what am *I* doing with it? and it turned out to be a weapon. She knew that people must be, at bottom, like herself, and this was enough to justify—to make imperative—any measures she could take against them. And if everybody had been, at bottom, what Gertrude thought she was, she would have been right to behave as she behaved, though it would have been better simply to curse God and die."

Gertrude hates with ferocity Benton's composer in residence, Gottfried Knosperl Rosenbaum, a large, rumbling Austrian Jew whose encompassing humanity is the unbearable antithesis to her hatred of life. She is cruelly satirical of Rosenbaum, whom she calls "the God-descended bud of the rose-tree," the more so because her anger makes no impression on him. He is impervious to her hatred. Gottfried, on the mythic level, is clearly what his name suggests, the principle of good, or God, in contrast to Gertrude's principle of evil, or the devil. Gottfried is gentle, compassionate, understanding, but also sometimes wise and remote beyond even his wife's understanding. But it, after all, is not necessary, or possible, to understand the motive force of goodness. It is enough to be aware of it. His allegorical function is evident in many details about Gottfried, though it is never intrusive. He is, for instance, a musician, harmonious of soul. He is fond of the young, and all but worshipped by the young and innocent Constance. His home is filled with old and beautiful and heterogeneous objects, like the world itself, rich and varied as life. Jarrell even makes him a composer, a creator—albeit a modest one, and his one famous work is a tone poem called, appropriately enough, "Lucifer in Starlight," in which he figures forth the great and suffering gap between heaven and the fallen angel. If this all seems to be overt, it can only be said that it is too delicately done to be obvious. None of the reviewers of the book seems to have noticed it. Jarrell makes Gottfried sufficient and fascinating wholly on the human psychological level. He is a huge, bear-like, elderly man, who dresses in absurd, woolly sweaters, and likes to play tennis with his students. He is an elderly artist transplated from Europe to the New World, and he and his wife carry with them all the rich cultural baggage of the old world. The Rosenbaums are childless, somewhat overburdened by past times and experiences, sad, profound, ironic. They understand—and do not at all understand—the strange new world of America to which the tragedy of Nazism has exiled them. Anyone who has ever known elderly, cultivated exiles would recognize the tone and quality of the Rosenbaums as special, without recourse to a manifest allegorical interpretation of them.

The dualism set up between Gottfried and Gertrude is the most obvious symbolic suggestion among many which make Jarrell's intention, on one level, clearly allegorical. The book is full of sly references and symbolic jokes. The president of Benton, for instance, is an institution of a man, totally self-satisfied, unquestioning, and happy. He is more a cliché than a person, but he doesn't know it. He has only a single peculiarity. He had been an Olympic diver before "being called" to Benton, and his greatest pleasure is still to swim and dive, to be suspended in the womb-like medium of water, a kind of limbo for the half-alive. Jarrell's choice of this somewhat esoteric avocation for his college president has distinct mythic overtones. In the classical limbo, a shadowy, womb-like place, no one suffers, but no one truly exists either, either in pain or pleasure. Psychologically the president is all the smug, faceless conformists of the world doing their appointed tasks and thereby freeing the creative souls for perils and ecstasies of awareness. It is just another tossed in bit of playful allusiveness that Jarrell gives us in making the president's two

Afghan hounds dislike him. Their names, delightfully appropriate, are Yin and Yang. It is clear at once that these opposing, polar principles could not possibly like the president of Benton, that faceless man-in-the-middle. Whenever he takes them for a walk he loses them almost at once to any definite personality who comes along, whether it be the Victorian innocent, Miss Batterson, or the cursed Gertrude.

It would take a monograph to explore completely all the rich allusiveness of *Pictures from an Institution*, for Jarrell was not only a sensitive, perceptive, and comically gifted man; he was also an unusually erudite one, whose novel offers a happy hunting ground for the tracking down of allusive and elusive references.

II

Jarrell's novel, it seems clear, has suffered critically from its wit as Adlai Stevenson's political career suffered from his wit. There is an assumption, which even our most astute minds seem unable to overcome, that if one is witty one cannot be profound, or, as Benton's president might say, "sincere." *Pictures from an Institution* has suffered both from reviewers who didn't understand it at all, like Anthony West, and from reviewers who thought it was terribly funny and nothing more, like Francis Steegmuller. West in an influential *New Yorker* review begins by saying he is disappointed in Jarrell because he has written a book about an author, a situation he compares at great length to a man looking at himself in a mirror looking at himself in a mirror. This implies the absurd suggestion that the artist who uses himself as material is on the wrong track; that Thomas Mann, Henry James, James Joyce, Thomas Wolfe, Gide, and a host of others, would have been *sounder* if they had written, say, historical novels instead of all those self-centered portraits of the artist. But this is scarcely less outlandish than West's reaction to the main characters. He dislikes Gertrude because she is *inhuman*, but he prefers her to Rosenbaum, because he is *too human*. He offers, as a critique of the humane and compassionate Rosenbaum, a philosophical position which is his own and quite opposed to Jarrell's. Speaking of Rosenbaum, he says: "It is not enough to believe, in a soupy, emotional way, in life, which cares no more for man and his works than it does for stones and fish; it is necessary to believe in man and in certain rational concepts of human behavior." But the essence of Gottfried is precisely that he goes beyond the narrow, people-oriented view which dwells on its own rationality because it fears the broad comprehensiveness of the world. Gottfried is immensely—though never soupily—understanding of people, but he believes in a broader concept, in a process of life which is often sad and oftener absurd, but he cannot hate it. If this "yea" to life is what West refers to as "soupy," then it seems plain that West's own position is close to that of the redoubtable Gertrude whom he prefers: "She had never had a nightmare; this was her nightmare. She looked at the world and *saw*, and cried out, her voice rising at the end of the sentence into falsetto: 'Why, it wouldn't fool a *child!*' "

Steegmuller, with far less space at his disposal in a *New York Times* review, does at least offer homage to Jarrell's wit. Unfortunately he is so overwhelmed by the pyrotechnic display that he misses everything else. He says, for instance, "It is scarcely surprising that in a performance of such kaleidoscopic brilliance, the elements of coherence and staying power should to a certain extent be sacrificed." This is a startling sentence. Staying power, the ability to keep up the fireworks is precisely one of the remarkable qualities of the book. Jarrell, furthermore, is the most lucid and coherent writer to be found anywhere. One can only suspect that Steegmuller means, perhaps, "cohesion," because he says, a few lines later, that "the book lacks conventional novelistic architecture." What "conventional novelistic architecture" means is a bit difficult to determine if one searches for it in some novels which have been called great, say *Tristram Shandy*, perhaps, or *The Immoralist*, or *The Stranger*, or *Herzog*. To demand "conventional" architecture is to ask for dead form. Presumably, Steegmuller means that Jarrell's novel lacks structure.

In a sense this remark is justified. *Pictures from an Institution* does lack the plot development of much customary fiction. The book is not architectural. It is musical in form and therefore somewhat obscure to readers who do not expect this.

Jarrell was deeply interested in music, as the book itself makes clear. That he saw his book in musical rather than architectural terms seems evident from the title he gave it. *Pictures from an Institution*, like Moussorgsky's *Pictures at an Exhibition*, is a series of portraits, but they are interwoven, contrapuntal portraits, balanced and moving in relation to each other, as well as in relation to his several levels of development. Each portrait is conditioned by the fact that it is of a human being interacting with other human beings against the theme (in the bass) of Benton College, USA. But all of these characters exist on a triple thematic level. We see them as riotously funny stereotypes of humanity; as separate, sentient, and suffering individuals; and as allegorical figures in a mythic drama. It is a complex musical score Jarrell has composed—intricate, full of recurrent motifs, grace notes, and distant echoes.

As Jarrell, the narrator, remarks in the book, "Nothing ever happens at Benton." What he means is that although life goes on there as it does everywhere, *plot*, the lines of external action we associate with conventional fiction, is not particularly apparent. It is amusing that Gertrude, who is writing a novel about Benton and is intensely concerned with facts and with structure, might well be producing the kind of novel suggested by the phrase "conventional novelistic architecture." Jarrell says of her book: "The fact that nothing much ever happened at Benton made her even more impatient with Benton; it was not simply raw, but dead, unresisting material. She felt justified in paying no attention to it except as a giant nursery of facts, facts that would cover, with their mild, academic ivy of verisimilitude, the girders of a plot that could have supported the First National Bank."

Jarrell, himself, did not write—perhaps could not, almost certainly would not—write Gertrude's kind of book. Nothing much happens, but this is not the same thing as saying that *Pictures from an Institution* has no structure. Its structure is internal, as harmoniously conceived as music, the parts interwoven as carefully as those in a toccata and fugue. The music begins with the entrance of the serpent into Eden and ends with her departure. In between it paints the good, the wise, the innocent and the foolish as Jarrell explores with gaiety, insight, and all the brilliant verbal devices of the poet those who live in the garden. The lack of typical architecture in his book is not a flaw. It is a perception.

III

Jarrell's book has been assessed in a number of curiously limited ways.

It has been codified as a "college novel," one of those dubious categories which equate the substance of a work with its locale. Benton College is, of course, a locale, but its inhabitants are as universal as Everyman. One might as well call *Remembrance of Things Past* a French bourgeois novel and feel that one has thereby summed it up and explained it. The life of the college conditions some things about the characters; any locale must. But the characters are fundamentally of the world; they are human beings wherever they live and they portray humanity to the degree that their creator was capable of understanding human life. Jarrell was deeply capable. The book has also been seen as a malicious exercise in wit at the expense of very specific people. This narrow view has provided numbers of people with amusing after-dinner conversation of the "You know who *Gertrude* is, don't you?" variety. It has been seen as a joke book, stuffed with wit to beguile a weary hour. It has been seen as a clumsy exercise in fiction by a poet with no sense of architecture. It has even been seen as mushy emotionalism by a woolly-headed romantic.

Pictures from an Institution is far more complex and profound than any of these views suggest. It is a study of a group of people by a man of insight and vision, who saw how strange and wonderful humanity is and who could not help but laugh, and could not help but understand. It seems likely that this warm, brilliant, and compassionate novel will, more than his poetry, be the work by which Jarrell's creative stature will be judged.

To Benton, with Love and Judgment: Jarrell's *Pictures from an Institution*

Suzanne Ferguson*

Renouncing plot in its title, *Pictures from an Institution* remains true to its promise. Its major characters neither act nor develop; its putatively major events are reported but not dramatized; in the events that *are* dramatized—a dinner party, a funeral, the "Art Night" of a women's liberal arts college—nothing of consequence happens, and no causal relationship among these events is established. Most of the chapters are named for particular groups of characters, but vignettes and anecdotes about other characters appear in each one. The numerous aphorisms—used both for description and for narration—and allusions seem to project aspiration for a permanent place in a rhetorical *Book of Records* rather than a history of the novel. In some notes toward a lecture now in the Berg Collection of the New York Public Library, Jarrell wrote, "My book has no plot, no action, no sex, no violence, . . . no sweep, no scope." Antinovel? Metafiction? In part, no doubt, for it persistently calls into question the project of representing "life" in a novel.

Yet, for all the fun it has at the expense of the conventions of the realistic novel and of that peculiarly narcissistic subgenre, the academic novel, *Pictures from an Institution* is also a mock-epic prose poem in which Randall Jarrell attempts to come to terms with several of his life-long obsessions. On its title page he calls the book a "comedy"; it is also a meditation upon American character, American education, and the nature of good and evil in modern culture. Its structure reflects a dialectical opposition of two impulses in Jarrell's character: to judge and to love, damn and praise.

In setting out to write a prose fiction of some length, Jarrell apparently recognized two demands that he could not adequately fulfill by writing poems or essays: to confront very directly his experiences as a teacher in postwar American colleges and to allow his own ambivalent feelings toward the aspects of human nature and culture revealed in that setting to work themselves out in a series of confrontations of character and situation. In these confrontations, or juxtapositions of "pictures," Jarrell tests his own values and conflicting attitudes.

*This essay was written especially for this book.

In *The Poetry of Randall Jarrell*, I remarked the deep core of didacticism in Jarrell's work, his tendency to want to teach his audiences—readers and friends as well as pupils—his enthusiasms in the world of the arts and in the arts of living: sport, philosophy, psychology. In suggesting that a motivating impulse of *Pictures from an Institution* is the impulse to teach its audience, I do not mean to imply that it is an "apologue," arguing like *Rasselas* or *The Confidence Man* some reasoned, abstract world view. Yet there is more than a hint of apologue (and its inversion, satire) in the book's coyly self-conscious rejection of plot, in its extended analytical descriptions of the characters, in its consideration of abstract issues of national character, the relations of life to art, the relation of good to bad art, the follies of progressive education. If, on one level, the book is a compendium of all Jarrell's enthusiasms (usually referred to specifically, by name) and an indictment of his bêtes noires (usually attacked in general), on another level *Pictures* appears to be Jarrell's own struggle with a demon, the demon of judgment which constantly demands discriminations among high and low, good and bad, wise and foolish, sophisticated and ignorant, as the fundamental human activity.

As a critic and professor, Jarrell's task was to discriminate between good and bad art. To him, the good in art was not only beautiful but accurate in its observation of life: True with a capital *T*. The value of "great" writing or painting or music resides in truth-telling about the human experience, truth-telling about reality and wishes, as well as in excellence of style.[1] In his criticism, Jarrell did not hesitate to rank Kipling, Christina Stead, and others among the very good but not the very best of writers after weighing precisely both their artistry and the depth and accuracy of their vision. Reading his poems and his novels, we sense that he made such judgments not only in his criticism, but that, either from instinct or training, he habitually measured not only art but the whole quality of life with similar clear-eyed and austere standards. However, Jarrell knew, too, that while we need such evaluations, we also need sympathy, compassion, and forgiveness for our sins. The judge of others needs these things not least among mortals, as Jarrell shows in his characterization of Pilate in "Eighth Air Force."

In *Pictures from an Institution*, Jarrell presides over his own case against the world and himself, finding both to be reprehensible and lovable. His ideal characters, the Rosenbaums and Constance, are both strong and weak, sweet and bitter (or, in Constance's case, sweet and bland); but even his "worst" characters, Gertrude Johnson and President and Mrs. Robbins, are allowed at least touches of humanity and affection. While the chief targets of satire in the book are the essential folly and stupidity of progressive higher education and the ignorant self-righteousness of those who complacently perpetuate that folly, in the world of Benton College the greatest evil is finally unkindness. Here as in the world of

Jane Austen, the worst crime is the humiliation of the weak and defenseless, whether out of unthinking hubris or the deliberate but misguided desire to reveal the "truth," to teach someone a lesson. In satirizing hubris, the satirist himself becomes self-righteous. Considered from different perspectives, Truth itself has limitations, means different things even, at different times and to different persons: hardly a discovery, but an observation that Jarrell instinctively found difficult to accommodate, since his desire so clearly was that the true and the good should be one and eternal in a paradise never to be lost.

What his character Gertrude does in "smoking" heads for her novel is in a sense what Jarrell also does in presenting most of the characters and themes of his novel.[2] The difference, we are asked to believe, is that Jarrell sees also good in the beings whose follies and blindnesses he impales, whereas Gertrude sees only the folly and blindness. "She saw the worst: it was, indeed, her only principle of explanation. Consequently she seemed to most people a writer of extraordinary penetration. . . . She knew that people must be, at bottom, like herself, and this was enough to justify—to make imperative—any measures she could take against them. And if everybody had been at bottom, what Gertrude thought she was, she would have been right to behave as she behaved, though it would have been better simply to curse God and die."[3] In Jarrell's judgment, however, Gertrude is not what she thinks she is, and so, although her ignorance of peoples' better nature and her snobbish aggressiveness are made fun of, her wit, her affection for Sidney, and her own vulnerability to loneliness are seen with sympathy, even admiration.

Jarrell's struggle between judgment and unjudging love is most strongly reflected in the main metaphoric pattern of the book, in which Benton is an earthly paradise[4] whose inhabitants seem mostly unaware that they are threatened with loss as they enact the roles of humans tempted (some not very strongly) by the apples of knowledge. Into this Eden comes a cynical Satan, Gertrude Johnson, expecting and sometimes tempting "these mortals" (in the title of her most recent book) to prove their folly. God, repeatedly invoked in seemingly playful and conventional ways, remains remote from the activities, allowing Gertrude free rein for "going to and fro in Benton and . . . walking up and down in it" (131; cf. Job 1:7). Her chief opponent, in terms of values, is Gottfried Rosenbaum: "If a voice had said to her, 'Hast thou considered my servant Gottfried Rosenbaum, that there is none like him in Benton, a kind and a clever man,' she would have answered: 'I can't *stand* that Gottfried Rosenbaum' " (134; cf. Job 1:8). Although she cannot tempt him, she baits him, to her own discomfiture. Complementary patterns of allusion and metaphor repeatedly emerge—from Jonah as from Job, from the story of St. George and the Dragon, from *Comus* and *Faust*. In these as well as other allusive motifs—those invoking *Der Rosenkavalier*, "The Witch of Coös," "Hansel and Gretel," "Lucifer in Starlight," *The Ghost*

Sonata (which Jarrell calls *The Spook Sonata*)—the themes of knowledge and ignorance, judgment and forgiveness, pride and foolishness press into the surface of the narrative.

Jarrell's ambivalence about judgment appears prominently in his narrator's relationship to Gertrude, whom M. L. Rosenthal has seen as "discharg[ing] the hostile and supercilious side of Jarrell's critical intelligence."[5] A poet-teacher, as Gertrude is a novelist-teacher, the narrator frequently agrees with Gertrude's judgments about other characters' failings, although he disassociates himself from her acerbic desire to find evil in everyone. Like Gertrude's, his observations of the Bentonites come from a devilish "going to and fro in Benton and from walking up and down in it." The narrator is basically an observer rather than a participant in life, a type seen with suspicion in American fiction from Brockden Brown to Fitzgerald. It is in his voice that the most trenchant criticisms of progressive education are sounded; and with Gertrude, he condemns the trivia and silliness of "Art Night." Unlike Gertrude, however, he believes in the possibility of good in people and thinks that he has found it in Constance and the Rosenbaums, whom Gertrude loathes and slanders because they do not fit her debased conception of human nature. He shows his ability to appreciate the good in the unlikeliest places when he admires Miss Rasmussen's wonderful statue "The East Wind," although he has trouble recognizing the good when it appears in the context of grotesque exaggeration and physical gracelessness, as in Flo Whittaker: "after you had been with [her] you didn't know what to do—honesty and sincerity began to seem to you a dreadful thing, and you even said to yourself, like a Greek philosopher having a nervous breakdown: 'Is it right to be good?' " (45).

Jarrell is ambivalent, too, toward Benton, where the system of progressive education leaves its students ignorant of facts but learned in social consciousness. Though Benton displays only too clearly the absurdities of postwar progressive colleges, it is repeatedly seen as a kind of paradise:

> In Spring the air was full of apple-blossoms, and Benton was like—like Spring everywhere, *but more so*, far, far more so; in Winter the air was full of snowflakes, the red-cheeked snow-booted girls stood knee-deep in their pedestals of snow, and the frost-crystals of their windowpanes were not frost-crystals at all but cut-outs, of Matisse's last period, that had been scissored from the unused wedding dress of Elaine the Lily Maid of Astolat; in Autumn all Benton was burning, and the students walked under the branches of the fire—how was it that they walked among flames, and were not consumed?—and picked the apples the blossoms had grown into and threw the cores on the tennis courts. . . . (218)

In this paradise, or lotus-land (one hardly knows which), the students are prepared for *Life*, its apologists claim, but Jarrell-the-narrator knows that is not so:

They said, over and over and over: *What is the good of learning about Spinoza if you do not learn about Life?* (And this is true: how much better it would be if we could teach, as we teach Spinoza, life!) They had heard intelligent people say, as intelligent people say with monotonous regularity, that one gets more out of one's reading and conversation at college than one gets from college itself. Benton decided, with naked logic: Why not let that reading and conversation *be* college, and let students do the ordinary classwork on the outside?—if they felt that they needed to; for some of it might profitably be disregarded, all that part that is, in President Robbins' phrase, boring. (83–84)

Education at Benton consists largely in developing the students' sense of guilt—guilt for their own privileged position in society: "Many a Benton girl went back to her nice home, married her rich husband, and carried a fox in her bosom for the rest of her life" (221). Having "sloughed off the awful protean burden of the past: of Magdalenian caves and Patmos and palm-leaf scriptures from Ceylon; of exiles' letters from Thrace or the Banks of the Danube; of soldiers' letters from the Wall—the Roman Wall, the Chinese Wall" (221), Benton's students have no cultural experience to enrich their imaginations and comfort them in times of trouble. To them the Blatant Beast is "Something in a long poem that none of *you*'ll ever have to read" (199), as both Gertrude and the narrator tell one of them; to Jarrell, clearly, that is a loss not only to the student but to the general richness of society.

This kind of criticism, and there is much more, is typical, in content if not expression, of conservative reproaches against progressive education, not just in college novels, but in the real world. Atypical, and almost surprising in Jarrell, whose own standards are distinctly conservative, is the equanimity with which the misprision is accepted. His satire of "Benton"—Sarah Lawrence, primarily—is decidedly benign.

A crux for the conservative educator is the whole issue of teaching creative arts: writing, painting, sculpture, musical composition, and dance all get attention in the novel. Virtually all of Jarrell's pronouncements on art in his criticism suggest that, like many who earn their daily bread by teaching creative writing, he believed that the most valuable aspect of a work of art comes from something which cannot be taught or even learned. "A good poet is someone who manages, in a lifetime of standing out in thunderstorms, to be struck by lightning five or six times. . . ."[6] What is the justification, then, for attempting to "teach" creativity? It is a question Jarrell dares not ask directly, even in the novel, although it lies at the heart of his ambivalence toward the values represented in Benton.

Although they are not taught the tradition, from which they might learn not only mankind's abiding concerns but the glories of its achievement, Benton students learn all the most modern techniques: welding sculptures, composing from tone rows, manipulating fictional point of view. Like much of the rest of the educational process at Benton, the creative arts courses become a kind of therapy. The longtime creative writing teacher, Gertrude's predecessor Miss Batterson, has adapted perfectly to this theory. Only her gifted students baffle her, because their work never

> seemed to be helping their development as much as the work of the stupider students was helping *theirs*. . . . Miss Batterson's Unconscious, going back to childhood for the word, felt that it was mean of the best students so plainly to dislike the others' work; the others liked theirs, didn't they? And certainly all work, dropped into the mechanism by which she had learned to judge, did look extraordinarily alike. (88–89)

Surely there is a special poignancy in Jarrell's position here. As a teacher of creative writing and a critic, how often he must have longed to say, like Gertrude, "Do you want me just to give your story a grade, or shall I go over it with you and tell you what's wrong with the point of view?" (201); yet we learn from his students' written tributes how extremely patient and kindly a teacher he in fact was.[7] A confirmed Freudian, he knew, just as Miss Batterson did, that their stories helped his students, whether they were "good" stories or not.

The teacher is inextricably compromised in whatever falsehood is perpetrated by the offering, for "credit," of instruction in a creative art. One problem with the students' art, in life as in the novel, is that it is so utterly imitative of the teachers'. The sole example of student writing described, Sylvia Moomaw's story of "a bug who became a man," is a blending of the style of her teacher, Gertrude, with that of her model, Kafka; the narrator says, "she had adjusted herself . . . to Gertrude, to Kafka, exactly as if each had been Sylvia Moomaw" (201). The students of painting imitate their teacher's paintings of animals, "beasts of prey, in forests and marshes, all looking like feral Florence Nightingales" (231). When they are *not* imitations, the works frequently have no subject at all. The sculptures at "Art Night" are described in some detail. A sample:

> Some of the statues looked like improbably polished *objets trouvés*, others looked as if the class had divided a piece of furniture among themselves, lovingly finished the fragments, and mounted the result as a term's work. . . . After looking at ten or twenty of these statues you muttered to yourself, "I wish wood didn't *have* any grain"; a few more and you were sorry that there is such a thing as wood—were sorry, that is, until you came to the Ores and Metals section of the sculpture. . . . [The welded statues] were made, apparently, of iron twine, with queer undigested knots or lumps or nodules every few inches, so that they all looked like representations of part of the root-system of the alfalfa plant, or that of almost any legume. Sometimes a statue had four legs and was an animal; sometimes it had two legs and two arms and was a man. But sometimes it had neither arms nor legs, and was an abstraction. (229–30)

The narrator's judgment here and his approval of Gertrude's hilarious commentary on the students' performance of the *Spook Sonata* (adapted by one of their teachers) remind us that, once a work is displayed, it will be judged not as therapy or a learning experience, but as art.

The teachers' art, too, is judged. Some of their compositions are only marginally superior to the students' innocent imitations, as in the case of the painter's and most of the sculptress' work. Even Rosenbaum recognizes himself, and is recognized by the narrator, as a minor composer. The descriptions of his work provide Jarrell with an opportunity for fanciful *sprezzatura* that places it as it characterizes it. One of Rosenbaum's best-known pieces is in honor of Bach; its theme (in imitation of that of *Die Kunst der Fuge*) uses the letters of Bach's name as the notes of a tone row,

> and there were four movements, the first played on instruments beginning with the letter *b*, the second on instruments beginning with the letter *a*, and so on. After the magnificent group that ushered in the piece (bugle, bass-viol, bassoon, basset-horn, bombardon, bass-drum, bagpipe, baritone, and a violinist with only his bow) it was sad to see an Alp horn and an accordion come in to play the second movement. (136)

Other Rosenbaum favorites are a cantata on Frost's "The Witch of Coös," with "the most idiomatic writing for skeleton that I've ever heard—one *ostinato* figure, half glissando xylophones and half violinists hitting their soundboxes with their bows" (135),[8] and the tone poem, "Lucifer in Starlight," "which the more advanced orchestras played . . . almost as the less advanced played *The Sorcerer's Apprentice*" (258). The descriptions themselves are full of energy, but they do not describe great art.

Clearly, although they shelter many producers of "art," both students and teachers, the groves of academe are not seen by Jarrell as the nurturing ground of great artists. Even here, however, one may be struck by lightning. Miss Sona Rasmussen, the Finno-Japanese "potato-bug" sculpture teacher—to appreciate whose aesthetic theories "you would have had to be an imbecile"—abandons her welding briefly at term's end to carve from a railroad tie something astounding:

> The railroad tie had become a man, a man who floated in the air as the foetus floats in the womb; his pressed-together arms and legs, his hunched-up shoulders, his nudging face were indicated in broad burnt lines or depressions. . . . He was part of the element he inhabited, and it and he moved on together silently: his limbs, blunted by their speed, were still. (274–75)

This quasi-magical transformation demonstrates a key principle of Jarrell's critical faith: that there is a grace beyond craftmanship that paradoxically makes the work of art *live*.

Gertrude's novels will never be so transfigured precisely because their impulse is so rational, so "scientific": "Gertrude dissected to murder." Her novel about Benton invites comparison with Jarrell's novel about Benton. Obviously, hers will also be highly crafted. Unlike his, it will have a plot because, though she usually has minimal plots, she senses that "a plot that could have supported the First National Bank" (216) will be necessary to give plausibility to the improbable characters she has taken from the life. One Bentonite, Jerrold Whittaker, is too implausible to use at all: "Seventy or eighty years ago I could still have got away with him, but nowadays—not a chance! He's just too good to be true. . . . My readers wouldn't believe in that man for a minute" (95). Jarrell's novel, since it is telling the "truth," lacks plot: as his narrator points out to Gertrude, nothing happens at Benton. He can also use too implausible characters such as Jerrold.

The thematic dialectic of judgment and love is reinforced structurally, in *Pictures*, by a dialectic of verisimilitude and artifice. Despite the fact that they are composed of a tissue of witty apothegms, Jarrell's characters mostly have the air of being drawn from life; and since its publication *Pictures from an Institution* has always had the reputation of being a *roman à clef*. In a letter to John Crowe Ransom written in late 1952 Jarrell defends himself against the charge that President and Mrs. Robbins "are" Dr. and Mrs. Henry Taylor, president and first lady of Sarah Lawrence when Jarrell taught there in 1946–47, and in a letter to Philip Rahv in the summer of 1953 he discusses the similarities of Gertrude to Mary McCarthy ("the same general type") and Jean Stafford. The Rosenbaums, he admits in a letter to Hannah Arendt, are loosely based upon her and her husband.[9] Both the narrator and Gertrude have characteristics of Randall Jarrell; in the lecture notes mentioned earlier, Jarrell writes, "I'm perfectly willing to have people think Gertrude Johnson me, or part of me," but not an "actual lady novelist." These individual and composite characters, presented at one level as the types one finds in academe, are nonetheless endowed with idiosyncracies and anecdotes that radiate the authenticity of things really heard and seen in life: for example, Miss Batterson's anecdote of her father's cow, killed and eaten by Union soldiers while, a boy, he watched helplessly from his treetop hiding place. The account of Gertrude's dinner party is no doubt a composite, but all habitués of academic dinner parties will recognize not only the dismal evening but the rush to the all-night restaurant that must follow.

The anecdotes are close to home; the descriptions, wildly exaggerated and impossibly elegant in their rhetoric, are nonetheless homely in content. Mrs. Robbins, who "felt that the pilgrim's earthly progress is from drawer to drawer, and that when we are all dead the Great Game will be over," pours tea "as industrial chemists pour hydrofluoric acid from carboys" (13); Flo Whittaker, whose "skirt looked as if a horse had left her its second-best blanket; the sweaters looked as if an old buffalo, sitting by a fire of peat, had knitted them for her from its coat of the winter before" (45), is a wife and mother of two, but is "surely, the least sexual of beings; when cabbages are embarrassed about the facts of life, they tell their little cabbages that they found them under Mrs. Whittaker" (46). The domestic threatens magic, and the mysterious becomes domesticated: Else, the Rosenbaums' maid, is "the Witch from *Hansel and Gretel*. She had decided that it is safer to feed than to eat people, but she smiled her old smile—I could never look at her without feeling behind me for an oven" (41). However devastatingly accurate and funny these descriptions seem, none is really cruel. One imagines the characters—or their models—saying, as Karl Shapiro did of one of Jarrell's reviews of his poetry: "I felt as if I had been run over but not hurt."[10] The same blend of narratorial condescension and rueful identification prevails in these portraits as in such poems as "A Girl in a Library" and "Lady Bates."

The "pictures" from the institution are not simply portraits, however, as Jarrell makes clear in his chapter titles, the first five of which name pairs or groups: "The President, Mrs., and Derek Robbins"; "The Whittakers and Gertrude"; "Miss Batterson and Benton"; "Constance and the Rosenbaums"; "Gertrude and Sidney." These may be regarded as "conversations" in the painterly sense, not because the characters named in the titles converse in a literal way but because their portraits are juxtaposed so as to reflect upon each other in complementary and contrasting ways. The remaining chapters, "Art Night" and "They All Go," suggest a broader canvas but still no motivated action. The activity, such as it is, goes on in the readers' minds as they attempt to come to terms with their own need to judge these characters, this institution.

In the lack of developed dialogue or a sustained plot, Jarrell makes a virtue of necessity. His poems and children's books confirm the suspicion that he could not—any more than Gertrude usually can—construct a traditional plot, possibly because he saw human affairs in terms of accident and of forces beyond human control. The characters of the novel, like those of the poems, are isolated individuals whose most successful means of communication is the mutual perception of works of art. Jarrell builds his composition of individual figures and groups with minute, deliberate strokes upon strokes, like Seurat with his bathers or his Sunday-afternoon-relaxing bourgeois. Like painted figures, the characters are caught in movement but static, monumental in the changing but unchanged landscape of Benton. Their significant personal affairs are kept deliberately offstage: we witness neither of the terrible quarrels between Gertrude and President Robbins; we are not privy to the Rosenbaums' decision to "adopt" Constance. Yet these are virtually the only events—other than Gertrude's realization that she could not get along without Sidney—that the book offers in the way of incidents that might have formed the basis of a plot. (The usual business of academic novels—academic politics, hiring and firing, the seduction of students by teachers and vice versa—is mercifully absent.)

The structural pattern that emerges from the juxtaposed portraits is not static, however, for it portrays the tension of opposites constantly merging with and being reflected in each other as Jarrell alternately scourges and praises his characters. The unself-conscious complacency that will later be associated with the Benton faculty and students in general is first seen in President Robbins, who early on is characterized as "an institution," but an institution somehow like St. George, since he must battle the dragon, Gertrude, to preserve the faith. Gertrude's skepticism is her destructive—but perhaps also purgative—fire. Not only a figure of the Satan of Genesis and Job, Gertrude is also "the witch" who leaves "the forest" at the end of the narrative; but there are other witches, too—Else, Mrs. Robbins, Fern Whittaker (Flo and Jerrold's nasty daughter), and, surprisingly, Irene Rosenbaum. Indeed, it appears that any wise woman has witchlike qualities. Those who lack them are saintly and somewhat monstrous innocents: Miss Batterson, Flo, Constance, Sylvia Moomaw.

The male characters also present a configuration of oppositions. There are the basically institutional sorts who display only brief moments of humanity; in addition to Dwight Robbins, these are Jerrold Whittaker and the memorably null "Head" of the large public university English department which hires away Miss Batterson—an expert on Cowper who is thought by most who hear that name to be an expert on Cooper. Their opposites are the flawed humans, Gottfried Rosenbaum and the narrator, who by constantly compromising their own values manage to live in harmony with the institutions. Comparable with the female innocents is Sidney, Gertrude's possession "as a baby is its mother's." The two snake-loving boys—Derek Robbins, in most respects so ordinary, and John Whittaker, brilliantly precocious—form a gratuitously implausible juxtaposition that makes fun of Freudian interpretations of behavior and the conventions of fiction even as it keeps us keyed into the theme of a lost paradise.

The book is shot through and through with images figuring the motif of the "fall" into knowledge as a recognition of mortality. Wisdom seems, inevitably, wisdom about what is wrong with things and people. To bring wisdom, as Gertrude does, is to bring evil: truth makes people unhappy, not free. Gertrude's "truths," derived from the principle of extrapolating the worst possible motives—to her, greed or sex—are seen as relatively trivial truths if not actual mistakes in the face of the more profound recognition of aging and the drift toward death experienced by the narrator, by Rosenbaum, and once, fleetingly, by Gertrude herself. Those who can see and accept such truth are—like the Marschallin of *Der Rosenkavalier*—the heroes of Jarrell's mythology. Gottfried and Irene Rosenbaum, guided by the great works of art they know and love (not having been educated at Benton), do accept that truth and find what passes in this world for contentment, some of the time at least. To preserve Constance a little longer from having to come to terms with that truth (having lost her family in childhood, she had been in a sense immunized from recognition), or to prevent her from learning a wrong "truth," or to satisfy their own need to hold close a little of her innocence and potentiality for life, they take her into their family, doing as Gottfried would have done to himself: "I want," he says, "some people to come from another planet and to make me their pet" (152). Not only does the narrator share that ambition (262), so did Jarrell-the-poet: see "A Sick Child" and "Hope."[11]

The significance of this wish is great. For Jarrell it seems to go back to the time in his childhood when he sat as Ganymede for the sculptors of the Nashville replica of the Parthenon. They wished to adopt him and take him away to a world Jarrell even then sensed was quite different from the resolutely middle-class, unintellectual, unimaginative world of his mother and her family; but of course his mother refused permission, not telling her son of the offer. Had he known of it, he was to say later, "I'd have gone with them like *that*."[12] The longing to find one's own ideal family is reflected in all Jarrell's children's books, as it is in the Rosenbaums' adoption of Constance, Miss Batterson's adopting of Benton (in preference to the interesting but incompatible group Rosenbaum meets at her funeral), or Gertrude's "adopting" of Sidney. That family, that ideal home, constitutes the lost Eden, recoverable only in dreams and works of art. One enters that world in sleep and in the moment of creation, in the same way as the "East Wind" of Miss Rasmussen's inspired sculpture hovers in the air "as the foetus floats in the womb" (274–75). To awaken is to fall into knowledge, to be cursed with discrimination, the need to judge. Only grace frees fools from folly and the knower from knowledge, as the narrator admits: Miss Rasmussen "was a potato-bug who had been visited by an angel, and I decided—decided unwillingly—for the rest of my life to suffer potato-bugs gladly, since angels are not able to make the distinctions that we ourselves make between potato-bugs and ourselves" (276).

After knowledge, there is forgiveness. Out of the clash of personalities and values, Jarrell salvages affection for the humanity represented in his "pictures" and brings his dialectical structure to a resolution. Like Gertrude, the narrator has "misjudged" Benton, and he feels a willingness for it to misjudge him in return. "I signed with it a separate peace. There was no need for us to judge each other" (276). As the narrator, so the author: after impaling the errors and asininities of progressive education on a thousand barbs of aphorism, after dissecting the "wicked" inhabitants of the institution with his comic scalpel, Jarrell makes a separate peace with the world of his novel in the benign and sunlit atmosphere of its close. He seems to have arrived at the benediction Constance remembers from St. Augustine and applies to Rosenbaum: "I want you to be" (4). This statement, introduced so early in the novel, is a touchstone to which the narrator returns several times in the course of his story (36, 60,

269) and, implicitly, at the end. Emerging from the tensions of opposed judgments, Jarrell-as-narrator accepts Miss Rasmussen's one miracle, as a sign from the Providence that rules the world as the novelist rules the novel, and decides to love.

Notes

1. Keith Monroe's "Principle and Practice in the Criticism of Randall Jarrell," above, pp. 258–60, documents these themes in Jarrell's essays.

2. Noted by John Crowe Ransom in "The Rugged Way of Genius," *Southern Review*, NS 3 (1967), 270–73 (reprinted in *Randall Jarrell, 1914–1965*, 165–70); and M. L. Rosenthal, *Randall Jarrell* (Minneapolis: Univ. of Minnesota Press, 1972), pp. 38–39.

3. Randall Jarrell, *Pictures from an Institution* (New York: Knopf, 1954), pp. 188, 191; hereafter cited in the text.

4. This argument is adumbrated in somewhat different form by Sylvia Angus in "Randall Jarrell, Novelist: A Reconsideration," *Southern Review*, NS 2 (1966), 690–93.

5. Rosenthal, p. 38.

6. Randall Jarrell, *Poetry and the Age* (New York: Alfred A. Knopf, 1953), p. 48.

7. Summarized in Sister M. Bernetta Quinn, *Randall Jarrell* (Boston: Twayne Publishers, 1981), pp. 131–42.

8. My colleague Richard D. Altick reminded me that Saint-Saëns used xylophones for the skeletons of "Danse Macabre" in 1874; perhaps Rosenbaum is here shown to be even less avant garde than the narrator assumes.

9. The letters were shown to me by Mary Jarrell. They will appear in the edition of letters to be published by Houghton Mifflin.

10. Karl Shapiro, *Randall Jarrell* (Washington: Library of Congress, 1967), p. 3. Reprinted in *Randall Jarrell, 1914–1965*, p. 199.

11. *Complete Poems* (New York: Farrar, Straus & Giroux, 1969), pp. 53, 307.

12. Reported by Mary Jarrell in "The Group of Two," *Randall Jarrell, 1914–1965*, p. 286.

The Poet, Truth, and Other Fictions: Randall Jarrell as Storyteller

Kathe Davis Finney*

The fiction of a lyric poet automatically raises questions about its motivation. What need prompts a poet to write a story instead of a poem? Why does the craftsman of the minute particular extend himself to the painful length of a *novel*? Randall Jarrell seems to have felt the narrative impulse particularly strongly: even apart from the strong narrative line apparent in much of his poetry, he compiled five anthologies of fiction, wrote four storybooks for children (one almost novel-length), and, most conspicuously and popularly, wrote the wonderful novel *Pictures from an Institution*.

Jarrell's discussions of fiction, as well as his fiction itself, make apparent that his motivation has to do with his interest in a problematic raised by all art, but one which fiction makes most explicit: the relation between fiction and reality. As narrative fiction is traditionally the mimetic genre, its forms have seemed appropriate to raise explicitly the question always implicit in the art of fiction-making: what is real ("really" real), and how do we know? How accurate are our perceptions; what reality do they have? How much do we the perceivers—and more, we the conscious inventors—invent our own realities in the act of perception.

Jarrell's contemporary and friend Delmore Schwartz articulated in "The Isolation of Modern Poetry" (1941) the popular notion that the alienation of the modern poet is what accounts not only for his obscurity, but also for his limitation almost exclusively to lyric forms, rather than to narrative or dramatic forms.[1] Since the time of Blake, explains Schwartz, it has become "increasingly impossible for the poet to write about the lives of other men." The only available subject has come to be "the cultivation of his own sensibility," including his own life and other poetry.[2]

> For writing about other poetry and in general about works of art is the most direct way of grasping one's sensibility as a subject. But more than that, since one can hardly write about one's sensibility, one can only write lyric poetry. Dramatic and narrative poetry require a grasp of the lives of

*This essay was written especially for this book and appears by permission of the author.

other men, and it is precisely these lives, to repeat, that are outside the orbit of poetic style and poetic sensibility. An analogous thing has, of necessity, happened in the history of the novel; the development of the autobiographical novel has resulted in part from the inability of the novelist to write about any one but himself or other people in relation to himself.[3]

(The "modern poetry" Schwartz refers to is particularly that of Yeats, Eliot, Stevens, and Pound.) The real merits of this argument are less important than the fact that it, or the idea it expressed, was widely accepted. With many of his contemporaries, Jarrell was very consciously the inheritor of a historical and cultural condition of dispossession, his sense of alienation exacerbated by personal circumstances, including a broken home, as well as by his academic training and the pressures of a reality that included the Depression and *another* war. But the very events which intensified the sense of dispossession he shared with the preceding "Lost Generation" made it impossible for him to accept that generation's solutions. "The middle generation," as John Berryman dubbed his contemporaries, or "The Last Generation," in Schwartz's parodic phrase, fought not only against their own alienation, but also against the lyric closure and formalist aesthetic which were its artistic correlates, and the solipsism which was its logical conclusion. The older poets had integrated the personal with the social and the philosophical in the pursuit of the impersonal; the younger ones pursued the same integration to the point of personal revelation.

Jarrell reacted against an autotelic idea of art and the related complex of values not in simple opposition, however, but dialectically, opposing only by assimilating and transcending. He began deep in "the modern tradition." Not merely highly intelligent, but also highly intellectual (and highly educated), Jarrell used his learning to search for a way of writing and being that would go beyond the merely learned: intellectual, rational, conventional. He both celebrated and deplored our book-bound condition, what we have since learned to call intertextuality. Not yet quite appalled by a Borgesian vision of the infinite library, he composed works full of other works, presenting and nostalgically seeking authority for his own authorship while at the same time illustrating the benighted state of those who live by books (or words, or ideas) alone.

Both an avid reader and a merciless critic of the poets of the "high modernist mode," Jarrell was also the student and friend of such critics as John Crowe Ransom, Allen Tate, Robert Penn Warren, R. P. Blackmur, and others of the best and best-known codifiers and apologists of those poets and of New Critical aesthetic values.

He shared Schwartz's interest in philosophy, though always partial to its most literary manifestations (e.g., Goethe). He was deeply read in European literature in general, almost obsessively so in German. And Kafka in particular struck a deep chord in Jarrell's being, perhaps partly because of *his* father-preoccupation, as well as other obvious affinities. Jarrell quotes and refers to Kafka often in his introduction and essays and is especially fond of citing Kafka's dream narratives as examples of pure story.

Most importantly, the psychological knowledge which had been news to the generation of the twenties was for the middle generation a matter of established fact and serious study. Jarrell's bachelor's degree was in psychology, and he knew Freud in particular deeply and well. Freud seemed to address Jarrell's personal problems in his preoccupation with the role of the father, as well as his psychological version of the myth of the Fall and the sense of loss that it explains. Most of all Freud was important, to Jarrell as to the literary world in general, for *The Interpretation of Dreams*. Freud not only redefined "mind" so that it was no longer equivalent to consciousness, but by the same token he asserted the reality of the mental world. As Edward Said points out, "The *Interpretation* deals as much with the nature of psychological reality as with the meaning of dreams." He adds, "the book's fascination lies in the fact that Freud does not choose between illusion and reality until the very end," and discusses the way in which Freud himself used techniques developed by late nineteenth- and early twentieth-century writers to deal with the inadequacy of language as mimetic.[4] Dream, as a window on the unconscious, depicts a reality equal to if not profounder than that of the waking world. "There is a reality behind the outer reality," Jarrell says in *Pictures*; "it is no more real than the other, both are as real as real can be, but it is different."[5] The artist as the bringer of this subterranean truth to the public can be understood then as both alienated and essential (as Edmund Wilson, for instance, explained him by means of the Philoctetes myth in *The Wound and the Bow*, published in 1931).

This complex of factors and influences caused Jarrell to question both internal and external realities in ways he could best deal with in fiction rather than poetry. His narratives took Jarrell toward a postmodernist solution to the problems of dispossession, though he did not quite arrive there. He sought a nondualistic formulation of man's place in the world, and rejected—or tried to reject—the dichotomies of subject and object, life and art, without finding a fully satisfactory formulation for his insights. He explored at least tentatively the idea of the shared human world as constitutive of human reality (including personal identity), but the idea was not clearly articulated or fully developed enough to serve as a real or personally enabling solution.

Though moving beyond the high modernist aesthetic meant moving toward narrative, Jarrell could not go back to traditional narrative any more than he could retreat to mere subjectivism or expressionism. Consequently his fiction is post-Joycean, though not obviously so: short on plot, heavily autobiographical (as Schwartz said it must be)—if only in disguised form—with fictionality itself as one of its subjects. Jarrell wrote, that is, a fiction moving strongly in the direction of what we now call metafiction.

In his essay "Stories," Jarrell reflects upon the word *story*: it means, he says, both history ("truth") and fiction. "A story, then, tells the truth or a lie—is a wish, or a truth, or a wish modified by a truth."[6] But after Freud the opposition between truth and wish is no simple one. "The truths that he systematized, Freud said, had already been discovered by the poets; the tears of things, the truth of things, are there in their fictions" (145). Reality may stand in opposition to the pleasure principle, but "truth" does not necessarily lie with reality: "The wish is the first truth about us . . ." (140).

By embodying the truth of wishes, story both clarifies and expands our selves. In *Pictures from an Institution*, the familyless girl Constance, "adopted" by the Rosenbaums, finds an emotional correlative of her life in the Grimms' fairy tale (entirely "unrealistic," of course) "The Juniper Tree." Weeping "in joy for herself and her happiness and in grief for her own stupidity and the world's," she ends "no longer conscious of the world except as the brimming margin of herself, a boundary that was not a boundary."[7] Jarrell was, Karl Shapiro says, "the poet of the *Kinder* and the earliest games of the mind and heart."[8] And his motive for writing children's stories was likewise, I think, his own wish to convey the archetypal or psychologically primal truth of wishes.

But even in the children's books, the issues of truth and reality are addressed directly. *The Gingerbread Rabbit* may be read as an illustration of the reality of the fictional, or "merely" mimetic. The title character is confected by a doting mother who is inspired by a large real rabbit. The story itself is an imitation of the traditional children's tale of the gingerbread man, as well as an imitation of life: dedicated "to my little Mary," the book begins with the mother's asking herself "What can I do for a surprise for my little Mary. . . ?"[9]

Coming "to life," as we say, the gingerbread rabbit immediately encounters perceptual relativity. Confronted with the common figure of speech, "Just look at yourself," the rabbit tries literally to do so, but finds disparate reflections in a spoon, the side of a pan, and the window glass. The last pleases him: " 'Why, I'm beautiful,' said the rabbit." But that judgment of reality is challenged by the rolling pin, the mixing bowl, and the paring knife, who point out that he is neither wooden nor round nor a paring knife.

Having run away to the woods, the rabbit encounters a different form of deception: a fox who, perceiving the gingerbread rabbit's inadequate knowledge of reality, poses as a rabbit. He is exposed when the original rabbit happens along and explains in effect that reality is that which does not need to be labeled as itself: "A real rabbit doesn't need to tell you he's a rabbit." Now, as "the real thing," this rabbit is equally in a position to challenge the authenticity of the gingerbread rabbit, but instead takes him home to his wife. Like the Rosenbaums, the rabbit couple decides to adopt the parentless child. Thus supplied with a parentage, the gingerbread rabbit has been, in Borges' phrase, successfully "inserted into reality."

The mother's solution to the loss of her creature is to make an imitation of *him*: a stuffed "gingerbread" rabbit. The little girl's delight in the toy's realism—"He looks exactly like a gingerbread rabbit"—is tempered by a fear of its consequences:

> "He looks very like a real rabbit, too. . . . If I just saw him out in the yard and went up to him I'd expect him to run right off into the forest."
> "Oh *no!*" said the mother. "He wouldn't do that. Surely he wouldn't do that!"
> And he never did. (54–55)

So—because this is a children's story and a happy ending depends upon it—the mother is permitted to be right. But her denial is in the face of having just confronted the very danger the little girl articulates. The rabbity portion of the happy ending presents an inverted form of the same issue. The gingerbread rabbit is delighted at having escaped a danger which his new "parents" consider never existed: "And the other two rabbits were too polite to tell him that it wasn't a giant at all, but just a mother and her little girl" (55). It is true that the mother had no plans to eat the gingerbread rabbit: to an accusing squirrel she protests, "Do you think I'm a cannibal?" Her remark is part of Jarrell's gentle humor, but is perhaps also intended to show the mother's sympathetic sharing of the child's perspective, from which animals are all anthropomorphic, or "human." More seriously, it may mean that the rabbit is human by virtue of being a human imitation, a human creation. Still, the mother is certainly a physical "giant" to the rabbits, even if not a fairy tale ogre, and like the mother's assurance to her daughter, the rabbits' benign view is founded on a wish.

The Bat-Poet, though also a children's book, is a more sophisticated story which raises the same issues in more explicit form. The title bat begins his poetic career in alienation: when the other bats change locations he is left behind and, cold and lonely, suffers from insomnia. In a comic reversal of the human situation, he is unwillingly exposed to all the strange activity of the daytime. Waking to the unaccustomed daylight, "he would just hang there and think."[10] Out of the strangeness he begins to make poems. His model is the mockingbird, whose song he has long listened to and loved. But no more than Gertrude in *Pictures* can the bat manage a tune: "his high notes were all high and his low notes were all high and the notes in between were all high." With practice however he manages some lyrics: "If you get the words right you don't need a tune" (5).

Uninterested in the daytime world, the other bats are even less interested in poetry, and charge him with familiar faults: it does not make sense, "And it's just not real." As a senior poet, however, the mockingbird is impressed, though he suffers from an also familiar artistic vanity, and requires the bat's admiration for his latest composition, "To a Mockingbird." Imitating the master in more ways than one, the bat-poet also writes a mockingbird poem, which impresses the rest of his audience, a chipmunk, with its mimetic accuracy: "It really is like him. . . . You wouldn't think he'd drive you away *and* imitate you. You wouldn't think he could" (30). But just because it *is* so mercilessly accurate, the chipmunk predicts that the mockingbird will not like the poem. The chipmunk is right. "The mockingbird exclaimed angrily: 'You sound as if there were something wrong with imitating things.' 'Oh no,' the bat said" (31).

In children's books, at least, poets can end happily, and the bat-poet does so, though significantly enough he achieves happiness, through reintegration with his community, only when he ceases to be a poet. Struggling to write a bat poem, he settles finally on his own babyhood as subject. Requiring neither observation nor invention, "It was easier than the other poems, somehow: all he had to do was remember what it had been like and every once in a while put in a rhyme" (34–35). He takes the completed poem out to the barn to say to the other bats, but they are asleep. Practicing his poem for when they wake up, he too falls asleep for the winter, "snuggled closer to the others" (43).

The Animal Family most vividly offers the truth of wishes. A sustained idyll written in the last year of Jarrell's life, the book deserves full separate treatment of a sort I can not give it here. It does not deal with art *per se*, but like *The Gingerbread Rabbit* affectionately parodies traditional fairy-tale form and motifs, and in many ways, especially in its concern with the family romance, it is the most Freudian. Fantasy that it is, it incorporates portions of Jarrell's own life: "Daily, like a small glacier," says Mary Jarrell, "it gathered up objects such as deerskin rugs from Salzburg, the new window seat we'd added, the Gucci hunting horn over our brick hearth and our female satyr figurine from Amsterdam."[11]

The plot is so simple and so without conflict as almost not to be a plot. A hunter, living alone "where the forest runs down to the ocean," takes a mermaid for a companion. This early part of the book is a study in extreme differences in perception, the consequences of such differences in and for language, and human fulfillment achieved finally through human love. The two begin by teaching each other words: "then he would pat his leg and say 'Leg! Leg!' and the mermaid, looking as if a leg were a very queer thing either to have or to have a word for, would repeat the word in her liquid voice."[12] In her eagerness to be "landish," she learns much more quickly than the hunter, but "sometimes the land was so different that the mermaid would learn a word in a few seconds and after a half-hour's explanation still not know what it meant" (20). So it is when the hunter attempts to explain a house, all its furniture, and its function: " 'To keep from getting *wet*?' the mermaid said despairingly" (23).

The mermaid is animallike, certainly inhuman, in her unity with her environment and in her freedom from the problems of consciousness. She cannot comprehend the hunter's need to stave off boredom; "she never understood, even, what it meant to be bored" (44). She lives in a perpetual present, with no fear of the future or of death, no sense of loss, no nostalgia. Explaining why she feels no pain at the thought of her dead sister, she says, "She was then. Why do you want her to be now too?" (52). Yet in time "home" to her comes to be that strange dry place the house, with its anomalies of clothing and fire. "The hunter and the mermaid were so different from each other that it seemed to them, finally, that they were exactly alike; and they lived together and were happy" (54).

Happy as they are, the hunter begins to long for a son, without knowing that he does; the truth of this wish is brought to him by a dream. He finds a bear cub, who becomes for a time their child substitute: "When he would walk across the room on his hind legs, reach for something on the table, and then cram it into his mouth, he looked like a little boy in a bearskin" (73). After the bear is grown, the hunter brings home a baby lynx ("the lynx from the Washington Zoo," says Mary Jarrell).[13] " 'Another boy,' said the hunter" (103); "it was the way the bear used to be when he was little, only more so. A lot more so" (104–05).

Finally, as the title to the penultimate chapter announces, "The Lynx and the Bear Bring Home a Boy": a boy left on their shore by the same storm that killed his mother. Once again an unforthcoming nature is outwitted by adoption, that is, by human invention and love. Before long the boy is convinced he has lived with them always, and that their story of how the animals found him is a delightful fiction. "He *knew* that the hunter was his father and the mermaid his mother and had always been" (156–57). And just as if they were, he embodies both of their loves and talents, swimming as easily as he walks, learning to speak with "that watery sound" of the sea people as well as with the "walnut sound" of the land.

Mothering the boy and loving the hunter, the mermaid learns their perceptions. Her own kind do not understand her defection to the land, as she explains to the hunter; thinking of themselves as people, naturally enough, they call her "The one who lives with the animals" (167). But by the same token, she has come to view them from (what we consider) a human perspective: "They don't know how to be bored or miserable," she says. "When my sister died, the next day I'd forgotten and was happy. But if you died, if he died, my heart would break" (170). By becoming a member of "The Animal Family" (named ironically and yet not), the mermaid has fallen into the human world of mortality, the fall necessary to know the redemptive power of love.

Though the hunter has not mastered the mermaid's ways as she has his and the boy's both, he is utterly accepting of her *and* the boy, expressing his contentment with "Let and live let," the mermaid's variation. Against all ordinary probability, then, the couple transcend their different language, different elements, different *realities*, to achieve a happiness that I suppose one must say both is and is not human. Not merely the "truth" but the reality of such a vision of wish-fulfillment is asserted by the epigraph to the little novel: "Say what you like, but such things do happen—not often, but they do happen."

Pictures from an Institution, written for adults, presents by contrast the surface of "the outer reality." But just as Gertrude Johnson, the novelist within the novel, writes books which are unquestioningly read as experimental, though their "grammar, syntax and punctuation were perfectly orthodox" (187), so Jarrell, in *this* apparently conventional novel, is preoccupied with the metafictional concerns of the "reality behind the outer reality." For adults, the primary access to the "reality behind" is through art, and the forms and functions of art are a major concern of the novel. The "pictures" are, like the bat-poet's, portraits of a series of individuals, but seen socially: in pairs or in groups, and within their institutional setting. (That the nature of the institution is not specified in the title is of course a commentary on academics, or maybe is even more general: we are all institutionalized in some sense.) The institution is Benton, a "progressive" women's college. Characters, and scenes in which they are variously (and artfully) combined, are juxtaposed as, quite explicitly, contrasts among alternative realities, and the novel has as its profoundest theme the problematic nature of "reality."

Pictures is a novel of one day, though that fact, established on the first page, is so little insisted upon that it can go unnoticed until the last page. Without a plot in any conventional sense (the chronology of the day is not significant, nor significantly pointed to, and no structuring conflicts are presented and resolved), the novel is exquisitely patterned as a minuet. But not obviously so: Jarrell seems to regard plot as inversely proportional to action, in that plot is the artificial imposition of pattern upon the events of life. Precisely because nothing happens at Benton, Gertrude can write there her first novel with "a real Plot" (214), "a plot that could have supported the First National Bank" (216). Jarrell's own structure is not such a Plot, but rather a series of arrangement of characters, or "pictures" of those characters.

The organization is based most fundamentally on two characters in polar opposition, Dwight Robbins, the president of Benton, and the visiting novelist Gertrude Johnson. Externally Robbins is like the mermaid, at one with his element, "so well adjusted to his environment that sometimes you could not tell which was the environment and which President Robbins" (11). One of these times occurs near the end of the book, when, diving into the swimming pool, the president shows himself in perfect harmony with nature and the intelligible universe. "Intelligible? Surely. 'What's there unintelligible about it?' he would have asked . . ." (253). Undivided himself, he perceives no divisions, no insoluble conflicts, in the world. The narrator leaves him in middive, and that is the reader's last vision of him, "hung there upon the Wheel of Things" (253). Like the bear in *The Animal Family*, "He's got a real gift for getting along in the world"[14]—and is just about as human. He is prelapsarian—not so much innocent as prior to that human distinction: "President Robbins had no complaints about this Paradise, the world. The Tree of Knowledge of Good and Evil *is* the Tree of Life, he knew; and President Robbins lay sleeping in its branches, his parted lips smelling pleasantly of apples" (10). Having escaped his own personal fall into the knowledge of death, he is, not immortal, but exempt from time: "he possessed, and would possess until he died, youth's one elixir, Ignorance" (16).

But the human environment is double, consisting of society as well as nature, or nature only as seen *through* culture: President Robbins' "sea" is a concrete pool. Hence Robbins' state of integration involves an almost complete identification with his institution, and of it with him: "He had not evolved to the stage of moral development at which hypocrisy is possible. To him the action was right because it was his—he had never learned to judge his own act as though it were another's. . . . He had the morals of a State; had, almost, the morals of an Army" (72). He is, then, inhuman in two opposed directions.

The consciousness the president so utterly lacks is what Gertrude has most of. First of all, she suffers an extreme Cartesian split. A nondescript "mousy woman" (65), she is "a pale, pale, almost wholly unsaturated brown" all over: "This is what you saw. Yet when you knew her how different it all looked; Gertrude's spirit shone through her body as though the body were an old pane of glass, and you thought, 'My God, how could I have been so blind!' " (5). She is so far from being at one with the environment that she scarcely touches it, or it her: "Every place was like every other to her; . . . Wherever she went, she went in Gertrude" (65–66). Her isolation, the dispossession effected by her consciousness, is part of what makes Gertrude human, and her utter unwillingness to accept anything which might be illusion—even reality—and her consequent inability ever to be happy, are treated with an odd tenderness by Jarrell. But "her vision was too penetrating" (187): "She looked at the world, and *saw*, and cried out, her voice rising at the end of the sentence into falsetto: 'Why, it wouldn't fool a *child*!' " (197). This penetration, though it is what has made her a writer, finally proves a fatal flaw for a writer, for it makes her, in a different way, as inhuman as President Robbins. Seeing *through* life, instead of seeing life, "she did not know—or rather, did not believe—what it was like to be a human being" (189). Seeing life only as material for art, Gertrude misses the essence of life, and hence finally also of art. Her failure is symbolized by two deficiencies: she is tone-deaf, and she does not dream.

> For just as many Americans want art to be Life, so this American novelist wanted life to be Art, not seeing that many of the values—though not, perhaps, the final ones—of life and art are irreconcilable; so that her life looked coldly into the mirror it held up to itself, and saw that it was full of quotations, of data and analysis and epigrams, of naked and shameful truths, of facts: it saw that it was a novel by Gertrude Johnson. (214)

But this is a criticism that very seriously undercuts itself—not only by that casual but devastating "not, perhaps, the final ones," but also in its catalog of elements, which moves on from the characteristics of a novel to the inclusiveness of life. Who of us does not live a life filled with "quotations, . . . naked and shameful truths," and all the rest? And the implication is one Jarrell makes clearer elsewhere in the novel: by acting on our wishes, we help to shape reality. In some sense, we are all writing the novels of our own lives.

The paradoxical fact that art is produced by the same consciousness that splits us, that keeps us from unmediated animallike being in the world (but which in turn is what makes us human), and art's consequent paradoxical quality as both more and less "real" than life, constitute an antinomy that Jarrell did not really resolve, though he saw that it must be gotten beyond.

Gertrude is like the mockingbird, who compliments the bat-poet on his metrics and technique when the bat has tried to capture the quality of experience. Yet there can be no question of Jarrell's admiration of such concern with technical accomplishment, and of the impulse behind it. He says of the mockingbird, "He always had a peremptory, authoritative look, as if he were more alive than anything else and wanted everything else to know it"; and "every part of him had a clear, quick, decided look about it." Mary Jarrell quotes that sentence, and says that Jarrell used it first of his cat, and that it summed up his appreciation of any activity done as it ought to be done: "They were Kitten's qualities and Randall wanted them from tennis partners and automobile mechanics and critics. At certain intellectual moments Randall had that look himself. . . ."[15] At the same time, the mockingbird is not, naturally, human.

The bat-poet *is* human, in the same way that the Rosenbaums' cat is said to be "just human" (268). He draws his best poem from his own past, but this return to self, which also returns him to communal bat-life, overcomes his alienation only as it also overcomes his art.

At the end of *Pictures*, Gertrude is also thinking of writing a novel about her own kind, about—"here for the smallest part of a second, she hesitated—'about a writer' " (267). Clearly Gertrude is in no danger of fully rejoining the furry sleeping tribe, but her discovery that she is as dependent on her husband as he on her—that she loves him, in short—has turned her in a new direction, one which, followed far enough, would eliminate her art.

The one person at Benton over whom Gertrude does not triumph is the composer Gottfried Rosenbaum. He is Gertrude's opposite number, entirely lovable on the same principle that makes her so unlovable:

> His automatic acceptance of everybody was a judgment of mankind crueller, perhaps, than Gertrude's impatient rejection of everybody. She had great expectations for humanity, expectations which any human being disappointed; anybody satisfied Gottfried's expectations. The thought of how he had acquired these expectations was a disagreeable one. (169)

But Dr. Rosenbaum, though famous—"Of *course* he's famous! He's in the *Britannica*, in the article on Schönberg," explains one of his students (139)—falls short of major art. He confesses it freely, and even the adoring Constance can see: "and how she hated seeing!—that when you listened to *Wozzeck* or *Le Sacre du printemps* or Bartok's quartets something happened to you that was different from anything that happened to you while you listened to even the best of the works of Gottfried Rosenbaum" (257). Why this should be is not explained; Dr. Rosenbaum himself "said equally 'Failure is the common condition of composers—or common composers; I am no different from my kind' " (257). One may infer some connection between this failure and his lowered expectations. Yet his most notable success seems to emerge from the same knowledge. "A tone poem called *Lucifer in Starlight*," it is a piece which gives "these people, so used to 'coping with reality,' a different intuition: that the world is too much for even the devil to cope with, but also. . . . But also what? They could not say . . ." (259).

The novel presents two examples of successful art. Both embody an inhuman as well as a profoundly human quality. Irene Rosenbaum's singing career has been over for a long time, and her voice is gone, but "when she sang you decided that a singer does after all need a voice to sing, but you did not decide this until several minutes after she had finished singing." Her art is so complete it has gone beyond the conventions of art to what Jarrell calls "a Higher Regularity," and so achieved apparent artlessness:

> She did what she did because there was nothing else possible to do, and when she had done it she did not know what she had done: or so you felt, hearing. This was a delusion, of course; . . . she once talked for half an hour about Lehmann's, Schøtz's, and *her* ways of singing the song from the *Dichterliebe* that begins, *Ich grolle nicht*. (164)

Consistent with Jarrell's views throughout, art goes beyond art to reconnect with life, while yet bringing to life something it does not have without art. Irene's singing is this kind of Supreme Fiction:

she could not have sung a scale without making it seem a part of someone's life, a thing of human importance. Yet when the song and her voice said: *We are all dying*, something else about her voice—a quality that could not be localized, that all the sounds possessed together and none possessed apart—said to you also: *Whoever dies?* Over feeling and act, the human reality, her voice seemed to open out into a contradicting magic of speculation and belief, into the inhuman reality men discover or create. Her voice pushed back the boundaries of the world. (164–65)

The other example of successful art in the novel is in fact produced artlessly, almost accidently. Sona Rasmussen, Benton's art teacher, half Japanese, half Norwegian, "was a fat, tiny, shiny woman: with a different paint job, and feelers, she would have looked exactly like a potato-bug—I used to think of her as part of a children's story . . ." (227). Her art, metal sculpture, and her ideas about art are of a corresponding level: "Some of what she said was technical, and you would have had to be a welder to appreciate it; the rest was aesthetic or generally philosophic, and to appreciate it you would have had to be an imbecile" (230). Nonetheless, and with no change in her aesthetics, Miss Rasmussen produces one sublime piece of sculpture:

> The railroad tie had become a man, a man who floated in the air as the foetus floats in the womb; his pressed-together arms and legs, his hunched-up shoulders, his nudging face were indicated in broad burnt lines or depressions, so that you could hardly tell whether the man had been drawn or modelled; he was there. He fitted into the rectangle of the railroad tie as a cat, fast asleep, fits into the circle of itself. . . . He was part of the element he inhabited, and it and he moved on together silently: his limbs, blunted by their speed, were still. Even his muzzling mouth and pressed-flat nose were still, so that I remembered *The arrow in its flight is motionless*. . . . (274–75)

He is not a man, however, but "the East Wind." The figure epitomizes the human, reminding the narrator of "*Ur*-men," but also transcends it. And so does Miss Rasmussen, by virtue of her creation. Though her accomplishment is not accounted for, as Irene's is, by a lifetime of ardent intelligent crafting, the narrator is no less awed: "She was a potato-bug who had been visited by an angel, and I decided—decided unwillingly—for the rest of my life to suffer potato-bugs gladly, since angels are not able to make the distinctions that we ourselves make between potato-bugs and ourselves" (276).

So through art the self pushes back its own limits, and pushes back the boundaries of the world, the boundaries of "reality." Language artful enough ("If you get the words right you don't need a tune") alters the world as it is altered by it, and salvages for the waking world the insights of dream. These reflections occupied Jarrell to the end.

The novel ends with the reassertion of the narrator's bond of love and family, a bond essentially like Gertrude's with Sidney, though more powerful, and perhaps more like the bat-poet's reintegration with his group. From the now deserted campus, the narrator calls his wife to ask if she can pick him up, and the novel's final words are her reassuring "Of *course* I can. I'll be right over" (227). But just previously the narrator, cleaning out his office for departure, has arrived at an even more connubial understanding with Benton itself:

> I felt that I had misjudged Benton, somehow. . . . and I was willing for Benton in its turn to misjudge me. I signed with it then a separate peace. There was no need for us to judge each other, we said, we knew each other too well; we knew each other by heart. Then we yawned, and turned sleepily from each other, and sank back into sleep. (276)

Mary Jarrell chose to close the volume of tribute and memoirs, *Randall Jarrell, 1914–1965*, with a poem Jarrell would have included in the book he was planning at the time of his death. Called "A Man Meets a Woman in the Street," the poem presents the man admiring the woman and wishing she would turn to look at him. "A wish come true is life," he says, and in the poem it does come true and does become life: not only does she turn, she is his wife, as he, though not the reader, has known all along. In this idyllic moment the wish is reality, and, united in love with another person, the speaker feels himself for a moment free of the human separation from the natural world. Having begun with a distinction between how the birds and he began the day,

> I wished as men wish: "May this day be different!"
> The birds were wishing, as birds wish—over and over,
> With a last firmness, intensity, reality—
> "May this day be the same!" (301)

Jarrell ends the poem by correcting himself:

> We can't tell our life
> From our wish. Really I began the day
> Not with a man's wish: "May this day be different,"
> But with the birds' wish: "May this day
> Be the same day, the day of my life." (302)

Yet even then he cannot get beyond feeling that what is quintessentially human stands in opposition to the perfect unity we seek in love and art:

> My wish will have come true. And yet
> When your eyes meet my eyes, they'll bring into
> The weightlessness of my pure wish the weight
> Of a human being. . . . (301)

Like love, the magic even of fully achieved art remained a "contradicting magic" for Jarrell; "the inhuman reality men discover or create" is as close as he got to a formulation of the unity he wished.

Notes

1. *Selected Essays*, ed. Donald A. Dike and David H. Zucker (Chicago: University of Chicago Press, 1970), p. 4.

2. *Selected Essays*, p. 10.

3. *Selected Essays*, p. 11.

4. *Beginnings* (Baltimore: Johns Hopkins University Press, 1975), p. 161.

5. *Pictures from an Institution* (1954; rpt. New York: Farrar, Straus and Giroux, 1962), p. 178.

6. *A Sad Heart at the Supermarket* (New York: Farrar, Straus and Giroux, 1962), p. 140.

7. *Pictures from an Institution*, p. 265.

8. "The Death of Randall Jarrell," in *Randall Jarrell, 1914–1965*, ed. Robert Lowell, Peter Taylor, and Robert Penn Warren (New York: Farrar, Straus and Giroux, 1967), p. 223.

9. *The Gingerbread Rabbit* (New York: Macmillan, 1964), p. 1.

10. *The Bat-Poet* (New York: Macmillan, 1964), p. 2.

11. "The Group of Two," in *Randall Jarrell, 1914–1965*, p. 296.

12. *The Animal Family* (New York: Pantheon, 1965), p. 16.

13. "The Group of Two," p. 296.

14. *The Animal Family*, p. 96.

15. "The Group of Two," p. 280. She also explains that, like *The Animal Family*, *The Bat-Poet* was based to an unexpected extent on actuality: Randall wrote it " 'out in Nature' " in a hammock, watching "the half-tamed [animals] we fed." These also had their human "actual" equivalents: "In Life, Frost and Cal [Lowell] were Mockingbirds; Michael di Capua and I were Chipmunks, of sorts; and Bob Watson and Randall were Bats" (p. 290).

The Translations

[From "Jarrell and the Art of Translation"]

Ingo Seidler*

. . . .

II

Disregarding a few isolated exercises, Randall Jarrell's translations are mainly of four authors: Rilke (ten published poems, nine of them in *The Woman at the Washington Zoo*, 1960, and, with the German alongside, in A. Flores, *Anthology of German Poetry*, 1960; one in *The Seven-League Crutches*, 1951); Mörike ("Forest Murmurs," in *The Woman at the Washington Zoo*; "The Forsaken Girl," in *Ladies' Home Journal*); Corbière ("Le Poète Contumace" and "Rondels pour Après," both in *The Seven-League Crutches* and *Selected Poems*, 1955); and finally Goethe (*Faust*, a work in progress, parts of which are being published for the first time in the present issue). [When Jarrell's translation of *Faust I* was finally published in 1976 by Farrar, Straus and Giroux it kept all it had promised: this is our generation's English *Faust* (I.S., 1980).]

Seen against Jarrell's own work, none of his four authors will, in spite of their great diversity, surprise his reader, nor will, upon a closer look, his selection from their *oeuvre*. In the case of Rilke particularly, one cannot help but think that some of those poems might have been written by Jarrell himself: significantly, he is partial both to Rilke's childhood poems and to the poet's preoccupation (especially pre-eminent in the early years of the First World War) with death. Although Jarrell may in some cases have been the first to attempt a translation, other translations are at the present available for all of his. His accomplishments can, therefore, be considered both against the originals and with reference to parallel efforts. And though comparisons may be odious, they seem altogether necessary in the face of competitive renderings of one text.

As a rule, Randall Jarrell has made no attempts to rhyme his translations, even where the original is rhymed; free, or rather "ordinary accentual-syllabic verse" (his term) replaces the verse schemes of the

*Reprinted from *Analects*, 1, No. 2 (1961), 40–48, by permission of the author. The original first section of the essay, on general problems in poetic translation, is omitted here.

originals. By this liberty, the merits of which will have to be discussed in some detail later, he has made room for a relatively close fidelity without having to compromise the idiomatic quality of his English. As will be confirmed in individual comparisons, Jarrell's translations, therefore, usually surpass his competitors' on two scores: what he gives are always English poems that can be read as such, without begging for embarrassing concessions; at the same time they tend to be closer to their models than are most competitive attempts.

While all of Jarrell's selections are quite typical of their creators, not all seem to me to be representative of the best in them. Thus a poem like Rilke's youthful "Lament," although it can boast at least five different English translations, is hardly a very significant achievement when compared to the poet's later work. Jarrell's concentrated translation compares very favorably with the more verbose efforts of most of his competitors. While he does not waste a single word, some of the other translators allow the challenge of rhymes to get in their way. Thus, "Und einer von allen Sternen / müsste wirklich noch sein" is rendered as "Of all the stars there must be far away / A single star which still exists apart," by one rhyming translator; Jarrell, on the other hand, gives a concise "And surely, of all the stars, / one still must be." Likewise, "Ich möchte aus meinem Herzen hinaus / unter den grossen Himmel treten," translated as clumsily as "I long to still my beating heart / Beneath the sky's vast dome" (by the translator of before), remains a satisfying image in Jarrell's "I would like to walk / Out of my heart under the great sky." On the other hand, this poem contains one of the few instances where Jarrell quite needlessly, and in fact harmfully, substitutes for one very definite concept another, equally definite, but entirely different in meaning and tone. Where Rilke suggests the high-strung sensitivity and anxiety of his speaker by letting him suspect that in a *boat* which just passed by, something fearful was said, Jarrell, for no reason that is apparent to me, substitutes *car* for boat. He does, it is true, attain by this a rhyme, but since the rest of the translation is unrhymed, this seems a flaw rather than a desirable effect. Was *car* to make things more "contemporary"? But the whole poem is romantic, soft and entirely *fin de siècle*. Still, the lion's paw of the poet comes out beautifully at the end of the poem when Jarrell, and only he among the translators, seizes an opportunity actually to improve Rilke by making use of a possibility that was denied the German by his syntax. Following a ray of a star back to its source, Rilke had to put the white city, to which this star is finally likened, into the penultimate line to round off his relative clause. Jarrell, in his medium, could do what Rilke surely would have liked to do, clinching the whole poem tight by a very satisfying "I believe I know / Which one endures; / Which one, at the end of its beam in the sky, / Stands like a white city."

Much subtler a poem and a greater challenge to the translator is Rilke's short "Evening," also an early work, but already abounding in very Rilkean and all but untranslatable linguistic refinements. Again, Jarrell seems to be making the best of "Zu keinem ganz gehörig," by his terse "not wholly either's." More difficult, the line "unsäglich zu entwirren," rendered as "inexpressibly to disentangle" by one translator, drove another, Mr. MacIntyre, into the despair of "unspeakably confused." Jarrell's "inscrutably to disentangle" seems to me to tax English about as much and certainly in the same way that Rilke's line does German—thus the unconventional quality of Rilke's line has itself been translated. We only part company when Rilke, speaking of someone's life, calls it "bald begrenzt und bald begreifend" and Jarrell reproduces this by "bounded by everything, or boundless." Surely, *boundless* does not do justice to the meaning of *begreifend*, and Mrs. Norton's "now circumscribed, now comprehending" is much closer to Rilke's intention.

That one of Rilke's greatest early poems, "Childhood" (1905), would be attractive to a poet understanding childhood as sympathetically as does Jarrell, is very natural. Yet the poem poses grave problems of translation. An irregular, but incredibly rich rhyme scheme, supported by interior rhymes, assonances, alliterations, half rhymes and other acoustic correspondences, suggests even more the strange universe of the child, with all its imagined connections, surreal identifications and never-ending surprises, than does the *meaning* of the words. To disregard almost completely this enchanting musical structure seems to me to do some real and irreparable harm to the poem and I would, for one, gladly sacrifice some accuracy, if by this the musicality of the poem were saved. For this work at least, I plead Verlaine's "La musique avant toute chose." Apart from this, there is one passage where Jarrell, who generally follows his text very piously and successfully, suddenly leaves it and inserts a whole two lines, turning his effort into an adaptation rather than a translation. Where Rilke reads "Männer und Frauen; Männer, Männer, Frauen / Und Kinder, welche anders sind und bunt," Jarrell gives "Men and women, men, men—black and tall / And going slowly, as if in their sleep, / Beside the sudden white and blue and red / Children." Admittedly, to translate *anders* and *bunt* each by an entire line is a case of poetic particularization that is not in itself reprehensible. What I would question is that it improves Rilke's poem significantly, and what I would object to is that Jarrell thus destroys a structurally essential feature of the poem, namely the repetition of the word *anders* (other) in stanzas one, two and four of Rilke's text. The contrast between the little world already mastered and the great, vaguely menacing, but *unqualified* "other" seems to me to be almost the *leit-motiv* of the poem and to eliminate it a genuine loss. One other detail concerns Rilke's line, "und Schrecken lautlos wechselnd mit Vertrauen." Jarrell's "And one's fear changing silently to trust" is too final and comforting, for *wechselnd* suggests that the process may be any moment reversed. Leishman's "and fear and trust changing in subtle ways," seems closer to the mark. On the other hand, Leishman's rhymes drive

him into translating "O immer mehr entweichendes Begreifen" by a weak
and wordy "O thoughts that fade into the darkness, straying / alone,"
when Jarrell can give a somewhat too solid, but honest "O knowledge
ever harder to hold fast to." And a veritable touch of genius appears in
our poet's rendering of Rilke's wonderful coinage, "o schweres Zeitver-
bringen." Mrs. Norton's "O heavy spending of time," while being quite
literal, does not really accomplish quite the same in English, nor does
Leishman's, "o time that creeps away," make me very happy. Jarrell gives
"o leaden waiting-out of time," and whoever can *taste* Rilke's line, besides
understanding it, will surely see that *that* is what he wanted.

Although entitled "The Grownup," "Die Erwachsene" is really
another poem about childhood, or at least, about leaving what
Hofmannsthal called the magic state behind. A very beautiful poem, unmistakably Rilke, and recreated to perfection by Jarrell. Even such
unlikely English nouns as "the flying, fleeting, faraway, / the monstrous
and the still unmastered," wonderfully imitating Rilke's "das Fliegende,
Entfliehende, Entfernte, / das Ungeheure, noch Unerlernte," sound
perfectly natural and convincing within the translation. And how sensitively he succeeds in echoing Rilke's meandering, never-ending, qualify-
ing and subqualifying, smoothly flowing sentences, of which three make
up the entire sixteen line poem—in German and in English.

Equally successful is Jarrell in his version of Rilke's "Washing the
Corpse," a poem that seems to live on an extraordinarily subtle interplay
of piety and irony in describing the washing of Christ's body by two most
ordinary and unsubtle charwomen. Not the slightest nuance seems to me
to be lost: this is the poem, the *whole* poem—in English.

And a third short and very fine translation is "The Child," marred
only slightly by one of the few (if not the only) dictionary mistake that I
found in all of the Rilke translations. In "klar und ganz wie eine volle
Stunde, / welche anhebt und zu Ende schlägt," the word *anheben* has
nothing to do with "lift up" or "raise." Instead, it means "to begin, to set
out," and the sentence ought not to read "which is raised and strikes its
end," but "clear and entire as a completed / Hour that sets out to strike
its end."

In a certain sense, "The Great Night," of 1914, but not published in
Rilke's lifetime, might be considered a more mature "Lament." While the
initial situation in both poems is the loneliness of an unusual sensitivity, in
the later poem the dilemma is stated in a much more accomplished manner and the speaker reconciles himself to his isolation more convincingly:
the night becomes the understanding *thou*. Rather a difficult poem to
translate, yet, except for a few possible alterations or additions, Jarrell's
version seems highly commendable. The very first word, *anstaunen*, to
me is more than "to look at": "to gaze, stare, marvel at" would seem to be
closer. Rilke's daring *unüberredete Landschaft* appears well translated by
"landscape not yet won over," but the fact that a room was *mitfühlbar*

("sympathisable") gets lost in Jarrell's version and "alles Weinens . . . un-tröstliche Gründe" seems better rendered by Leishman's "inconsolable grounds of infinite crying," than by Jarrell's "spring of all our tears, the spring that is never dry." As to the last two lines, "Dein auf weite Ernste verteiltes/ Lächeln trat in mich ein," both Leishman and Jarrell seem to prove what one might have suspected beforehand: they absolutely defy translation—who has ever heard of "earnestnesses"?

"Death," another posthumously published poem of 1915, with a grim, surrealist *humour noir* quality about it, poses fewer problems to the translator than most—at least if he does not struggle, like Leishman, with obstinate rhymes. Quite free, but very convincing is Jarrell's rendering of "Sind sie denn hier vernarrt/ in dieses Essen voller Hindernis?" "They munch away/ At their own frustrations so insatiably" does not retain a single word or concept of the original, yet, the spirit undoubtedly is there.

In his translation of Rilke's "The Olive Garden," Jarrell allows the language to rhyme itself, occasionally and quite casually, still never sacrificing his English to meet a rhyme. Leishman who insists on im-itating Rilke's rhyme scheme line by line is again forced to add and distort in several instances. Thus, Rilke's economical and unambiguous lines, "Ich bin allein mit aller Menschen Gram,/ den ich durch Dich zu lindern unternahm,/ der Du nicht bist. O namenlose Scham . . ." are not just toned down as Leishman replaces "der Du nicht bist," by "thee whom I cannot find," but he scrambles up his syntax to the extent of giving, for Rilke's first line, "I am alone with all men sorrow name" (sic!)—and all that to get a rhyme for "claim," itself a weak and rhetorical substitute for Rilke's *unternahm*. The embarrassing consequences of slavishly imitating a rhyme scheme (which with Rilke himself was obviously not rigidly predetermined) could hardly be demonstrated more strikingly. How natural, by contrast, Jarrell's line flows: "I am alone with all men's sor-row— / All that, through Thee, I thought to lighten,/ Thou who art not. O nameless shame. . . ." Or compare their two renderings of Rilke's "Die Nacht, die kam, war keine ungemeine." For Leishman's awkward, thin and abstract "The night that came requires no specifying," Jarrell has a calm and poised "The night that came was no uncommon night." Only in the last stanza does it seem that Jarrell's version might be improved. For one, he leaves out entirely Rilke's important "zu *solchen* Betern," filling in a not very meaningful "For men beseech." Jarrell's line, "who lose themselves, all things let go," sounded considerably less strained in Rilke's German ("Die Sich-Verlierenden lässt alles los"). And the final line of the poem, "ausgeschlossen aus der Mütter Schooss," suffers greatly, so it seems to me, if *Schooss* (womb or lap in Rilke's idiosyncratic spelling) is translated by "heart." Jarrell's familiarity with Rilke's work might have reminded him that *Schooss*, not *Herz*, is the poet's symbolic scene for the perfectly protected existence. And although admittedly all of us have left our mother's womb and few her heart, for Rilke the most terrible form of being exposed is not "to be shut from one's mother's heart," but (and this is Leishman's here preferable rendering) to be "disincluded from one's mother's womb."

If Rilke's poems on childhood and on death prove particularly fascinating for Jarrell, the poet's "Requiem for the Death of a Boy," of 1915, can almost be expected among his translations, and so it is. Again, Jarrell gives a sympathetic, close and yet idiomatic reading and again, his competitor, Leishman, has to resort to circumlocution and some distortion to secure his rhymes. Whatever corrections one might suggest for Jarrell's translations are, with one exception, minor. Thus, Rilke's third line, "nun schon so lang und ganz von weit erkannt," does not seem to me to refer to the dead child's distance to the world of the living (Jarrell's "So far off now, already so long ago"), but rather to the boy's great proficiency in recognizing animals—"for so long already, and from far away." Both translators, amusingly, bowdlerize Rilke's "Glas voll Wein," Leishman giving "glass filled to overflow," Jarrell even "glass of milk." Surely nobody would take Rilke as suggesting some slightly degenerate central European precociousness (with a Gallic leaning toward alcoholism) in the boy. And when Jarrell translates "Dass man das machen kann: / ein Pferd aus Holz," by "you can make one, / A wooden horse," the profound astonishment ("how is it possible?!") of the boy is lost. Greater is the loss—and this is perhaps the only serious objection to the present translation—when Jarrell, for once, streamlines four very important verses: "Sah ich den Bach, wie hab ich da gerauscht, / rauschte der Bach, so bin ich hingesprungen. / Wo ich ein Klingen *sah*, hab ich geklungen, / und wo es klang, war ich davon der Grund," to read: "Whenever I would see the brook I'd race it, / And the brook raced, too, and I would run away. / Whenever I saw something that could ring I rang, / And whenever something sang I played for it." Clearly, Rilke's point is—and a very Rilkean point it is—that the child, whenever he sees a brook or "a ringing," undergoes a metamorphosis and becomes himself the rippling brook or the ringing bell. By eliminating the kinaesthetic paradoxes and taming the verse, the identification is not completed and the image spoiled.

In spite of our occasional disagreements, to me Randall Jarrell's approach in translating Rilke is the most sensible. His versions are the most readable I have yet seen in English. If it is true, as Dryden suggested, that to be a thorough translator of poetry a man must needs be a thorough poet, perhaps it also holds that a thorough poet, if he chooses to try, must needs be a thorough translator.

III

A poet like Randall Jarrell, his head filled (among other things) with *Märchenflausen*, should have a weak spot for that unique mixture of Swabian earthiness and classical grace, the poetry of Eduard Mörike

(1804–1875). The poet's simple and slender poem, "The Forsaken Girl," does not just sound like an anonymous folksong; for most of the many people who can sing it, it has become one, too: they have long forgotten that Mörike wrote the text. Much longer, chattier, and more *gemütlich* is the other Mörike poem of Jarrell's, "Forest Murmurs," a romantic idyll in classical distichons, yet so very German: with its fairy-tales, little girls, old trees, sweet nightingales and wishful phantasies. Besides being a piece of *Kulturgeschichte* of a by-gone time, "Forest Murmurs" is quite a respectable piece of craftsmanship. Compared with Rilke's highly charged and carefully balanced little word machines, it is, of course, a different and lighter kind of poetry, and, because of its plottiness, relatively easy to translate. The challenge would seem to be not to lose, somewhere in the course of translation, the charm and freshness of the lines, and Jarrell has admirably avoided falling into this trap. How delightful, after all the sugary and cute, diluted brews prepared by armies of "commercial artists," the story of Snow-White sounds: "Because she was so beautiful, the Queen, the vain one, hated her / Fiercely, so that she fled, made her home with dwarfs." What a Homeric line to describe the peasant girl: "Bronzed and stalwart, the maid; noon blazed on her cheeks." And about the Muse: "Her kingdom is the impossible: impudent, frivolous, she ladles together/ All that's unlikeliest, gleefully gives her prizes to half-wits./ Allowed three wishes, her hero will pick the silliest." How could one get tired of it?

If Mörike's naiveté appeals to Jarrell, the lover of fairy-tales, the sophisticated and capricious verse of Tristan Corbière (1845–1875) with its constant shifts between wit and sentimentality, empathy and dry mockery, with puns, jokes and literary allusions thrown in, brings out another side of our translating poet. Jarrell has translated two works of the fascinating Breton playboy, and it comes rather as a surprise that they should be of such different quality. For one, he has given us a superb translation of *Le Poète Contumace* and for another, an all but superfluous adaptation of four of the five *Rondels pour Après*. I have gone to some trouble comparing Jarrell's versions to the ones in MacIntyre's book of Corbière translations; *Le Poète Contumace* has few lines that I do not prefer in Jarrell's unrhymed, colloquial, yet infinitely more imaginative rendering; in the *Rondels*, there are few that I would not rather take from MacIntyre. With both works, Jarrell tends to be further away from the original text. But while in the first work the distance seems to be just sufficient to enable him to make full use of his imagination and great linguistic resources, in the *Rondels* he leaves out, adds, twists about and re-writes whole lines in a way that is always at odds with the letter and often with the spirit of the French text—yet his adaptations do not seem to make for very convincing poetry in English either. Let me furnish a few illustrations. In the first of the four, *Sonnet Posthume*, Corbière has a very straightforward "Qui dort dîne." MacIntyre renders it by an equally straightforward "who sleeps dines." Jarrell's version reads, "The hungry sleep and are fed?" And referring to the hay on which the corpse is to be bedded, Corbière has a grim, but clear "A tes dents viendra tout seul le foin," in MacIntyre's version "All you'll chew is hay." Does not Jarrell's "Your tongue is all grass," altogether miss the point? Less objectionable (his is an adaptation) is Jarrell's rendering, "The last fields are all flowers," for "La plus aimée est toujours la plus loin." Also, to call "un sacristain très bien," "a well-to-do sexton," instead of (MacIntyre's) "an immaculate sacristan" will do little harm. But if Corbière's incredibly bitter "les premiers honneurs t'attendent sous le poêle" is reproduced by "here under the pall, the first prize is waiting," the pun for whose sake the line was undoubtedly written—*first* as against *last* honors—is pitilessly destroyed.

The second *Rondel* seems more successful, although I do not know why neither of the two translators rendered "Les caveaux sont sourds," by, "The vaults are deaf." MacIntyre has "Graves are deaf and dark" (he needs a rhyme for "remark"); Jarrell even, "You are not listening."

The third contains some of Jarrell's strangest excursions. Why does "C'est le chandelier de ton lit d'auberge," become "It's as light as day?" Why must "Pour les pieds-plats, ton sol est maudit," be changed to "They drive you out in the cold, those flatfeet," when a direct, "For those flatfeet, your soil is cursed" would make perfect sense? And why the effort of translating, in the lines of "Seuls, le vent du nord, le vent du midi / Viendront balancer un fil-de-la-Vièrge," the word *balancer* by "to weigh in their great scales," if "to swing" (or MacIntyre's "to set aquiver") seems to work so much better?

And in the fourth and last *Rondel*, would not "dungeon flowers" translate "fleurs d'oubliettes" better than "Solitary's flowers"? Does not "Ne fais pas le lourd" simply mean, "Don't act dumb," "Don't play the dullard," and not (as MacIntyre has it) "Don't make it heavy," but even less (Jarrell's) "Go, little poet"? If Corbière has "Les bourgeois sont bêtes—", why does Jarrell replace *bourgeois* by "grown-ups"? And finally, there is the line, "Boîtes à violon qui sonnent le creux." MacIntyre translates this, quite literally, as "fiddle-boxes that sound hollow. . . ." But Jarrell suggests, "a sound box / For your penitentiary's last siren." If the benevolent reader gets it, he is quicker than I. It took me ten minutes. And what I finally thought I got was certainly no longer Corbière.

The situation is quite different, in fact it is reversed, when we look at Jarrell's translation of Corbière's *Poète Contumace*. MacIntyre's rhymes hamper him all along. Thus, Corbière's "Fier toujours d'avoir eu, dans le temps, sa légende," becomes an almost unreadable "Of having its old-time legend always proud" (to rhyme with "crowd"), when Jarrell can give us a nice and terse: "As vain as ever: it had its memories." And Jarrell, not MacIntyre, realizes that the poet is using a hunting image in speaking of "Un poète sauvage, avec un plomb dans l'aile"—this *plomb* is not just "lead weighing down his wings," it's a shot. But even without rhyming, MacIntyre frequently lets go both his text and his reader's imagination. "Faisant, d'un à peu près, d'artiste, / un philosophe d'à peu près, / Râleur de soleil ou de frais,/ En dehors de l'humaine piste." with Corbière, becomes a rather weak and sapless "making almost a philosopher/ of an artist only by half,/ a noon-and-evening grumbler/ aside from the human path" with MacIntyre. How much closer, how much funnier and how much livelier is Jarrell's: "Making, from something almost like an artist, / Something almost like a philosopher;/ Rain or shine, always complaining;/ Off any human track."

There are, it is true, some instances where the cards are stacked differently. "Le sait-il bien lui-même?" is not well reproduced by Jarrell's very assertive "He knows!"; and for Corbière's wonderful pun *viveur vécu* ("verlebter Lebemann" would do it nicely) Jarrell had, in a criticism of McElroy's earlier Corbière translation, two or three wordings that I would prefer to his present "dilapidated body"—was it "wasted wastrel" and "spent spendthrift"? *Castagnoles* are indeed not *castanets*, but pomfret, a Breton fish, and "la folle du logis" is not a witch, but the imagination, or a crotchet, as MacIntyre has it. Both translators bowdlerize "Belles nuits pour l'orgie à la tour," and neither seems to know that "d'après nature" does not mean "back to nature," but "true to nature, life-like." Yet the few instances where Jarrell might be improved do not tip the scales.

Corbière's idioms (for which MacIntyre sometimes finds no equivalent at all) are beautifully imitated: "Mon coeur fait de l'esprit": "My heart's cracked jokes." Or the following opportunity: "Dans mes dégoûts surtout, j'ai des goûts élégants." With MacIntyre this becomes a dull "Especially in my dislikes my taste's above the average." Jarrell saves both the idea and the pun: "In my distastes especially, I had good taste." Or, and this, I promise, is the last example, "Et c'est pauvre: adorer ce qu'on aime!" MacIntyre's "and it's flat: to adore what's dear," is itself irretrievably flat and no match for Jarrell's simple, "And that's pitiful: to worship what one loves."

To those who can't read *Le Poète Contumace* in the original, I shall hand Randall Jarrell's translation; the *Rondels pour Après* I shall not mention again. . . .

For some time, Randall Jarrell has been working on a translation of *Faust*, that monumental hybrid "Überdrama" of Jarrell's "own favorite daemon, dear good great Goethe." Unless statistics lie, (in Frantz: *Half a Hundred Thralls to Faust*, University of North Carolina Press, 1949), a quarter of a million English Fausts, in 48 different translations, had, by 1949, come off the various presses; in the last decade, these figures have been well surpassed. Every conceivable approach has been tried, from Bayard Taylor's painstakingly metric version, faithfully imitating even the change of masculine and feminine line endings, to free prose adaptations like Abraham Hayward's. Strangely enough, it was Taylor's mid-Victorian version that, going to fifty editions, has proved most successful so far. But to the unprejudiced reader, it is quite obvious that Taylor's language of 1870 has aged much more than has Goethe's of 1830. And it seems no less evident that every generation both needs and deserves its own version of the classics. If we eliminate Louis MacNeice's rather imprecise rendering on account of being incomplete, the most popular modern rival versions seem to be Philip Wayne's, C. F. MacIntyre's, and G. M. Priest's.

For different reasons, the part of Jarrell's translation that I saw seems to have the edge over all of them. Wayne's rhymed version, although it has a pleasant Oxford (or is it Cambridge?) snap in the lighter scenes, resorts to all too many quaint and old-fashioned clichés and tricks ("Nay, nay . . . ," "Pray have no fear . . .") to be considered a recreation in a truly contemporary medium. Also, in spite of Wayne's impressive vocabulary, his strict rhyming scheme forces him too often to replace Goethe's imagery by his own. Still, I would prefer his work to the two others, by MacIntyre and G. M. Priest. Both of them have, at one time or another, been acclaimed as the best available, the latter (if we are to believe the blurb) even reminding Thomas Mann of Luther's translation of the Bible! But for one, Priest's version is quite frankly eclectic, for another, he too, has to fill in words like "yonder, always, whither, fain," etc., to make his rhymes come out. The result can be quite painful at times. "Dazu hast du noch eine lange Frist," becomes "For that, a respite long doth still exist." Who would not prefer Jarrell's "Your credit's good—forget it!" Goethe's "Dazu hast du eine volles Recht" is rendered by a pedantic "Your perfect right to that I'll not deny"; Jarrell has "That's your prerogative." Or, even worse, for "Beglückt, wer Treue rein im Busen trägt," Priest gives "Blest he whose bosom is with breachless faith replete." How much more poetic is Jarrell's "Happy the man who bears within his breast / pure faith, pure trust." And so one could go on.

C. F. MacIntyre (with whom Jarrell also rivalled in his Corbière and Rilke translations) spoils his work mainly by his annoying habit of paraphrasing concrete images by more general, abstract terms. Thus, "Um Lebens oder Sterbens willen" becomes "to provide for contingencies"; Jarrell has at least a nicely Mephistophelian "in case of accident," for "Das Streben meiner ganzen Kraft/ Ist grade das, was ich verspreche," MacIntyre has: "The goal of all my struggling's been just this/ that I now promise"; with Jarrell, "To keep striving with all my might: that is exactly what I'm promising." Or, for an even more drastic example, compare the following—Goethe: "Dazu hast du ein volles Recht; / Ich habe mich nicht freventlich vermessen. / Wie ich beharre, bin ich Knecht,/ Ob dein, was frag' ich, oder wessen." MacIntyre: "Stand on your legal rights./ My action is not rash. I'll not regret it./ As soon as I stagnate, I become a slave./ So what does it matter whose I am?" And Jarrell's superior wording: "That's your prerogative. But this is no rash boast./ As soon as I stand still I'm a slave:/ Yours, someone else's, what's the difference?" Then there are MacIntyre's mistranslations. "Ein solcher Diener bringt Gefahr ins Haus," does not mean "A servant like you must cost too dearly" (MacIntyre); Jarrell's "Your sort of servant is a risky business" is much closer both in meaning and in tone. "Allein ich will" is not "That's what I want," but (Jarrell): "But I will"; "Möchte gern was Rechts hieraussen lernen" is not "I want to learn something out here that's practical," but more like Jarrell's "I'm here to get a real education."

Looking at Jarrell's translation critically (and I have only seen the two scenes published here [i.e., in *Analects*]), I should like to make the following observations. First of all, there are a number of minor mistranslations. Thus, *Ströme* is not "streams," but "torrents"; *undurchdrungen* not "impenetrable," but (as yet) "unpenetrated"; *ehrbar* not "careful" but "honorable"; and *Muhme* not "cousin" but "old aunt." Secondly, I still have not been able quite to reconcile myself to the loss (except in a few final couplets) of *rhyme*. It is true, all the rhyming translations seem to prove that it can't be done. Still, I am not quite happy with this argument. Friedrich Schlegel has already, in a letter to A. Hayward of 1832, expressed the doubt that a prose translation can do the work justice. Goethe himself was ambivalent on the issue. While he held that it is "by rhythm and rhyme that poetry becomes poetry," he also thought that "the truly instructive and quickening element is that which remains of the poet after he has been translated into prose." To be sure, Jarrell does not translate into prose, but into free, unrhymed verse. Yet, what I miss is the snappy quality, the pleasant clicking effect, that Goethe accomplishes by his *rhymes* and that give his lines greater sensual appeal and greater finality. How eminently satisfying are Goethe's two famous lines, summing up man's middle years, after they have been acoustically prepared for by two previous, rhymable lines: "In jedem Kleide werd' ich wohl die Pein / Des engen Erdenlebens fühlen./ Ich bin zu alt, um nur zu spielen,/ zu jung, um ohne Wunsch zu sein." To translate this by "I am too old just to play./ Too young to keep living without wishes," is perfectly correct—but the life is gone. And the same "clicking device" is used with great ingenuity throughout the play to heighten certain *comic* effects: if a long emotional speech of Faust's is finally interrupted by one of Mephistopheles' dry remarks, the rhyme, with which he mockingly echoes one or the other of Faust's fondest ideas, accounts for at least half the fun.

Still, perhaps these features of the play will have to be reserved for those who can read it in the original. In all other respects, Jarrell's contemporary, concrete, lively and thoroughly poetic lines make for the most attractive *Faust* translation that I have read, and if it is true that every generation needs its version of the classics, Randall Jarrell may well be writing the English *Faust* for ours.

Jarrell's Translations: The Poet as Elective Middle European

Richard K. Cross*

It must have looked to Randall Jarrell's contemporaries during the fifties as though he were at the peak of his form. *Poetry and the Age* (1953) confirmed his stature as a critic; *Pictures from an Institution* (1954) represented a breakthrough for him into a new genre; and the *Selected Poems* (1955) drew together the best work from the four volumes published between 1942 and 1951 that had established his reputation as a poet. And yet there must have been readers who observed that the *Selected Poems* contained but two fresh pieces and that relatively few new poems were appearing in the quarterlies. "A wicked fairy has turned me into a prose writer," he used to tell his wife.[1] A very able writer of prose at least, one may think; still it is easy to grasp the plaintive note in his jest.

Even those who had remarked the falling off in Jarrell's productivity as a poet may well have been surprised to open *The Woman at the Washington Zoo* (1960), his first book of new verse in nine years, and to find that translations, mainly from Rilke, comprised more than a third of it. A few poems that he had rendered into English—one each by Gregorovius and Mörike and several by Corbière and Rilke—had come out in magazines over the preceding dozen years, but these hardly served to indicate the amount of time and effort that Jarrell had been investing in translation. In the years that ensued he brought out translations of eight folk tales, five from the Grimms' collection and three from Bechstein's, as well as two Radauskas poems; however, only since Jarrell's death in 1965 have the appearance of *The Complete Poems* (1969), containing seven previously unpublished Rilke lyrics, and his translations of Chekhov's *Three Sisters* (1969) and Goethe's *Faust, Part One* (1976), made plain the full extent of his commitment. Jarrell began most of these projects and completed many of them during his dry spell in the fifties. No doubt factors other than the difficulty he had writing his own poetry moved him to undertake the translations, but it seems unlikely that they would have engaged so considerable a portion of his energies had he not experienced that block. The poet appears to have devoted himself to translating writers he particularly admired partly because the endeavor seemed worthwhile in

*This essay was written especially for this book and appears by permission of the author.

310

its own right but also because he hoped, by aligning himself with the genius of a Goethe or a Rilke, to summon his own more modest muse. Whether the labor of translation did indeed smooth the way for the verse in *The Lost World* (1965), his last volume and one of his two or three best, is debatable, but it almost surely helped him to maintain equilibrium while he waited for the poems to come.

One might expect a poet of Jarrell's school—out of Eliot by way of Ransom and Tate—to take a strong interest in the French symbolists. There is not much in either Jarrell's poetry or prose, however, to suggest a particularly deep interest in anything French. Important exceptions are his passion for Proust and his translations of Tristan Corbière's *Le Poète contumace* and four of the five *Rondels pour après*. Jarrell's version of the former balances adroitly between fidelity to the letter of the original and to its spirit. The following examples are representative of his ingenuity in coming up with an equivalent idiom: Corbière's apostrophe to his hermit poet—"mon vieux, triste et faux déterré"—Jarrell renders as "poor old sport, have they dug you up without a permit?"; in lines somewhat less freely adapted, "un mur si trouvé que, pour entrer dedans, / On n'aurait pu trouver l'entrée" becomes "a wall so holey that no living man / Had ever come in through the doorway."[2] Jarrell does not attempt to duplicate the rhyme schemes of the poems he translates; indeed his versions often do not rhyme at all. In "Le Poète Contumace," however, he does introduce subtle rhymes that at least sometimes approximate Corbière's design and that, in any case, work well in themselves. Consider, for instance, stanza four:

> One year, the tenant of this low tower
> Was a wild poet with a ball in his wing
> Fallen among owls: the venerable owls
> Who, from some height, considered him.—He respected
>   their holes—
> He, the only paying owl, as his lease stated:
> *Twenty-five écus a year: door to be replaced.*

Brief quotations can only hint at Jarrell's effectiveness in capturing and sustaining the singular amalgam of irony, humor, and self-pity in Corbière's poem of nearly two hundred lines.

"Afterwards" (135–37), Jarrell's adaptations from the *Rondels pour après*, is much less impressive—a contention I shall illustrate with examples from the second poem in the sequence. Rendering "Les caveaux sont sourds" as "You're not listening" catches but a fraction of its sense and dissipates nearly all its chill, while giving "Jeter leur pavé sur tes demoiselles" as "To throw bricks on your bottle of fireflies" alters the meaning of the line with no apparent warrant and loses the play on "pavé" and "demoiselle" in the sense of paving beetle. Perhaps Jarrell meant his "bottle of fireflies" to link up with the "voleur d'étincelles" in the refrain. If so, he might better have translated "étincelles" literally as "sparks" rather than making the phrase over into "little thief of starlight," a change that strikes me as indicative of his tendency to soften Corbière's wry confrontation in the *Rondels* with the specter stalking him.

It would be a mistake, though, to dwell on the lapses in "Afterwards" and to neglect the genuine affinity between Corbière and Jarrell evident in "Le Poète Contumace" and a poem like "A Girl in a Library." Jarrell's coed cannot elicit anything like the passionate reaction to which his Breton counterpart's Marcelle gives rise, but the two poets' ruminations on the women are, nonetheless, informed by comparable blends of mocking distance and tender sympathy. Both men were witty sophisticates who, for reasons of their own, found the provinces more congenial than great cities and whose irony reflects the tension that life in such circumstances can generate.

Anyone who surveys the list of Jarrell's translations will infer, correctly, that he was concerned much less with the West than with the heart of Europe. "I believe my favorite country's German," he remarks in "Deutsch Durch Freud" (266–68; the title plays on the Nazi slogan *Kraft durch Freude*). The "country" in question is less a place than a tongue and the culture it potentiates. That the poet only half-knew the language seems not to have diminished its appeal in the least:

> A Feeling in the Dark
> Brings worlds, brings words that hard-eyed Industry
> And all the schools' dark Learning never knew.
> . . . .
> If God gave me the choice—but I stole this from Lessing—
> Of German and learning German, I'd say: Keep your
>   German!

One cannot take Jarrell's self-deprecation too seriously, though, and not just on the ground that he is an inveterate ironist. Of more consequence is the fact that, while one may quarrel with points of diction or syntax in his translations, there are very few outright errors in them. He may have enjoyed "reading Rilke / Without *ein Wörterbuch*," but we have it on Mary Jarrell's word that when the time came to produce English versions her husband reached for the Wildhagen and Héraucourt.[3]

Hannah Arendt recalls Jarrell as having been "completely at home in the strange and intense poetry of German folk tales and folk songs."[4] Introducing his translation of *The Golden Bird and Other Fairy Tales of the Brothers Grimm*, a collection intended primarily for young readers, Jarrell remarks: "Some grown-ups are surprisingly fond of the stories: I know a poet who has written poems about Hansel and Gretel, Sleeping Beauty, the Frog Prince, and Cinderella."[5] That poet, is, of course, the translator himself. His versions of the Grimms' "Snow-White and the Seven Dwarfs," "Hansel and Gretel," "The Golden Bird," "Snow-White and Rose-Red," "The Fisherman and His Wife" and of Ludwig Bechstein's[6] "The Rabbit Catcher," "The Brave Flute Player," and "The

Man and the Wife in the Vinegar Jug" are, all of them, readable and reliable. Naturally they are not altogether flawless. One might, for example, object that giving the fox's cautionary refrain in "The Golden Bird" as "you'll be in a mighty bad fix" veers toward slang in a way not justified by "sonst möchte es dir schlimm ergehen" or that calling the couple's initial (and final) abode in "The Fisherman and His Wife" a pigsty rather dresses up the "Pissputt" of the original, but reservations of this sort do not amount to much in comparison with the pleasure these translations offer. If my response and that of my four-year-old daughter may be taken as representative, Jarrell is quite right about the breadth of their appeal.

Given the poet's attraction to folk tales, it is understandable that he should have been drawn also to that most amiable Swabian Eduard Mörike, whose *Wald-Idylle* he translates as "Forest Murmurs" (253–55). The poem recounts the speaker's experience reading Grimm one day in a wood that comes to seem as enchanted as it might in one of the tales. In the course of the morning he tells the story of Snow White to a neighbor's child from the village and ends by allowing himself a series of deliciously whimsical reflections on his relation to the muse of fairy-tales and his desire for the neighbor girl's older sister that become, almost, a *Märchen* in their own right. Mörike's poem is cast in long, leisurely, unrhymed lines that pose few obstacles to the translator. Partly on that account but also, doubtless, because its matter was so dear to Jarrell's heart, "Forest Murmurs" is one of his most successful translations. He has a version of another Mörike poem as well, a lovely, simple ballad entitled *Das verlassene Magdlein*. "The Forsaken Girl" (456) adapts the lyric quite freely, e.g., "Treuloser Knabe" becomes "Dear one, wicked one." It is not among Jarrell's most inspired efforts, but it is a reasonably good facsimile.

His version of Ferdinand Gregorovius's "Lament of the Children of Israel in Rome" (447–51) is in some respects anomalous. The poem is incidental to Gregorovius's labors as an historian of Rome in the Middle Ages; its interest for Jarrell, who translated it only a few years after the Holocaust, probably lay in its moving tribute to the Jews' power of endurance. The "Lament" is not, on the whole, remarkable as art, but a number of its stanzas do possess a kind of stiff dignity, of which the following is a fair sample:

> By the waters of the Tiber
> We set up, with silent weeping,
> Poorly, and with unhewn stones,
> The sanctuary of Thy temple;
> And we traced upon the walls
> Thine emblems, Lord, that we might still
> Remember, when they met our gaze,
> Thy house's old magnificence.

The project that consumed more of Jarrell's time than any other between 1957 and 1964 was his translation of *Faust, Part One*, an undertaking rooted in his sense of kinship with the poet he calls "my own favorite daemon" (267) and his belief that Goethe's theme remains central to the experience of the West: "If our world should need a tombstone, we'll be able to put on it: HERE LIES DOCTOR FAUST."[7] Appalled by the nearly Spenserian artifice of many earlier *Faust* translations, Jarrell meant, his widow relates, to render it in an idiom "neither imitation German nor imitation English, but plain English intended for readers and playgoers."[8] The language of his version is indeed comparatively colloquial; its tonal range is, however, considerably narrower than Goethe's. It is a style better suited to the banter of Martha and Mephistopheles than it is to the more exalted moments in the drama. Consider, in that connection, the following passage from *Wald und Höhle* (lines 3345 ff.) where Faust is compelled to recognize the impasse into which his passion for Gretchen has driven the two of them:

> What good's this ecstasy within her arms?
> What if I warm myself against her breast—
> Shall I not, always, feel her misery?
> Am I not homeless? fugitive? the monster
> Without aim, without peace, that like a cataract
> Plunges from rock to rock, in greedy rage,
> Down into the abyss?[9]

Jarrell's rendering conveys the sense of these lines accurately, but it substantially diminishes their force. "Ecstasy" is in a different key than the "Himmelsfreud" of the original, a word distinctively Goethe's own but one that any peasant could understand; Jarrell's term seems clinical by comparison. In any case, the reference to heaven is not just a rhetorical fillip, and no translator should casually discard it. "Homeless" is weaker than "Unbehauste," which might better be translated by a less common word like "unhoused." Much more serious than these points of diction is the fact that Jarrell's lines read, in spite of their being blank verse, almost as though they were prose. His having jettisoned rhyme exacerbates the difficulty, since Goethe's rhymes are integral to the logic and music of his stanzas to an extent not characteristic of most of the other works Jarrell translated. Without them, especially in a passage whose emotional coloration is as intense as that in the one we have been considering, the verse suffers a diffusion both of energy and focus.

I have discussed Jarrell's *Faust* translation in much greater detail elsewhere and rather than try to rehearse my argument in the limited space available here, it seems more sensible to refer the reader to the other essay.[10] It may be worthwhile, however, to repeat a sentence from that piece linking Jarrell's fascination with Goethe to his own oeuvre, in which there is hardly a poem that "does not manifest one or more elements of the Faust 'syndrome': restlessness of the heart stemming from conflicting or repressed impulses; impatience with all manner of constraints and a resolve to transcend them; love of nature and solitude and, at the same time, distress at feeling cut off from the folk; dread of aging and the loss of love; disenchantment with the kind of self-consciousness that alienates one from the unreflective vitality of one's early years; a sense of the radical imperfection of both the self and its world and corresponding need to strive toward fuller being; recognition that the freedom demanded by the Faust figure entails great suffering." No Jarrell poem represents the ensemble of these qualities more vividly than his splended "Woman at the Washington Zoo," which ends with the plea: "You know what I was, / You see what I am: change me, change me!" (216.)

There is no evading that imperative, since as Rilke reminds us: "da ist keine Stelle / Die dich nicht sieht. Du musst dein Leben ändern."[11] If any poet had a claim on Jarrell rivaling Goethe's, that poet was Rilke. All of the Faustian attributes cataloged above pertain to Rilke as much as they do to Jarrell—similarities the latter would have been quick to affirm, as he was any hint of a resemblance between himself and writers he admired. "I shall never forget," he recounts in *Poetry and the Age*, "hearing a German say, in an objective, considering tone, as if I were an illustration in a book called *Silver Poets of the Americas*: 'You know, he looks a little like Rilke.' "[12] (Mary Jarrell tells a parallel anecdote about the innocent vanity with which her husband responded to someone's having likened him to Chekhov.)[13] The affinity between these two—in Rilke's phrase—"bees of the invisible" goes beyond matters of character or theme, significant as those are. For Jarrell the Rilkean "Dinggedicht," striving to speak not so much about as *for* the thing it contemplates, must have seemed an apotheosis of the symbolist tradition in which he had been schooled. The doctrine of correspondence essential to such poetry is quite clearly formulated in Rilke's "Evening Star" (485):

> The star far off separates yet how could I see it
> If there were not inside me the same star?
> We wish on the star because the star itself is a wish.

Versions of eighteen Rilke lyrics, the majority of them from *Das Buch der Bilder* and *Neue Gedichte*, appear in *The Complete Poems*. Jarrell made no attempt to translate a representative selection of the Bohemian master's poems but chose rather to do those that reflected one or another facet of his own sensibility. They do not include the famous anthology pieces like *Herbsttag* or *Der Panther* or *Das Karussell*. In general Jarrell's strategy is, once again, to avoid rhyme but to remain close to the literal sense and, whenever possible, the syntax of the original. He does not hesitate to deviate from common usage when Rilke's verse calls for it, e.g., "the landscape, not yet won over, / Darkened as though I was not" in "The Great Night" (238) faithfully renders the equally unidiomatic lines "die unüberredete Landschaft / finsterte hin, als wäre ich nicht." No translator has managed to reproduce the nuances of imagery and cadence in that remarkable poem, composed by Rilke on the eve of the Great War and reminiscent in both theme and manner of Baudelaire, with greater exactitude than has Jarrell in lines like these:

> The closest things
> Didn't bother to make me understand. The street
> Crowded itself up to the lamp post; I saw that it was strange.
> Out there a room was clear in lamplight—
> Already I was part; they sensed it, closed the shutters.
> I stood there. And then a child cried. And I knew
> The mothers in the houses, what they were—knew, suddenly,
> The spring of all our tears, the spring that is never dry.

His version is quite literal until the last line, which resolves with considerable ingenuity the problem of rendering "und wusste / alles Weinens zugleich die untröstlichen Gründe."

Both poets were intrigued by children, whose capacity for wonder and dread so vastly exceeds that of most adults. Thus it is natural that Jarrell, whose early years had been as full of misery as Rilke's own, should have undertaken to translate "The Child" (245), with its poignant image of the boy "dressed in his little dress," excluded from the grown-ups' sphere and incomprehensible to them, or that other, more ambitious poem, "Childhood" (242–43), which plays the "leaden waiting-out of time" in the schoolroom off against the "gleaming and ringing" of streets and the large freedom of parks. It may be that translating such poems (along with reading Proust) helped Jarrell to recover and grapple with the experience he relates in "The Lost World" sequence. Just as Rilke employs youthful promise as a measure of adult shortcomings in "The Grown-Up" and "Faded," so Jarrell does in "Next Day" and "Gleaning." The same sense of miraculous potentiality, the power of desire to engender out of thin air its own fulfillment, which informs Rilke's "Unicorn" (482)—

> They nourished it, not with grain
> But only, always, with the possibility
> It might be.

—undergrids Jarrell's "Seele im Raum" whose title is borrowed from a Rilke poem.

The American poet's obsession with death appears to lie behind the translations of "Washing the Corpse," with its Lawrentian stress on the otherness of those who have died and on their continuing power over the living, and "Death," a steely meditation of men's propensity to resist the inevitable: "One has to pull the present from their mouths, / The hard present, like a dental plate" (246). Those who died young held a peculiar fascination for Jarrell, as they did for Rilke, who imagines Jesus in "The Olive Garden" (417–18) facing his end estranged from the Father and indeed from all parents:

> Who lose themselves, all things let go;
> They are renounced by their own fathers
> And shut from their own mothers' hearts.

"Hearts" represents a curious substitution on Jarrell's part; the original has "Schooss" ("lap" or, better here, "womb"), which offers an apter, more vivid closing image.

Another Rilke translation in this vein is "Requiem for the Death of a Boy" (247–49), where the newly dead child tries to assimilate his experience among the living, grown suddenly strange, to the still less familiar condition in which he now finds himself. Especially moving are the lines on the wooden horse, in which varying states of animation commingle:

> When you call it a horse, why isn't it a lie?
> Because you feel that you're a horse, a little,
> And grow all maney, shiny, grow four legs—
> So as to grow, some day, into a man?
> But wasn't I wood a little, too,
> For its sake, and grew hard and quiet
> And looked out at it from an emptier face?

Requiem auf den Tod eines Knaben, composed in November 1915, commemorates the loss of a single child in a time when communiqués from the front and newspaper headlines threatened to reduce death to a matter of statistics. Jarrell's wartime poems perform a comparable function. One thinks first of the airman in "The Death of the Ball Turret Gunner," whose end is depicted as a state-sponsored abortion, or the flyboys in "Eighth Air Force" (143) who "play, before they die, / Like puppies with their puppy," but the civilian victims in "Come to the Stone" and "Protocols" belong in this category as well. For Jarrell as for Rilke beauty was conceived in terms of fearful symmetry: "Denn das Schöne ist nichts / als des Schrecklichen Anfang, den wir noch grade ertragen."[14]

"During almost all the War-years," recalled Rilke in 1920, "I was . . . waiting in Munich, always thinking it *must* come to an end. . . . For me, the open world was the only possible one, I knew of no other: what did I not owe to Russia,—it has made me all that I am, from there I inwardly set out, all the home of my instinct, all my inward origin is *there*!"[15] Nothing in Jarrell's life corresponds to Rilke's early pilgrimages to Russia—his visits to Tolstoy, his deep respect for the peasants' piety, his awe before the immensity of the steppes—but, through acts of imaginative appropriation, the American partly became in sympathy what his Bohemian counterpart had been in fact: a Middle European with a pronounced tilt toward the East. Like Rilke, Jarrell revered the great nineteenth-century Russians, although his devotion had a more secular cast to it. One indication of where the boundary of the latter's kinship with Rilke lay resides in his special affinity for Chekhov rather than for Tolstoy or Dostoevski.

Before we take up the bond with Chekhov, though, I should like to pause briefly to consider another facet of Jarrell's Eastward leaning, one scarcely attributable to Russophilia, viz., his interest in the Lithuanian writer Henrikas Radauskas, three of whose poems he translated. The accent in each of these falls on the warped images, wry humor, and acute sense of dislocation one associates with surrealism. "Guess what smells so," Radauskas asks in the opening line of "The Winter's Tale" (250), which goes on:

> You didn't guess.
> Lilies? Lindens? No. Winds? No.
> But princes and barbers smell so,
> The evening smells so, in a dream.

"In a Hospital Garden" and the prose poem "The Fire at the Waxworks," with their imagery of burning, torsion, and collapse, are not simply oneiric in character but downright nightmarish. A Lithuanian of Radauskas's generation might well see these tactics as less a matter of subjective distortion than of holding the mirror up to a history gone awry.

Among the many writers about whom her husband cared, reports Mary Jarrell, "the one he thought of as being the closest to his own nature as an artist and a man was Chekhov."[16] The two men worked primarily in different genres, of course, but they did indeed share a delicacy of feeling and perception as well as the technical finesse needed to embody that sensibility in art. Beyond that they had in common a disposition to gentle melancholy hedged with that irony, more compassionate than critical, we have already remarked in Jarrell's poetry. He chose to translate *The Three Sisters*, his widow tells us, "not only because it was his favorite Chekhov play; it was his favorite play."[17] His feeling for it is evident in the sensitivity with which, aided by Paul Schmidt's literal translation, he has rendered its lines into an English that comes close to being a transparent medium for Chekhov's characters as they endeavor to disclose or mask their affections and dislikes, their hopes, anxieties, and ennui.[18]

Just how thoroughly Jarrell had taken critical possession of the drama becomes clear in the nearly sixty pages of notes that accompany the translation. "*The Three Sisters*," he comments, "is as well-made as an Ibsen play in that everything is related to everything else, except that Chekhov relates things in a musical way." He goes on to say that the dramatist diffused leitmotivs in a way that enabled him "to relax the essential structural framework the play is built on. In the exchange of themes, overly defined edges of characterization and situation are blurred and, to him, more realistic. In particular, Cherbutykin's 'What's the difference?' is his own special leitmotiv that, however, is borrowed by nearly everyone at sometime or other."[19] Although they remain in comparatively rough form, Jarrell's notes are rich in the sort of insight one finds in his essays and that is at least as crucial to the task of translation as philological competence.

Since the style of the translation mirrors Chekhov's in not calling attention to itself and since it attains its effects cumulatively, quotation tends to do it violence. Still, one can hardly resist some attempt to convey

its flavor. The lines below are drawn from Olga's speech—"her big aria,"
Jarrell calls it—at the close of the play:

> Time will pass, and we shall be gone forever, they will forget us—they'll
> forget our faces, our voices, and how many of us there were, but our suf-
> ferings will change into joy for those who will live after us, happiness and
> peace will come on earth, and they'll be reminded and speak tenderly of
> those who are living now, they will bless them. . . . It seems as though a
> little more and we shall know why we live, why we suffer. . . . If only we
> knew, if only we knew!"[20]

Olga's lines summarize Chekhov's response to the counterpoint of mean-
ingfulness and futility that runs through *The Three Sisters*. That response
remains, at bottom, a question rather than an answer—a question about
the persistence of meaning even in the least promising circumstances,
even if God alone knows what it is.[21] Its roots lie in the Russian tradition
of suffering as a spiritual resource, a legacy that has continued intact
down to our own day, as the examples of Anna Akhmatova, Nadezhda
Mandelstam, and Alexander Solzhenitsyn demonstrate.

It is not Jarrell's heritage by birthright, but the tragic wisdom it embodies accords with his world view. The speaker of "A Game at Salzburg"
(67–68) engages in a traditional Austrian form of play with a three-year-
old girl:

> She says to me, softly: *Hier bin i'*.
> I answer: *Da bist du.*

For her the issue is one of personal reassurance; for him it concerns,
ultimately, our worthiness to exist:

> In anguish, in expectant acceptance
> The world whispers: *Hier bin i'*.

It is the game whose odds Pascal has reckoned.

Notes

1. Mary von Schrader Jarrell, Afterword to *Goethe's Faust: Part One*, trans. Randall
Jarrell (New York: Farrar, Straus and Giroux, 1976). p. 281.

2. "Le Poète Contumace," *The Complete Poems* (New York: Farrar, Straus and Giroux,
1969), pp. 123–28. The translation initially appeared under the title "The Contrary Poet" in
the August 1950 issue of *Poetry*. Subsequent page references to *The Complete Poems* appear
in the text.

3. *Faust*, p. 290, "As for actually speaking German," Mrs. Jarrell says, "Randall
didn't—but mostly because he wouldn't. . . . He could have conversed . . . but he was shy of
sounding absurd" (p. 288).

4. "Randall Jarrell," in *Randall Jarrell, 1914–1965*, ed. Robert Lowell, Peter Taylor,
and Robert Penn Warren (New York: Farrar, Straus and Giroux, 1967), p. 5.

5. (New York: Macmillan, 1962), p. iii.

6. *The Rabbit Catcher and Other Fairy Tales* (New York: Macmillan, 1962).

7. Prefatory note to *Faust*, p. v.

8. *Faust*, p. 285.

9. *Faust*, p. 193.

10. "You Must Change Your Life," *Parnassus*, 10 (Fall-Winter 1982–83).

11. Rainer Maria Rilke, "Archäischer Torso Apollos," in *Ausgewählte Werke* (Wiesbaden: Insel-Verlag, 1951), I, 155.

12. (New York: Alfred A. Knopf, 1953), p. 7.

13. "The Group of Two," in *Randall Jarrell, 1914–1965*, p. 278.

14. "Die Erste Elegie," *Duineser Elegien*, in *Ausgewählte Werke*, I, 245.

15. Quoted in J. B. Leishman, Introduction to *Duino Elegies*, by R. M. Rilke, trans. J. B. Leishman and Stephen Spender (New York: Norton, 1963), p. 11.

16. Afterword to Anton Chekhov, *The Three Sisters*, trans. Randall Jarrell (New York: Macmillan, 1969), p. 99.

17. *The Three Sisters*, p. 99.

18. Anyone in doubt about the playability of Jarrell's version of *The Three Sisters* should consult the New York reviewers' verdicts on the 1964 Actors Studio production. See especially the reviews of Howard Taubman in the *Times* and Norman Nadel in the *World-Telegram* of 23 June 1964.

19. *The Three Sisters*, pp. 110–11.

20. *The Three Sisters*, p. 96.

21. Jarrell glosses Olga's words to her sisters as follows: "Partly she is saying they *will* pass and be forgotten, but also, that in the end, remembrance exists, and not forgetting. She tells them that some meaning is destroyed, but some holds out bravely, means to persist, *must* persist, making an enclave of meaning in the middle of comparative meaninglessness. Finally, she says that when we can't manage to get meaning into our lives, meaninglessness is accepted as meaning that we don't understand" (*Three Sisters*, pp. 119–20).

INDEX

Note: Because many of Jarrell's critics have imitated his technique of endlessly listing and comparing, this index could have been much longer. To give it useful direction, I have attempted to list only significant references, especially in cases of duplication of information.

S.F.

Abstract-Expressionism, 86, 92

Adams, Charles, *Randall Jarrell: A Bibliography*, 7

Aeschylus, 110–11, 148

Aiken, Conrad, 261, 263

Altick, Richard D., 283n.

Analects, 6

Andersen, Hans Christian, 56, 65, 234–35

Angus, Sylvia, 8, 266–71, 283n.

Apuleius, 79

Archetype, female, 5, 101–19. See also Jung, Mother Goddess

Archetypal journey, 143–48

Arendt, Hannah, 120, 279, 312

Arnold, Matthew, 1, 28, 50, 51, 83, 85, 86, 87, 88, 89, 94, 95, 97, 99, 100, 210, 228–29, 263

Auden, W. H., 2, 21, 28, 34, 43, 47, 49, 67, 68, 78, 83, 85–86, 89, 91, 96, 99, 154, 178, 204, 219, 236, 246, 253–54, 256, 258, 261

Augustine, Saint, 68, 282

Austen, Jane, 274

Babbitt, Irving, 45

Bach, Johann Sebastian, 278

Bachofen, Johann Jakob, 110–11

Baynes, H. G., 70

Bechstein, Ludwig, 310

Beck, Charlotte, 6, 191–202

Bellow, Saul, 270

Belmore, H. W., 202n.

Benamou, Michel, 241–45

Berg Collection, 9, 272

Bergson, Henri, 80

Berkeley, Bishop, 80

Bergman, Ingmar, 205

Berryman, John, 3, 4, 43–45, 87, 96, 120–21, 285

Bierstadt, Albert, 215

Bishop, Elizabeth, 49, 90, 261

Blackmur, R. P., 43, 129, 253

Blake, William, 257

Blatant Beast, 276

Bly, Robert, 204

Booth, Philip, 3, 33–35, 99

Borges, George Luis, 285

Bosch, Hieronymus, 215, 224

Botticelli, Sandro, 38

Bradbury, Ray, 222

Breughel, Pieter the elder, 211, 215, 219, 221, 222, 224

Brooks, Cleanth, 6, 246

Brown, Norman O., 99

Browning, Robert, 21, 141

Bruno, Giordano, 231

Burchfield, Charles, 207

Cambon, Glauco, 6

Campbell, Joseph, 77

Campbell, Roy, 50

Camus, Albert, 270

Carpaccio, Vittore, 224

Carroll, Lewis. See Charles Lutwidge Dodgson

Carruth, Hayden, 3, 24–28

Cézanne, Paul, 224

Chekhov, Anton Pavlovich, 47, 50–52, 211, 217–18, 223, 226, 310, 318–19. See also Jarrell, translations

Ciardi, John, 63, 226, 246
Clark, Sir Kenneth, 222
Cole, Thomas, 215
Coleridge, Samuel Taylor, 104, 111, 212–13
Comfort, Alex, 252–53
Constable, John, 207
Cooper, James Fenimore, 281
Coralli, Jean, 72
Corbière, Tristan, 2, 28, 30, 84, 143, 298, 304–06, 310–12
Cornelius, David K., 240
Cowley, Malcolm, 97
Cowper, William, 281
Crane, Hart, 78
Cross, Richard K., 8, 310–20
Cummings, E. E., 48

Dante, 26
Dawson, Leven M., 238–39
de la Mare, Walter (John), 44, 84
Derrida, Jacques, 164
Dickens, 154
Dickey, James, 3, 5, 39, 163, 177
Dike, Donald, 297n.
Dodgson, Charles Lutwidge, 60
Donatello, 121
Donoghue, Denis, 6, 179
Dunn, Douglas, 186
Dürer, Albrecht, 38

Eliot, T. S., 19, 41, 46, 66, 242, 244, 257, 261
Emerson, Ralph Waldo, 126
Empson, William, 43–44
Erie, Charles Maine, 204
Existential psychoanalysis, 88–89

Fein, Richard, 149–62
Ferguson, Frances, 7–8, 163–75
Ferguson, Suzanne, 8, 200, 234, 272–83; The Poetry of Randall Jarrell, 1, 5, 9, 273
Fiedler, Leslie, 120, 125, 126
Finney, Kathe Davis, 8, 284–97
Fiske, John, 72
Fitts, Dudley, 161
Fitzgerald, Robert, 121
Five Young American Poets, 3, 15–16
Flint, R. W., 255n.
Flores, A., 298
Fowler, Russell, 6, 176–90
Francesca, Piero della, 121, 224
Fränkel, Hermann, 79–80
Frantz, Adolf, 306

Frazer, Sir James George, 140–41
Freud, Sigmund, 1, 2, 6, 17, 47, 70, 74, 83, 84, 85, 86, 87, 96, 98, 104, 105, 106, 145, 146, 147, 166, 167, 168, 172, 187, 188, 212, 228–29, 236, 277, 281, 286, 287, 289
Fromm, Erich, 118n.
Frost, 2, 3, 23, 28, 34, 44, 53, 90, 121, 123, 126–27, 129, 130–31, 137, 246–47, 250, 259, 260, 261, 262, 264; "An Answer," 123; "Design," 262; "Home Burial," 46, 49, 137; "Provide, Provide," 121, 130–31, 263; "The Witch of Coös," 274
Frye, Northrop, 242
Fugitives, 9

Galileo, 78, 231
Garnett, Edward, 44
Gide, André, 269, 270
Gillikin, Dure Jo, 7
Giselle, 72–73
Glick, Nathan, 6
Goes, Hugo van der, 220–22, 224
Goethe, Johann Wolfgang von, 86–87, 89, 90, 94, 95, 191, 285, 298, 306–09, 310, 311, 313–15; Faust, 274. See also Jarrell, translations
Graham, W. S., 3, 21–24, 25–26
Graves, Robert, 46, 103, 107, 110, 113, 119, 259, 260
Gregorovius, Ferdinand, 310, 313
Grenfell, Sir Wilfred Thomason, 24
Grimm, Jakob and Wihelm, 63, 64–65, 77, 79, 96, 121, 142, 144, 166, 167, 176, 187, 215, 234–35, 287, 310; "The Fisherman and His Wife," 215, 313; "Frog Prince," 209; "Hänsel and Gretel," 69, 75–76, 102, 147, 235, 274, 280
Groddeck, Georg, 47, 83, 86, 87, 88, 92, 93, 95
Grünewald, Mathias, 222
Guiney, Mortimer, 6

Hagenbüchle, Helen, 5, 7, 101–19; The Black Goddess: A Study of the Archetypal Feminine in the Poetry of Randall Jarrell; 5, 116–17n.
Haggin, B. H., 127
Hartman, Geoffrey, 122
Hayward, Abraham, 307, 308
Heade, Martin Johnson, 215
Hegel, Georg Wilhelm Friedrich, 87–88, 248–49

Heidegger, Martin, 93, 106
Hoffman, F. J., 6
Homer, 79
Housman, A. E., 43, 119n.
Humphrey, Robert, 6
Humphries, Rolfe, 87
Hyman, Stanley Edgar, 263

Imagism, 187

James, William, 50, 80, 218
Jarrell, Mary von Schrader, 7, 183, 191,
    212, 217, 222–23, 226, 283n., 289, 290,
    293, 296, 312
Jarrell, Randall:
—Books:
    The Animal Family, 4, 55–57, 59, 210,
    289–91; *The Bat-Poet*, 4, 57, 58, 174–75,
    223, 227, 288–89; *Blood for a Stranger*,
    2, 17–18, 27, 153, 154, 178, 232, 233:
    The Complete Poems, 3, 9, 37–41, 82,
    99, 191; *Fly by Night*, 4, 57–60; *The
    Gingerbread Rabbit*, 57, 59, 287–88;
    Kipling, Auden & Co., 4, 48–53; *Little
    Friend, Little Friend*, 3, 19, 27; *Losses*,
    3, 21–26, 63, 150; *The Lost World*, 2, 3,
    33–37, 189, 223; *Pictures from an Insti-
    tution*, 4, 54–55, 244, 251, 266–83, 284,
    291–96; *Poetry and the Age*, 4, 41–45,
    250; *The Rage for the Lost Penny*, 2, 3,
    96, 97; *A Sad Heart at the Supermarket*,
    4, 53, 82, 94, 95; *Selected Poems*, 3, 30–
    31, 199; *The Seven-League Crutches*, 3,
    27–30, 140–48, 234; *The Third Book of
    Criticism*, 4, 45–47; *The Woman at the
    Washington Zoo*, 3, 194
—Translations
    Goethe's Faust, Part I, 4, 211, 298, 313–
    15, see also Goethe; *The Golden Bird
    and Other Fairy Tales*, 96, 312–13, see
    also Grimm; *The Rabbit Catcher and
    other Fairy Tales of Ludwig Bechstein*,
    215; *The Three Sisters*, 4, 211, 226,
    318–19
—Individual poems:
    "Absent with Official Leave," 77;
    "Aging," 134; "Augsburg Adoration," 38;
    "Bamberg," 188; "Bats," 38; "La Belle
    au Bois Dormant," 143–44; "The Bird of
    Night," 174; "The Black Swan," 29, 71–
    72, 154, 234–35; "The Bronze David of
    Donatello," 32, 243, 244; "Burning the
    Letters," 23, 77–78, 142, 151–52; "A
    Camp in the Prussian Forest," 24; "The

Carnegie Library, Juvenile Division,"
    63–64, 215, 237; "A Child of Courts,"
    233–34; "Children Selecting Books in a
    Library," 178–80, 215; "Christmas
    Roses," 17; "Cinderella," 93, 94, 169,
    170, 171; "A Conversation with the
    Devil," 30, 76, 189, 249; "A Country
    Life," 22, 23, 205–06; "The Death of the
    Ball Turret Gunner," 2, 29, 52, 155–58,
    169, 171, 172, 238–240, 244, 317; "A
    Description of Some Confederate
    Soldiers," 142; "Deutsch Durch Freud,"
    40, 140, 145, 215, 217–18, 312; "The
    Difficult Resolution," 229, 231: "The
    Dream of Waking," 76; "Eighth Air
    Force," 52, 93, 141, 158–62, 169, 172,
    174, 180, 317; "The Elementary Scene,"
    98, 203–04, 236; "The Emancipators,"
    78; "The End of the Rainbow," 32, 208–
    215, 226, 243; "An English Garden in
    Austria," 207; "Esthetic Theories: Art as
    Expression," 114–16; "The Face," 36, 80,
    146, 197–98; "Fear," 232; "Field and
    Forest," 37, 207; "For an Emigrant," 18,
    92, 153; "A Front," 153; "A Game at
    Salzburg," 28, 319; "A Ghost, A Real
    Ghost," 80, 204, 214, 236; "The Girl
    Dreams That She Is Giselle," 73; "A Girl
    in a Library," 28, 39, 92, 132–34, 187,
    216, 312; "Hohensalzburg: Fantastic
    Variations on a Theme of Romantic
    Character," 29, 64–67, 79, 144, 225;
    "The House in the Wood," 107; "A Hunt
    in the Black Forest," 107; "The Iceberg,"
    144, 232; "In the Ward: The Sacred
    Wood," 140; "In Those Days," 92,
    134–35; "The Island," 148; "Jerome,"
    169–71, 174; "Jonah," 30; "The King's
    Hunt," 74; "The Knight, Death, and the
    Devil," 28; "The Learners," 149;
    "Leave," 207–08; "The Lines," 79; "A
    Little Poem," 232; "London," 145; "The
    Long Vacation," 18, 230; "Loss," 147;
    "Losses," 38, 76, 149; "The Lost Chil-
    dren," 135; "The Lost Children,"
    232–33; "The Lost World," 39, 92, 189;
    "Love in its separate being," 16, 232;
    "The Märchen," 63, 64, 101, 140, 142,
    215–16, 229, 231, 235; "A Man Meets a
    Woman in the Street," 92, 138–39; "The
    Memoirs of Glückel of Hameln," 231;
    "The Metamorphoses," 79, 153; "The
    Meteorite," 206; "The Mockingbird,"
    223; "Money," 22; "Mother, Said the

Child," 153, 233; "Nestus Gurley," 32, 224, 244; "New Georgia," 147; "Next Day," 36, 40–41, 136–37, 197–98; "The Night before the Night before Christmas," 28, 68–71, 94, 225, 230, 236; "90 North," 17, 116, 195–96, 230, 232; "Nollekens," 30; "The Old and the New Masters," 34, 40, 219–22, 226; "An Old Song," 80; "O My Name It Is Sam Hall," 21; "On the Railway Platform," 97; "Orestes at Tauris," 109, 110, 111–114, 147; "The Orient Express," 28, 146, 232; "A Pilot from the Carrier," 153; "Pilots, Man Your Planes," 21, 149, 151; "The Place of Death," 80; "The Player Piano," 39; "The Prince," 195; "Protocols," 153; "A Quilt-Pattern," 29, 74–76, 102, 105, 107, 142–43, 213, 230, 235; "The Range in the Desert," 94; "A Rhapsody on Irish Themes," 73, 103, 104, 214, 219; "The Rising Sun," 208; "Second Air Force," 218–19; "Seele in Raum," 28, 93, 137–38, 172, 177, 181–89, 199, 200–01, 316; "A Sick Child," 188, 195; "The Sick Nought," 149, 150; "Siegfried," 145, 149, 150, 156, 231; "The Skaters," 214, 232–33; "The Sleeping Beauty: Variation of the Prince," 65, 141; "A Soul," 30; "The State," 95; "A Story," 17, 91; "The Survivor among Graves," 231; "Terms," 148; "Thinking of the Lost World," 92, 135–37, 194, 223, 227; "Transient Barracks," 146; "Utopian Journey," 230; "Variations," 102; "The Venetian Blind," 73, 80, 144; "A Well-to-Do Invalid," 95; "Well Water," 37, 51; "When you and I were all," 97; "The Wide Prospect," 79, 231; "Windows," 92, 243; "Woman," 93, 104, 108, 132; "The Woman at the Washington Zoo," 32, 36, 105, 174, 198–99, 241–45

—Translations of poems:
"The Breath of Night," 206; "The Child," 194, 195–96; "Childhood," 194; "Death," 206; "Evening," 206; "Faded," 197; "Lament," 206; "The Reader," 192; "Requiem for the Death of a Boy," 194–95; "The Unicorn," 199–200; "The Widow's Song," 197

—Essays:
"The Age of the Chimpanzee," 84, 86, 220–22, 226; "The Age of Criticism," 127, 128, 250, 263; "Changes of Attitude and Rhetoric in Auden's Poetry," 85;

"The End of the Line," 82, 98; "Fifty Years of American Poetry," 247; "To Fill a Wilderness," 92; "From the Kingdom of Necessity," 83; "The Intellectual in America," 93, 250, 263; "An Introduction to the Selected Poems of William Carlos Williams," 218; "John Ransom's Poetry," 189; "Kafka's Tragi-Comedy," 94; "The Obscurity of the Poet," 92, 250; "Poetry and the Age," 45; "Poetry in a Dry Season," 85; "Poetry in War and Peace," 84; "Poets, Critics, and Readers," 49, 250; "On Preparing to Read Kipling," 87; "Reflections on Wallace Stevens," 248; "Robert Frost's 'Home Burial,'" 84–85; "A Sad Heart at the Supermarket," 250; "The Situation of a Poet," 84: "Some Lines from Whitman," 30, 44, 252; "Stories," 163–68, 287; "The Taste of the Age," 94, 99, 250; "To the Laodiceans," 44, 129, 262; "A View of Three Poets," 90; "The Woman at the Washington Zoo," 246

—Critical Problems and Issues:
Aesthetic, 1; attitudes, 177, 181; biography, 7, 64, 203, 205–06, 212, 217, 222–24, 282; compared to other twentieth century critics, 48; concept of self, 228–37; critical perspective, 42, criticism, 122–31, 246–65; devices of criticism, 261–64; dramatic gift, 35; fictional subjects, 286–87; as fiction writer, 284; German influence, 31; humor, 262–64, intelligence, 27; irony, 35; landscapes in, 203–227, letters, 7, 9; manuscripts, 8–9; "modernism," 3, 17–18, monologues, 22, 53, 176–78, 187; *Pictures from an Institution*, genre of, 272–73, lack of plot, 270, musical form, 270, roman à clef, 271, structure, 280–81, theme of the fall, 281; post-modernism, 16; prose style, 41, 46; realism, 21, 23; reputation, 176; reviewer, 97, 256; "sentimentality," 2, 51; style, 2, 3, 5, 9, 15, 33, 99, 177, 179, 243–45; style of criticism, 262: style in translation, 298–99; symbols, 19, 117n.; symbolism, wood, 140–48; translations, 32, 298–320; translations of Grimm, 57; versification, 15, 20; voice, 163–175, 178–79; wit, 4, 19, 40

—Themes and images:
1, 5, 6, 8, 27, 31, 34, 150, 176, 249, 298; of aging, 36; of childhood, 149, 155, 193–94, 228–29; of children in trans-

lations, 316; Christian, 67, 159; of criticism, 250; of death, 76; death of children, 238, 240; dream, 17, 149, 229; humanitarianism, 6; mirror, 183, 213–14, 226; metamorphosis, 63–81; mother, 154, 157; myths, 67; Necessity, 2, 63, 145–46, 253; nightmare, 157; nihilism, 231; reality, 258–59; sexual themes in children's books, 58–59; unconscious, 101, 257–58; war, 33, 149–62, 180, 238–40; wishes, 296; women, 39
Jeffers, Robinson, 17
Job, Book of, 274, 281
Johnson, Samuel, 273
Joyce, James, 267, 269
Jung, Carl Gustav, 5, 67–68, 102, 104, 106

Kafka, Franz, 96, 99, 277, 285–86
Kant, Emmanuel, 218
Kardiner, Abraham, 91
Kazin, Alfred, 120
Keats, John, 217, 238
Kenyon, Theda, 66
Kierkegaard, Sören, 169
Kinzie, Mary, 8, 228–37
Kipling, Rudyard, 46, 47, 50, 83, 84, 91, 99, 254, 273
Kisslinger, Margaret, 12
Klein, A. M., 86
Kokoschka, Oskar, 222–23, 224
Kunitz, Stanley, 6

Laing, R. D., 99
La Rochefoucauld, 166, 167
La Tour, Georges de, 84, 220
Lechlitner, Ruth, 3, 17–18
Leishman, J. B., 202n., 300–01, 302, 303
Lessing, Gotthold Ephraim, 217
Levertov, Denise, 204
Lewis, Wyndham, 126
Locke, John, 80
Logan, John, 3, 32–33
Lowell, Robert, 3, 27–28, 44, 48, 49, 51, 80, 83, 90, 98, 121, 131, 132, 151, 163, 176, 205, 224, 259, 261, 262, 264, 266
Lucas, John, 4, 48–54

McCarthy, Mary, 54, 251, 279
McElroy, Walter, 84, 306
MacIntyre, C. F., 193, 300, 304–06, 307, 308
McKay, G. W., 192–93
MacLeish, Archibald, 20, 246, 251–52, 261

MacNeice, Louis, 307
Maguire, C. E., 5
Mahler, Gustav, 191
Malraux, André, 251
Marc, Franz, 222
Marchen. See Grimm, Jakob and Wilhelm
Marx, Karl, 20, 47, 69
May, Rollo, 88
Mazzaro, Jerome, 6, 7, 82–100, 236
Melville, Herman, 273
Meredith, George, 274
Meredith, William, 3, 35–37
Metcalf, John, 4, 54–55
Meyers, Jefferey, 7
Mid-Century American Poets, 63, 246. See also John Ciardi
Mills, Charles De B., 70
Miller, Arthur, 95, 97
Milton, John, 115, 206, 274
Mörike, Eduard, 298, 303–04, 310, 313
Monroe, Keith, 8, 256–65, 283n.
Moore, Marianne, 46, 52, 64, 155–56, 204, 260, 261
Mother archetype, 102, 103, 104, 106, 108, 110, 111, 114. See also archetypal female, Carl Gustav Jung
Moussorgsky, Modest, 270

Nadel, Norman, 320n.
National Book Awards, 82
Nemerov, Howard, 3, 86
Neumann, Erich, 104, 106
New Criticism, 44, 49
Newton, Isaac, 231
Norton, M. D. Herter, 301

Oedipus complex, 58, 103
Ovid, 70, 79–80, 81, 242
Owen, Wilfred, 24, 27, 29, 53, 97

Péguy, Charles, 244
Plato, 68
Pope, Alexander, 19
Potter, Beatrix, 57
Pound, Ezra, 90, 258, 260, 261
Priest, G. M., 307
Pritchard, William, 7, 120–39
Proust, Marcel, 187, 271, 311
Pushkin, Alexander Sergeevich, 92, 133
Pyle, Ernie, 52, 87, 97, 161

Quartermain, Peter, 12
Quinn, Sister M. Bernetta, 5, 7, 63–81, 102, 189, 203–27, 234

Radauskas, Henrikas, 310, 317, 318
Rahv, Philip, 279
Randall Jarrell, 9
Randall Jarrell 1914–1965, 5, 6, 9, 120–21, 163
Ransom, John Crowe, 1–2, 3, 6, 15–16, 27, 120, 185, 204, 246, 247, 252, 259, 263, 279
Read, Herbert, 24
Rich, Adrienne, 225, 227
Rideout, Walter, 6
Rilke, Rainer Maria, 1, 2, 3, 30, 31, 32, 88, 110, 177, 183, 188, 191–202, 218, 242, 257, 261, 298, 299–303, 310, 311, 315–17; *Das Buch des Bilder*, 193; *Duino Elegies*, 193; *Gedichten des Jahre*, 194; *Neue Gedichte*, 193; *Sonnets to Orpheus*, 199; *Das Stunden-Buch*, 192; "The Child," 301, 316; "Childhood," 300, 316; "Death," 302, 316; "Evening," 299; "Evening Star," 315; "Fourth Elegy," 194; "The Great Night," 301, 315–16; "The Grownup," 301; "Lament," 299; "The Olive Garden," 302, 316–17; "The Panther," 198, 242; "Requiem for the Death of a Boy," 303, 317; "Seele im Raum," 199; "Soul in Space," 183; "Washing the Corpse," 301, 316. See also Jarrell, translations
Rimbaud, Arthur, 243
Robert, Grace, 72
Robinson Crusoe, 63, 148
Rodin, Auguste, 193
Roethke, Theodore, 46, 58–59, 96, 176, 204, 248
Roger-Marx, Claude, 225–26
Roualt, Georges, 159
Rosenberg, Isaac, 24, 52
Rosenthal, M. L., 3, 6, 29–30, 98, 275
Ruitenbeek, Hendrik M., 88
Ruskin, John, 259
Russell, A. E., 205

Said, Edward, 286
Sarah Lawrence College, 276, 279
Sartre, Jean Paul, 80, 88
Schlegel, Friedrich, 308
Schmidt, Paul, 318
Schwartz, Delmore, 3, 4, 19–20, 41–43, 78–79, 89, 284–85
Scrutiny, 49
Seidler, Ingo, 8, 298–309
Sendak, Maurice, 57, 59
Seurat, Georges, 280

Shakespeare, William, 19, 124
Shapiro, Karl, 3, 7, 30–31, 53, 82, 89, 120, 263–64, 280, 287
Sharistanian, Janet, 6, 7, 8, 246–55
Shelley, Percy Bysshe, 238
Skira, Albert, 219
Spengler, Oswald, 90
Spender, Stephen, 17, 24, 48, 177, 320
Spinoza, Baruch, 6, 51, 80, 251, 276
Stafford, Jean, 279
Stead, Christina, 273
Steegmuller, Francis, 269–70
Stein, Gertrude, 244
Stevens, Wallace, 46, 47, 49, 83, 123–24, 129, 151, 209, 241, 246, 247, 248–49, 258, 260, 261
Stevenson, Adlai, 269
Stevenson, Robert Louis, 204
Strauss, Richard, 36, 80, 274, 281
Strindberg, August, 274–75
Surrealism, 187
Su-Su, 209, 212
Swan Lake, 71–72
The Swiss Family Robinson, 210
Symbolists, French, 311

Tate, Allen, 2, 44, 97, 204
Taubman, Howard, 320n.
Taylor, Bayard, 307
Taylor, Eleanor, 7, 254n.
Taylor, Dr. and Mrs. Henry, 279
Taylor, Peter, 6, 7, 224
Tennyson, Alfred, Lord, 21
Thomas, Dylan, 27, 219
Tolstoy, Leo Nikolaevich, Count, 46–47
Transcendentalism, 187
Travers, P. L., 4, 55–57
Tristram Shandy, 266, 270
Turgenev, Ivan Sergeevich, 50, 52, 166, 167
Turner, J. M. W., 214
Tyler, Parker, 5, 88, 140–48

Uccello, Paolo, 224, 225
Unitas, Johnny, 138
UNC-Greensboro, Manuscript Collection, 9
Updike, John, 4, 57–60

Valéry, Paul, 167, 241
Van Doren, Mark, 44
Vendler, Helen, 3–4, 37–41, 45–47, 82, 91
Verlaine, Paul, 300
Vermeer, Jan, 121
Vuillard, Edouard, 212, 225–27

Wagner, Richard, 191
Warren, Robert Penn, 204, 218; *Understanding Poetry*, 246
Wayne Philip, 307
West, Anthony, 269
White, E. B., 60
Whitman, Walt, 2, 122–23, 181, 246, 252, 259, 260, 261, 262, 264
Wilbur, Richard, 50, 87, 122, 261
Wilde, Oscar, 82, 95
Williams, Oscar, 50, 82
Williams, Tennessee, 48
Williams, William Carlos, 2, 44, 46, 49, 53, 84, 86, 87, 89, 90, 207, 246, 247, 258, 260, 261, 264

Winters, Arthur Yvor, 3, 43, 50, 251–52, 261
Wolfe, Thomas, 217
Wordsworth, William, 50, 94, 124, 154, 193, 228–29, 260
Wright, James, 204
Wright, Stuart, 7, 9

Yeats, William Butler, 165, 217, 246, 247–48, 257, 260

Zaturenska, Marya, 262–63
Zucker, David, 297n.